showing at the same time that cross-cultural studies may be used as a second "royal road" to Man's unconscious mind.

The presentation of the exhaustive source material on which this work is based will enable further workers in this field to extend and, if necessary, to amend, the implications and the conclusions of the present work.

This book adds another indispensable inch to the bridge which will one day, and inevitably, link the social and psychological sciences, and weld them into an indissoluble whole.

INDEX • BIBLIOGRAPHY • CHARTS

Dr. George Devereux is an internationally recognized authority in anthropology and ethnopsychiatry. He has done field work among the Hopi, Mohave, Yuma and Cocopa Indians, the Karuama Pygmies and Roros of Papua, New Guinea, and the Sedang Moi of Indochina. He has taught in the University of Wyoming, Wellesley College, Columbia University, University of Southern California, University of Haiti, the Menninger School of Psychiatry and the Topeka Institute for Psychoanalysis, etc. He has done research in Worcester State Hospital and other psychiatric hospitals. He has held numerous fellowships and his publications include some ninety articles and three books.

A STUDY OF ABORTION IN PRIMITIVE SOCIETIES

A STUDY OF ABORTION IN PRIMITIVE SOCIETIES

A typological, distributional, and dynamic analysis of the prevention of birth in 400 preindustrial societies

BY GEORGE DEVEREUX

THE JULIAN PRESS, INC., NEW YORK

Published by The Julian Press, Inc.
251 Fourth Avenue, New York 10

Printed in the United States of America
by H. Wolff, New York

ACKNOWLEDGMENTS

Thanks are due the following copyright holders for permission to reprint passages from works indicated:

American Ethnological Society, for "Disease, Religion and Society in the Fiji Islands," by D. M. Spencer.

American Geographical Society, for *The Manners and Customs of the Rwala Bedouins,* by Alois Musil.

Bernice P. Bishop Museum, for "The Ethnology of Pukapuka," by Ernest and Pearl Beaglehole.

Bureau of American Ethnology, for "Arapaho Child Life and Its Cultural Background," by M. I. Hilger; and for "Chippewa Child Life and Its Cultural Background," by the same author.

Catholic Anthropological Conference, for "Illegitimate Birth Among the Gunantuna," by Joseph Meier.

Clarendon Press, for *Both Sides of Buka Passage,* by Beatrice Blackwood.

Columbia University Press, for *The Individual and His Society,* by Abram Kardiner.

East African Medical Journal, for "The Custom Observed As Regards Miscarriage Among the Barotse," by V. M. Kammer.

William Heinemann, for *The Fijians,* by Sir Basil Thomson.

Journal of the Royal Anthropological Institute of Great Britain and Ireland, for "Depopulation in Espiritu Santo, New Hebrides," by J. R. Baker; and for "The Medicine, Surgery, and Midwifery of the Sinaugolo," by C. G. Seligmann.

The Macmillan Company, for *The Golden Bough,* by Sir J. G. Frazer.

Macmillan & Company, Ltd., for *The Ila-speaking Peoples of Northern Rhodesia,* by E. W. Smith and A. M. Dale.

William Morrow and Company, for *Growing Up in New Guinea,* by Margaret Mead (copyright 1930), and *Male and Female,* by the same author (copyright 1949).

Oceania, for "A Cargo Movement in the East Central Highlands of New Guinea," by R. M. Berndt.

Oxford University Press, for *The Muria and their Ghotul,* by Verrier Elwin.

Peabody Museum, Harvard University, for "Some Sex Beliefs and Practices in a Navaho Community," by F. L. Bailey.

Routledge and Kegan Paul, Ltd., for *Sorcerers of Dobu,* by Reo Fortune.

Viking Fund Publications in Anthropology, for "Truk: Man in Paradise," by Thomas Gladwin and S. B. Sarason.

To Carleton S. and Lisa Coon
in friendship

FOREWORD

The purpose of the present work is threefold. It seeks

1. To develop a typology of practices and attitudes pertaining to abortion, both as an experiment in the construction of typologies and as a means of providing an objective proof for the valid and generally accepted—but, oddly enough, never systematically proven—axiom that cultural diversity demonstrates the tremendous plasticity and variability of human behavior.

2. To provide, by means of a large body of data, an empirical basis for two major theorems:

   a. *The methodological thesis* that the intensive analysis of the context and implications of a particular institution in a single tribe or of the still proverbial Viennese neurotics can—as both Durkheim and Freud indicated—yield universally valid conclusions, and that the selfsame propositions could also be derived from a study in breadth of the variations of the same culture-trait or institution in a large number of societies. This general methodological proposition may, as far as *practical* implications are concerned, be thought of as the equivalent of the mathematician's ergodic hypothesis. The chief merit of this methodological thesis seems to be that it justifies simultaneously, and by identical means, both studies in depth and studies in breadth.

   b. *The substantive thesis* that, were anthropologists to draw up a complete list of all known types of cultural behavior, this list would overlap, point by point, with a similarly complete list of impulses, wishes, fantasies, etc., obtained by psychoanalysts in a clinical setting, thus demonstrating, by identical means and simultaneously, the psychic unity of mankind and the validity of psychoanalytic interpretations of culture, both of which have hitherto been validated only empirically.

3. To present fairly exhaustive source material on the topic under investigation, so as to enable future workers, as well as critics, to carry further and to correct, whenever necessary, and with the least effort, the implications and conclusions of the present work.

Although it must be admitted that the concrete topic (abortion) was chosen more or less accidentally, it so happens that it is ideally suited for demonstrating the above theorems. In the first place, the number of theoretically possible modes of abortion behavior is sharply limited by the fact that pregnancy and abortion both are physiological processes, so that biological factors automatically place a limitation upon an indefinite proliferation of culturally devised techniques and attitudes. At the same time, the fact that abortion always involves trauma and stress, and is closely linked with areas of conflict between superego, ego, and id, renders it particularly suitable for psychoanalytic study. Last, but not least, the fact that—for obvious reasons—abortion does not occupy anywhere a focal position in culture and that a good many possible actions and attitudes related to abortion are, in Linton's terminology, either cultural alternatives or optional elements (i.e., behavior which is, to an appreciable extent, individually motivated and shaped) compensates implicitly for the usual lack of adequate and specific psychological data concerning named individuals, which bedevils every student of the psychological dimensions of primitive cultural behavior. In other words, given the nature of data usually found in anthropological works, it would be almost impossible to write a major depth-psychological study about—to take an example at random—primitive potters in general, simply because in pottery work most of the behavior observed is fairly rigidly standardized and therefore, except in the few areas where pottery has become an art, yields no really significant clues as to *individual* choice and motivation.

Since the foregoing propositions are validated in this work on a rather large scale, it is hoped that they will prove to be useful as basic propositions also in other comparative studies which combine the cultural with the depth psychological approach.

In the final accounting, the chief purpose of this work is to add another inch to the bridge which, one day, will inevitably link the social and the psychological sciences, and weld them into an indissoluble whole.

ACKNOWLEDGMENTS

The writer is indebted to many persons who have encouraged him to write this work, and have facilitated its completion.

Harold Rosen, Ph.D., M.D., aroused the writer's interest in the problem of abortion, by asking him to contribute to a volume which he was editing on *Therapeutic Abortion* (New York, Julian Press, 1954) a chapter on abortion in primitive society. When the chapter was completed, Dr. Rosen drew the attention of the publisher, Mr. Arthur Ceppos, to the fact that this material could advantageously be expanded into a volume, and kindly authorized both the writer and the publisher to reprint the chapter in question from *Therapeutic Abortion.* This chapter now forms, in a slightly revised version, Part One of the present volume.

The late Professor Ralph Linton greatly facilitated the writer's work in the Human Relations Area Files through his counsel, through lending him his secretary, and by offering him —as on so many previous and subsequent occasions—his hospitality during the writer's stay in New Haven. On this, as on so many other occasions, the writer's debt of gratitude toward this great scientist and great man is much more considerable than Professor Linton would ever allow him to acknowledge in his lifetime.

Professor George Peter Murdock helped the writer gain access to the Human Relations Area Files on the best possible footing, advised him on the most efficient way of using these files, and allowed him to try out on him some of his theoretical ideas concerning this material. Professor Murdock, and also Professor Clellan S. Ford—to whom the writer is likewise indebted for his interest—through their intensive questioning as to what theoretical use, beyond the establishment of a typology, the material collected by the writer could be put, made the writer grasp, all of a sudden, that his data represented an ideal body of facts for proving certain of his views on the relationship between "culture and the unconscious," which are now set forth in the chapter of the same title.

Miss Claire M. Vernick, Professor Linton's secretary, rendered invaluable help for three strenuous days, by "pulling" for the author the slips found in the Human Relations Area Files.

Mrs. Anne Davis, custodian of the Human Relations Area Files, greatly facilitated the work in the files by her practical advice and infinite patience.

Mr. Herbert H. Williams, and several graduate students of the University of Pennsylvania working under his direction, located and copied numerous texts to which the writer had given them often altogether inadequate bibliographic clues.

Dr. E. M. Loeb, Miss Marianne L. Stoller, and Mr. R. K. Lewis kindly provided him with unpublished field data, which are acknowledged in the proper place.

Last, but not least, the writer is indebted to his publisher, Mr. Arthur Ceppos, for his interest and, above all, for patiently putting up with several postponements of the delivery of the final copy, which became unavoidable as a result of the writer's change of residence and position while this work was under way.

The writer wishes to specify that this work is not sponsored by the Devereux Foundation and that no material from the files of students of that Foundation has been used in its preparation. Indeed, most of the manuscript was completed before the writer joined the staff of the Devereux Foundation. Nonetheless, the writer is indebted to the Devereux Foundation for allowing him, at times when deadlines had to be met, to devote some time to putting finishing touches on the manuscript, and also for placing at his disposal at such times some clerical help.

Without the joint efforts of the above-mentioned this book could not have come into being, though the writer alone is responsible for its ultimate contents and no doubt far from negligible shortcomings.

George Devereux

April 2, 1954

CONTENTS

PART TWO: CULTURE AND THE UNCONSCIOUS

PART THREE: SOURCE MATERIAL

PART FOUR: TABULATION OF TRAITS

PART ONE

TYPOLOGY

1. INTRODUCTION

The purpose of this section is to illustrate the range of attitudes and behavior patterns which may occur in connection with a given institution. The institution of abortion lends itself especially well to a demonstration of man's extreme plasticity, partly because physiological realities themselves set a certain limit to possible variations, partly because abortion is a relatively marginal and therefore not highly elaborated institution, and partly because of an inherent defect of our data—i.e., because the topic of abortion is not one which anthropologists have taken particular pains to explore in detail, so that it is quite probable to suppose that our data on almost every tribe are relatively fragmentary. (This assertion can be easily confirmed by noting how, whenever we have material from several authors on the abortion practices of a given tribe, these data complement—and sometimes contradict—instead of simply duplicate one another. Cf., to take examples more or less at random: *Fiji, Azande, Tiv, Dahomey*. For contradictions, cf. the *Haida*.) If, now, even fragmentary data yield so wide a variety of phenomena, it is legitimate to state that the present study provides an unusually convincing proof of man's plasticity and variability of behavior.

As stated in the Foreword to this volume, the present section (Part One) was the first to be written, and originally was part of the book *Therapeutic Abortion* edited by Dr. Harold Rosen. It therefore included originally only data derived from some 330 primitive tribes, plus some data on 20 historical and modern nations: the Aztec, the Inca, eighteenth-century Japan, ancient China, nineteenth-century China, ancient India, ninetenth-century India, Achaemenid Persia, Islamic Persia, ancient Assyria, the Jews of the Old Testament period, ancient Egypt, nineteenth-century Egypt, the Arabs of the Khalifate period at the peak of their civilization, nineteenth- and twentieth-century urban Arabs,* nineteenth-century Turkey, classical Greece, ancient Rome, the Visigoth Kingdom, and nineteenth-century rural Hungary. Although, in the writing of the present volume, the emphasis has shifted from abortion in *all* societies to abortion in *primitive* societies, in revising this section we have simply added further typological refinements or items derived from the study of some 70 additional tribes, and have *not* eliminated references to selected practices of the 20 nations previously listed. This was done because, in the typological section, as distinct from the interpretative one, the *context* in which a given behavior item occurs is relatively unimportant, so that the nonspecialist's inability to grasp at a glance the full implications of a practice occurring in a highly complex national culture, such as that of the *Greeks,* is no obstacle to the proper classification of a given cultural, behavioral, or attitudinal item within the framework of a simple typology.

As regards the typology itself, it emerged from the study of the facts themselves—insofar as anything at all may be said to come from letting facts "speak for themselves." In other words, while we explicitly recognize the socio-cultural basis of *all* methods of classification (27), as well as the fact that linguistic categories (which differ from language to language) unwittingly provide us with a classificatory frame of reference (65), we may confidently state that the *idea of classification* is present in all cultures, and that the very simple categories which we have used—such as motivation, techniques, attitudes, penalties, etc.—are, to the best of our belief, likewise present in all cultures and expressible in all languages. We might add in passing that, to the best of our knowledge, this is the first time that, in constructing his frame of reference, an anthropologist has specifically taken into consideration the necessity of using only "universal categories," or, at least, has specifically *stated* that he has done so.

Examples. With exception of one or two obvious practices, each custom or belief will be illustrated by means of an example. The effort has been made to draw as many of our examples as possible from a relatively small but representative group

* Contemporary tribal Arabs, as distinct from urban Arabs, are counted among the tribes.

of tribes, because it was felt that too many strange-sounding names would merely confuse the nonanthropologist reader. Whenever possible, we have chosen examples which can be found in one of the secondary sources, especially when we were able to collate the secondary source with the primary ones. By citing primarily data derived from fully listed secondary sources, we enable the reader to locate the unlisted primary source, via the fully listed secondary source, without too much effort. This policy explains why relatively few of the 400-odd tribes on which data were collected are mentioned in this section. Certain examples are cited repeatedly, in order to illustrate the multidimensionality of even a single practice or incident.

Bibliographic Note. It seemed desirable not to encumber with an elaborate set of bibliographic footnotes a section already topheavy with innumerable facts. Since the sourcebook section contains all the primitive data referred to in this section, it might have seemed simplest to mention only the tribes referred to, leaving it to the reader to refer back to the sourcebook section for the authority for any given statement. This, however, seemed somewhat cumbrous, since the anthropologist in particular likes to know at a glance on whose authority a given statement was made. On the other hand, in order not to overload the text itself with too many different names, it seemed desirable to use in this chapter as many facts culled from major secondary sources as possible, and to cite this same secondary source as the authority, even when the fact itself had been traced back to its original source. This policy of bibliographic simplification may or may not seem wholly satisfactory to all readers, but it has, at least, the merit of being a consistent and planned one. For this reason, the actual sections dealing with typology are preceded by a brief bibliography, which includes the abbreviations used to refer to the items it contains. It lists only the handful of major secondary sources used and one primary source which deals with a fairly large number of tribes. These works are referred to in the text by certain abbreviations or initials (e.g., HDBK or AH) placed in parentheses after the *italicized name of the tribe* to which they refer. When the data were derived from primary sources, the italicized name of the tribe is followed, in parentheses, by the full family name of the authority for that statement. Thus, the reference "*Tikopia* (Firth)" means that our authority for that particular statement about the Tikopians is Professor Raymond Firth. Since many of these names in parentheses are familiar to anthropologists, even such abbreviated references may enable them to appraise the reliability of a given statement without having to refer first to the sourcebook section to check the authority for a given fact.

PRINCIPAL SOURCES

AH Hrdlička, Aleš. *Physiological and Medical Observations among the Indians of Southwestern United States and Northern Mexico.* Bureau of American Ethnology, Bulletin 34, Washington, D. C., 1908. (Primary source)

GPM Murdock, G. P. *Our Primitive Contemporaries.* New York, 1934. (Secondary source)

HA Aptekar, Herbert. *Anjea.* New York, 1931. (Secondary source)

HDBK Steward, J. H., ed., *Handbook of South American Indians.* Bureau of American Ethnology, Bulletin 143, Washington, D. C., 1946–50, 6 vols. (Mostly a secondary source, with some primary material)

HK Hovorka, O. v., and Kronfeld, A. *Vergleichende Volksmedizin.* Stuttgart, 1908–1909, 2 vols. (Secondary source)

HRAF Human Relations Area Files, Yale University. (Almost entirely primary material, including even some unpublished data)

NH Himes, Norman. *The Medical History of Contraception.* New York, 1936.

NM Miller, Nathan. *The Child in Primitive Society.* London, 1928. (Secondary source)

PB Ploss, Heinrich, Bartels, Max, and Bartels, Paul. *Das Weib in der Natur- und Völkerkunde.* New edition, revised by Reitzenstein, Ferdinand Baron von. Berlin, 1927, 3 vols. (Secondary source)

WGS Sumner, W. G. *Folkways.* Boston, 1906. (Secondary source)

2. MOTIVATION

Many kinds of motives operate in the causation of induced abortion. These motives fall, broadly speaking, into the following general categories:

(I) *Spontaneous and subjective conscious motivation* of the woman herself, who, for a variety of reasons, and without anyone—except perhaps her lover—putting pressure on her, decides to abort either to avoid some inconvenience, difficulty, or penalty, or in order to achieve a personal end; and *abortion under pressure* from individuals or from the tribe as a whole.

(II) *Subjective but unconscious motivation.* The woman may, "accidentally on purpose," behave in a manner which will cause what she herself may "believe" to be a "miscarriage," or else may maneuver herself into a position where she is put under pressure to abort.

(III) *Involuntary abortion through assault.*

(IV) *Involuntary abortion by magical means,* where the woman does not even know that she is being aborted, and imagines that she has a miscarriage.

I. CONSCIOUS MOTIVATION

A. *Medical and Biological Considerations*

"PROPHYLACTIC" abortions are known to occur in primitive society. *Purari* (Williams) women abort simply because they are afraid of childbirth. The *Apinayé* (*Nimuendajú*) primipara dreads birth, and hence aborts. It has been falsely alleged that *American Indian* (PB) women abort halfbreed babies because their pelvises are supposedly too small for such large babies. *Mataco* (HDBK) women abort the first fetus, in order to make subsequent births easier. In *Suau* (Williams) girls who are "too young" are made to abort. At the peak of *Arabic* (PB) culture, an eminent physician deemed abortion legitimate if the woman was "too small," but recommended that the abortion should be performed not by a physician but by a midwife. Among the *Bafiote* Negroes (PB), girls who had led overly free lives are afraid of delivery in their riper years, and therefore abort. In *Turkey* (HK) women abort if it is feared that the birth will be a difficult one. A *Zuni* (Stevenson) medicine man told a woman that she was going to have triplets, which would kill her. She therefore aborted. In *Central Celebes* (WGS) women abort lest their perineum should tear during birth, a torn perineum being considered extremely shameful.* *Ashanti* (Rattray) women whose adultery becomes known through other means than their own confessions are made to abort, in order to save them from the dangers of such an adulterous childbirth. *Dayak* (Grabowsky) women abort if they are believed to be pregnant with twins, one of which is thought to be a monster. *Efik* (Hewan) women abort to prevent miscarriages or the birth of children who will die in infancy.

THERAPY. If a pregnant *Dahomeyan* (Hazoumé) woman is ill, the fetus is formally tried, and if it is found guilty of having caused her illness, it is aborted in order to cure the mother.

"EXTREME" YOUTH, which is culturally defined, may be a reason for abortion. The very young *Suau* (Williams) girl is aborted by her mother's sister. Among the *Owambo* (PB) a girl is not supposed to give birth before she undergoes the puberty rites. Among the *Masai* (Fox) it is shameful for a warrior to impregnate an uninitiated girl, and he must wipe out this shame by killing an enemy. Leakey adds that the pregnant uninitiated girl must be initiated at once, the burden of the rite being borne by the seducer.

"ADVANCED" AGE is also a matter of cultural definition. *Chagga* (Raum) women must not bear children after their daughters are married. If a woman wishes to continue to bear

* The *Sedang Moi* (Devereux) dread a prolapsus uteri, and are as reluctant to mention the word for it as they are to utter the term for clitoris. (Female phallus phantasy?)

children, she uses an amulet to delay her daughter's puberty. (See also the *Bafiote* case previously cited.) In the *Torres Straits* (HA), where elderly parents of young children are ridiculed, older women abort their pregnancies. In *Formosa* (Campbell-Candidius), on the other hand, only women over thirty-four or thirty-seven years carry their babies to full term.

EUGENIC THEORIES, both real and fictitious, sometimes motivate abortions. Eugenic infanticide is recorded for *Formosa* (Wiedfeldt). *Masai* (Merker) women have to abort the children of alien, old, or sick fathers. The prevention of the birth of monsters is another "eugenic" measure. The *Jivaro* (Karsten) believe that demons can father monsters, and therefore abort such evil fetuses. Such monsters are conceived if a woman who is undergoing a contraceptive or sterilizing treatment disregards the dietary rules associated with this treatment. If she then bathes in the river, a demon enters her vagina in the shape of an insect or small fish, and causes her to conceive a monster.* The offspring of legally defective *Jivaro* marriages are also believed to be monsters, and must therefore be aborted. (See also the *Dayak* data previously cited.)

SOCIAL PROPHYLAXIS is related to "eugenics" at least psychologically. *Achewa* (Steytler) women abort adulterous bastards, because their birth would result in misfortunes for the community.

BIRTH CONTROL is so broad a category as to be almost meaningless for a study of motivation. It describes the effects of an act, and not its motivation, which may be economic, ritual, customary or something else. Almost the only datum which belongs primarily in this category is a practice recorded from *Fiji* (PB), where women legitimately, but too frequently, pregnant will abort, because they are afraid of ridicule. In *Formosa* (Campbell-Candidius) women abort all their pregnancies—sometimes as many as sixteen—until they are thirty-four to thirty-seven years of age. The motivation of this practice is not at all clear, since the sources simply mention "shame" or unspecified "religious" motives. In numerous tribes women are not expected to bear more than a limited number of children, and therefore

* Lewis Cotlow (*Amazon Head-Hunters,* New York, 1953) states that he was an eyewitness to the invasion of a *Jivaro* girl's vagina by a small fish called *canero* or *candiru.*

abort either their first or their last pregnancies, or, as in *Fiji* (PB), also one or more intermediate ones, simply because it is "customary" to do so. In many cases we do not know whether we are confronted simply with inadequate data or with some definite kind of motivation which was forgotten after the practice became customary or fashionable.

B. *Political Causes*

DYNASTIC FACTORS. In order to safeguard the senior male branch of the royal house of *Uganda* (GPM) from competition, princesses are not permitted to marry. They lead promiscuous lives, and their babies are either aborted or killed at birth. This policy may represent an attempt to shift from a matrilineal to a patrilineal royal succession. Dynastic rivalries may have been responsible for the fact that in the *Turkish* (HK) Sultan's harem one of his wives, who was called the "bloody midwife," plied her trade openly. In *Brunei,* Borneo (PB) half the noble girls remain single and practice abortion. In *Bali* (PB), the Prince of Badong's slave concubines must report to him when they are pregnant, and are then aborted by him. It is not clear whether dynastic considerations operate here, or whether they must abort to safeguard their beauty. *Aztec* (Bancroft) data show, however, that even in harems only some pregnancies are aborted. In *Borneo* (Roth) the jealousy of the other inmates of the harem may force a pregnant woman to abort.

ABSOLUTISTIC EXCESSES played a role in mass abortions on *Nukuoro* (Eilers). When Queen Kauna lost her son soon after birth, she ordered all small boys to be killed, so that her subjects would share her sorrow. Then, still not content, she ordered all pregnant women to abort.

CONQUEST. Two former Spanish-dominated areas, the *Antilles* (Las Casas) and *Guam* (Thompson), have the sad distinction of being the only places where native women aborted to save their children from the alien yoke, slavery, and abuse. These mass abortions went hand in hand with mass suicides, and represented a more or less definite attempt at race suicide. By contrast, data indicate that native slavery was more lenient by far than that of the Spaniards, since only two instances of abortion among the slaves of native tribes could be located. Among the *Toradja* (Kruyt) and the *Baholoholo* (HA), slave women aborted because they did not wish to bear children who would also be slaves. General demoralization and "loss of vigor" due to acculturation, as causes of abortion, are reported from much of Melanesia and New Guinea (*Suau,* Williams), and from the *tribes of the Montana in the Bolivian East Andes* (HDBK). The unsuitability of mission life is blamed for increases in the abortion rate of the *Australians of New South Wales* (PB). Carr-Saunders claims, however, that missionary teachings decrease the incidence of abortions. While this may be true in some instances, it is known that in parts of *Melanesia* (HA) an increasing apathy about bearing children is related to the decline of headhunting and to the gradual disintegration of other major and nuclear native institutions. This is directly attributable to missionary labors. In *Fiji* (Thomson) Christianized Fijian girls abort in order not to be expelled from the Church. In the *Torres Straits* (HA), on the other hand, changed economic conditions resulting from conquest led to a decrease in the number of abortions. Parents began to desire sons who could be gainfully employed, and the existence of a class of "prosperous" male workers who were able to buy wives created a demand for young girls. The secular laws of the conquerors also influence the incidence of abortion. The suppression of infanticide in *Samoa* (PB) and in the *Society Islands* (PB) by white authorities led to an increase in abortions. A *Mohave* (Devereux) schoolgirl aborted because she was afraid of what reservation authorities might do both to her and to her lover. The appearance of a culturally doubly marginal class of halfbreeds in native society also affected the rate of abortions. Among the *Quapaw* (Currier), halfbreeds abort more frequently than do full-blood Indian women.

MISCEGENATION is closely related to conquest. The relevant data will be covered under the heading Improper Paternity. (See also *Quapaw* data preceding.)

C. *Social Structure*

IMPROPER PATERNITY. Many tribes abort children fathered by unsuitable persons:

1. The father is unknown: *Tikopia* (Firth).
2. The father raped the mother: *Korea* (Japanese law) (Materi).

3. The father had access to the woman through "error": *Korea* (Japanese law) (Materi).
4. The father is not married to the girl. (Very widespread) In *Fiji* (Thomson) girls usually abort only those bastards whose fathers belong to the lower classes.
5. There are "several fathers": The *Wogeo* (Hogbin) believe that all premarital children have several fathers, and the girl's protestations of fidelity to one lover are not believed.
6. The father is a close relative of the girl, so that the cohabitation was incestuous: *Gunantuna* (Meier), *Sedang Moi* (Devereux).
7. The father is an alien: *Tucuna* (HDBK).
8. The father is neither a native Cuna, nor a Frenchman: *Cuna* (Nordenskiöld).
9. The father is a prisoner of war or a slave: *Tupinamba* (Magelhães de Gandavo) (See Cannibalism.) *Toradja* (Kruyt).
10. The father's marriage to the mother is unlawful: *Jivaro* (Karsten).
11. The father is a prince, and the mother is his slave concubine: *Badong, Bali* (PB).
12. The father is the owner of the slave-girl: *Turkey* (PB).
13. The father, though he is the woman's lawful husband, is dead: *Pima* (Grossman). (See Economic Factors.)
14. The father is not the married woman's husband: *Azande* (Hutereau).
15. The father is neither the woman's husband nor a person who has lawful sexual access to her: *Western Arnheim Land* (Berndt and Berndt).
16. The father is a demon: *Jivaro* (Karsten).

SOCIAL PRESSURE is sometimes put on the girl or woman to abort. A variety of persons may put such pressure on her:

1. The lover: *Kgatla* (Shapera).
2. The husband. (See Economic Motivation, Jealousy, Sexual Taboos.)
3. The girl's mother: The *Chagga* (Raum) mother is ashamed of her unwed daughter's pregnancy, and urges her to abort.
4. The girl's sisters: *Wogeo* (Hogbin).

5. Tribal opinion or authority reflecting customary attitudes. (See Eugenics, Improper Paternity, Miscegenation, Politics, Jealousy, "Prophylaxis," etc.)
6. The medicine man: Zuni (Stevenson). (See Prophylaxis.)

Ways of dealing with, or of punishing, private persons who put pressure on women to abort, or have knowledge of the latter's intention to do so, are discussed in the section on penalties for abortion.

AGREEMENT ON ABORTION. In *Keisar* (PB), women abort without the husband's knowledge or consent, after they have had two children. *Crow and Assiniboine* (Denig) husbands urge their wives to abort, but do not acknowledge this openly. Among the *Omaha* (Dorsey) a husband frankly told his wife to abort. In *Buin* (Thurnwald) abortion is agreeable to both parents.

D. *Economic Factors*

NOMADISM may play a great role in abortions. The *Mataco* (HDBK) abort because they are seminomads. The *Caduveo,* a *Guaycuru* group (WGS), abort because they are afraid that their husbands might leave them behind. This may, however, backfire in certain cases, since the *Kaingang* (Santin de Prade) left behind the chief's wife, who was ill from a miscarriage when they had to leave their village.

ECONOMIC FACTORS play a tremendously important role in the motivation of abortion. Missionaries, travelers, and government officials sometimes disguise the genuineness of this motivation by saying, *e.g.,* that the *Hottentots* (PB) abort because they are "lazy." Anyone familiar with the tremendous economic burden which primitive women carry, and with the great poverty of many groups, will take a more charitable view. Needless to say, the concept of what is actual economic want is determined by culture. In *Malekula* (Deacon), where wealth is the main avenue to social prominence, women abort so as to be able to work in the gardens and contribute thereby to the family's economic success. The *Papuans of Geelvink Bay* (Rosenberg) declare: "Children are a burden and we get tired of them. They destroy us." By contrast, the *Munda-Kolh* (PB) abort because they are genuinely poor. The *Gilbert Islanders* (HA) abort because their soil is barren. Sometimes women abort during the first part of marriage. In *New Britain* (PB) it is not proper to have children during the first two to four years of marriage—perhaps because the couple is just settling down. By contrast, *Turkish* (PB) women abort after they have borne two children, one of which is a boy, because their husbands do not care to support more than two children. In *Keisar* (PB), women have adopted the two-child system, though without the knowledge and consent of their husbands. In times of famine *Ngali* and *Yumu* (Róheim) women abort to feed the fetus to the children already born. The mother herself also partakes of the flesh of the fetus, because she is "meat-hungry." The *Pima* (Grossman) widow who has several living children may abort her posthumous baby, because in this tribe the dead man's property is destroyed, and she is therefore afraid of being left destitute. In this connection, we can once more underscore the cultural basis of the conception of "poverty" by contrasting the *Pima* with their neighbors, the *Mohave* (Kroeber), who also destroy the dead man's property but do not (Devereux) abort posthumous babies, since someone, be it but a friend, will always give shelter and subsistence to the widow and her brood.

DIFFICULTIES OF CHILD REARING are hard to separate from economic motivation, and, like the latter, are sometimes lumped together under the heading of "laziness" by superficial reporters. Here again, one is likely to take a more charitable view if one has had occasion to watch a primitive woman take care of a large brood. The only convincing evidence that the troubles of child-rearing motivate abortion comes from *Ugi* (Elton), where women abort their own children and then buy larger children from other tribes, some of which breed children for paid adoptions. As with the concept of "economic stress," cultural factors determine precisely what "too much work" means. The *Hottentot* (PB) are said to abort because they are "lazy," though, considering the nomadic mode of life of this desert tribe, one has to admit that numerous children would be a tremendous burden for most women. Where—theoretically at least—women could conveniently rear more children than they do, the motivating factor is not specifically "laziness"—which is a negative motivation at best—but some positive factor represented by the appeal of some other activity which cannot be pursued if one has too many children. These motives are discussed under special headings.

UNWELCOME HEIRS. In *Fiji* (Thomson), a lady of rank who marries outside her own village aborts her children, so that no little "outsider" would have a lien on the land held by her own lineage.

E. *Family Dynamics*

ILLEGITIMACY PER SE is a wholly meaningless motivational category, though, needless to say, the abortion of illegitimate children is extremely widespread, even where neither the unwed mother nor her bastard are penalized in any way. In *Dobu* (Fortune) Kadi, Alo's daughter, who aborted her bastard, was severely beaten about the body with a club by her maternal uncle Kopu, who had a socially recognized and corporeally enforceable right to a male heir from his sister's daughter's womb. The *Navaho* (Bailey) feel that no girl has a reason to abort, since neither she nor her bastard are penalized. The *Zuni* (AH) mother who notices that her daughter is illegitimately pregnant urges her not to abort, lest she become sterile. The *Chagga* (Raum) father curses the man who causes his betrothed daughter to abort, since, should she die, his claim to compensation disappears. The abortion of bastards in areas where neither the mother nor the child are penalized is, thus, not motivated by "illegitimacy," but by reasons which have to be discussed under separate headings.

In brief, "illegitimacy" is a primary reason for abortion only where the mother, her kin, and/or the child are penalized.

PENALTIES ON THE MOTHER:

1. Death: The *Massawa* (PB) father must hang his premaritally pregnant daughter.
2. Beating: In *Wogeo* (Hogbin) a girl's sisters beat her because her attempted abortion was unsuccessful.
3. Unspecified: *Flathead* (Turney-High) girls abort because they are afraid of their relatives.
4. Shame: The *Akamba* (Lindblom), as well as many other tribes which authorize premarital intercourse, despise the girl who becomes illegitimately pregnant.
5. Impaired eligibility: The *Kgatla* (Shapera) girl will abort if she is engaged to a man other than her baby's father, for fear that the match may be broken off. If not

engaged, she will abort in order to pass as "unspoiled," and be therefore able to contract a good marriage.

6. Increased eligibility: Among the *Konyak Naga* (von Fürer-Haimendorf) the engaged girl cohabits with any man she desires. However, if she becomes pregnant, she must immediately break off her liaison, and marry her fiancé. Although we have no concrete data on this point, we must mention the theoretical possibility that if the girl is in love with her current lover, she may be impelled to abort in order to postpone her marriage to her previously selected fiancé.

PENALTIES ON THE LOVER: In the *Admiralty Islands* (Parkinson) pregnant girls abort in order to save their lovers from being killed later on by their husbands. *Bangala* (Weeks) women abort to protect their lovers from having to pay a fine.

PENALTIES ON THE GIRL'S KIN: The *Chagga* (Raum) mother will urge her pregnant unwed daughter to abort, lest she shame her mother. The *East Indian* (PB) prostitute widow will abort to save her family from shame.

PENALTIES ON THE BASTARD

1. Death: The *Gunantuna* (Meier) bastard is supposed to be killed, and the mother who fails to do this is scolded.
2. Cannibalism: The *Tupinamba* (Magelhães de Gandavo) son of a prisoner of war and of a *Tupinamba* girl is eaten. The mother often aborts her baby in order to prevent this from happening.
3. Ridicule: The *Masai* (Hollis) call the bastard "child of seduction" or "child of the fireplace." Though the *Pima* (Parsons) discriminate against bastards, they are said to become quite frequently chiefs or great men.
4. Lack of social status: The unclaimed or only half-*Mohave* (Devereux) bastard has no "gens" and "no name, or a funny name." The *Tucuna* (HDBK) bastard has no sib or moiety affiliation.

ADULTERY. Jealous husbands sometimes require their adulterously pregnant wives to abort. *Azande* (Hutereau) husbands consult the *benget,* to find out whether their pregnant wives are carrying their own children. If the *benget* states that the pregnancy is adulterous, the husband forces his wife to abort, and then proceeds against her as in regular divorce actions. Among the *Ashanti* (Rattray), if a woman's adultery comes to light otherwise than by her own confession, it is legitimate to make her abort, in order to "save her life," which such a pregnancy endangers. In *Rome* (PB) the satirist Juvenal advised a deceived husband to give his wife abortifacients, lest she give birth to a half-Ethiopian child. Needless to say, in societies where others than the husband have lawful access to women, the wives are not required to abort the children of such persons. The *Western Arnheim Land* (Berndt and Berndt) woman does not abort the children of those of her husband's kin who have lawful access to her. Yet a *Masai* (Maguire) husband was so jealous of a man of his own age-group that he forced his wife to abort the latter's child. In *Pukapuka* (Beaglehole), a woman aborts (miscarries ?) if she plans to commit adultery. However, even in primitive society, some husbands prefer to close their eyes rather than risk a scandal. In *Buka* (Blackwood) an adulterous woman sometimes pretends that her pregnancy is legitimate and this will be tacitly accepted both by the husband and by the community, though they know the true facts in the case. Yet, most *Buka* husbands being less complaisant, adulterously pregnant women usually try to abort. The abortion of adulterine bastards is extremely widespread, especially where adultery is penalized, and therefore need not be further documented.

MARITAL DISCORD often leads to abortion. A *Copper Eskimo* (Jenness) beat his wife, thereby causing her to abort. *Tupinamba* (Thevet) and *Australian women of Victoria* (PB) abort if they are angry with their husbands, while *Jivaro* (Tessman) women would not abort for such a reason. *Crow* and *Assiniboine* (Denig) women abort if they are deserted. In *Fiji* (PB) a woman may abort to annoy a husband whom she suspects of infidelity or (Williams and Calvert) who has just taken a second wife. *Dusun* (Staal) women abort after bad dreams only if they know that their husbands have failed to do their duty.* There is indirect evidence that such hostile actions may have also a magical implication. An *Araucanian* (HDBK) unwed mother sometimes kills her little son and roasts his testicles in a hot pot, to make

* The *Harney Valley Paiute* (B. Whiting) woman throws away her live baby if she is hostile to its father.

her faithless lover impotent. This rite is called *koftun*. In societies where babies are greatly desired, the possibility of aborting or of committing infanticide places a powerful weapon in the hands of the woman. In *Rome* (Kiefer) one of the earliest recognized reasons for divorce was the mother's poisoning of her children. The *Minyan,* or, if one prefers, *Colchic* (Euripides) case of Medea's revenge is also relevant in this context.

PROTECTION OF YOUTHFUL BEAUTY. Abortion in order to protect the beauty of the woman occurs in many areas. *Samoan* (PB) girls are specifically interested in protecting their breasts. The belief that childbirth, while the mother is still young, ages a woman is reported from the *Orinoco area* (PB), though in that same general region some tribes believe that childbirth in youth enhances a woman's beauty (Gilij). In view of the brittleness of many primitive marriages, this motivation often reflects not so much vanity as practicality. Thus, in *Brunei* (PB) prominent men retire their concubines after their first or second pregnancy. As a result the concubines prefer to abort.

COITUS TABOOS DURING PREGNANCY AND LACTATION are extremely common causes of abortion. Sex is so strictly banned from *Chagga* (Raum) pregnancy that, if the pregnant woman "menstruates" or if her husband has a voluptuous dream, she must abort. In *Malekula* (Deacon) and in the *Mount Hagen* district (Gitlow) the wives of monogamous men abort more frequently than those of polygamous ones. This taboo is, thus, an important factor in the motivation of polygamy, and also of infidelity. The *Abipone* (Dobrizhoffer) wife aborts because she is afraid of being repudiated during the taboo period, or fears that her husband might take another wife. *Persian* (Chardin, PB) women abort because they fear that their husbands might get involved with other women while they are pregnant. In *Truk* (Gladwin) women abort because they themselves are unwilling to forego the pleasures of intercourse. *Chagga* (PB) women who become pregnant during the lactation period are so severely criticized that they will abort in order to avoid a scandal. In *Malekula* (Deacon) the wife aborts because both spouses desire to continue cohabitation.

DISLIKE OF THE PARENTAL ROLE is a motive which is difficult to appraise. Only a few of the sources consulted specifically refer to this attitude in connection with abortion. In *Alor* (Du Bois) the women are said to reject the maternal role. Among the *Kai* (Keysser) and the natives of *Buin* (Thurnwald), both sexes reputedly reject the parental role. The same is apparently true of the *Papuans of Geelvink Bay* (PB), who say they get tired of their children, and that their children destroy them. We know that *Marquesan* (Linton) women are very rejecting mothers, since they prefer to lead the promiscuous life which the shortage of women in these islands makes possible for them.

DISAPPOINTED PARENTHOOD. A *Navaho* (AH) woman who loses several children in a row may give up hope and abort her subsequent children. Under similar conditions *Mohave* (Devereux) women only "sterilize" themselves.

MOURNING. A *Chagga* (Raum) woman aborts if she conceives within two months after the death of a child.

WIDOWHOOD. A *Pima* (Grossman) widow with several children may abort her posthumous child. She is afraid of being left destitute, because it is customary to destroy all of the dead man's property. (See also Economic Motivation.)

CLASS-LINKED ABORTION. In *Tahiti* (AH) members of the society of the Areoi were allegedly pledged to do away with their children. *Rome*'s decline (AH) was characterized by the prevalence of abortion among the upper classes. By contrast, among the *Baholoholo* (HA) it was the slave woman who aborted, so as not to bear future slaves.

F. *Miscellaneous Customs and Attitudes*

CANNIBALISM is at the root of two types of abortions whose motivations are diametrically opposed to each other. Some *Central Australian* (Róheim) women abort in order to feed the fetus to their starving children. In that region small children are also killed in order to feed them to their older siblings (Róheim). Among the *Tupinamba* (Magelhães de Gandavo), prisoners of war are sometimes given a local girl as a bedfellow or wife. The offspring of such a union is then eaten, since it belongs to its father's kin, whose feelings they wish to hurt by this action. Sometimes, however, the *Tupinamba* wife of the prisoner does not like the idea of having her child eaten, and therefore aborts it, in order to safeguard it from such a fate.

ABORTION TO DEMONSTRATE THE TECHNIQUE. A group of *Mbaya* (PB, Azara) women was asked by Azara how abortion is performed. A pregnant woman promptly lay down and let two old women belabor her belly with their fists, until blood spurted from her vagina. She aborted a few hours later. The casualness of this demonstration is the more striking as this operation is painful, may cause lifelong illness, and is sometimes fatal. In *Dobu* (Fortune), Nela, who had had many abortions but who was not pregnant at the time, publicly chewed the abortifacient sample which she had given the anthropologist, to show that the secret drug she was giving him was not a treacherous poison.

DREAMS AND OMENS. If a *Dusun* (Staal, Rutter) woman dreams twice that she will die in childbirth or that her child will be deformed, and, in addition, knows that her husband does not fulfill his obligations, she will ask a priest to pray over her. If the dream recurs nonetheless, she asks a midwife to abort her. If a *Chagga* (Raum) husband has a voluptuous dream, he demands that his wife abort, because pregnancy requires that all sexual aspects of marriage be suspended for the time being. In *Pukapuka* (Beaglehole), if the lightning strikes or a meteor falls nearby, it means that the child has been incestuously conceived and has to be aborted.

RELIGIOUS REASONS, without further specification, are reported from *Formosa* (Campbell-Candidius) and from *India* (PB). *Mafulu* (Williamson) women abort if they are not in a position to provide a pig for the feast required of women before they give birth.

THE EMOTIONS MOTIVATING ABORTION are chiefly shame, fear, and anger. Of these, shame is the most important, since it is the chief inhibitor of disapproved conduct in primitive society. Fear of penalties is also a common motive, while anger toward the husband or lover is a somewhat less usual reason for aborting. A large variety of other emotional nuances is also mentioned, but all of them belong ultimately to one of the foregoing categories, with the possible exception of the sheer casual bravado mentioned in connection with abortion for purposes of demonstration. A *conscious* sense of sin, as distinct from a sense of having trespassed and as distinct also from shame, is apparently not a major motive for abortion in primitive society. Yet it is conceivable that guilt feelings in the strict sense may have motivated certain abortions in *Ashanti* (Rattray) society. (See following.)

II. SUBJECTIVE BUT UNCONSCIOUS MOTIVATION

The existence of motivation of this type is partly inferential. The *Mohave* (Devereux) women knew that the penalty for the violation of certain pregnancy taboos was miscarriage, but allegedly never deliberately violated such taboos in order to abort. However, if they lost several children in a row, they did sterilize themselves by burning the last dead infant's cradle, instead of breaking it and throwing it into the river. Shortly after these lines were first published elsewhere, the existence of this hypothetical motive was fully confirmed by the *Maori* (Goldie) technique of procuring an abortion by committing a sacrilege, for which the penalty is miscarriage. The *Efik* (PB, Hewan) women tested the "quality" of their pregnancy, by taking a certain drug during the third month. Too large a dose of this drug sometimes caused them to abort. *Dobu* (Bromilow) women deliberately abort by means of "accidents." They play games so boisterously that they fall down heavily on their bellies, and produce what others may believe to be simply miscarriages. It is entirely possible that some primitive women, though not consciously planning to abort, "accidentally on purpose" behave in a manner which produces abortions masquerading as "miscarriages." Since in many areas standard means of abortion consist in lifting or carrying heavy loads, or in working too hard, a woman, unconsciously desiring to abort, may "accidentally on purpose" overexert herself, just as some modern women "accidentally on purpose" forget to follow the rules laid down by their obstetricians, or just "happen" to fall down the stairs. Some *Chippewa* (Hilger) data permit us to infer that some "miscarriages" allegedly due to overwork—which is known to produce miscarriages—may be abortions procured "accidentally on purpose," for unconscious reasons. We may also suspect that among the *Ashanti* (Rattray)—where a woman whose adultery becomes known otherwise than through her own confession must abort—some women may manage to have their adultery become known "accidentally on purpose," being perhaps motivated by an impulse to confess and to atone, as well as by an unconscious desire to abort. This, however, is a matter of inference only.

III. INVOLUNTARY ABORTION CAUSED BY ASSAULT

We found very few references—one of which is legal—to assaults seemingly *consciously calculated* to cause a woman to abort. A *Copper Eskimo* (Jenness) angrily beat his wife in a manner apparently calculated to cause an abortion. Unfortunately, we do not know the causes of this quarrel. *Assyrian* (Sigerist) law viewed both assaults causing miscarriage and voluntary abortions as acts which deprive the husband of his offspring. The assailant was severely punished in accordance with the lex talionis, while women who aborted deliberately were—significantly—impaled.

The *"accidental"* aborting of a woman is seldom mentioned. The *Persian* King Cambyses (Herodotus) was reproached by his pregnant sister-wife for having killed their brother Smerdis, thus stripping the house of their father Cyrus of its members. "Then Cambyses was wroth, and sprang fiercely upon her, though she was with child at the time. And so it came to pass that she miscarried and died." This, of course, further depopulated the house of Cyrus. A revealing light is shed on this episode by the flattering speech which Croesus shortly thereafter addressed to Cambyses, whom other courtiers had just declared superior to his father Cyrus. Croesus offered subtler flattery, declaring Cambyses inferior to his father, *because he had not yet left behind him a son like Cambyses.* This flattery was offered shortly after the miscarriage of Cambyses' unborn child! Among the *Masai* (Hollis), if a man cohabits with a pregnant woman and thereby causes her to miscarry, the neighborhood women beat him and strangle and suffocate as many of his cattle as they can—a punishment similar to that inflicted on abortionists. The *Mohave* (Devereux) believe that *violent* coitus, as well as oral or anal cohabitation with a pregnant woman, may injure the fetus. The *Masai* and *Mohave* data suggest that coitus with a pregnant woman is accompanied by body-robbing fantasies. We therefore suspect that if a pregnant woman is assaulted in such a manner that she "accidentally" miscarries, the assault reflects unconscious body-robbing and sibling rivalry (Cambyses' case) impulses. The fact that *Assyrian* law equates such assaults with voluntary acts calculated to make a woman abort, i.e., views both as acts which rob the husband of his offspring, confirms this suspicion. The final victory of a man who was delivered by a Cesarean over the wicked king (Shakespeare: *Macbeth*) is worth remembering in this context, since this Cesarean operation is described in words which make it seem an act of violence rather than an operation.*

IV. INVOLUNTARY ABORTION MASQUERADING AS MISCARRIAGE

WITCHCRAFT MOTIVATED BY MALICE may cause a *Mohave* (Devereux) woman to abort.

WITCHCRAFT ON BEHALF OF A PRINCIPAL occurs among the *Achewa* (Steytler), where a magician, using a little boy as a cat's paw, causes a woman to abort so as to get hold of the fetus, which he then uses in erecting a furnace for his principal, who is a smith.

THE GHOST OF A WOMAN WHO DIED IN CHILDBIRTH may abort a *Nias* (Chamberlain) woman.

THE DEVIL causes *Lepcha* (Gorer) women to abort. In the *Marquesas* (Linton) many women had a male familiar spirit, the *fanaua,* who was either the spirit of an ancestor or a male spirit in love with the woman. Such familiar spirits, and more especially those in love with the woman, would, at her bidding, abort certain women whom she disliked.

VARIOUS SUPERNATURALS may cause *Ashanti* (Rattray) women to abort. This can be counteracted by drugs.

* The *Lamba* (Doke) husband is obliged to rip open the belly of his dead pregnant wife, in order to deliver the dead baby. The manner in which this has to be done is so gruesome that many husbands shrink from it and prefer to hire a substitute at considerable expense to themselves.

TRIBAL ELDERS among the *Tiv* (Abraham, Downes, East) give a primipara suffering from the discomforts of pregnancy a supposedly curative but actually abortifacient drug, in order to make her abort, so that they can use the fetus for certain earth rites.

A MALICIOUS CO-WIFE sometimes causes an *Ashanti* (Rattray) woman to abort.

MEDICINE MEN sometimes cause *Witoto* (Whiffen) women to abort for their own protection and purposes.

3. ALTERNATIVES TO ABORTION

Perhaps the psychologically most interesting avenue of approach to an understanding of abortion is an examination of substitutes and alternatives for abortion.

MARRIAGE is a less common alternative than one might expect. In *Ponape* (Hambruch, Eilers) a pregnant girl was supposed to marry her lover. A *Wogeo* (Hogbin) girl whose attempted abortion was unsuccessful was beaten and ridiculed by her sisters for being unable to make her lover marry her.

"CONTRACEPTION." The *Songosor* (Eilers) girl expects her lover to remove his semen from her vagina with his finger. If he refuses to do so, the girl will grant him no further favors, even though in this group bastards are nothing to be ashamed of.

INFANTICIDE. If a *Gunantuna* (Meier) girl fails to abort her bastard, she may kill it. More important from our point of view is the relatively recent substitution of abortion for traditional forms of infanticide in *Samoa* (PB), the *Society Islands* (PB) and elsewhere, under white pressure. It has been stated for *Mala* (Hopkins), and for other *Melanesian* groups as well, that the substitution of abortion for infanticide led to a decrease in "racial vigor."

SUICIDE. *Buka* (Blackwood) women sometimes killed themselves when they did not succeed in aborting their adulterine bastards. Lactating *Chagga* (Raum) women, pregnant by their husbands, will try to abort, and if they fail, sometimes commit suicide.

FLIGHT. A *Kgatla* (Shapera) girl, pregnant by someone other than her fiancé, fled the tribe.

CONDONEMENT. *Buka* (Blackwood) husbands sometimes claim the paternity of an adulterine bastard, in order to avoid a scandal. The community does not challenge this obviously false claim.

4. THE FREQUENCY OF ABORTION

Statistical data on abortion in primitive society are mostly either unavailable or else both unreliable and skimpy. The data available are of several types:

GENERAL PREVALENCE. We meet with such general statements as "abortion is very common," or "on the increase," or "very rare," or "absent."

PERCENTAGES. In *Alor* (Du Bois) 10.5% of 121 pregnancies were aborted or miscarried. Of 44 *Kgatla* (Shapera) women studied, 8 either admitted that they had aborted, or were known to have done so. In *Fiji* (Thomson) 35 out of 448 mothers of families had had miscarriages and/or abortions.

INDIVIDUAL FREQUENCIES reported are of the following kinds: In *New Ireland* and *Lavongai* (Parkinson) sixteen- and seventeen-year-old girls admit 3 to 5 abortions. In *Formosa* (Campbell-Candidius and others), where women abort all pregnancies until they are thirty-four to thirty-seven years of age, some women had had as many as sixteen abortions. Among the *Chukchee* (Bogoras) three women provided accurate data: one had 5 living, 2 dead, and 5 aborted children; the second had 7 living, 3 dead, and 3 aborted children; and the third had 6 living, 2 dead, and 2 aborted children. (Another passage makes one wonder, however, whether miscarriages were meant.)

FREQUENCY IN TIME. In a Mu'ò'ng (Cuisinier) village, one abortion and 3 clandestine births occurred in the ten months during which the village was studied.

CUSTOM AS AN INDEX OF FREQUENCY yields fairly precise but nonnumerical data. The *Mataco* (HDBK) custom of aborting all first conceptions simply establishes that two unspecified numbers are equal. In addition, information of this type gives no clues to the frequency of additional and differently motivated abortions.

5. THE TIME OF THE ABORTION

Women attempt to abort from the first moment of pregnancy until the very last stages thereof. The *Kgatla* (Shapera) women take a drug to expel the semen immediately after coitus. In *Yap* (Senfft) women seek to abort when they miss their first menses. The *Sinaugolo* (PB) abort only while the baby is still believed to be a bloodclot. The *Swaheli* (PB) believe that one can abort as late as two to four months after conception. The *Masai* (PB) prefer to abort during the third month. The *Dahomeyan* (Herskovits) abortifacient is useless after the third month. The *Navaho* (AH) probably abort only after there is quickening. *Persians* (PB) abort as late as the sixth or seventh month. In *New*

Guinea (Keysser), women abort even in advanced pregnancy. The *Ao Naga* (Hutton) abort a few days before actual delivery. A *Hopi* (Beaglehole) girl killed her baby while she was actually delivering it, by squeezing it to death between her legs.

A brief comment about abortions occurring as late as the last two just cited may not be superfluous. One may ask why the woman cannot wait a few days, or, in the *Hopi* case, a few minutes, before disposing of the child by infanticide, with far less risk to herself. One suspects that, in addition to self-punitive mechanisms and to rationalizations that the child is less fully alive within the womb than after it is born, these women may be afraid that once they see their babies, they may not be able to kill them. A native remark suggesting this interpretation will be cited in the section on Attitudes.

6. TECHNIQUES OF ABORTION

As many women, modern as well as primitive, have discovered, it is difficult and dangerous to terminate a pregnancy at will. It is, hence, rather surprising that in the entire literature consulted there were but few references to natural factors facilitating voluntary abortion. Abortion among the *Mohave* Indians (Devereux) is sometimes facilitated by venereal disease. Since such diseases also occur in numerous other primitive societies, this may explain why some seemingly ineffective or crude abortifacient techniques are often successful. Thus, it is possible that the *Hopi* (Beaglehole) were able to cling to the belief that a girl can abort simply by wishing it, only because the "somatic compliance" was appreciably facilitated by venereal disease. Other ailments probably play a similar role. The *Rhadé Moi* (Jouin) specifically mention spontaneous abortions during attacks of malaria. Even structural impairments of the reproductive system, due perhaps to inadequate maternal care, may facilitate abortion. This is suggested by the *Central Celebes* (WGS) practice of aborting in order to forestall the possibility of a perineal tear, which is deemed to be shameful.

I. THE DISCOVERY OF TECHNIQUES

OBSERVATION. In the case of miscarriages due to mechanical injuries, to effort or to jolting, even superficial observation may suggest a causal connection and enable the primitive to adapt an observed accident to the deliberate production of abortions. In the case of drugs, starvation, loss of blood, etc., several observations and more than usual ingenuity may be needed to transform the lesson of a fortuitous occurrence into technical "progress."

TRANSPOSITION OF TECHNIQUE. Some techniques are straightforward adaptations of obstetrical practices to abortion. A *Chinese* (PB) drug, prescribed for the expulsion of an already dead fetus, could be used also as an abortifacient. The *Opata* (AH) shake both the parturient woman and the woman who wishes to abort. The *Mohave* (Devereux) prescribe stallion meat just before delivery, "to kick out the baby," but intimate that, taken prematurely, it could cause an abortion or a miscarriage.

HOSTILITY may well suggest suitable means, as witness a *Copper Eskimo* (Jenness) husband's savage abuse of his wife, and the *Persian* Cambyses' (Herodotus) aggression against his sister-wife.

SUICIDALNESS is probably a powerful motive force behind the invention of abortifacient techniques. This may explain why jumping from high places is highly characteristic of *Melanesians* and *Papuans,* as a means both of committing suicide and of aborting. [See also the *Ila* (Smith and Dale) data.]

TRUE INVENTIVENESS does not seem to be characteristic of any of the primitive tribes studied, at least not in connection with abortion producing techniques.

BORROWING. Many *Ainu* (Pilsudski) women use Japanese abortifacients.

EXPORTATION OF TECHNIQUES. The *Semang* (Schebesta) do not

use abortifacients, but sell certain abortifacients known to them to their *Malay* customers.

REJECTION OF NEW TECHNIQUES. A *Chippewa* (Hilger) woman resented the advice given to her by a white woman.

II. TECHNICAL DIFFERENCES

NUMBER OF TECHNIQUES. Although the small number of techniques at the lower end of the scale may be due to inadequate reporting, the only abortifacient recorded for the *Loyalty Islands* (PB) is the drinking of hot sulphur spring water, while the culturally not more advanced *Pima* (AH) use mechanical means, heat from the sun and hot stones, starvation, drugs, the unique effort technique of climbing a rope and letting oneself fall, and the equally unique technique of burial up to the waist.

SOCIAL DIFFERENCES. In the *Canary Islands* (PB) rural people had their herbs and urbanites their expert abortionists.

TRIBAL DIFFERENCES, even between closely related groups, were often considerable: As regards the various *Apache* (AH) tribes, the *Jicarilla* used herbs and probably also mechanical means. The *Mescalero* used "drugs"—including a fermented one—and instrumentation, one form of which, the bent wire, is thought not to be an aboriginal technique. The *San Carlos* used mechanical means and drugs. The *White Mountain* group used mechanical means and external pressure on the *fundus uteri.*

CULTURAL LEVEL. If we disregard such lower extremes as the *Tasmanians* (GPM), who used only mechanical means, and such upper extremes as *Rome* (PB) or the *Arab Khalifate* (PB), where many techniques were known, the number and variety of techniques used do not seem closely correlated with the degree of cultural development. However, here too the incompleteness of our data may make this conclusion unreliable.

AREAL DIFFERENCES are too complex to discuss in a brief chapter, except to mention our impression that jumping is predominantly characteristic of *Melanesians* and *Papuans* and of such culturally somewhat related areas as *Alor* (Du Bois) and *Truk* (Gladwin). Outside this area, it is mentioned as a custom for the *Ainu* (Pilsudski) and the *Chippewa* (Hilger), and perhaps for classical *Greece* (PB). The remaining data (*Navaho,* Bailey; *Pima,* AH) almost certainly refer to individual cases rather than to custom. The *Navaho* case, in particular, is almost certainly an instance of individual improvisation. *South American Indians* (HDBK)—who gave numerous valuable drugs to modern medicine—seem much addicted to abortifacient medication. Sea water as an abortifacient draught is, for obvious reasons, limited to seacoasts, but this does not explain why it should be used so only in the *Pacific Ocean* area. Likewise, only camel-herders would know the irritant properties of camel-sputum, which does not explain why it is reported as an abortifacient only from *Siwah Oasis* (Cline). Chopped hair is a commonly used poison in *Southeast Asia,* which makes its appearance as an abortifacient among the *Menomini* (Hoffman), and apparently nowhere else, doubly puzzling. These, and similar, areal distribution problems cannot be solved until we have reasonably *accurate* data from at least 100 widely scattered tribes, rather than *incomplete* ones from some 400 cultures.

III. SPECIFIC TECHNIQUES

ANESTHESIA

In *Ponape* (Hambruch-Eilers) the woman prepares herself for abortion by drinking kava. Since this is the only reference to drugs purporting to alleviate the pains of abortion in primitive society, it should be mentioned that in *Samoa* (Mead) the chewing of large quantities of kava is supposed to cause abortion.

ABORTIFACIENT MANEUVERS

A. *Effort*

Hard work in general is reported from many areas. Types of work involving rhythmic movements of the pelvis seem especially popular. Thus, *Hopi* (Beaglehole) girls squatted and ground corn in the metate for hours on end.

LIFTING heavy objects is mentioned for the *Kwakiutl* (Ford).

CARRYING HEAVY LOADS is reported from *Malekula* (Leggatt). A puzzling technique is reported from the *Navaho* (Bailey), who supposedly carry a log "on top of the baby."

CLIMBING—and especially climbing a smooth tree—is recorded from the *Purari* (Williams). In addition to climbing a coconut palm, the *Miriam* (Haddon) woman also bumps her belly against the trunk while she is ascending and descending it, thus combining effort with jolts and with mechanical means.

PADDLING. After climbing a smooth tree, the *Purari* (Williams) woman paddles her canoe toward the Baroi River to the west. No other direction will do. Hence, in this tribe, the effort technique is combined with magical means.

B. *Jolts*

JUMPING UP AND DOWN seven times was prescribed to a harp-player by no lesser personage than Hippocrates, father of *Greek* (PB) medicine and classical opponent of abortion.

JUMPING FROM HIGH OBJECTS, such as rocks or trees, is reported from *Alor* (Du Bois) and from many *Melanesians* and *Papuans*. A *Pima* (AH) girl repeatedly pulled herself up on a suspended rope and then dropped down.

JOLTING ONESELF AGAINST A STONE WHILE SQUATTING is reported from *Alor* (Du Bois). Since it is specified that one does this in a squatting position where, one assumes, the knees protect the abdomen, this technique must be viewed as jolting rather than as a mechanical abortion, as we define it.

DIVING INTO THE SEA, from an overhanging ledge or from another elevation, is reported only for the *Gunantuna* (Meier).

SHAKING. The *Opata* (AH) woman is grasped by the hips from behind, and is shaken exactly as though she were in regular labor.*

C. *Heat Applied Externally*

HOT WATER is poured on the belly of the *Sedang* (Devereux) woman, though this may scald her.

HOT ASHES are put on the abdomen in *Kroë, Sumatra* (PB).

* Since nineteenth-century upperclass Occidental women frequently tried to abort by riding horseback, it is noteworthy that this technique is not mentioned for any primitive tribe. On the contrary, the only reference to primitives riding horseback in *this* connection assigns exactly the opposite purpose to this sport: in a certain tribe where the women aborted quite freely, a woman wishing to carry her baby to term rode horseback in order to strengthen the fetus. Unfortunately the exact reference to this custom was permanently mislaid, so that we are obliged to quote it from memory and can assign it only tentatively to the *Mataco Indians*.

HOT COALS, wrapped in an old shoe sole, are put on the *Kalmuck* (PB) girl's belly, just above the uterus. She supports this and other skin irritations stoically.

WARM STONES are put on the belly, and are used to rub it, in *Tikopia* (Firth).

A HEATED COCONUT HUSK is used by *Kiwai* (Landtman) women, who lie across it so that its heat will go inside and kill the baby.

A BIG FIRE is made by the *Manja* (Vergiat) woman, who then cleans the fireplace, sprinkles water on it, and lies down on her belly, steaming her abdomen.

LYING IN THE SUN for a long time occurred among the *Pima* (AH) centuries ago.

D. *Skin Irritants* seem to be related to external applications of heat.

VARIOUS IRRITATING DEVICES are used by the *Kalmucks* (PB).

IRRITATING LEAVES are rubbed by the *Taulipang* (Koch-Grünberg) on the skin.

BLACK BEETLES are collected by *Aranda* (Basedow) women, who roast them, reduce them to powder, and then rub this into their armpits and on their bellies and pubes.

LARGE TONCADIRA ANTS are made to bite the *Taulipang* (Koch-Grünberg) woman's body. These ants are also taken internally (See Drugs).

SKIN IRRITANTS ARE COMBINED WITH TOPICAL APPLICATIONS on *Eddystone Island* (Rivers). A *meka* leaf is heated and rubbed on the belly, and four *tingi* leaves are held under the vulva. (Whether "under" does, or does not, imply contact is not clear from the text. The whole practice may be purely magical.)

BATHS, though commonly used in Europe, are mentioned only for *Fiji* (Thomson) and *Micronesia* (Matsuoka). The *Gunantuna* (Meier) practice of diving into the sea is apparently not a bathing but a jolting technique. (See also Manipulation of the Genitals.)

E. *Weakening of the organism* is accomplished in two ways:

STARVATION. The *Pima* (AH) girl seeks to abort by starving herself. Certain *Amazonas Indian tribes* (Tastevin) diet to the point of starving themselves while taking sterilizing drugs.

BLEEDING. Both *Persian* (PB) and *Kgatla* (Shapera) women bleed themselves on the foot. The *Bukaua* (PB) proceed more radically, and make incisions on the belly, the elbows, the knuckles, the fingertips, and the heels, with a certain sharp grass. *Persian* (PB) women also use leeches to bleed themselves.*

F. *Mechanical abortion* is defined here as any technique which seeks to damage the fetus through the abdominal wall.

THE GIRL'S OWN WEIGHT, either of itself or supplemented by special contrivances or movements, is used in many areas to produce abortion. The *Pima* (AH) girl simply lies face downward for a long while. The *Gunantuna* (Meier) girl lies down on a mat and presses her belly against it. The *Wappo* (Driver) girl rolls around on her belly. The *San Carlos Apache* (AH) girl leans across the edge of a box. The *Assiniboine* and *Crow* (PB) girl thrusts a stick into the ground so that its top is about two feet above ground. Then she leans her belly against the top of the stick and rolls her belly around.

A WEIGHT may be placed on the belly and may even be rolled around on it. The *Miriam* (Haddon) women place a basket full of yams on their bellies. The *Aymara* (HDBK) roll a stone on the belly.

A CONSTRICTION BELT around the waist is used by the *Manus* (Mead). Pondramet's wife used this device with fatal results. The *Hottentot* (PB) place the sash just above the uterus, to stop the growth of the fetus. In *Eddystone Island* (Rivers) they put on a belt made of a creeper which lies across the road, and also utter a formula, thus supplementing constriction with magic. In *Nufor Island* (PB) the woman first puts on a tight belt, and then has someone step on her abdomen, thus supplementing constriction with gross traumatic crushing. In *Bukaua* (PB) the pregnant woman is pulled through a tree fork. It is not clear whether this is magic or constricting pressure.

BURYING THE WOMAN TO HER WAIST is recorded only for the *Pima* (AH). It is not clear whether or not this represents constriction.

SQUEEZING. The *Kwakiutl* (Ford) mother clasps her pregnant daughter's waist from behind. This is a common obstetrical

* Cf. the *Sedang* (Devereux) case history for a mention of leeches, to explain away bleeding after abortion.

manipulation among many Indians. In *Suau* (Williams) it is the chest which is squeezed, since during early pregnancy the fetus is believed to be high up in the torso. In *New Britain* (Danks) they grab the waist on both sides and press and work the fingers into the belly, to compress it. The *Kamchadal* (PB) squeeze the baby to death in the womb so that, when it putrefies, it comes out in pieces.

MASSAGE AND RUBBING. The *Dusun* (Staal) smear oil on the belly and then massage it. The *Cahita* (Wagner) rub an "abortifacient" paste on the belly, but in Wagner's opinion it is the rubbing which is effective. In *Bukaua* (PB) they rub the body with tapa-cloth. *Samoans* (PB) massage and knead the abdomen. The *Miriam* (Haddon) press the belly with a bamboo. This technique is also used to remove the baby from the womb of a woman who dies in childbirth. A rolling-pin type of pressure is used in *Persia* (PB.) In *Pukapuka* (Beaglehole) deep massage is believed to be more effective if the abortionist's hands are first dipped into hot water.

MASSAGE AROUND THE UTERUS, with "crooked thumbs" is practiced at *Mt. Hagen* (Gitlow). The *White Mountain Apache* (AH) apply pressure on the *fundus uteri.*

PRESSURE WITH A POINTED OBJECT is a relatively skilled operation. The *Yana* (Gifford and Klimek) apply pressure with the thumbs and fingernails. (See also "The girl's own weight," preceding.)

PINCHING THE BELLY is reported from *Java* (PB.)

TWISTING THE BELLY is done by the *Angami Naga* (Hutton).

GRASPING THE UTERUS through the abdominal wall, and twisting and squeezing it until the fetal connections are detached, is done by the *Zuni* (AH).

FEELING FOR THE HEAD, grasping it through the abdominal wall, and then hitting it sharply with a stone, is practiced by the *Ao Naga* (Hutton) a few days before birth.

SQUEEZING THE BABY between the thighs, as it emerges from the womb, is done among the *Hopi* (Beaglehole).

THE GROSS TRAUMATIZATION OF THE BELLY is widely practiced. In *New Britain* (PB) the belly is hit from both sides with the thumbs and fingers. A *Harney Valley Paiute* (B. Whiting) smote his wife's stomach, which public opinion considered "pretty mean." If the *Payagua* (PB) woman already has several children, they belabor her belly with fists. The *Murngin* (Warner) abort a woman by getting on her on their hands and knees. A *Queka Kwakiutl* (PB) medicine man knelt on a woman's belly. An angry *Copper Eskimo* (Jenness) husband threw his wife on the snow and rolled his foot on her belly. In the *Torres Straits* (PB) the abdomen is hit with a stone. The *Greenland Eskimo* (PB) use the stick wherewith they stretch wet footwear, and the *Smith Sound Eskimo* (PB) use a whip-handle or some other object to smite or to poke the abdomen several times a day. The *Miriam* (Haddon) woman stands with her back against a tree, and two men, holding a pole horizontally, push hard against her belly. The *Assiniboine* and the *Crow* (PB) woman lies down on her back. A plank is put across her stomach, and several women step on and hop up and down on it, until blood spurts from the vagina. A *Pima* (AH) girl repeatedly ran wildly at a closed door, striking it with her abdomen. Pseudo-accidents are also used to traumatize the abdomen. In *Dobu* (Bromilow), girls play games boisterously and make themselves fall down heavily. In many tribes, such as the *Miriam* (Haddon), gross traumatization is resorted to only after other methods fail, while among the *Tasmanians* (GPM) only such crude methods were known.

G. *Manipulation of the Genitals*

The *Romans* (PB) rubbed the organs. Old *Mohave* (Devereux) women knew how "to reach inside and choke the baby"—presumably meaning thereby a violent manipulation of the cervix. In *Fiji* (Thomson) the pregnant woman first squats waist-deep in water and is subjected to a vaginal examination by an old "wise woman," who tries to ascertain by this procedure precisely what remedy should be administered. This diagnostic manipulation sometimes suffices to make the woman abort. Similar "diagnostic" manipulations in supposedly "simple menstrual troubles" often produce "accidental" abortions in *Fiji* (Quain).

H. *Coitus*

The *Masai* (Leakey) believed that coitus may cause a pregnant woman to abort.

I. *Instrumentation* can be of various types. The *Masai* (Leakey) insert a sharp stick into the vagina. The *Chagga* (Raum) insert the midrib of a leaf into the uterus. In *Fiji* (PB) women preferred to insert two sticks instead of just one. In *Persia* (PB) a hook is used to break the membrane. The *Mescalero Apache* (AH) woman had another woman insert a bent wire into her uterus—a technique which, according to Hrdlička, may not be aboriginal. In *Hawaii* (PB) a kind of wooden stiletto, whose handle represented Kupo, the god of abortions, was used.* The *Japanese* (PB) did not seek to pierce the fetal membrane, but preferred to insert a pointed root, anointed with musk—which they also took internally as an abortifacient—between the fetal membrane and the wall of the uterus. Considerable skill was shown by two groups in inserting the instrument. Among the *Batak* (PB) a kind of peashooter propelled the midrib of a leaf, or a bamboo sliver, into the mouth of the uterus. The *Eskimo of Smith Sound* (Bessels) took considerable precautions not to injure the vagina during instrumentation. Needless to say, primitive instrumentation often had tragic results. Infections and severe injuries to the cervix, including open wounds, have been reported by physicians practicing in *India* (PB). In *Hawaii* (Handy *et al.*) archaeologists even found in a cave a pointed stick near the remains of a female who presumably died as a result of instrumentation.

J. *Inserting foreign bodies* into the uterus and leaving them there is commonly practiced. The *Romans* (PB) inserted papyrus into the orifice of the cervix, while in *Mainate, India* (PB) a small stick is put into it. In *Turkey* tobacco, or an olive stem, is left in the cervix. The *Japanese* (PB) insert a thread of silk covered by musk into it. At the peak of *Arab* (PB) medical progress, the mouth of the cervix was first opened with emollient pessaries, and then a ball of wool strewn with irritant substances was put into it. A simpler method is practiced in *Fezzan* (PB), where a ball of tobacco, or cotton soaked in the juice of *Colotropis procera,* is inserted into the birth canal. The *Romans* (PB) also used dry sponges.

* Bartels (PB) suspected that this selfsame instrument may also have been used to dilate the orifice of the cervix to facilitate conception, but this view is violently disputed by von Reitzenstein (PB).

K. *Irritant pessaries* were used by *Arab* (PB) physicians, who also caused women to carry certain drugs in the vagina. The *Romans* (PB) used pessaries.

L. *Local medication* has also been reported. *Arab* (PB) physicians opened the cervix with an instrument and injected irritating substances. The modern Egyptians of *Alexandria* (PB) irritate the uterus with laurel, pepper, etc. A douche of *elixirium proprietatis Paracelsi* was used in *Turkey* (HK). The *Romans* (PB) fumigated the organs with the help of an instrument called the embryosphactes, whose description is not known.

M. *Clysters* were used by the *Efik* (Hewan), though they are, interestingly, not reported as abortifacients from the numerous Indian tribes who had aboriginal bulbed enema syringes.

N. *Drugs taken internally* as abortifacients are reported from most areas of the world. Some of these drugs have known and appropriate effects, while others are frankly semimagical. No attempt can be made to list their infinite variety. Only their general classification can be attempted.

PROVENIENCE:

1. Herbs and plants are the most commonly listed abortifacients.
2. Insects: The *Taulipang* (Koch-Grünberg) pound large Toncadira ants and take this paste in water left standing outdoors overnight.
3. Animal secretions: In *Siwah Oasis* (Cline) the foam from the camel's mouth is taken. Musk is used in Japan (PB).
4. Animal products: The *Menomini* (Hoffman) chop up the tail hairs of the blacktail deer and administer them in bearfat, causing gastric irritation and hence possibly also uterine contractions. The *Menomini* themselves believe, however, that the fine spicules of hair dart forward like magic arrows and search out the life which is to be destroyed.*

* This surprising technique is almost certainly reliably reported, since *Lkungen* (Boas) women eat the sharp leaves of *Carex sp.* which supposedly "cut" and kill the unborn child. In both instances the abortion may be due to an irritation of the gastrointestinal tract. Indeed, in *Fiji* (Thomson), the abortionists know that their drugs irritate the bowels.

5. The *Jivaro* (Karsten) use raw eggs, and the *Masai* (Merker) goat dung.
6. Fossil organic matter: The Tatars (PB) of South Russia use both amber and amber water.
7. Inorganic matter: The *Persians* (HK) use emetic of copper sulphate. *Baholoholo* (HA) women drink water from the smith's fire bucket, which contains iron sulphate, an emmenagogue.
8. Water: Sea water is drunk in *Suau* (Williams), and boiled (hot?) sea water in *Yap* (PB). The Loyalty Islanders (PB) drink water from a hot sulphur spring.

SIMPLES VS. COMPOUNDS. Several simples have just been listed. However, the *tribes of the Amazonas* in *Brazil* (Tastevin) add to all their drugs a "corrective" second drug.

DRECKAPOTHEKE pure and simple does not seem to be used. Indeed, the camel's sputum mentioned above has irritant properties, and the powdered bodies of the Toncadira ants presumably contain formic acid. The *Masai's* (Merker) goat dung may perhaps cause nausea and vomiting. This absence is noteworthy, since Dreckapotheke, though rare among primitives, is not absolutely lacking even in primitive gynecological practice. Thus, some *Navahos* (Stewart) use mule's rectum boiled with certain plants, as a sterilizing substance.

POLYVALENT DRUGS are common. Some *Manja* (Vergiat) drugs are also used as aphrodisiaca. Among the *Nama Hottentot* (Laidler) Klipsweet, boiled and strained, is, in small doses, a favorite medicine for children. In larger doses it is administered for the treatment of the inadequate flow of birth waters and for menstrual difficulties. In large doses it is an abortifacient. The *Efik* (PB) have a drug which, in moderate quantities, "tests the quality of the pregnancy," while in larger doses it is an abortifacient.

CHARACTERISTICS. Emetics are used in *Persia* (PB). Laxatives are taken among the *Aymara* (HDBK). Strong purgatives are administered in *Gilan, Persia* (PB). Emmenagogues are reported from *Lesu* (Powdermaker). Astringents are taken by the *Lampong* (PB). Sternutators have been reported from *Rome* (PB). The *Cahita* (Wagner) give convulsants. Toxic substances are used as abortifacients in *Annam* (Dê), and probably also in *Wogeo* (Hogbin). In *Fiji* (Thomson) the female abortionists know that their abortifacient drugs initially irritate the bowels. Because of its appearance, a certain abortifacient drug is called "the frothy drink." It is not clear, however, whether its abortifacient qualities are directly ascribed to its frothy appearance. The *Muria* (Elwin) use alcohol.

PREPARATION. The most common form in which drugs are taken is a decoction, infusion, or "tea." In the *Torres Straits* (PB), two leaves are chewed together. The *Mescalero Apache* (AH) use a fermented vegetable drug, while the *Manja* (Vergiat) let one of their drugs, made of a paste of crushed seeds, germinate. In *New Caledonia* (PB), green bananas are made into hot mush. (It is suspected that a secret drug is added to this mush.) The *Menomini* (Hoffman) chop the tail hairs of the blacktail deer into fine spicules and mix them with bearfat, the latter being apparently simply a vehicle for the former. In the case of a certain magic abortifacient, the magic drug itself is *not* eaten. The *Kai* (PB) boil a kernel found in the cassowary's excrement with vegetables, and then eat the vegetables only, since they feel that the soul-substance of that kernel—which is its "active" part—has communicated itself to the vegetables.

MODE OF ADMINISTRATION. Most internal medications are taken only internally. However, the *Japanese* (PB) use musk both as a local irritant and internally. The *Buka* (Blackwood) take their abortifacient internally, but also rub some of it on the abdomen. The *Jivaro* (Karsten) pour a raw egg directly into the mouth of the woman. Only a few drugs are chewed, as among natives of the *Torres Straits* (PB), or eaten, as in *New Caledonia* (PB). Most drugs are liquid infusions, which are drunk, as among the *Aymara* (HDBK). The *Gunantuna* (Meier) supplement drugs with magic rites known to the women.

TEMPERATURE. Hot water (*Yap*, PB), warm infusions (*Aymara*, HDBK), and hot food (*New Caledonia*, PB) are most common. One infers, however, that the *Taulipang* (Koch-Grünberg) take their emulsion of powdered Toncadira ants cold, since they put it in water left standing outdoors overnight.*

PHARMACODYNAMICS are an extremely ill-explored subject. Some native groups may be taking effective medication for the wrong reason, or, like the *Kai* (PB), they may take ineffective

* The *Mohave* (Devereux) say that cold water is contraindicated during menstruation, pregnancy and childbirth.

drugs for imaginary reasons. We have already mentioned that the *Menomini* (Hoffman) chopped deer hair may be effective because it sets up a gastrointestinal irritation, although the *Menomini* themselves believe that these spicules act like magic arrows, which seek out the life they are supposed to destroy. The *Kai* (PB) use a kernel found in the feces of the cassowary, which may be pharmacologically entirely ineffective, though the natives feel that its effectiveness lies in its soul-substance. We also mentioned that in the case of the *Cahita* (Wagner), who rub a drug on the abdomen, the *rubbing* rather than the *drug* may cause abortion. The *Algerian Arabs* (PB) have a drug which, in their opinion, causes the fetus to shift its position, thus making abortion easier. The *Dahomeyan* (Herskovits) abortifacient is ineffective after the third month of pregnancy. The *Mano* (Harley) hold, however, that their abortifacient is so potent that an abortion may be caused even by simply inhaling its fumes, or by using a pot in which the abortifacient had been boiled. The *Lampong* (PB) use an astringent drink.

SOURCE OF DRUG. Most drugs used are native; only some are imported. (See section on Abortionists.)

IMAGINARY DRUGS. *Chaco Indian* (HDBK) legends speak of marvelous abortifacient drugs, but real abortions are mechanically induced.

OVERDOSES OF HARMLESS DRUGS. The *Bakongo* (Weeks) believe an overdose of kitchen salt to be an abortifacient.

ANTI-ABORTIVES. The *Ashanti* (Rattray) have a drug which counteracts the attempts of witches, supernaturals, and malicious co-wives to abort a pregnant woman.

O. *Magical abortifacient means* discussed in this section are limited to those which the woman herself uses. Magical abortifacient practices of which she is the unwilling victim are discussed in the section on Motivation.

MAGICAL GARMENTS. An *Ainu* (Pilsudski) girl simply slit her lower garment to her waist. This "technique" was unknown to all others, who were amazed when they heard of it.

MAGICAL POSTURE. The *Manja* (Vergiat) girl sits on a certain plant in order to abort.

MAGICAL FOOD. The *Kai* (PB) take a kernel found in the feces of the cassowary, and boil it with vegetables. It is only the vegetables that are eaten, since the kernel's "soul substance," which is its "active" principle, communicates itself to the vegetables.

MAGICAL DRINK. The *Agaria* (Elwin) drink water in which virgin iron was steeped.* The *Algerian Arab* (PB) woman drinks water in which the ink wherewith certain sacred words were written on the bottom of the cup is dissolved. She also recites a magical formula.

MAGICAL BATH AND SHAMPOO. The *Lampong* (PB) medicine man speaks the girl's initials into a lemon, and utters prayers while the girl is bathed. Whenever he squeezes a drop of lemon juice on her head, he urges the unborn and as yet unformed child to emerge before its time, so as not to shame its mother. The lemon is then ceremonially stuffed into the hollow of a *rimba* tree. This treatment is usually supplemented by astringent drinks and massage.

MAGICAL AMULET. The *Turkish* (PB) hodja brings with him an amulet, which has the picture of a long-beaked bird on it. This so irritates an imaginary bird—which comes into being in the womb at the time of the conception and flies away at birth—that it breaks the fetal membrane prematurely and departs.

SYMPATHETIC MAGIC. The *Taulipang* (Koch-Grünberg) throw a gourd on the fire. If it bursts, the fetus will also burst.

UNSPECIFIED MAGIC is mentioned for many tribes, including the *Purari* (Williams) people.

MAGIC AVAILABLE BUT NOT USED. *Mohave* (Devereux) women *could* abort by deliberately violating any of a number of pregnancy taboos, but they never take advantage of this possibility. By contrast, *Maori* (Goldie) women sometimes deliberately commit sacrilege for which the penalty is miscarriage.

DRUGS VS. MAGIC. Many primitives differentiate clearly between what they consider as drugs and what they consider as magic. *Lesu* (Powdermaker) abortifacients are deemed to be drugs. Hence, unlike the magician, the drug-dispensing abortionist is paid after his treatment proves effective, and not in advance.

* The context is not clear enough to enable us to decide whether this water—like that found in the *Baholoholo* (HA) smith's firebucket—contains iron sulphate, which is an emmenagogue.

P. *Psychogenic abortion.* It is quite conceivable that many purely magical drugs, and many pharmacodynamically ineffective or inappropriate medicines as well, may in fact "cause" abortion by psychogenic means. The *Hopi* (Beaglehole) even go so far as to say that a girl can abort by simply wishing it to happen. This may well be so, since psychoanalytic literature contains numerous reports that repeated psychogenically induced miscarriages ceased to occur as a result of psychoanalysis.*

7. PHYSICAL CONSEQUENCES OF ABORTION

Most statements on this subject are exceedingly vague, and it is almost impossible to determine whether such remarks as "many women pay for their crime with their lives" or, conversely, "this brutal abortive technique seems to have no deleterious aftereffects" are native statements or the statements of the observer and, in the latter case, whether they are based on facts or on personal bias and wishful thinking. This being said, the following data seem moderately reliable:

Among the *Ainu* (Pilsudski) a woman became a chronic invalid, and finally died as a result of repeated abortions. *The Indians of the U. S. Southwest* and of *Northern Mexico* (AH) do not greatly fear the risks of abortion. The *Cahita* (Wagner) abortifacient drug temporarily induces violent spasms and even total rigidity. Among the *Kaingang* (Santin de Prade) the whites found in an abandoned village the wife of a chief. Because of a

* The writer himself had in research psychoanalysis a *Plains Indian* woman who for years tried in vain to conceive. Eventually she did become pregnant, but miscarried the child after a couple of months, during a break in her analysis.

recent miscarriage, she was too ill to flee with the rest of the group. The *Zuni* (AH) believe that girls who abort become sterile. The *Kgatla* (Shapera) hold that frequent abortions spoil the blood of the woman and make her permanently sterile. The *Mataco* (Karsten) abortifacient drug is also believed to sterilize the woman for a period of two to eight years. The sterilizing after-effects of *Azimba* (Angus) abortifacients must, later on, be counteracted by means of certain special drugs. A sample of a vague and probably biased statement is that the women of *New Ireland* and *Lavongai* (Parkinson) who abort are so weakened that they die young.

The literature contains only one reference to the deterrent effects of a near-fatal case of abortion. When the *Koyukuk Eskimo* (Marshall) learned that a girl almost died of her abortion, this frightened them so much that no further abortions occurred until the time of Marshall's study.

8. THE ABORTED FETUS

There is little information on the disposal of the aborted fetus and on eschatological beliefs pertaining to it.

I. DISPOSAL OF THE FETUS

DISPOSAL OF THE ORDINARY FETUS. Some *Arapaho* (Hilger) fetuses are buried like adults, while others are disposed of in the same manner as the placenta usually is. Among the *Chippewa* (Hilger) miscarried fetuses were buried like adults, while aborted ones were buried under the floor of the mother's wigwam, or under the root of the tree from which the abortifacient was prepared, or anywhere under the ground. The *Navaho* (Bailey) often simply throw the fetus away. The *Cheyenne* (Hoebel) and the *Kgatla* (Shapera) do the same, but sometimes (accidentally on purpose?) so carelessly that the fetus is found and an investigation takes place. The *Navaho* (Bailey) hide the fetus or put it in a cave. The *Mohave* (Devereux), though practicing cremation, bury fetuses informally and at once.* In *Annam* (Brodrick), where elaborate funeral rites are customary, the fetus is buried informally because it has no soul as yet. If the *Rhadé Moi* (Jouin) woman aborts in or near the village, the fetus is wrapped in an old blanket and is buried in the cemetery. When abortion takes place in the fields or on the road, the fetus is buried on the spot. Both practices contrast with the ritualism of ordinary *Rhadé* burials. Among the *Lepcha* (Gorer), if the fetus was thrown in the river, the priest afterward waved thorny or stinging plants above the river and the parents sacrificed an animal, to discourage the devil responsible for this death from repeating his performance. The *Tiv* (East) fetus is buried by small boys behind the village. The *Achewa* (Steytler) fetus is buried in the refuse heap. When the *Kgatla* (Shapera) find a fetus, they put it in a small pot and bury it in a "cool" place—i.e., in the girl's hut or somewhere in the shade. The *Thonga* (Junod) women bury a fetus which was not properly disposed of by its mother in the mud by the river, where, being "cool," it will not prevent rain from falling. The *Pedi* (Junod) perform rain-rites both where the fetus was found and at its ultimate resting place. In *Hawaii* (Pukui) the aborted fetus was put in the water, entrusted to the care of the gods to whom fetuses belong.

DISPOSAL OF FETUSES ABORTED FOR MAGICAL PURPOSES. The magically aborted *Achewa* (Steytler) fetus is recovered from the rubbish-heap by the magician, who reburies it, mixed with "medicines," at the spot where the new furnace of the smith who had hired him to cause an abortion and obtain a fetus will be erected. The *Tiv* (East) elders, who abort a primipara by

* The *Mohave* (Devereux) dispose of unwanted babies and puppies by burying them alive. A deserted *Mohave* woman revenged herself on her child's father by causing her child—who was not killed at birth, but who died some years later as a result of a seemingly genuine accident—to be buried in the local white cemetery, instead of cremating it according to *Mohave* custom.

magical means, use deception to delay the burial of the fetus until nightfall. Then the fetus is taken to the ritual place, its throat is cut, and its blood is made to drip into a pot. The bloody water is then smeared on a special sacred object, and the elders also wash their hands in it. The rest of the water is sprinkled over the farm and into the well of the tribal keeper of this sacred object. Abraham adds that the fetus' feet, hands, ears, nose, and liver are cooked and then scattered over the keeper's farm. He also specifies that the bloody water is not poured from the pot, but that the sacred object is immersed into the pot, and the water is scattered over the farm and dripped into the well by using this sacred object as a sprinkler. The fetus' navel cord is preserved, and is annually immersed into water which is then scattered on farms and dripped into wells with the sacred object used as a sprinkler.*

THE CANNIBALIZED FETUS. In times of famine *Central Australian* (Róheim) women abort in order to feed the fetus to its older siblings.

II. POST MORTEM SOCIAL STATUS OF FETUS

Among the *Manus* (Mead) the mother does not distinguish in retrospect among miscarried, stillborn, and shortlived infants. They are named, and ritual gifts are subsequently exchanged in their name.

III. THE ESCHATOLOGY OF THE FETUS

This topic is even less well explored than the disposal of the fetus itself. This may be due to the fact that in *Annam* (Brodrick), fetuses are not credited with the possession of souls, while the *Mataco* (Métraux) feel that fetuses and children are not in-

* The following information, bearing on *infanticide,* may suggest the desirability of a further investigation of this topic. The deserted *Araucanian* (HDBK) woman kills her baby and roasts its testicles in a hot pot, in order to make her unfaithful lover impotent. The fact that this practice has a special name (*koftun*) suggests that it is fairly customary.

dependent beings. By contrast, the *Manus* (Mead) go so far as to name aborted fetuses. The *Rhadé* (Jouin) consider the ghosts of fetuses most dangerous, and address them in prayers: "You *genii* of the *manes* of aborted fetuses, you to whom no rice has been offered, to whom no water has been given, for whom no fire was stoked, you who were left in the orchid of the brač tree, do not get angry!" The ghosts of fetuses have access to Heaven, and Aé Dié, master of the universe, so readily listens to them that they can send misfortunes to mankind. They are under the tutelage of the nourishing goddess H'bia Dung Day, who feeds and mothers these children who never lived on earth. The *Hopi* (Beaglehole) believe that if a girl aborts repeatedly, the ghosts of her aborted fetuses will conspire against her and destroy her to prevent her from killing further unborn children. (These data are in line with beliefs from other areas regarding the malignancy of the ghosts of children killed at birth, and of women who die in childbirth.) In *Mangareva* (Te Rangi Hiroa), children born dead, *i.e.,* both aborted and stillborn children, were given names and were later deified under different names; *e.g.,* the child Te-Ma-Omotu, born dead, was deified under the name of Te Agu. The *Maori tiki* may represent stillborn or aborted children, though this is not a point on which there is agreement among anthropologists. The *Maori* call abortion "the excrement of the gods." The *Hawaiians* (Pukui, Handy *et al.*) had a very elaborate eschatology pertaining to fetuses.

IV. MOURNING

In *Tami,* New Guinea (Keysser) the woman who aborted wears a short mourning net, corresponding to the European's "half mourning" attire.

9. THE ABORTIONIST

In most cases the woman herself performs the abortion, sometimes using singularly complicated or painful means to achieve her purpose. There are seemingly equally frequent references to assistance provided by unspecified old women. Expert or inexpert "midwives" practice both in advanced societies—such as *Moslem Persia* (PB) and ancient *Rome,* from whose *sagae,* who practiced abortion, the modern French term for midwife, *sage-femme,* is said to derive (PB)—and in primitive societies, such as *Fiji* (PB). In the harem of the Sultan of *Turkey* (HK) the official abortionist—called the "bloody midwife"—was one of the Sultan's own wives. In *India* (PB) barber women assist women wishing to abort. A *Mohave* (Devereux) schoolgirl was assisted by her schoolmates. Both medicine men and medicine women practice in *Bali* (Weck). Among the *Wolof* (PB), the medicine men of *Cayor* are especially skilled abortionists. *Inca* (HDBK) midwives —who were also abortionists—acquired their powers through visions, through having borne twins, or through undergoing certain rites.

Physicians are sometimes more squeamish than medicine men and midwives about functioning as abortionists. In *Greece* (PB), Hippocrates forbade the physician to perform abortions, but took pity on a pregnant harpist and prescribed exercises calculated to produce it. At the peak of *Arab* (PB) medicine, a famous physician, Abdulkhasem, conceded that abortion may sometimes be a therapeutic necessity, but urged that the operation itself be performed by midwives and not by physicians. Sages also assist with abortions. Safe abortifacients were allegedly invented for the benefit of future generations by the wise men of *China* (PB), who admonished pregnant women not to resort to less safe, strange, and untried means. Semireligious persons and even priests, such as *Turkish* (PB) hodjas and *Algerian* (PB) talebs, also helped women to abort.

Laymen are also known to be professional abortionists. In *Lesu* (Powdermaker), the knowledge of abortifacients is limited to men who learned this art from their maternal uncles, and who make a handsome profit out of it, due to the *Lesu* custom of ostentatiously overpaying everyone. In *Ugi* (Elton), the knowledge of abortifacient drugs is the monopoly of certain women. Among the *Kiwai* (Landtman), the experts are old women, who warn young women not to try to induce an abortion unassisted, because in doing so they risk their lives. All *Gunantuna* (Meier) women know about abortifacients, this knowledge being handed down from mother to daughter. The *Azande* (Czekanowski) have no professional abortionists. Among the *Riff* (Coon) women's markets sell abortifacients, but this is kept secret from the men. Aliens and minorities are often a source of abortifacients. The *Malay* (Schebesta) buy theirs from the *Semang,* who allegedly do not use such drugs themselves. The *Tiv* (Abraham) obtain their supplies from the "Uke" (probably the *Jukun* or the *Hausa*). *Algerian Arab* (PB) women buy their supplies from stores run by *Jewish* women. The *Kgatla* (Shapera), who prefer European chemicals to their own drugs, buy washing blue, ink, etc., from unsuspecting *white* storekeepers.

Abortionists practice with various degrees of concealment. In Constantinople, *Turkey* (PB), there were famous abortion "factories" openly plying their trade. Among the *Riff* (Coon), drugs are sold openly in the women's market, but this is kept secret from the men. Regarding the *Bukaua* (Lehner), we are told that the men don't even want to know anything about matters pertaining to abortion.

The woman's own relatives are seldom mentioned as abortionists. A *Sedang Moi* (Devereux) father aborted his daughter whom he himself had impregnated. The *Truk* (Gladwin) woman is assisted by her mother. *Suau* (Williams) girls are assisted by their maternal aunts. The *Murngin* (Warner) seem to be the only tribe where women are aborted by their sisters. Brothers and male relatives do not seem to function as abortionists. A *Walapai* (Kroeber *et al.*) husband aborted his own wife. The

Muria (Elwin) lover must help his unwed girl friend, while the *Buka* (Blackwood) lover assists his married mistress.

Friends and well-wishers commonly assist women seeking to abort. A *Mohave* (Devereux) schoolgirl was aborted by her schoolmates. *Assiniboine* (Currier) girls receive help from their friends. In the *Torres Straits* (Hunt), the girl is assisted by two unspecified men.

Persons aborting a woman, or forcing her to abort, against her spontaneous wishes, form a separate category. A *Copper Eskimo* (Jenness) husband abused his pregnant wife in a manner which could not fail to cause her to abort. The slave concubines of the Prince of Badong in *Bali* (PB) must report to him as soon as they know that they are pregnant, and are then handed an abortifacient by him. Juvenal ironically advises the deceived *Roman* (PB) husband to give his wife (against her will?) an abortifacient, lest she bear him an Ethiopian brat. Small *Achewa* (Steytler) boys are the unsuspecting cat's paws of magicians who wish to abort a woman. *Tiv* (East) tribal elders abort a primipara for magical purposes, without the latter's knowledge and consent. A *Masai* (Maguire) husband forced his wife, who was pregnant by another man, to abort. Custom obliges an *Ashanti* (Rattray) woman, whose adultery comes to light otherwise than through her confession, to abort "for her own safety." The *Masai* (Merker) cause women pregnant by an old or ailing man to submit to abortion. The *Cuna* (Nordenskiöld) forced women pregnant by a father who was neither a Cuna nor French to abort. The *Gunantuna* (Meier) law more or less requires the abortion of bastards and especially of incestuous children. *Lepcha* (Gorer) women may be aborted by the devil. *Ashanti* (Rattray) women may be aborted by supernaturals, by witches and by malicious co-wives. The ghost of a woman who died in childbed causes *Nias* (Chamberlain) women to abort. In addition, members of the *Wogeo* (Hogbin) girl's own family may put pressure on her to abort, to save themselves as well as her from public humiliation. In *Fiji* (Thomson), ladies of rank who marry outside their own village must take an abortionist with them as a member of their train.

Special Payment Rites: Lesu (Powdermaker) abortionists are not considered magicians. Hence, they are paid after, and not before, they perform their task.

Attitudes toward abortionists and penalties inflicted on them will be discussed in another section.

10. ATTITUDES

VARIABILITY OF ATTITUDES. Contrary to our stereotype of the primitive, attitudes toward an abortion—or toward a failure to abort—may vary even within the same family. Certain individuals may even display attitudes at variance with the tribal standard. Both points are proven by *Wogeo* (Hogbin) data.

MYTHICAL VIEWS ON ABORTION. The *Mohave* (Devereux) believe that since every human activity had a mythical precedent, abortion too must have had one. It must be conceded that no published (Kroeber, Bourke) or unpublished (Devereux) version of the *Mohave* creation myth mentions this incident, and that none of the writer's informants knew it. Nonetheless, they felt certain that a precedent *was* set at the time of creation. Why did they hold this view? In the first place, the *Mohave* creation myth is not static—it is "dreamed," and each person embellishes it in accordance with his inclinations. Thus, a future medicine man who will specialize, *e.g.*, in obstetrics, may "dream" the obstetrical portion of the creation myth. The *Mohave* say that long ago certain witches could abort a woman magically. It is to be assumed that, in accordance with *Mohave* (Kroeber, Devereux) practice, this matter became known because these witches boasted of their deeds. Now, the claim that one has such powers automatically implies that one has "dreamed" the corresponding mythical precedent. Today no witch knows how to abort a woman magically, which, in theological terms, means that there is no one today who knows the relevant mythical precedent through having "dreamed" it. The *Mohave* specify, however, that any forgotten therapeutic rite can be revived whenever someone happens to "dream" the corresponding portion of the creation myth. The conclusion is therefore inescapable that even though there is not a soul today who actually knows this mythical precedent, tomorrow someone may claim to know it because he "dreamed it," his dream having been motivated either by his wish to cause an abortion or by his wish to specialize in the cure and prevention of abortions. We hold that such a chronologically recent "mythical" episode would be a true and bona fide part of the *Mohave* creation myth, which is still in a process of evolution and will remain in a state of evolution as long as any trace of *Mohave* religion is believed in even by a single individual.

THE ABSOLUTE JUSTIFICATION OF ABORTION is the most extreme form of social approval, and is usually based upon some general principle. As regards *Greece* (Ellis), Zeno was of the opinion that unborn children had no souls, and this fact was deemed to justify abortions. The *Sedang* (Devereux), whose custom penalizes abortions, justify it emotionally, by asserting that until the child suckles it is more or less just like a piece of wood. In explanation of this paradox, it should be stressed that the *Sedang* loathe their gods and often declare that they submit to the unreasonable and onerous laws and customs which the gods had foisted on them only because they are unable to defy the gods, whose invisibility alone protects them from the superior courage and cunning of their rebellious human slaves. In other words, the *Sedang* obey and enforce the law against abortions, as they obey and enforce many other divine laws, simply from fear and despite the fact that they deem these laws unjust, unreasonable, or just plain silly.*

CONDITIONAL JUSTIFICATIONS specify that only certain types of abortions are to be socially sanctioned. The *Gunantuna* (Meier) practically demanded that bastards and, a fortiori, incestuously conceived children, should be gotten rid of. In *Wogeo* (Hogbin), a girl was beaten and scolded by her sisters when her attempted

* In the same way the *Sedang* heartily approve of premarital coitus, which the gods forbid, and disapprove of premarital masturbation and homosexuality, which are permitted and which they are obliged to practice because an unreasonable law of the gods denies them a more normal form of sexual gratification.

abortion failed, while her parents observed an icy silence. In *Korea* (Materi), Japanese law legalized the termination of a pregnancy which was due to rape or "error." Turning now to *Greece,* Plato (Rep. V) felt that the fetus should be aborted if the father and the mother were overage or if the child was incestuously conceived. Aristotle (Polit. VII: 16) felt that abortion was justified whenever the parents had had their normal quota of children. In *Cochinchina* (PB) it was no crime to abort a bastard. In *Atjeh* (PB) the husband's consent sufficed to justify an abortion. The *Jivaro* feel that monsters—which may result from impregnation by demons or from legally defective marriages—are not human at all and that, since their birth causes epidemics and misfortune, it is legitimate to abort them. Hence *Jivaro* husbands do not object if their wives want to abort for so legitimate a reason. The upper classes in *Yap* (HRAF)—though frantically trying nowadays to have children, in order to survive—did not approve when the missionaries began to impose western morals, including taboos against abortion, even upon the lower classes. They felt that those of inferior clay—*i.e.,* former payers of tribute—should not be encouraged to breed unchecked. In brief, they viewed the imposition of Christian morality as an attempt to exterminate them. The *Pima* (Grossman) justified the abortion of the lactating woman, deeming this to be in the interest of the baby which was already born. They explained that the mother loved the baby she could see more than the one she could not see. In *Futuna* (Burrows) the aborting of bastards was decided upon by a vote of the women of the neighborhood. Once the women voted for the abortion, they could make the woman abort, even if she herself had no desire to get rid of the fetus.

APPROVAL BY THE GROUP AS A WHOLE. Although abortion is extensively and rather openly practiced in many societies, few groups give it unqualified approval. The *Choroti* (Karsten) approve of the abortion of premarital pregnancies, and so do some other groups.

APPROVAL BY ONE PART OF THE GROUP. The *Kgatla* (Shapera) disapprove of abortion and say that "the knot of the cradle-skin is a flower" even if the child is a bastard. Yet abortions are seldom given any publicity, since the women tend to stick together. In *Hungary* (newspaper reports), peasant women conspire to promote the one-child (egyke) system but know better than to let their menfolk and the officials know about this.

TOLERANCE mostly reflects indifference. In *Fezzan* (PB), there simply is no law against abortions. In nineteenth-century *Turkey* (BP) there was such a law, but it was allegedly so obscurely worded that the judges could never figure out whom they were supposed to punish. Nineteenth-century *Chinese* (PB) laws were fairly severe on paper, but, since the mandarins were more interested in finding mitigating circumstances than in enforcing the law, few persons were punished, and the situation as a whole amounted to toleration. In *Buru* (PB), abortion was generally tolerated.

OPPOSITION TO ABORTION ranged from mild resignation to deep horror. In *Dobu* (Fortune), when Nela, who was not pregnant at that time, chewed some abortifacient (to show that it was not a treacherous poison) before giving it to the anthropologist, and her full breasts became flat as plates the next day, her husband Kopu just said casually: "That is the way of its evil—always." Yet Kopu himself, where his socially important blood-kin, rather than a mere wife, was concerned, felt strongly enough to beat his sister's daughter for aborting, and thus denying him an heir. In *Ponape* (Hambruch, Eilers), abortion is not punished, but is deemed improper. The *Tarahumare* (Bennett and Zingg) call it an "ugly" act. A *Harney Valley Paiute* (B. Whiting) was called "pretty mean" for aborting his wife by traumatizing her abdomen. In *Alor* (Du Bois) abortion is disapproved of, but is no great secret. In biologically and culturally still "vigorous" *Mala* (Elton), public conscience condemns abortion, which increased in the other *Solomon Islands* when "vigor" declined. In *Yap* (Senfft) abortion is deemed shameful. In *Truk* (Gladwin), it angers the relatives. The *Northern Paiute* (Stewart) say that only "modern" girls, who drink and fornicate, do such things. The *Orang Laut* (WGS) deemed it a horror and did not regard such an abomination possible. A *Cherokee* (Mooney) informant had trouble "understanding" what the anthropologist meant by abortion. When he finally "understood," he was horrified, exclaiming that one might as well cut off the head of a five-year-old child, and that it was outright murder. After this conversation his regard for whites appears to have decreased. The *Doreh Bay* (PB) term for abortion is: "To kill the belly." All *Flathead*

(Turney-High) words meaning abortion have as their root the word "murder." The *Navaho* (Bailey) say that if a girl aborts, people might suspect that she had cohabited with a dog or had committed incest. Religious and related attitudes also enter into the picture. In *Annam* (Dê), an attempt is made to prevent abortion. They try to make the man marry the girl and therefore lower the bride price. Yet, though in *Annam* (Dê) abortion is no crime, it is felt (Brodrick) that only bad and impious people do it. In *Bali* (Covarrubias), abortion is deemed to be criminal and related to black magic. The *Jews* (WGS) and the *Moslems* (PB) alike considered it a heathen abomination, the latter adding that it is a most damnable crime, implicitly forbidden by the Koran as a kind of murder. *Ancient India* (WGS) compared it to the crime of crimes: the murder of a Brahmin. It should be stressed that even people who practice abortion may condemn infanticide. The *Macusi* (Farabee) practice abortion and (Schomburgk) contraception but not infanticide, and those who heard of infanticide among the *Pirara* were horrified. A unique view is that of the *Greek* Herodotus, who considered the *Persian* King Cambyses' fatal assault on his pregnant sister-wife as an additional proof of that king's madness. This is significant, since the *Greeks* notoriously practiced abortion and the exposure of unwanted children (Oedipus). Apparently, Herodotus objected more to Cambyses' manner of doing this deed than to the deed itself. Such an attitude is fairly typical of *Greece*. The *Bontoc Igorot* (Jenks) mother objects to her unwed daughter's abortion, fearing that the girl might become the mistress of many men instead of the faithful wife of one man.

ABSENCE OF SECRETIVENESS. In *Cootch* (PB), one mother boasted of having had five abortions. In *New Ireland* and *Lavongai* (PB), sixteen- and seventeen-year-old girls openly mention that they had had three or four abortions. Among the *Assiniboine* and the *Crow* (Denig), the topic of abortions is discussed in public. Married *Turks* (PB) asked unashamedly for abortifacients. Furthermore, even though *Turkish* (HK) law forbids abortions, some abortionist institutions were well known and tolerated.

SECRETIVENESS. The *Malay* (Favre) word for miscarriage is related to a Javanese word which means simply "to escape" or "to pass unnoticed." The *Murngin* (Warner) woman aborts in secret because she fears that her baby's father might be angry. In *Eetar Island* (PB) abortion is a great secret. Among the *Guaycuru* (Sanchez Labrador), girls abort in secret, although, even if this became known, it would not prevent them from finding new suitors. Married *Guaycuru* women practice abortion more openly, because they need not fear that their husbands will repudiate them.

SUSPICIOUSNESS is inseparable from secretiveness. Whenever a woman bears a crippled baby, the *Mohave* (Devereux) suspect that the mother had tried to abort it. In *Dahomey* (Herskovits), where it is believed that a woman's face changes early during pregnancy, if no signs of advanced pregnancy appear after such a change has been noted, abortion is suspected.* If a *Kgatla* (Shapera) girl's appearance changes too suddenly, an inquest is held. If after a reasonable time a *Riff* (Coon) wife bears no child, she is suspected of having aborted and is divorced.

EVASIONS AND LIES are to be expected in groups where abortion is performed in secret or is penalized, or if the interrogator is a member of the white race, whose representatives are known to oppose abortion. As regards the *Aleut* (Shade), the investigator tried to question a suspected abortionist, Jenny of Nikolski, about such techniques, but found her evasive and admitted that they ended up discussing basketry.† A *Sedang* (Devereux) father, who both impregnated and aborted his daughter, and then palmed her off on an unsuspecting husband, pretended that she had cohabited with other men. The daughter herself, when she was asked about the blood on the lower part of her body, explained that she had been bitten by leeches.‡ A *Buka* (Blackwood) lover, who successfully helped his married mistress to abort, naïvely broadcast such evasive remarks as: "See! She is not pregnant! She is menstruating!" It may not be inappropriate to comment briefly on the nature of these evasions, which substantiate the hypothesis advanced elsewhere (23) that every lie, other than a simple denial, affirms in its latent content that which its manifest content seeks to deny or to distort. (Abortion

* If a *Murngin* (Warner) woman has a stillbirth, the husband suspects her of having smothered her baby.

† Baskets and other containers are well-known symbolizations of the vagina and the uterus.

‡ *Persian* (PB) women abort by allowing leeches to suck their blood.

and basketry, abortion and leeches, gratuitous advertising of the fact that the woman is *not* pregnant.)

11. SOCIAL ACTION

I. THE BASIS FOR SOCIAL ACTION

A. *The Social Status of Abortion*

ABORTION AS A PERSONAL MATTER. Old *Germanic* (WGS) tribal law did not penalize the woman who aborted, since it was her right to do so. Only the person who helped her was punished. The *Taulipang* (Koch-Grünberg) hold that abortion is a strictly personal matter, the girl's body being her own, to do with as she pleases. Although *Macusi* (Schomburgk) women may, apparently, abort quite freely, the *Macusi* were horrified when they were told that the *Pirara* tribe practiced infanticide.

ABORTION AS A FAMILY MATTER. Unless the *Jakun* (WGS) husband chooses to beat his wife for having aborted, she goes scot free. He may, however, beat her to death and not be penalized for having done so. The *Choroti* (Karsten) consider abortion strictly a family matter. Very few of the 400-odd groups examined oblige a private person to take action.

ABORTION AS A CLUB MATTER. The officials of the *Muria* (Elwin) *ghotul* (clubhouse) usually oblige the boy who impregnated a girl to give her an abortifacient, but also demand that such matters be concealed from the rest of the village.

ABORTION AS A CRIMINAL MATTER. The *Cheyenne* (Hoebel), who were of the opinion that the unborn child has a legal personality and a tribal status, felt that abortion was a wholly criminal matter, since it involved violence within the family, where no blood-feud is possible.* The *Xosa* (Kropf) chief collected a fine, because he lost a follower through abortion. The *Visigoth Kingdom* (WGS) viewed abortion as a crime against the state. *Tribal Germanic* (WGS) law only considered the abortionist as a criminal.

ABORTION AS A SIN, in the religious sense, will be discussed in connection with calamities following abortion. The *Jews* (WGS) called abortion a heathen abomination.

B. *The Need for Action*

A PERSON OR GROUP IS HARMED by an abortion.

1. Deity: The contaminating evil spread by a woman who aborted may communicate itself even to the goddess Sedna, among the *Eskimos of Baffin Land* (Boas).
2. Cosmic order, and especially rainfall, on which mankind depends for its survival, is upset by an abortion occurring among the *Thonga* (Junod).†
3. The state of the *Visigoths* (WGS) was felt to be damaged by abortions.
4. The chief of the *Xosa* (Kropf) was deemed to have lost a retainer through an abortion.
5. The community was threatened by calamities among the *Mojo* (HDBK). (Cf. also "Cosmic order" above.)
6. The husband's rights were felt to have been interfered with by the aborting *Assyrian* (Sigerist) woman.
7. The father of the betrothed *Chagga* (Raum) girl curses the abortionist, because, if his daughter dies, his claim to an indemnity disappears.
8. The family in general may object among the *Gunantuna* (Meier).
9. The maternal uncle, from whom the child would inherit in a matrilineal society, may feel harmed by the abortion, as among the *Dobu* (Fortune).

* Contrary to the commonly held opinion, we feel that the police powers of the state are not a substitute for vendettas, but represent an attempt to mete out justice in precisely the kind of intrafamiliar tort which shocks the community and in which blood feud is not possible.

† This notion must be sharply differentiated from the doctrine that abortion is against (abstract) natural law. The concept of natural law is not common among primitives, and even the *Sedang* (Devereux), who do have a related concept, do not bring abortion within its scope.

10. The woman herself may risk various unpleasant natural consequences. (See other sections.)
11. The lover himself is never stated to have been harmed by an abortion.

SUPERNATURAL CALAMITIES may result from abortion. Since the *Rwala* (Musil) fear women who miscarried or had stillbirths, we may assume that they also fear those who aborted. The *Sedang* (Devereux) woman who aborts jeopardizes the welfare of her village. If a *Pedi* (Junod) man cohabits with a woman who aborted, it will poison him, so that he shrivels up and dies within a week. The *Venda* (Stayt) believe that a man would die of consumption if he lay with a woman who has aborted. They also forbid such a woman to go near the cattle lest the livestock become sterile. She may not resume marital relations with her husband until both are purified. *Barotse* (Kammer) women who miscarry are dangerous to women of childbearing age, because the latter too may miscarry if they come in contact with a woman who miscarried, before she has been purified. Even the house and the clothes of such a woman are dangerous to other women. The *Mojo* (HDBK) drown the aborting woman at once, lest the village be ravaged by an epidemic of dysentery. The *Pedi* (Junod) believe that no rain will fall until the country is set right by means of elaborate rain-rituals. If a secret miscarriage or abortion occurs among the *Thonga* (Junod), the women perform certain rain-making rites, and any man who intrudes on them must answer riddles in the foulest possible language, borrowed from the circumcision rites. Among the *Eskimo of Baffin Land* (Boas), if a premature birth (or abortion) is not made public, some man may unwittingly come in contact with the woman, and be thereafter avoided by the seals. Even the seals may be affected by such an occurrence and take this evil to the goddess Sedna, who would then also be harmed by it.

II. PREVENTION

A. *Reassurance*

The *Zuni* (AH) mother who notices that her unmarried

daughter is pregnant urges her not to abort, and assures her that all will be well.

B. *Restraint*

The *Masai* (Leakey) parents, if they know that their unwed daughter is pregnant, will try to prevent her from aborting.

C. *Condonement.*

Among the *Buka* (Blackwood), women usually abort their adulterine bastards. However, some husbands prefer to pretend that the bastard is their child rather than have a scandal. The community connives in this pretence. The *Kwakiutl* (HRAF) bastard, too, is usually claimed by the husband, in order to avoid a scandal. It may not be a mere coincidence that both the *Kwakiutl* and the *Buka* are much preoccupied with prestige in terms of wealth, and with the display and ostentatious giving away of wealth.

D. *Deterrent Examples*

The fact that a *Koyukuk Eskimo* (Marshall) girl almost died from her abortion frightened other women sufficiently to stop all abortions for quite a length of time.

E. *Public Measures*

In the second half of the eighteenth century, *Japanese* (Tsuchiya) peasant women were so poor that they practiced abortion on a large scale. The state passed laws to curb this practice. Honjo adds that all pregnant women were registered, and that the state and the feudal lords made considerable efforts to discourage abortions.

F. *Ritual Measures*

After an aborted *Lepcha* (Gorer) fetus has been thrown into the river, the priest performs a ceremony and the parents offer a sacrifice, to prevent the devil responsible for this event from repeating his evil deed.

G. *"Medical" Measures*

An *Ashanti* (Rattray) drug prevents the malicious abortion of a woman by witches, supernaturals, and ill-disposed co-wives.

III. PROCEDURE

A. *Detection of the Aborting Woman*

Both in a *Kgatla* (Shapera) and in a *Cheyenne* (Hoebel) case, the fact that an abortion had taken place became known when a fetus was found. In both tribes, official attempts were made to identify the culprit by examining the breasts of all women of childbearing age. In the *Cheyenne* case, Hoebel specifies that this technique of detection was improvised for the occasion. In the *Kgatla* case, the technique of detection may have been a traditional one. In a *Sedang Moi* (Devereux) village people wondered why a girl had blood on her legs and skirt, and some days later her newly acquired husband noticed that she had milk in her breasts. Among the *Chinese* (PB), the woman suspected of abortion is examined by a midwife. The Chinese book *Si Yuen Li* even describes a "chemical" test for abortion: if mercury is introduced into the vagina and darkens, abortion has taken place. Among the *Kgatla* (Shapera), if a girl's appearance changes too suddenly, an inquest may be held to determine whether she has aborted. Among the *Eskimos of Baffin Land and Hudson Bay* (Boas), the woman herself is required to announce that she gave birth prematurely. The *Riff* (Coon) wife who bears no child within a certain time is suspected of having aborted, and is divorced. A *Mohave* (Devereux) woman who gives birth to a crippled child is believed to have attempted to abort it.

B. *Mitigating Circumstances*

The father of *Greek* (PB) medicine and author of the medical prohibition against abortion, Hippocrates himself, relented in the case of an unfortunate harpist and recommended exercises likely to cause abortion. Though *Chinese* (PB) mandarins could punish abortion quite severely, they inquired less into the offense itself than into the circumstances justifying it, so that many abortions remained unpunished. Among the *Sanpoil* (Ray), the chief imposed fewer lashes on a young offender than upon an "older" (second?) offender. The *Turkish* (PB) situation was even more peculiar. In the nineteenth century there were laws against abortion, but they were supposedly so poorly worded that the judges could never figure out whom the law meant to punish, so that hardly anyone ever was penalized. Japanese law in *Korea* (Materi) legalized abortion when pregnancy was due to rape or "error."

C. *Aggravating Circumstances*

A *Kabyle* (J. G. Frazer) woman who aborts under her husband's roof is killed.

D. *Clemency*

The *Ila* (Smith and Dale) believe that adultery with a pregnant woman may cause stillbirth. If such a stillbirth actually occurs, there may be a public outcry, and the people may demand the death of the lover. However, the elders usually persuade the people to be content with a fine.

IV. PENALTIES

A. *Supernatural Penalties*

MAN-INDUCED SUPERNATURAL PENALTY. The *Chagga* (Raum) father curses anyone who causes his betrothed daughter to abort, because, if she dies, his claim for a compensation disappears.

VICTIM-INDUCED SUPERNATURAL PENALTY. If a *Hopi* (Beaglehole) girl aborts repeatedly, the ghosts of her fetuses conspire against her and kill her, so that she will not be able to kill further fetuses.

DIVINE PENALTIES. The *Palaung* (Milne) believe that a woman who aborts will be punished in her next incarnation. The *Annamese* (Sallet) abortionist goes to the ninth hell.

B. *Natural Penalties*

The *Zuni* (AH) believed that a girl who aborts will be sterile. For this reason, when a mother noted that her daughter was illegitimately pregnant she urged her to bear her child, and told her that all would be well. A certain *Zuni* girl, who aborted in the first decade of this century, was placed in warm sand by an old woman for 10 days to prevent her "drying up." *

* Burial up to the neck in hot sand is a fairly common therapeutic, pubertal, menstrual, and postpartum measure in that general area (Devereux).

C. *Human Penalties* for abortion are either private or public. In addition, there is also an intermediate range of social, or socially sanctioned, penalties, such as contempt, ridicule, and the right to divorce the aborting woman.

PRIVATE PENALTIES ON THE WOMAN:

1. Scolding and anger faced the *Truk* (Gladwin) girl who aborted.
2. Beatings were not uncommon. In *Dobu* (Fortune), Adi, daughter of Alo, was severely beaten about the body with a club by her maternal uncle Kopu, who had a socially recognized and corporeally enforceable right to an heir from his sister's daughter's womb.
3. Killing: A *Jakun* (WGS) woman who aborted could be beaten by her husband with a club, and nothing was done to him even if she died of the beating. Yet abortion was so much a private matter that if the *Jakun* husband did not choose to punish his wife she went unpunished. In the opinion of the *Chimariko* (Driver), a husband would kill his aborting wife.

PRIVATE ACTION AGAINST THIRD PERSONS:

1. Damages: The *Azande* (Lagae) husband is entitled to a compensation, amounting in value to twenty knives, from his aborting wife's father. If the father refuses to pay, the husband complains to the chief.
2. Substitute killing: If an *Azande* (Hutereau) husband whose wife aborted does not succeed in getting either a fine or a substitute wife from his wife's father, he kills either his wife or one of her siblings in revenge.

SEMIPRIVATE PENALTIES:

1. Divorce is a common private penalty for abortion. In *Yap* (Senfft), abortion is shameful and a cause for divorce, but it is not legally punishable. Among the *Riff* (Coon), the suspicion of abortion is ever present in the minds of men, so that, if a wife does not bear a child within a reasonable length of time, she is suspected of abortion and is divorced. Needless to say, actual abortion is also a cause for divorce among the *Riff*.

2. Ridicule: In *New Caledonia* (de Rochas) people sometimes point out a woman who aborted and remark: "There goes one who took the banana cure." (See Techniques.) Among the *Assiniboine* and the *Crow* (Denig), abortion was freely discussed in public and was laughed at as something ludicrous.
3. Contempt: The *Jakun* (WGS) despised a girl who aborted. She lost her standing in the community, women despised her, men did not want her for a wife and her parents punished her in a degrading manner. The *Munda Kolh* (Jellinghaus) disapprovingly contrasted the behavior of a woman who aborts with the childless couples' longing for offspring.
4. Indirect criticism: In *Rome* (CS) women who did *not* abort were deemed worthy of special praise.

PUBLIC PENALTIES ON THE WOMAN:

1. Fines: The *Sedang* (Devereux) girl who aborts pays a fine to her village because, by her forbidden act, she has put the souls of her fellow villagers in jeopardy. Among the *Xosa* (Kropf), the chief collects a fine of four or five heads of cattle because he has lost a potential subject. The fine to be paid by the woman may be demanded from her husband, if he knew of her plan, or else from her lover or from her family, even if they knew nothing about it. *Mongol Oirat* (Riasanovsky) law provides that the fine to be paid for aborting a woman has to be proportionate to the age of the fetus.
2. Beating: The *Chinese* (PB) inflicted the bastinado—a hundred strokes—and three years' exile. A nineteenth-century *Creek* (Foreman) law punished abortion with fifty lashes. The *Sanpoil* (Ray) chief had the aborting woman whipped. Anywhere from a few to as many as one hundred lashes on the back were given. Old offenders were punished more severely than young ones.
3. Exile, to the primitive, is nearly as severe a punishment as death. The *Chinese* (PB) woman was condemned to one hundred strokes and was exiled for three years. A *Cheyenne* (Hoebel) woman was exiled until the next arrow renewal ceremony took place—a terrible punish-

ment in the Plains, which were in a state of constant warfare.

4. The death penalty was imposed among the *Aztecs* (GPM), except if the woman was aborted to save her life. The *Assyrians* (Sigerist) impaled the woman who aborted. The *Mojo* (HDBK) drowned such women at once, lest the village should suffer an epidemic of dysentery. The same "punishment" was also inflicted on the *Mojo* woman who was unfortunate enough to have a miscarriage.

PUBLIC PENALTIES AGAINST ABORTIONISTS AND ACCESSORIES. The *Germanic* (WGS) tribes punished the abortionist but not the woman. The *Xosa* (Kropf) chief fined those who made or administered an abortifacient. The *Masai* (Maguire) husband or lover who made a woman abort was beaten by the women, who also clubbed one of his oxen to death and ate it ritually, at a meal which neither men nor pregnant women were allowed to attend.* Furthermore, if a *Masai* (Hollis) man caused a pregnant woman to abort by cohabiting with her, the women flogged him, and suffocated with their garments as many of his cattle as they could. The *Assyrians* (Sigerist) punished the abortionist, as well as a man whose assault caused a woman to abort, in accordance with the lex talionis. The *Chagga* (Raum) father cursed anyone causing his betrothed daughter to abort, because if she died of it his claim for compensation disappeared.

PUNISHMENT OF RELATIVES. If an *Azande* (Lagae) woman aborts her own husband's child, her husband complains to her father and demands a fine to the value of twenty knives. He may also demand a substitute wife. Hutereau adds that if his demands are not complied with, he may kill one of his father-in-law's children. Yet, if the child is adulterine, the husband can oblige his wife to abort and can then divorce her. The fine which the aborting *Xosa* (Kropf) woman has to pay to the chief may be demanded from her husband if he knew of it, or from her lover or her family, even if they knew nothing of her intentions.

* This double exclusion appears to equate men and pregnant women, which, in view of the equation baby = penis, will not surprise the psychoanalyst.

V. NONPUNITIVE MEASURES

A. *Confession* that one has aborted—or simply miscarried—is very important to groups which believe that contact with an aborting woman may be harmful. An *Eskimo* (Boas) woman of *Baffin Land* has to confess her miscarriages and abortions, lest men should unwittingly approach her and be thereafter repulsive to the seals they seek to hunt. The seals themselves may also be contaminated by her and then carry the contamination to the goddess Sedna, who will also be affected by this unconfessed evil. Deathbed confessions of abortionists are known to occur in *Nigeria* (Harley).

B. *Purification Rites* are reported from several areas. Among the *Kgatla* (Shapera) and the *Pedi* (Junod), abortion endangers the "coolness" of the land, i.e., rainfall, so that the land must be set right by means of complex rituals. The same is true of the *Thonga* (Junod), where such purifications are exclusively feminine rites. Should a man intrude, he must answer riddles in the most obscene language, derived from the circumcision rites. Among the *Venda* (Stayt), both the husband and the wife have to be purified before they can cohabit again. The fine which the aborting *Sedang Moi* (Devereux) woman has to pay is, actually, more than a fine. It also restores the damaged integrity of the luck-soul of the village and of each and every inhabitant thereof. In addition, it also rehabilitates the soul of the woman herself.* It is, hence, both an economic and a ritual-purificatory sanction.

VI. MISCELLANEOUS

A. *Penalties for Not Aborting*

The *Gunantuna* (Meier) are angry if a bastard, and especially an incestuous child, is not disposed of, and scold the mother. In *Wogeo* (Hogbin), Sanemuk's sisters beat her when her attempted

* If a *Sedang Moi* (Devereux) murderer refuses to pay blood-money, his soul deserts him because it is disgusted with him.

abortion was unsuccessful, and even though her third sister came to her rescue, the latter also scolded her, while her parents maintained an icy silence. Among the *Muria* (Elwin), where boys must provide abortifacients for their pregnant girl friends, one boy told the deity in advance that the deity would be blamed if the abortifacient did not produce the desired result.

B. *Abortion as a Penalty*

The *Azande* (Hutereau) husband is entitled to make his adulterously pregnant wife abort. In connection with the problem of abortion as a penalty, it is illuminating to realize that the *Ashanti* (Rattray) abort an unconfessed adulterous woman for her own good, lest she die in childbirth. It should be added that in this tribe, where adultery is a capital crime equated with murder, adultery is believed to cause miscarriage. We must therefore assume that if the adulterous woman is aborted—allegedly for her own sake—this abortion, though masquerading as medical prophylaxis, is actually a substitute for the usual penalties which other capital offenses entail. The *Jukun* (Meek) believe that adulterous women miscarry spontaneously.*

C. *Compensation* for being aborted against one's own will has been recorded from two African tribes where a woman may be magically aborted without her knowledge or consent. Among the *Tiv* (Abraham) she is held to be especially favored by A'ondo, and is believed to bear a healthy offspring soon after her miscarriage. Among the *Achewa* (Steytler) the woman who was magically aborted in order that her fetus might be buried under a new smithy will eventually be presented with some hoes made in that smithy, but is supposed to be unaware of the reasons for being given these hoes.

* This belief may, conceivably, give a clue to the *Masai* (Hollis) theory that a man can cause a pregnant woman to abort by cohabiting with her, and that he should be punished for it.

PART TWO

CULTURE AND THE UNCONSCIOUS

1. BIBLIOGRAPHIC NOTE

Since this section is based on data found in the hundreds of works cited in the sourcebook, plus some additional ones, some policy had to be adopted to keep the terminal bibliography of this section within manageable limits and yet without loss of bibliographic accuracy. After several trials and errors the following policy was adopted:

1. Data found *neither* in the sourcebook *nor* in any of the works cited in the sourcebook are followed by a number in parentheses, which refers to the general bibliography to be found at the end of this book. E.g., the reference "*Angami Naga* (35)" indicates that we are using data from a work on the *Angami Naga* which is not cited in the sourcebook's bibliography on the *Angami Naga* because it contains no data on abortion.

2. Data pertaining to abortion which *are* found in the sourcebook are cited simply by giving the name of the ethnic group, since the reader, by referring to the sourcebook, can promptly identify the source of that statement, even where several works are listed for a single such group. E.g., the reference "*Masai*" indicates that the complete data are found in the sourcebook, under the heading "*Masai*," together with the full listing of the source from which that information was drawn.

3. *Collateral* data, *not* pertaining to abortion, but found in one of the works cited in the sourcebook, are cited in two ways:

   a. If we cite *collateral* data from the *only* work on a given tribe cited in the sourcebook, our text gives only the name of the group, since there can be no doubt as to the work from which these data were culled. Thus, collateral data about the *Muria* are cited simply as "*Muria*," since our sourcebook lists only one work on the *Muria*.

b. If we cite *collateral* data from *one of several* works on a given group cited in the sourcebook, the name of the tribe is followed in the text by the name of the author concerned. Thus, collateral data on the *Masai* found in Merker's work, but possibly not in the works of Bryk, Fox, Hollis, Leakey, Maguire, or Weiss, are cited as "*Masai* (Merker)."

While, at first glance, it may seem confusing and cumbrous to find, e.g., Merker's data referred to sometimes as "*Masai*" and sometimes as "*Masai* (Merker)" this mode of citation immediately tells the reader whether he can locate the actual data in the sourcebook, or whether, in order to verify them, he will have to consult Merker's volume itself. Likewise, no difficulties should arise from the fact that the citation "*Muria*" may indicate either data on *Muria abortion* reproduced in the sourcebook, or *collateral* data, *not* pertaining to abortion, found in Verrier Elwin's book on *The Muria and their Ghotul,* since the nature of the data themselves indicates which is the case in any given instances.

2. INTRODUCTION

After some preliminary methodological discussions, we propose to demonstrate in this section that a comparative study of primarily cultural data pertaining strictly to abortion in a large number of representative primitive societies yields conclusions duplicating those which may be reached by the intensive study, in context and in depth, of abortion in a single society.

The chief difficulty confronting us was to find a society whose conscious and unconscious attitudes toward abortion have been reported compendiously and analyzed in detail. A glance at our sourcebook section indicates that no single primitive tribe has been sufficiently studied in this respect to satisfy our demand for complete data and for a careful analysis in depth of these data. The same seemed to be true of all other non-European societies, and great historical cultures . . . with one exception so obvious that it took us a long time to notice the forest which was hidden from our sight by the trees.

It is well known that even nowadays every self-appointed "Nemesis of psychoanalysis" eventually brings up the fact that psychoanalysis, as a science or body of theory, was formulated on the basis of an intensive clinical study of a number of (culturally admittedly distinctive) middle-class Viennese neurotics. The manner in which opponents of psychoanalysis as a whole, or only of its applicability to all mankind, have sought to exploit this objectively perfectly correct statement has—understandably—obscured the very important and useful fact that, in its simplest and most literal sense, the body of psychoanalytic theory is probably the most penetrating set of conclusions ever drawn from the intensive study of a single social class, living at a certain point in history, in a distinctive cultural milieu, and one which is not even remotely duplicated in intensity or compendiousness by the very best existing ethnographic field reports.

In other words, we are entitled to turn the tables on those who sneeringly state that psychoanalytic theories are fully applicable only to an effete and neurotic Viennese bourgeoisie, living at a given point in history, in an amiable atmosphere of waltzes, Graustarkian court ritual, Hollywoodish uniforms, "Heuriger" wine, and good-natured "Schlamperei." This we may do by "accepting" their views—but only in order to indicate that psychoanalytic theory, inductively derived from an incomparably intensive study of such individuals, is equally applicable to all mankind.

In other words, the polemic aspect of our logical position is wholly subsidiary to the methodological point which we seek to prove, and which postulates the equivalence of conclusions reached from extensive studies in breadth and intensive studies in depth—which is precisely the view of both Durkheim and Freud.

Hence, in the following pages we take the position that we are not postulating a priori the universal validity of psychoanalysis. *As a methodological device,* we even go so far as to "deny"—for reasons of expository convenience—that there is a "science of psychoanalysis" in the sense in which there is a "science of physiology," and "postulate" instead that what goes under the name of "psychoanalysis" is simply a set of sociopsychological conclusions derived from the intensive study of the pre–World War I Viennese middle class. For the same reason, we view Freud, *in this context,* not as the founder of a new science, but as a most eminent and thorough sociologist and social psychologist, who did his field work among the natives of Vienna, and who formulated a series of general conclusions about the Viennese *only.*

If, after this methodological position is assumed, it can nonetheless be shown that Freud's conclusions about the Viennese have a universal applicability, both because they help us understand data pertaining to abortion in primitive societies and because these primitive phenomena almost automatically fall into several categories which constitute the conceptual framework of psychoanalysis, our thesis may be considered as proven.

We would like to add that this procedure and methodological device is far from illegitimate and specious, and cannot, in fairness, be viewed as a simple rhetorical tour de force. Indeed, ever since Abel, mathematicians have been familiar with a method of proof which consists in "inverting the problem," by taking as known that which is unknown, and working back from that point to what is, in fact, already known and established. If this procedure meets the high standards of legitimate mathematical reasoning, then the burden of proof that a similar procedure is *not* legitimate in the human sciences rests upon the self-appointed critic. Indeed, in the last resort, we have done nothing more than ask a question in an *answerable* manner, which means: in the *correct* manner. It is proper to remember in this context that the great mathematician Georg Cantor long ago proved, in his Habilitationsschrift, that it is more important to ask a question correctly than it is to answer it—presumably because a correctly asked question already implies its own answer.

We might add that this approach does more than take the

wind out of the sails of those who keep harping on the "Viennese background" of psychoanalytic theory. In other words, we "meekly" accepted their criticism, and then turned the tables on them by means of the hypothesis—already implicit in both Freud and Durkheim—that a single detailed study in depth can yield universally valid conclusions. It actually provides a logical basis for the assertion that psychoanalysis has a universal validity, which has hitherto either been simply affirmed, or else has been proven only empirically, by means of numerous examples. It is hardly necessary to stress that the confirmation of the universal validity of the principal psychoanalytic theories by means of examples, however numerous, can only create a *presumption* in favor of their universal validity, since it can always be suggested that eventually someone will (and usually does) turn up some data from the X-tribe which allegedly "disprove" some aspect of psychoanalytic theory. We hasten to add that such "refutations" usually show only that the critic is simply not familiar enough with psychoanalytic theory to realize that, just as the law of gravitation is not disproven by the existence of airplanes—which counteract the force of gravitation by means of buoyance and momentum, without, however, abolishing it—so the absence *on the conscious and culturally implemented level* of some phenomenon which, in the view of psychoanalysts, is a universal one, calls for nothing more than a description of the psychodynamic processes which keep that factor or phenomenon *in a state of repression*. We have made this point so often (*22, 24*) that it does not deserve still another detailed discussion in this context.

One last conclusion to be drawn from all this is that it is sometimes useful to pay attention even to seemingly senseless criticism, whose apparent illogicality and bias often simply disguise the fact that the critic has unwittingly hit upon a potentially productive problem, but was able neither to formulate it constructively nor to solve it meaningfully.*

* We hope to show in the near future that, by accepting the biased view that the psychoanalyst "directly influences" his patient, we can prove, even more conclusively than has already been done, that psychoanalysis is an experimental and inductive science, and that its procedures and problems are similar to those of other sciences dealing with almost imponderable phenomena.

3. METHODOLOGICAL CONSIDERATION

An attempt to interpret inferential psychological processes in individual primitives, whom the would-be interpreter has never seen in person, is open to almost the same type of criticism which can be advanced in regard to interpretations of the motivation of *successful* suicide.* In both instances interpretations have to be based upon inferences, and are always open to criticism, either on the score of overinterpretation or on that of under-interpretation. At this point one can engage in a nice game of intellectual tag, productive—to paraphrase Bertrand Russell—of heat rather than light, which gratifies little more than the scholar's obsessive impulses masquerading as methodological rigor. Methodology itself cannot point the way out of such methodological impasses. That can be done only by common

* Data based on the study of persons who have *unsuccessfully* attempted suicide do yield some clues, but are open to criticism on the score that, if a person is really determined, he can kill himself even when restrained and under constant supervision. Any psychiatrist can confirm this from his own experience. In this sense, then, the range of phenomena, from threats of suicide motivated by the desire to create a sensation or to blackmail someone, etc., to seemingly *bona fide* suicidal attempts which were frustrated at the last moment through the "chance" intervention of some external agency, forms a continuum. However, a very important *caveat* must be entered at this juncture against complete interpretative nihilism. Thus, if many last-minute "chance" rescues are admittedly suspect of having been unconsciously "engineered," one is equally entitled to ask precisely how many actually successful suicides were intended originally simply as exhibitionistic "attempted suicides," which "happened" to succeed through a "chance" failure of the rescuer to appear at the proper moment. Of course, at this point one may say that the "chance" failure was also an "engineered" one, and that the suicide was therefore a genuine one, and so on, *ad infinitum.* Due allowance being made for Lagrange's apt dictum that nature is not concerned with the analytical difficulties confronting the mathematician, somewhere or other a boundary must be drawn between excessive and obsessive methodological refinement-mongering, and naïve generalization-mongering.

sense, which—almost intuitively—warns one when one's quest for insight begins to deteriorate into an exhibition of subtlety.

Broadly speaking, two attitudes are possible in regard to attempts to interpret psychological factors in abortion in primitive society. One is the Durkheim-Freud thesis, that the meticulous analysis in depth of a single social or psychological phenomenon can yield universally valid results. The second is the currently much esteemed and admittedly very successful attempt to derive valid generalizations from the statistical analysis of sets of data pertaining to a large sample of cultures.

It is our *methodological thesis* that *identical* inferences can be derived from *both* approaches. In order to justify this view, we assume that we are entitled to construct a socio-psychological equivalent of, or counterpart to, the ergodic hypothesis of mathematicians, which postulates—on the basis of experience and convenience rather than on the basis of a generally accepted formal proof—that the results of a large number of consecutive tosses with one coin are identical with the results of a large number of simultaneous tosses with many coins. We feel that in the realm of human behavior—i.e., in the field of social and psychological science—the analogue of this hypothesis would be the assertion that information in breadth (comparative method) yields results or inferences comparable to information in depth (by means of a full analysis of all implications of a single datum or set of data). (Durkheim, Freud) Specifically, we feel that the errors caused by the specificity of information in depth are paralleled by the errors due to the noncompendiousness of information in breadth. A corollary of this view—that we can treat as "free associations" to our main topic *either* data from other segments of the culture one of whose traits is being investigated, and/or comparable data from other cultures pertaining to the identical segment or trait—will be expounded and justified further below.

As regards positive results, both data in depth and data in breadth necessarily, and regardless of whether we choose to recognize or to ignore this fact, lead us to a general theory of human society and of human nature. It is hardly necessary to add that the *particular* theories to which one is led by such data are partly dependent on such existential and "wissenssociological" factors as the investigator's training and his personal biases, both conscious and unconscious. These factors and biases should perhaps be stated, but need not be justified otherwise than by a display of one's results—if any.

4. CULTURE AND THE UNCONSCIOUS

It is always desirable that a new major insight should be generally accepted. However, there are ways and ways of accepting a new generalization. One can accept it wholeheartedly and make it one of the *Leitmotifs* of one's thinking. One can also "accept" it consciously, and yet be so ambivalent about it unconsciously that the very manner in which one "accepts" it sterilizes the new insight. When a new major truth is transformed either into a dogma or into a commonplace, we can be certain that it has undergone a process of sterilization and degradation in the minds of those who consciously profess to have accepted it, but unconsciously resist it to the uttermost.

The statement that impulses, wishes, fantasies, and other productions of the human psyche which are completely repressed in one society may be fully conscious and culturally implemented in another society is, today, almost a scientific commonplace. This means that, instead of being an axiom, it has become either a dogma or a platitude. In undergoing this metamorphosis it lost its provocative and thought-provoking character, and has consequently failed to stimulate attempts to explore all of its deeper implications.

One factor which facilitated the degradation and sterilization of this axiom is its apparent simplicity and obviousness which—somewhat on the lines of Edgar Allan Poe's *Purloined Letter* device—conceals the magnitude and depth of the problems which lie concealed behind its deceptively simple façade. One is forcibly reminded in this context of a great mathematician's advice: "Seek simplicity, but distrust it!"

The fate of any deceptively simple and obvious major theorem is always a partial misunderstanding and/or an "overinterpretation" thereof, which represents a defense against the acceptance of its real, deeper implications. One is reminded here of the avidity wherewith rank amateurs in physics have thrown themselves upon a completely misunderstood conception of the Heisenberg "indeterminacy principle," usually in order to support some semimystical, noncausal conception of nature as a whole, or of some segment thereof. As Bertrand Russell pointed out, such persons automatically assumed that in the expression "indeterminacy principle" the word "indeterminacy" was derived from the concept of "determinism," whereas, in fact, it refers simply to the process of "determining something by means of measurement." Specifically, the Heisenberg principle, in its original form, refers strictly and exclusively to the fact that, due to the disturbance created in certain microphysical processes *by the act of measurement itself,* it is impossible to determine *simultaneously* both the position and the momentum of a particle with the *same degree* of accuracy. The greater the precision wherewith we determine (measure) one of these factors, the less accurate becomes our determination (measurement) of the other factor. It is true, of course, that subsequently this very specific problem has given rise, even in highly competent circles, to speculations about whether or not this special finding had a bearing upon the causality problem ("determinism") itself, with Einstein reaffirming the deterministic view, and some nearly as eminent physicists taking the opposite position. However, it should be stressed that at this juncture we are passing from the realm of experimental and theoretical physics into the realm of philosophy and, in some respects at least, even into the realm of mere opinion.

A similar attempt to undermine the psychologically uncomfortable concept of causality has at its root a misunderstanding of the implications of statistical mechanics, especially as this science pertains to the kinetic theory of gases. It is quite certain that (even though our inability to solve the so-called "problem of three bodies"—of three or more bodies in relative motion to one another—and the sheer calculatory difficulty of analyzing mathematically the individual movements of very large numbers of gas molecules, have prevented us from developing a strictly mechanical, as distinct from statistical, theory of the behavior of gas models) each individual molecule continues to be thought of as moving strictly in accordance with the laws of classical mechanics. Thus, even though the total process unfolding itself within a closed system of gas molecules is, in a sense, irreversible, and illustrative of the drift toward entropy, each individual molecule continues to be thought of as being involved in classically mechanical—i.e., reversible—processes. In brief, the kinetic theory of gases means simply that *technical difficulties* rather than *philosophical principles* oblige us to "handle" findings pertaining to bodies of gases, and to certain other macrophysical processes, *as though* they were "truly" the products of chance.

These somewhat lengthy illustrative examples were felt to be necessary to underscore with sufficient emphasis the legitimacy of our supposition that major principles are often misunderstood—and misunderstood for emotional reasons—sometimes even by eminent scientists. Indeed, as regards the misunderstanding of the real and limited philosophical scope of the Heisenberg principle and of the kinetic theory of gases, it is not without interest to note that the (admittedly very eminent) opponents of Einstein's moderate views have repeatedly sought to use their overexpanded conception of indeterminacy (nondeterminism) as a means for denying that life, and especially human life, is subject to the psychologically highly anxiety-arousing law of entropy. (Cf. the Jeans vs. Donnan and Guggenheim controversy on this problem.) In fact, one eminent nuclear physicist even attempted to justify telepathy by means of considerations derived from the Heisenberg principle. (*41, 42*)

In brief, we reaffirm our position that the concept that certain things are repressed in one society and are culturally implemented in another society has been degraded and sterilized by a too hasty—that is, too ambivalent—acceptance, and that its real implications have therefore not been sufficiently investigated.

We are now prepared to examine more closely the further implications of this principle. Due to their complexity, we will have to start with certain basic principles and analyze them in some detail, in order to pave the way for a careful exploration of the complex problems hidden behind the simple façade of our basic thesis.

Some years ago Alexander Goldenweiser, in an unjustly neglected paper (36), enunciated the "principle of limited possibilities," which, very simply, states that the customs of tribe A in regard to a certain matter may resemble the customs of a distant tribe B in regard to the same matter only because there are just so many ways, and no more, of doing certain things. This sound and simple principle promptly suffered complete neglect, probably because it seemed to threaten some of the major logical foundations of various inductively oriented diffusion studies which absorbed much of the time and interest of the anthropologists of that period. In particular, it seemed to represent, at least by implication, a serious challenge to the hypothesis that unwritten culture history could be directly reconstructed from the geographical distribution of various culture traits. We shall return to this point in a moment, and will therefore content ourselves for the moment with simply saying that actually Goldenweiser's theory did nothing of the sort: It simply indicated that such direct inductive reconstructions of unwritten culture history were, perhaps, somewhat less convincing than many thought them to be, and that this decrease in logical certainty would have to be compensated for by greater cautiousness and better scholarship. That this demand was a legitimate one is clearly shown by the *increasing* sophistication and brilliance of many of the latest inductive reconstructions of culture history.

Indeed, it is important to remember that in the "diffusion vs. independent invention or convergent evolution" controversy, the prodiffusionist position has three—and only three—points in its favor:

1. *Logically,* it makes use of the principle of parsimony—and it was the *naïve* diffusionists' use of this principle which Goldenweiser sought to supplant by another conception of this principle.

2. *Psychologically,* its chief argument is the seductive rhetorical question: "Does man think, or merely remember?" (Spinden)

3. *Empirically,* it disposes of countless fully documented instances of diffusion and acculturation, whose mass contrasts

sharply with the meager driblets of truly convincing examples of independent invention which the moribund antidiffusionist philosophy can muster.

Another possible reason why Goldenweiser's valid principle found so little acceptance, and/or was felt by many to be so unchallenging and commonplace, may well be the fact that it was the *logical* counterpart or complement of Bastian's overhastily and quite cantankerously enunciated psychological theory of "Elementargedanken." (2) This latter principle represents a very imaginative expansion of the concept of the psychic unity of mankind, which—again!—has been so "readily accepted" that when someone like Bastian attempted to explore its deeper implications he elicited a great deal of adverse reaction—presumably because he would not let sleeping dogs lie. Briefly stated, Bastian challenged the diffusionist's *logical* position by asserting that the psychic unity of man implied that certain ideas (Elementargedanken) would arise everywhere when conditions were fairly comparable.

Due allowances being made for the fact that Bastian spoiled his case by presenting it practically in the form of an *obiter dictum,* and in his inimitably elliptical and confusing style, his views, while basically sound, were even more severely impaired by the fact that the simplest observation sufficed to show that a good many major ideas, which obviously possessed all the requisite characteristics of an Elementargedanken, did not, in fact, arise everywhere on the *conscious* and *culturally implemented level.* However, this defect was not pointed out either by Bastian's contemporaries or, so far as we know, by any anthropologist of the following generation.

Now (*habent sua fata libelli!*) it is, paradoxically enough, precisely this defect in Bastian's *presentation* of his basic theorem which, as we propose to show, is actually its most productive and most novel component. It must be readily conceded that neither Bastian nor his contemporaries were in a position to reach the conclusions which we are about to present, since at that time Freud had not yet begun his epoch-making investigation of the unconscious, and Ernest Jones and Géza Róheim had not yet enunciated their theory that things which are repressed in one society are often conscious and culturally fully implemented in another society. The point is that if we specify that Elementargedanken do, in fact, exist, but assume that they are repressed in tribe X and are conscious and culturally implemented in another tribe Y, our demonstration of the validity of the theory of Elementargedanken *in this modified form* becomes—as we propose to show—a relatively easy task.

As an aside, it may be suggested that the same may be true also of some other of Bastian's ideas, and may provide a tentative answer to the paradox—pointed out, with his usual sensitiveness, by Lowie (*53*)—that, despite his countless shortcomings, and despite the fact that today he is all but unread, Bastian was highly esteemed by many of his most eminent contemporaries.

The next question is why psychoanalysts, many of whom are also scholarly anthropologists, failed to revive Bastian's views, which in many ways dovetail so admirably with the principle of the psychic unity of mankind—without which, as we have shown elsewhere (*19*), psychoanalysis as a general human science, rather than as a special science pertaining exclusively, as some of its opponents still maintain, to Viennese neurotics, becomes unthinkable. We suspect that the classical psychoanalysts' neglect of Bastian's views may be partly due to the fact that, in its foggier implications, it shows an unfortunate kinship with Jung's mystical and wholly untenable theory of archetypes and of a racial unconscious. Perhaps it was in an attempt to avoid all resemblance with Jung that psychoanalysts—by means of a process which the writer, in collaboration with E. M. Loeb, described as "antagonistic acculturation" (*11*)—have, as regards Bastian, "thrown out the baby with the bath," and have lapsed instead into the kind of paleopsychological speculations which we have called "*pseudobiologia phantastica.*" In addition (and this is a far more serious matter) they have failed to enunciate *sufficiently often* and *sufficiently clearly* the fact that the psychic unity of mankind is a cornerstone of psychoanalytic theory, since without this axiom all psychoanalytic extrapolations from clinical data to cultural material become mere idle speculations and empty tours de force of no great consequence—which, needless to say, is not the case at all.

We cannot, in this place, restate *in extenso* the argument—presented in some detail elsewhere and illustrated by means of what we believe to be telling examples—that the human mind functions pretty much the same way everywhere, and never more strikingly so than in situations of stress, when tensions strip off the restraints of culture, and the "old Adam" emerges more or less in his pristine condition. (*19*) It was this latter finding which induced us to affirm elsewhere that a neurotic or, a fortiori, a psychotic, *Cheyenne Indian* or *Maori* resembles an American neurotic or psychotic *more* than a normal *Cheyenne* or *Maori* resembles a normal American. (*24*) We wish to repeat, however, in this context that this basic uniformity is not a thesis which requires that we predicate a theory of archetypes or that we engage in paleopsychological fantasies, since, as Feldman has pointed out, paleopsychological attempts to explain, e.g., the universality of the Oedipus complex, are worse than false; they are *unnecessary,* since each child's personal experience is sufficient to account for it. (*29*) Even less is it a supposition which enables us to ignore the influence of the specific cultural setting, since the same impulse or fundamental fantasy can be stimulated by various cultural influences and, conversely, can use equally well a great variety of cultural outlets and fields of action. Above all, the cultural setting will be decisively important in determining which impulse or fantasy will receive direct cultural implementation, which will receive indirect or substitute cultural implementation, and which will remain altogether unconscious, being kept in a state of repression either by means of culturally provided repressive devices or by means of individually evolved repressive devices unsupported by culture. (*24*)

It is hardly necessary to state that nothing said herein is intended, or can be used, as disproof of the amply proven theory of diffusion. If we mention this matter at all, we do so only because anything which can be *misconstrued* to imply an attack upon, or even a bypassing of, diffusionism is likely to elicit a somewhat overvigorous repudiation. In fact, it is specifically one of our basic theses that the very process of diffusion, which is a universal one, itself presupposes at least one universal uniformity of the human mind: the capacity to learn, and to integrate new learning with the rest of one's psychic material, in a manner both individually and culturally highly distinctive—which is, by and large, determined on the one hand by the specific ethos of the borrowing culture, and, on the other hand, by the basic personality structure prevailing especially in the borrowing group.

In the following discussion we accept as basic the following postulates:

1. The psychic unity of mankind, which includes its capacity for extreme variability.
2. The principle of limited possibilities, and
3. The finding that something which is out in the open and culturally implemented in one society is often repressed in other cultures.

The foregoing postulates have one important consequence or corollary: It is felt that *if all psychoanalysts were to draw up a complete list of all impulses, wishes, and fantasies elicited in a clinical setting, this list could be matched point by point by a list of all known cultural beliefs and devices drawn up by anthropologists.* This thesis, startling as it may seem at first blush, is, as Professor George Peter Murdock kindly pointed out to the writer, actually a quite plausible one, since fantasies and cultural items alike stem from the human mind, and, more specifically, ultimately from the unconscious. This view will, we believe, seem plausible—at least as a working hypothesis—to all who are willing to accept, at least tentatively, the principle of the uniformity of the human mind, and particularly of the unconscious human mind, though ultimately little more is required than a belief that there is something which may be called a science of *human psychology, as distinct from* a science of, e.g., *bird or rat psychology.* It is felt that this distinction, which is explicitly recognized to be possibly only a quantitative one, is wholly tenable regardless of whether or not one agrees with the frequently voiced logical principle that at a certain point quantitative differences become—or can, *in practice,* be treated as—qualitative differences.

Simple as this principle is, it is legitimate to demand that it be proven by means of empirical data. At this point it must be readily admitted that it would be altogether beyond the powers of any individual, or group of individuals, to develop a typology of all forms of human behavior and to match it with a typology of all fantasies recorded in psychoanalytic literature. Even the Yale University Human Relations Area Files, which are truly fabulous in scope, and are the product of the joint efforts of many fine minds and of a large team of investigators and collaborators, cover only some 200 groups. Furthermore, many workers have established the fact that valid studies could be made with the help of data pertaining to only 200 tribes, even though the present monograph shows that—at least as regards abortion—even without resorting to unnecessarily fine distinctions, the typology which could have been constructed by means of the data found in the Human Relations Area Files would not have covered the full range of the *finer shadings* of phenomena listed in the typology which was initially developed on the basis of some 350 tribes. Furthermore, it might be added that even after completing our typological study on the basis of 350 tribes (as against 200 Human Relations Area Files groups), in looking up data on some 50-odd additional tribes some further typological variations came to light, although it must be admitted that, after the 200 Human Relations Area Files tribes were covered, the principle of diminishing returns began to operate quite conspicuously.

In brief, it is felt that our present 400-tribe typology is fairly adequate and, as a working hypothesis, it may be assumed that no additional important data and insights of interest to us in the present context would have emerged had we covered 1,000 instead of "only" 400 tribes.

In further support of this view, it should be added that it is logically legitimate to suppose that, had our typological study involved a topic which anthropologists are accustomed to study in detail, instead of one which is of relatively marginal interest to most of them—as is shown by the fact that the Human Relations Area Files data contained information on abortion for only some 125 tribes—it is very probable that 200 tribes would easily have sufficed for the construction of a complete typology. This is best shown by the fact that there are relatively few types of kinship systems (*48*), though kinship systems are certainly far more complex than are abortion patterns and, being less limited by stringent biological possibilities, might, in theory, be expected to show a much larger range of variations. In fact, we suspect that for perhaps 90% of our tribes our information is spotty in the extreme: witness the fact that wherever we possess adequate information on a tribe (*Fiji, Masai,* etc.) the data cover many of the major categories listed in our typology. By contrast, differences seem to be largest between tribes on whom our information on abortion is extremely fragmentary or one-sided.

If this hypothesis is correct—and, on the basis of our data, we have but little choice in accepting it as correct—then there is a real justification, *even on this basis alone,* for our approach, which consists in an attempt to understand the real meaning of the customs reported for one tribe with the help of data reported preferably from neighboring, but sometimes also from remote, tribes. We wish to recall, however, that we also justified this interpretative technique on another basis, namely, by suggesting that data pertaining to a *definite* and *limited* cultural trait, such as abortion, which, moreover, is closely linked to biology, may be interpreted by treating (a) the rest of that culture, and (b) traits pertaining to abortion in other cultures, as "free associations" to the specific tribal practice under consideration. We can justify this latter thesis by showing that a *lie* about abortion uttered by a member of one tribe (*Sedang Moi*) reflected *actual practices* related to abortion in another tribe (*Kgatla*), and that an *Aleut* abortionist's *evasion* of questions about abortion contained *a series of symbols* clearly pertaining to the female reproductive apparatus.

This finding may explain why, in addition to our previously mentioned desire not to confuse the reader by references to too many tribes, we have used in our interpretative discussion mainly data from a limited number of tribes regarding whom our information on abortion is relatively complete.

We also have another, rather convincing—though admittedly indirect—proof in support of our view that even material derived from 350 tribes does, for all purposes, represent an adequate sample, at least for the formulation of a typology and for interpretative purposes. We found that our data from our original 350 groups did not contain a single example of attempted abortion by means of the deliberate violation of a taboo for which the penalty is miscarriage. Nonetheless, we mentioned this *possibility* in our typology. Subsequently it was found that precisely this means was resorted to by *Maori* women wishing to rid themselves of an unwelcome pregnancy.

Let us now consider briefly our main thesis, that material repressed in our society may be conscious and culturally implemented in another society. It may seem superfluous to demonstrate for psychoanalysts that one and the same fantasy may emerge in various persons, and to add that such fantasies may sometimes even have a culturally implemented counterpart. However, for the benefit of the students of social sciences, we propose to quote two such examples:

FAECES-EATING MONSTERS: The author is indebted to Miss Ruth Faison Shaw for a report that a child, after making a finger painting, told her that it represented certain monsters living in the plumbing, to which the child had to make daily food-offerings of faeces. Some time later the writer came across an identical fantasy in one of Ernest Jones's clinical papers. (*40*) So far, Jones's case material is the only published example of such a fantasy the writer has come across in his fairly extensive readings of psychoanalytic literature. We may now add that among the *Sedang Moi* of Indochina the writer himself witnessed the fact that, whenever a baby soils itself, its mother calls one of the scavenger dogs—which live largely on human faeces—to cleanse the baby's buttocks and the blanket in which it is wrapped . . . and it is significant in this context that the *Sedang* profess to be descended from a dog ancestor. Furthermore, he saw in the *Moi* jungles an official's outhouse which had a small side door under the seat so as to permit the official's servants to remove the faeces periodically. However, as it turned out, this never became necessary, because every time anyone used the outhouse a bevy of scavenger dogs and pigs came running, and devoured the faeces the very moment they were voided.

THE INVERTED PENIS: Various psychiatrists (*44, 66*) have reported from *Southeast Asia* the occurrence of an anxiety neurosis called *koro,* characterized by the panicky fear that the penis may withdraw into the abdomen. While they recognized this illness as being a genuine neurosis, the object of the anxiety itself —the withdrawal of the penis into the abdomen—was viewed by these writers as a wholly gratuitous fantasy. Yet, any ordinary textbook of urology contains descriptions of a condition called "luxation of the penis," characterized by a detaching of the shaft of the penis from the skin covering it, and by the withdrawal of the now loose penis into the abdominal or inguinal wall. Furthermore, we possess a detailed report (*57*) on a *German* ambulatory psychotic who repeatedly inverted his penis and made it disappear into his abdomen by literally turning it inside out. In other words, he stuffed his penis down his greatly dilated urethra, so that the glans finally emerged, in an inverted state, through a perforation just in front of the anus. The *Mohave* jokingly allege that this is precisely what male inverts would like to do. In this instance, in one culture area we find a cultural acceptance and implementation of a neurotic or psychotic fantasy or wish which has a genuine traumatic organic counterpart (luxation of the penis). In another area this fantasy is the subject of a joke. In still another instance this fantasy has been "acted out" by a psychotic belonging to a third culture area. (Additional data pertaining to this material were discussed elsewhere (25) and need not be further referred to in this context.) *

In the following pages we propose to examine a series of clinically observed and theoretically explainable unconscious attitudes and fantasies which seem to play a role in the motivation and justification of abortions. It may be argued that we should have proceeded inductively rather than deductively, first examining and presenting our set of data, and then reaching these broader formulations by induction. However, such an expository procedure would have been technically impossible due to limitations of space, and wholly spurious as well—even to the point of being little more than an empty gesture—since one cannot simply forget everything one knows (except, perhaps, when using the philosophical *tabula rasa,* and even that is far from certain) and, after having studied psychoanalysis, simply pretend never to have heard of the Oedipus complex. Such a procedure would be disingenuous in the extreme, and, what is more, wholly inappropriate in a study which specifically seeks to establish that the productions of patients which emerge from their unconscious are duplicated elsewhere by customs, beliefs, and traditional action-patterns. We did, however, use major psychoanalytic concepts simply as *initial* classificatory devices, and, from that point onward, proceeded inductively. The best proof of this is the fact that, on the basis of our primitive data, we were

* For the sake of completeness we should mention, however, that the *German* psychotic in question had lived for a number of years in *Japan.* However, this information is probably not significant in this context since, on the one hand, the *koro* neurosis has not been reported from *Japan,* nor even from *Northern China,* and, in addition, it is highly unlikely that a relatively uneducated man living in *Japan* would accidentally hear there of so rare and peculiar a condition occurring in another, though more or less adjoining country. This view is further supported by the fact that the inversion of his penis—which finally caused his death—was but one of the many weird and sadistic actions to which he subjected it.

able to reach at least some new theoretical conclusions regarding the unconscious background of abortion and certain related matters which, as far as we are able to recall, we have not found mentioned anywhere in the literature. We also confidently believe that our few inferred fantasies will eventually turn up in the analysis of patients who have aborted or have been indirectly connected with some abortion or miscarriage. We believe this precisely for the same reason which induced us to mention in our original 350-tribes typology the possibility of someone attempting to abort by the deliberate violation of a taboo for which the penalty is miscarriage; a custom which, as previously stated, did turn up, in precisely this form, in some very reliable *Maori* material.

It is also evident that we could not attempt simply to list all fantasies reported in psychoanalytic literature and to match these fantasies one by one, perhaps in alphabetical order, with some equivalent tribal practices. We deemed it sufficient to discuss the entire problem of the psychological motivation of abortion under certain broad headings, confident that if our ethnological data fitted these broad—but definitely not *too* broad—concepts perfectly, they would also fit specific variations thereof. So far as we have been able to ascertain, our ethnological data do not contain any trait which does not have a counterpart in some clinically reported and theoretically explained fantasy—which is precisely what our demonstration sought to achieve. If this assertion should seem inacceptable to anyone, the data contained in our sourcebook section should enable him to produce, with a minimum of effort, material which, in his opinion, contradicts our central thesis.

Perhaps the best proof of the fact that our approach to our ethnological data was unmarred by preconceptions is the fact that, originally, nothing more than a simple typological study was intended. Not until two eminent anthropologists—shortly before the completion of the sourcebook section of this work—asked the writer precisely what *problem* he sought to solve in his book, did it occur to him that something more than a typology might be indicated. Not until, under the impetus provided by these queries, he re-examined his data, with a view to finding some clue as to a suitable central problem, did it dawn upon him that his material was ideally suited for the demonstration of what has since become the central thesis of this work.* If the manner in which the central problem of the book was "found" is not an example of the process of induction, then we do not profess to know what genuine induction means.

5. CHOICE, MOTIVATION, AND THERAPEUTIC INDICATION

The following remarks seek to indicate what relevance, if any, the anthropologist's findings, obtained in the course of a cross-cultural study of abortion practices, may have for the practice of medicine in Occidental society, in particular as regards the criteria for possible "therapeutic indications for abortion." Since the writer is not a physician, he cannot hope to make a substantive contribution to the problem of whether or not such indications exist, nor to the problem of precisely what—if anything—does constitute a legitimate therapeutic indication for abortion. He may, however, hope to contribute something to a more realistic understanding of what, actually, is *meant* by the term "therapeutic indication," by subjecting the problem of choice and motivation and, therefore, also of "indications," to a searching analysis in the light of his cross-cultural data.

Let us consider first the meaning of the term "indications." It implies:

1. that there exist at least two possibilities of action and/or of purposive inaction

* As stated above, the material is ideally suited for this purpose both because it is a relatively limited one and because it is fairly closely linked to basic psychophysiological processes. This does not mean, however, that—given sufficient time and patience—precisely the same point could not be established also by means of, e.g., an exhaustive study of religious beliefs, etc.

2. one of which is given preference over the other alternative(s)
3. in terms of a motivation
4. which is explicitly stated
5. and which is deemed to be valid and legitimate in terms of
6. some value-system
7. whose hierarchical structure is revealed by one's choice.

This definition implies that—in one frame of reference at least—value may be defined as a hierarchy of choices, since the concept of value automatically implies a hierarchical structure of the value system. This is true even where seemingly only one value X exists, since the statement: "X is a value" implies that it outranks, or is hierarchically superordinated to, the—often not explicitly formulated—"value" "non-X." In brief, in the inductive and empirical approach to the study of values, the concept of choice is logically prior to the concept of a value hierarchy, which in turn is logically prior to the concept of value *per se*.

The statement that "under specified conditions the termination of pregnancy is therapeutically indicated" reflects a choice based upon a hierarchy of values in which physical and/or mental health are assigned value coefficients which are higher than the value coefficients assigned to certain other values which favor allowing nature to take its course.

Every pregnancy, however normal it may be and however joyfully it may have been planned and anticipated, involves certain physiological, psychological, and social adjustments which, in the broadest sense, represent "stress." Conversely, the artificial interruption of any pregnancy, however dangerous its continuation may be and however undesirable it may seem psychologically, socially, and economically, also involves basic physiological, psychological, and social readjustments which likewise represent "stress." (See next chapter.)

Our data show that the decision to abort, or not to abort, is made either by the pregnant woman herself, or by a person capable of imposing his will upon her, or by society as a whole. This decision results from a choice between two kinds of "stress," one of which is—rightly or wrongly—deemed to be less painful than the other. The relative intensities of the two alternative types of stress are appraised in terms of some value system. Insofar as an abortion is allegedly undertaken for the purpose of alleviating or forestalling some situation of stress, it may be described, in theory at least, as "therapeutically indicated," though in practice so broad a definition of "therapeutic indication" would hardly be acceptable to the thoughtful physician—and especially to the psychiatrist, who is aware that, even in the case of women seemingly determined to abort, powerful, though unconscious, instinctual and psychological forces demand that nature be allowed to take its course.

From the sociological and anthropological point of view, one major problem arises in this context. We have seen that when the woman herself, or someone else, decides that an abortion should take place, this implies that the abortion is *subjectively* viewed as "therapeutically indicated," since its assumed or nominal purpose is to alleviate or forestall one kind of "stress." Sometimes, this definition of the situation is in harmony with prevailing social codes and value systems. In other cases, the individual's decision is made in terms of a subjective system of values which is sharply at variance with more generally accepted social codes or value systems. In other words, what the individual deems to represent "therapeutic indications" for abortion, society may view as an entirely inadequate type of motivation, which does not satisfy social criteria for what constitutes a "good and sufficient"—i.e., "socially legitimate"—"therapeutic indication" for abortion. In brief, from the strictly sociological and anthropological point of view, social criteria, based upon existing systems of values, determine what *kinds* and *degrees* of stress are accepted as constituting a "socially legitimate" motivation of, or "therapeutic indication" for, abortion. As a rule, there exist fairly unequivocal criteria whereby the "social legitimacy" of a motivation may be determined. In other cases, however, the situation is considerably more equivocal. A typical example of such an ambiguous state of affairs is reported from matrilineal *Dobu* (Fortune), where a man's heirs are not his own children but the descendants of his sister. A certain *Dobuan* man accepted with vague indifference the repeated abortions of his wife but severely beat his sister's daughter, who had aborted his potential heir to whom he had a socially enforceable claim.

The social scientist who is wise enough to remain within his sphere of special competence has, thus, only one insight to contribute to the problem of what, if anything at all, constitutes a "therapeutic indication for the termination of pregnancy." This insight pertains to the objective fact that social attitudes, reflecting culturally anchored value hierarchies, determine what conditions–i.e., what *kinds* and *degrees* of stress–constitute a *socially acceptable* "indication," or a motivation which is in accordance with cultural standards, for the interruption of pregnancy. Whether or not such socially acceptable "indications" are legitimate in terms of a system of absolute and universal ethics is a problem wholly outside the realm of legitimate sociological and anthropological inquiry, and beyond the professional competence of the social scientist.

6. TRAUMA AND UNCONSCIOUS MOTIVATION IN ABORTION

The purpose of the present chapter is to justify the view that abortion invariably represents a trauma and is actuated by conflicts, which, after the completion of abortion, lead to additional conflicts and stresses. This demonstration was deemed to be necessary, since, unless the occurrence of trauma and the presence of neurotic motivational factors in general can be assumed at the very start of the discussion, a specific analysis of definite unconscious and/or neurotic factors in abortion would amount to little more than a seemingly gratuitous imputation of deep, dark, and unconscious motives to an act which, on the surface, so often seems to be motivated by highly rational and practical considerations.

1. *The Psychophysiological Vector.* It is a basic tendency of

the organism to permit the full and normal development of any psychophysiological process, once it is initiated, to resist any interruption or distortion thereof, and to react through malaise and anxiety to any such interruption or distortion. Needless to say, this malaise and anxiety need not be on a conscious level, and may be quite "convincingly" masked by an equally unconsciously determined pose of calm indifference. In fact, under the impact of other motivations—both social and endogenous—the frustration resulting from an interruption or distortion of a psychophysiological process may even be erotized or sublimated. Most of us, once we have swallowed our meal, would be extremely resentful if we were made to regurgitate it, and, if forced to do so, would be little inclined to resume our meal—yet this was precisely what took place at Roman feasts.* As an example of near-sublimation resulting from an interruption of a physiological process we may quote an authentic but little-known historical anecdote concerning Marshall Macdonald, one of Napoleon's chief officers. Macdonald, heroic but not particularly brilliant, was becoming considerably disturbed by an awareness that his increasingly obvious lack of strategic talent was rapidly causing him to fall into disgrace. To his misfortune, just as Napoleon and his marshals sat down to plan the strategy and tactics of the battle of Austerlitz, Macdonald experienced a violent need to void his stools, but did not dare leave the council of war for fear of completing his disgrace. In desperation he rose far above himself, outlined in a few words the main principles of the brilliant strategy which led to the victory of Austerlitz, and then ran for the bathroom. (*31*) †

Yet, on the whole, it is safe to say that, except under quite

* This oral perversion of "insatiability" has many roots, only two of which will be mentioned in this context. One is the perpetuation of the child's oral omnipotence fantasies. The second is an attempt to achieve orally what cannot be achieved genitally; insatiability being equated in this respect with perpetual potency. It is not by chance that Messalina was characterized by Juvenal as "lassata sed non *satiata*" after her sexual orgies. Juvenal's comment clearly reveals the deep oral sources of the sadistic, man-castrating and man-humiliating, nymphomania of frigid women.

† Given the hostile component in defaecation, it is plausible to suggest that this unexpected "sublimation" was greatly facilitated by the fact that Macdonald was expected to discuss war instead of, say, poetry or some less obviously aggressive activity. It might also be added that artillery tactics (!) played a particularly important role in the Austerlitz victory.

anomalous conditions, the interruption of any physiological process already set in motion is a severe source of discomfort; witness the tensions resulting from "necking parties." For this reason, even though some of our data indicate that primitive women sometimes abort for the most fatuous reasons (witness the case of the *Mbaya* woman allowing herself to be aborted in order to show Azara how it is done) we are not free to assume, even in such cases, that the interruption of pregnancy did not involve some severe, though perhaps unconscious, trauma.

An interesting, though subsidiary, point to be considered at this juncture is the validity of the reasons which impel some observers to allege that some primitive women abort with the utmost casualness, especially when such allegations do not represent some special pleading, such as: "Primitives are bestial and need to be ruled by whites, or [as the case may be] to be taught the ethico-religious outlook of Western civilization." A good example of an apparently genuinely candid remark is Karsten's statement that some *South American Indian* women make no more of an abortion than one might make of a tooth extraction. This "minimization by analogy" may sound very convincing indeed to the psychoanalytically unsophisticated, but will—assuming that the analogy is an aboriginal one—inevitably bring to the mind of persons familiar with dynamic psychology the symbolic implication of loss of teeth as representing castration or even death.

So far we have dealt primarily with basic biopsychological realities, which resist the interruption of any physiological process, once it is initiated. The normal pregnant organism "wishes" to stay pregnant until the child is ready to be born. It opposes considerable resistance to any factor or force which seeks to interrupt the pregnancy, regardless of whether this factor is illness, or an attempt to abort. As every physician knows, desperately ill and even severely injured or mutilated women have carried their children to term, and extraordinarily violent attempts to abort have occasionally failed.

It is equally well known that pregnancy involves a modification of the woman's endocrine balance, and also a number of other physiological changes, so that any premature interruption of pregnancy necessarily calls for extensive readjustments in the organism's balance, almost to the point of producing a "general adaptation syndrome" in Selye's sense.

So far, from the psychological point of view at least, we have dealt with factors which, on the psychological level, are represented partly by bona fide basic id-impulses and partly by impulses rooted in certain portions of the nuclear or body-ego. In the parlance of Occidental ethics, we have dealt with forces which jurists, theologians, and students of ethics have viewed as manifestations of "natural law." *

2. *Unconscious Factors.* The term "unconscious" is used here in the strict sense, to designate that which has never been conscious or that which has been conscious but has become unconscious as a result of repression or of other defensive maneuvers of the psychic apparatus. Psychoanalysts, though admittedly working chiefly with Occidental women patients, have found that pregnancy and normal childbirth have deep unconscious meanings, only some of which will be listed. According to Helene Deutsch (whose views on this matter are not *wholly* acceptable to this writer) some women feel that coitus culminates not in the orgasm, but in childbirth. (*6*) A sophisticated and far from frigid young woman, mother of several children, all of whom she delivered either without anesthesia or with a minimal amount of it, flatly declared: "Childbirth is a kind of orgasm—only more intense." There is quite a bit of psychoanalytic evidence to substantiate this psychological—but in our opinion, not necessarily biological or id-determined—meaning of pregnancy and childbirth, and also the existence of a fantasy of an indefinitely prolonged retention of the penis or fantasy of "interminable coitus," representing an imaginary means of acquiring a "*public*" penis. (The existence of this fantasy is also amply substantiated by the well-known unconscious equation: baby = penis.) Thus, a young married woman who found too obviously pregnant women both horrible and thrilling used to fantasy that, if she ever became pregnant, she would ostentatiously accompany her husband everywhere, so as to make a

* This statement is a purely descriptive one, and does not commit the writer either to an acceptance or to a rejection of the existence of "natural law," or of any particular concept of natural law. Least of all does it commit the writer to those conceptions of natural law which are invoked only when they are likely to make life more difficult for those against whom they are invoked.

show of her protruding belly, and to advertise thereby that she had cohabited with her husband—which she never dared to do when she and her husband were spending the night under the roof of her parents. In this instance the "perpetual cohabitation" and "retention of the penis" fantasies were also in the service of repressed, defiantly exhibitionistic wishes, which, while admittedly neurotic, were not wholly so, since they also served the mature need to emancipate herself from her parents, i.e. to cease being *primarily* a daughter and to begin being *primarily* a wife. Numerous other unconscious fantasies and wishes also militate in favor of the continuation of pregnancy and against abortion—so strongly, in fact, that in certain pathological instances the desire to retain the foetus indefinitely leads to prolonged and difficult childbirth.*

This does not mean, of course, that numerous unconscious factors do not underlie also the opposite desire: the wish to abort. However, it is our thesis that whereas at least some of the factors militating against abortion have never been conscious, and have their roots in the id and in the nuclear ego, unconscious factors militating in favor of abortion—and of psychogenic miscarriage—were always conscious at first, and became unconscious only as a result of repression. Their roots therefore reach into the conscious ego and into the superego, and their ultimate origin is to be sought in the external world, which is the source of all experience and of most of the content of both the ego and the superego. The woman who unconsciously hates her consciously beloved husband, and therefore wishes to castrate him or to deprive him of an heir; the emotionally immature married woman who deems it "sinful" to reveal by her pregnancy the fact that she is no longer a virginal daughter, ever faithful to her frustrating oedipal father; the pregnant native woman who failed to observe the taboo on coitus during lactation; etc., may produce a premature termination of her pregnancy either by means of a psychogenic miscarriage or else by deliberate abortifacient maneuvers. Indeed, even primitives seem to be aware

* It is impossible to resist the temptation of pointing out in this connection the support which a *real* understanding of psychoanalytic theory could give to students of ethics, including pastoral ethics. Unfortunately many potential beneficiaries of psychoanalytic insights reject them from sheer ignorance, because of a stubborn adherence to the principle "*credo ut intellegam,*" instead of to the Baconian principle "*intellego ut credam.*"

of the fact that a miscarriage can be brought about by simply wanting it.*

The point we seek to make is a rather simple one. It is felt that whereas several of the psychological factors which militate against abortion have the support of, and are the psychological equivalents of, powerful organismal processes, psychological factors, both conscious and unconscious, which militate in favor of abortion do not have such basic organismal processes at their root, and stem originally from the world of the ego, of the superego, and of external reality. The motivational processes militating in favor of abortion may have at their root either some very real situational factors (social disgrace, danger to life, and even—as in some *African* tribes—the decision of tribal authorities) or else they may be purely neurotically motivated.† It is felt, however, that it is extremely improbable that any woman ever decided to abort or consented to an abortion, even for excellent social reasons, without her decision being motivated, *in part at least, also* by unconscious and neurotic wishes. Indeed, it is hardly necessary to argue that often the best of reasons fail to impel man to perform even wholly rational and socially approved actions, unless his unconscious gives at least its conditional consent thereto. We must hasten to add, however, that, in the same sense, when a woman refuses to abort even where death or severe social penalties are certain, her decision is likewise at least partly motivated by unconscious and neurotic factors.‡

* A word of caution is necessary at this point. We have data of this type for two tribes only: The *Hopi* and the *Pukapukans*, and, in both instances, our authority are the Beagleholes. It should be stated at once that the Beagleholes' standing as reliable and psychologically alert field workers is, deservedly, of the highest. Furthermore, any anthropologist knows that, having obtained an interesting cultural tidbit from one tribe, he will remember to inquire about the same trait also in the course of his work with the next tribe he is investigating, and may, therefore, obtain a bit of information which he might otherwise not have "happened upon." The sole purpose of this footnote is to stress the desirability of obtaining similar information also from other tribes, particularly in view of the fact that we do have numerous and elaborately documented statements from a great variety of tribes regarding the *difficulty* of obtaining abortions, even by quite brutal means. Yet it should be added that psychophysiologically and psychodynamically the Beagleholes' data are definitely credible.

† It is hardly necessary to remind the reader that neurotic motivation also has its roots—at least indirectly—in distorting external experience.

‡ The correctness or falseness of this last statement has no bearing whatsoever upon the fact that a refusal to abort for any reason whatsoever may, as many

3. *Actual Motivation.* The foregoing considerations sought to elucidate some aspects of the motivation to abort (or not to abort) which we believe to have universal human validity—and, in our opinion, describe and define the dynamics of such motivational processes in any woman, be she a Chicago debutante or the mother of a starving Central Australian brood. There does not seem to be any indication that female animals ever abort deliberately, nor do we have concrete information regarding the possibility of "psychogenic" miscarriages in female animals. In fact, abortion seems to be one of the—far from numerous—genuine qualitative differences between animals and mankind. By contrast, many female animals practice infanticide, as do some male animals, of whom tomcats are perhaps the most notorious. Hence, insofar as it is possible at all to make a general statement about "human nature in the raw," it seems fairly reasonable to suggest that, were she left to herself, the non-neurotic human female would prefer not to abort. When she does abort, or miscarries for psychological reasons, this wish, decision, or "accident" is motivated by a combination of factors, some of which are frankly neurotic, while others reflect highly realistic socio-economic considerations. However, as stated before, even these realistic considerations would probably not be acted upon without some support from, or the consent of, unconscious neurotic wishes.

We must hasten to add, however, that in some instances these neurotic wishes are operative primarily in the set of actions which led to pregnancy in the first place, rather than at the moment when the abortion is actually decided upon.

We may consider under this heading a fictitious case, which will do as well as any real one could in leading us up to concrete data.

Let us assume that a neurotically motivated Southern woman cohabits with a Negro, while consciously or unconsciously aware

---

maintain, be in itself a wholly meritorious and ethical act. Indeed, many of the most admirable, creative, heroic, or saintly actions in the history of mankind have been motivated by neurotic wishes. In our opinion this does not detract in the least from their ethical excellence or from the magnitude of the benefits which mankind has derived from many noble acts so motivated. Whether the absolute refusal to abort for any reason whatsoever belongs to this category of noble actions is a problem on which there is no real consensus and which, furthermore, has no bearing upon the point which we are analyzing at this juncture.

that she does this at a moment when conception is very likely, especially since she is one of those women who conceive very easily. Let us suppose, furthermore, that she could have taken precautions but did not choose to do so, either intentionally or "accidentally on purpose." Chances are probably very high that not only was her cohabitation neurotically motivated * but also that some of this neurotic motivation consisted in the wish to abort eventually the child so conceived, partly perhaps in order to punish herself for her unconsciously ego-dystonic sexual deed; partly, one may venture to speculate, in order to "kill" her Negro lover and his child, perhaps as a substitute for crying "rape," etc. The best proof that this hypothetical example is more than idle speculation is provided by our data on the *Tupinamba,* who gave their prisoners of war a *Tupinamba* girl as bedfellow, in order to humiliate him later on by eating the baby born of this union. We know that this prospect so horrified some *Tupinamba* girls that they deliberately aborted the baby so conceived. Interestingly enough, we are not told that any of these couples ever did anything to prevent conception, either through abstinence, or through contraception. Let us now carry somewhat further our examination of our concrete *Tupinamba* data. We learn that the purpose of such abortions was to save the child, born on term, from being eaten as a gesture of hostility toward the captive father. However, the fact is that in neither case was the child permitted to live; it was simply spared the "indignity" of being cannibalized.† Even if we grant that the *Tupinamba* consider being cannibalized a special form of opprobrium, the aborting of a man's child is still an aggression toward him, even among the *Tupinamba.* Thus, the "considerately aborting" *Tupinamba* bedfellow of a captive is, in a way,

* This statement is a psychodynamic and factual one, and applies to the objectively defective reality-adaptation of a *Southern* woman who cohabits with a Negro. It would not be *necessarily* applicable to a *Frenchwoman* living in Paris and consorting with a socially eligible Negro man.

† Due allowance should be made, however, for the recurrent theme that the mother loves the already born child better than the unborn, especially after nursing it. Here we are dealing partly with social attitudes (since I know of no primitive society in which love, in the ordinary sense, is enjoined toward the unborn) but, I would venture to suggest, partly also with the primacy of vision and of other senses in the formation of social attitudes, such as the complex sentiment known as love. This point will be discussed more in detail in another context.

also committing an aggression against her lover by destroying his child, albeit in a culturally less "shocking" way. That this is not mere speculation is shown by the basic belief that cannibalizing the child will hurt the captive's feelings. At the same time she is also endangering herself, perhaps in order to punish herself for her exogamous sexual acts. Lastly, and most obviously, she is punishing and thwarting the members of her own tribe, who demanded this sacrifice of her maternal impulses, by making it impossible for them to achieve the very goal for which she was assigned to her captive lover in the first place. Thus, we find that an extraordinarily "realistically" motivated and culturally deeply understandable motive for abortion presumably involves, at the same time, also a supplementary stream of probably unconscious, aggressive, self-punitive and, in a word, neurotic motives, which were operative in the performance of the initial act of cohabitation—where abstinence would have achieved the same end with less discomfort—and in the final act of "pious" abortion as well.

We cannot attempt to examine here, one by one, all varieties of feminine motivation listed in the chapter on typology. Nor can we venture to do this in connection with the motivation of certain third persons or parties who, in various tribes, may put pressure upon, or may outright force the woman to abort. However, in this latter connection, we can and must stress that obligatory abortion, as a *punitive* measure, is repeatedly found in tribes—and apparently *only* in tribes—where illicit abortion is severely frowned upon and is specifically penalized. This is exemplified, for instance, by our *Ashanti, Azande, Masai,* and *Chagga* data, though among the *Azande* and the *Ashanti* it is the adulterous woman, among the *Masai* the girl who cohabited with an unsuitable person, and among the *Chagga* the pregnant, lactating woman, who is made to abort. We are dealing here with a very strict equivalent of one aspect of the concept of the "sacred," as defined by Durkheim: a ritual act is a specially authorized sacrilege. In this case the penalty demanded is an act which, if performed for private reasons, is severely punished. This correlation does not obtain between the taboo on voluntary abortion, and resort to prophylactic abortion: witness the occurrence of prophylactic abortions among the *Jivaro,* who place few restrictions on voluntary abortion. As in the case of voluntary abortion, decided on by the woman for realistic reasons, externally imposed abortion, especially of the punitive type, also seems to involve a certain amount of neurotic (vengeful) motivation on the part of the person or group enforcing compulsory abortion. This is shown by the fact that among the *Buka* many husbands prefer to pretend that their wives' illegitimate babies are theirs, rather than have a scandal and be forced to stand upon their rights. While it is open to debate just how accurate existing general techniques for the measurement of anxiety in various cultures—such as were developed by Horton (*39*) and by Whiting and Child (*64*)—are, it seems fairly safe to suggest that tribes in which abortion is culturally imposed upon the woman, for any reason whatsoever, but especially punitively, are tribes which, if not ascertainably *more* tense and anxious than others, happen to be tribes whose culture does not provide sufficient *other* outlets for narcissistic injury and/or specific or diffuse anxieties. This is a highly conservative and, in fact, quite innocuous suggestion and simply restates, in a specific context—abortion—the well-known fact that a radical interference with organic processes of any kind is always indicative of a compelling need to find an outlet for neurotic tensions and anxieties.

Nothing said in the preceding pages should be interpreted to mean that our data lend any support to the time-worn and shopworn—but tenacious—tendency to view primitives "as a bunch of neurotics gone savage," as someone (perhaps Horney in one of her less extreme moments) characterized some half-baked pseudoanalytic "interpretations" of primitive culture. No society is free from anxiety, and no known society has been indubitably shown to be absolutely free of abortion. The process of reproduction is a source of anxiety everywhere, and whether or not this anxiety—one of the many which arise in the course of living in society—is, or is not, permitted to find a *major* and *socially emphasized* outlet in voluntary or involuntary abortion depends on more factors, determined by the rest of the respective culture, than any single student, or even group of students, could adequately survey and factor-analyze. In the same sense the total social context will determine whether, in a given society, anxieties connected with reproduction will be manifested in a reproductive or nonreproductive context, or, conversely, whether anxieties *not* connected with reproduction will seek a preferential outlet primarily in the area of sexuality or in other areas. Which of these possibilities will actually materialize in a given group will depend primarily upon one consideration: Each society appears to define a certain area of cultural living as a "problem area." It will, therefore, tend to use this area as a preferential outlet for its tensions, and to assimilate other kinds of tensions to tensions arising in the traditionally defined "problem area," which is the cultural equivalent of what economists have often called "distressed areas." A general theory of this problem cannot be offered in this context, and will be dealt with in a forthcoming book. (*26*)

7. THE SIBLING-RIVALRY COMPONENT

Numerous tribes all over the world, which space children by means of a taboo on coitus during pregnancy and lactation, and/or by aborting pregnancies which follow too rapidly after a previous one, state that this is done in the interests of the child already born. As a *Pima* expressed it: The mother loves the child already born, which she can see, more than she loves the unborn child which is as yet invisible. This statement clearly suggests that the sensorium is deeply involved in the initial development of object cathexes . . . a finding whose implications cannot be discussed here. The *Sedang Moi* also correlate maternal love with sense impressions, *e.g.,* by proclaiming that until a child has suckled, it is like a piece of wood. By contrast, the *Arapaho* and the *Chippewa* are said to consider the unborn child as a human being, though the *Chippewa* buried only miscarried fetuses the way adults are buried, and disposed otherwise of the voluntarily aborted ones. As regards the *Arapaho,* it appears to have been a matter of personal preference whether a miscarried or aborted fetus was given a burial befitting human beings or was disposed of otherwise. However, the fact that the *Chippewa* made a distinction in the disposal of voluntarily aborted fetuses and of miscarried ones raises some doubts as to the absolute validity of the statement that they viewed all fetuses as definitely human. Our tentative reservations on this point are strengthened rather than weakened by whatever scanty data we do have from other tribes regarding the eschatology of miscarried or aborted fetuses. Among the *Maori,* the *Mangarevans,* and the *Rhadé Moi,* the aborted fetus becomes a kind of deity, whereas among the *Hopi* the fetuses of a repeatedly aborting girl apparently become some kind of demons, who gang up on her and kill her in order to prevent her from killing further fetuses . . . a belief which, in the entire body of our data, is duplicated only by a somewhat similar belief among the *Arapaho,* although there even the *unintentionally* miscarried fetuses may eventually attack and destroy their mother. This, in itself, raises certain doubts regarding the absolute validity of the statement that the *Arapaho* and *Chippewa* fetuses are considered human in the strictest sense of the term. Our chief point is that the conception that fetuses are nonhuman—regardless of whether this nonhumanness consists in defining them as good or bad supernaturals or as logs—is far more prevalent than the belief that they are truly human. Also, the fact that fetuses are often aborted in order to enable the parents to take better care of children already born—even to the extent that the *Australians* (Róheim, personal information) may feed the aborted fetus or the newborn child to its older siblings—clearly shows that they are not thought of as being on a par with children already born, whom the mother loves because she can see them (*Pima*), or because she has had the experience of nursing them (*Sedang*). This inference, which is based on specific cultural data—such as the finding that the newborn permitted to live a day or so is hardly ever killed afterward—is also plausible psychologically, since abortion, regardless of what some field workers may say, always seems to entail either conscious or unconscious feelings of guilt, witness the *Hopi* conception that aborted, and the *Arapaho* conception that miscarried, fetuses gang up on their mother and kill her. The defense against these feelings of guilt, reflected in the demonic conception of aborted fetuses, can take two forms: The aborted fetus can either be deified (*Maori, Mangareva*) or else the guilt can be denied and the fetus can be defined as something nearly inanimate (*Sedang Moi*) or as the absolute property of its parents (several *South American* tribes) who can do with it as they please. The most convincing proof of the fact that the deification of aborted fetuses is a defense against guilt is provided by our *Rhadé* data. There the dead fetuses, who never enjoyed the pleasures of life, are mothered by a female deity and have the ear of a male deity, whom they can induce to send misfortunes to mankind. In order to forestall this possibility, at their burial a formula is uttered which culminates in the plea: "Do not be angry with us"—an expression often found also in *Sedang Moi* prayers addressed to their gods, whom they consider powerful but malevolent.* The element of ambivalence toward the aborted fetus is quite clear in this example.

The sacrificing of the interests of the unborn or newborn child to those of its older siblings also implies the existence of a certain psychological or affective value-hierarchy, which subordinates the youngest child or the unborn baby to the older or already born child. The neonate's skull is battered in by hitting it against the older sibling's shoulder. (*Aranda,* Howitt.)

These data lead us to the problem of the attitude of children toward the spacing of subsequent pregnancies. We have reviewed elsewhere (22) the evidence regarding the *Northern Plains* of the United States, and have indicated that the *Sioux* child takes pride in the fact that its next youngest sibling was

* It may be mentioned at least in passing that the sole source of the power of *Sedang* deities is the fact that they can render themselves *invisible.* Until, in self-defense, they made themselves invisible, they were constantly outwitted and imposed upon by man's forebears. Whether this divine invisibility should, or should not, be tied up with the fact that the mother does not love the child until she had a sense experience—nursing—of the child, is a question which our data do not enable us to solve. However, we may at least intimate the possibility that the idea of supernatural beings may be rooted quite as much in one's feelings of omnipotence in the prenatal and early postnatal state, as in the child's conception of its parents' power. In the same sense, the characteristic invisibility or partial invisibility of supernaturals may be derived, perhaps, not only from the sometimes almost subliminal experience of the primal scene (parental coitus), but also from the invisibility and inferential existence of fetuses. These remarks are admittedly speculative, and in the present state of our knowledge deserve, at most, a footnote.

born several years after its own birth, since the child evaluates this as a proof that his parents loved him enough to refrain from coitus for a prolonged period of time. These data can be interpreted from two points of vantage:

1. From the viewpoint of the child, the spacing of births is a token of parental love, and their nonspacing a hostile gesture.
2. From the viewpoint of the parent, pregnancy and childbirth represent serious interferences with the marital relationship.

The first of these points will be discussed presently. The second will be examined more closely in the section on counter-oedipal factors in abortion.

We have very specific evidence that the natives themselves impute to the lactating child a considerable amount of hostility toward the unborn. The evidence pertaining to the *Mohave* was reviewed elsewhere (*12*); it being noted that the *Mohave* allege that the lactating child—who may be anywhere from one to three years old—still has an affinity with the maternal womb, and therefore so fiercely resents the intrusion of another baby into what he still considers "his original home" that he makes himself sick from spite, exhibiting severe gastrointestinal symptoms. The "clinical" observation itself is probably correct, since, despite much "scientific" sentimentalizing about the value of prolonged lactation, biochemical evidence unequivocally indicates that, after a certain number of months, the food value of the maternal milk begins to drop rather rapidly, so that the child is often literally suffering from a nutritional deficiency disease (*4*)—a fact which will not surprise dairy farmers who have long been familiar with the necessity of periodically reimpregnating ("freshening") their dairy cows. It is hardly necessary to add that the food value of maternal milk would decrease particularly rapidly in the course of a new pregnancy.

The next point to be considered is whether or not the jealousy which the *Mohave* impute to the nursing child is a genuine or a fictitious one. No psychoanalyst, and probably very few students of child behavior, will find anything extraordinary in the statement that even very small children are often aware of their mother's new pregnancy, and that they resent it to the point of fantasying attacks upon the pregnant maternal body

(body-destruction fantasies). Indeed, we have specifically suggested elsewhere that—among the *Mohave* at least—all feminine genital bleeding, be it due to defloration, childbirth, or simple menstruation, is more or less unconsciously conceived of as a result of an attack of the penis upon the womb. (*20*)

While the above considerations will seem commonplace to psychoanalysts and while their utilization would facilitate the demonstration which we are about to undertake, we will make allowances for the fact that such psychoanalytically commonplace findings are not readily accepted by some. Hence, even though it may make our demonstration somewhat more arduous a task than it has to be, we will not, for the time being, utilize this insight, and will proceed instead on the basis of the empirically established fact that the adult *Mohave impute* jealousy toward the unborn to the lactating child.

The reality of sibling rivalry is, we believe, sufficiently well established today, even in nonanalytic circles, to require no special proof in the present context. Traces of this rivalry persist throughout life, albeit often in a highly disguised form. It is therefore not at all surprising that *Mohave* adults, who at some early period of their lives have gone through the stage of sibling rivalry, should impute sibling rivalry also to nursing children—whether rightly or wrongly so, is a matter of no consequence in the present context. Indeed, the above information was obtained from a *Mohave* medicine man who, while drunk, boasted to the writer that he had bewitched his half-brother, because he was jealous of the preference which his mother had shown to the latter. (*15*) Yet, the informant had managed to disguise this hostility so well that when, after his informant's death, the writer mentioned this matter to old Mrs. Tcatc and to his interpreter, both expressed amazement, stating that no one—except his mortally sick nephew, whom the late shaman had treated in vain and to the best of his ability—had ever accused this shaman of being also a witch.

Let us now return to child-spacing by means of abortion, which is theoretically undertaken in the interest of children already born, and, in particular, in the interest of the next oldest child, who may still be nursing. Such a regard for the child's interest is fully compatible with what we know of the great kindness wherewith many primitives treat their children. At the same time, abortions so motivated also gratify the sibling rivalry —and, in the case of the *Australians,* also the cannibalistic— impulses of children already born . . . or, if one refuses to believe in the reality of infantile hostility toward the unborn sibling, one may say that such abortions serve as a prophylaxis against the occurrence of sibling rivalries after the birth of a new sibling.

The question now arises why natives who practice abortion for this reason *do* gratify their already born children in this respect. Indeed, it should be realized that even the most lenient primitive parents—and some of them are indeed lenient beyond anything the *Western* mind would consider reasonable or tolerable—draw the line somewhere and impose certain restrictions or inflict certain traumata upon their offspring.

We must therefore ask why any primitive parent should accommodate his already born child in this respect, since most of them know that abortion is a fairly dangerous, and certainly a very painful, experience? After all, even the native father—indulgent though he is—does not tell his uninitiated son about the initiation rites, and gives him no food reserved for adults. *(60)* We must therefore assume that this extreme considerateness is shown only because it also gratifies *some of the parents' own, more or less unconscious, wishes.* The nature and origin of these wishes are fairly clearly suggested to us by the assumption that adults *impute* to their children a hostility to the unborn. If they impute such wishes to them, then it is reasonable to assume that they do so because of their own unresolved, or only partly resolved, earlier sibling rivalry conflicts. And if we assume that this imputation is a valid one, and does, in fact, represent the actual psychological attitude of the nursing child (and on the basis of psychoanalytic experience we have to view this imputation as a realistic conception of the child's attitudes) we are led to ask the crucial question: Precisely what are the subjective factors responsible for the primitive parents' capacity to understand this undesirable, but real, trait in their children?

At this point a brief excursus into the psychological basis of knowledge and of insight into reality is unavoidable. There are a good many things in reality, right under our noses—and far less subtle than sibling rivalry manifestations—which we neither see nor comprehend. The fact is that when man does comprehend and does accurately describe some segment of reality, these are phenomena which we are not entitled to take for granted, simply because the comprehension and description are congruent with the facts. It is well to remember in this context Ackerknecht's brilliant, and insufficiently recognized, paper, which explains the "paradoxical" observation that cannibals—whose dietary habits certainly placed them in an excellent position for learning anatomy—never seem to have developed a science of anatomy, simply because they were not interested in *dissection* but only in (culinary) *carving*. (*1*) On a psychologically deeper level, we might suggest that the "carving" approach and the "dissecting" approach are actually mutually exclusive, and that the latter represents a defense against, and a sublimation of, the former. In other words, it is our view that the impulse to carve up a human body for cannibalistic purposes has to be repressed or sublimated *before* a science of dissection and anatomy can come into being. This statement can be generalized to apply to all other forms of knowledge as well.

In brief, we suggest that this extreme regard for the interests of the born child, which, tacitly in most cases and quite explicitly in the *Mohave* case, involves an *imputation* of sibling rivalry to the child, and an *awareness* of the child's sibling rivalry, is possible only because of the parents' own early and partially still unresolved sibling-rivalry experiences, and their consequent capacity to perceive the pressure of similar hostilities also in their own children. In other words, the parents have to identify with the nursing child in order to be able to understand the sibling rivalry problems of the latter and to impute sibling rivalry to it.

This identification of the parents with their children implies, however, also a regression to, and reactivation of, their own early sibling-rivalry problems. Such regressions are notoriously likely to occur in situations of stress, such as pregnancy and childbirth. How much of a crisis such events really are, is best demonstrated by Dr. Reo Fortune's finding that arguments between *Dobuans* and *Trobrianders* over whether the father has any role in the production of pregnancies—with the *Trobrianders* taking the negative position—are such traditional sources of conflict and vehemence between the two groups that they are laboriously avoided in all conversations. When, despite warnings received from his *Dobuan* friends, Fortune chose to discuss this topic with some *Trobrianders,* his *Dobuan* friend became so angry at him that he did not speak to him the rest of the day.

Our data seem to suggest that the spacing of births by means of abortions is *only consciously* motivated by a regard for the interests of the children already born, who—among the *Australians* for example—are actually fed the aborted or newborn baby; a highly startling example of *endo*cannibalism in an area where this trait is far from normal in any other context. Unconsciously, abortions nominally so motivated presuppose an identification of the parents with their children's sibling-rivalry conflicts, which, in turn, both presuppose and involve a regression of the parents to their own early sibling-rivalry problems. This inference is startlingly confirmed by the bitter exclamation of a *Papuan of Geelvink Bay*: "Our children destroy us!"

It now becomes desirable to indicate some possible dynamics for the suggested identification of the parents with their own children, in regard to sibling-rivalry conflicts.

The first, and most obvious, of these factors is the important role which older children play in primitive society, in caring for their newborn or very young siblings. That this task is often far from pleasurable, and represents drudgery at its worst, is shown by the remarks of an adult *Mohave* woman (*21*) who bitterly recalled that in her childhood she was bent almost double by the weight of the cradle which she had to carry around. In a sense, then, parental drudgery on behalf of the small child is quite likely to revive earlier memories of drudgery on behalf of a small sibling. The fact that, especially in economically marginal groups, this parental drudgery is very real indeed and that the care of the child often entails much self-denial, does not mean that parental resentment does not derive *additional support* from a revival of memories of drudgery on behalf of a sibling. Indeed, even rational actions often have an irrational substratum, as is shown by the fact that there are a good many rational things we could do and do not do, simply because they are at variance with, or derive no support from, our unconscious wishes and impulses.

Be that as it may, the following example clearly illustrates the identification of the parents with some of their children, although in this case the children identified with are the younger ones.

Among the *Sedang Moi* the writer once asked the widowed medicine woman A-Rua why she insisted on calling her adult oldest son "tao"—a kinship term meaning "older brother." She was surprisingly embarrassed by this question, and attempted to rationalize it by saying that she was simply trying to teach her younger sons to address their older brother properly. The tenuousness of this rationalization is made apparent by the fact that no other *Sedang Moi* woman, whether widowed like A-Rua or living with a husband, called her oldest son "older brother." It must be mentioned, however, that the kinship term "å," meaning primarily "younger sibling," also has the supplementary meaning "child," e.g., in the form "å a," "my child," or "ve å," the children. (It may therefore not be altogether a coincidence that the only nonmagical case of abortion reported in detail by the *Sedang Moi* concerned the impregnation of a daughter by her father.)

The second factor tending to revive memories of sibling rivalry in the parents is a more subtle one. Psychoanalytic experience indicates that one's spouse is often equated in the unconscious with one's parent of the opposite sex. As one of Griaule's *African* informants remarked: "At night, while but half awake, we sometimes call our wives 'mother.'" This may be due to the fact that sleeping beside one's wife may revive earlier memories of the warm closeness of the maternal body. If this inference is correct, it may help us to understand—partly at least—why one's mistress is more seldom equated with one's mother than is one's wife. As some wit once expressed it, "The only difference between marriage and an affair is that, in the latter case, one has to get up, get dressed, and go home afterward"; the implication being that one does not sleep beside one's mistress the way one sleeps beside one's wife, and as, in early childhood, one slept beside one's mother. To return to our main point: if there is a tendency to equate one's wife with one's mother, then it is similarly easy to equate one's unborn or newborn child with one's younger sibling, whose birth was one of the major traumata of one's childhood—as indicated, for example, by Leighton and Kluckhohn's analysis of the "dethroning" of the *Navaho* baby by the newborn. (*47*) This, however, is a problem which requires no further analysis at this juncture.

In the light of these considerations, it seems plausible to conclude that the spacing of births by abortion, while nominally (and partly realistically) motivated by regard for the welfare of children already born, is at the same time *additionally,* and presumably rather powerfully, motivated also by the parents' regression to early attitudes of sibling rivalry. These latter unconscious motives may, in turn, contribute extensively to the motivational force of the widespread aborting of children in order not to have to observe the coitus taboo during pregnancy and lactation, which will be discussed under the heading of counteroedipal attitudes.

8. COUNTEROEDIPAL CONFLICTS vs. SENSUALITY

We stressed in a previous study (*23*) that the problem of parental counteroedipal attitudes—which not only meet the child's oedipal ambivalences halfway, but, to a large extent, actually elicit them—has been a relatively neglected area of psychoanalytic research. The motives for this neglect were indicated in the aforementioned paper, and therefore need not concern us further in this context. On the other hand, our insight into even the dynamic psychologist's resistances against coming to grips with this problem oblige us to make a special effort to present our data and inferences in as convincing and detailed a manner as possible.

The basic datum: Many of our data on abortion indicate that the taboo on coitus during pregnancy and lactation, which prevails in numerous societies, is an important conscious motivation of the abortions of married women. Supplementary data from some other tribes (*Ainu,* etc.), where premarital license prevails, reveal that sometimes unmarried girls also abort, so as not to interrupt their participation in more or less carefree love affairs.

A. PRIMITIVE "VOLUPTUOUSNESS": Many of our earlier authorities—who were by no means always missionaries—sought to explain the data just referred to in terms of an extreme "voluptuousness" of primitive spouses. Superficially, the data seem to confirm this interpretation, since the abortions in question were obviously undertaken in order to make it possible for the spouses to continue indulging in sexual relations with each other. If we push our analysis somewhat further, the facts in question, and the problem of their interpretation in terms of "voluptuousness," can be discussed under three separate headings:

1. The role of sexuality in primitive society.
2. The role of sexuality in primitive marriages.
3. The hierarchical superordination of the sex drive to the drive toward maternity, which we also discuss in another chapter.

1. *Sexuality in Primitive Society.* It is admittedly difficult to appraise degrees of sensuality or the intensity of genital sexual drives. We know that *Baiga* (*28*) women accuse their husbands of infidelity if the latter do not cohabit with them several times a day,* while Gorer tells us that the *Lepcha* regularly cohabit several times a day. By contrast, a supposedly very sensual tribe like the *Mohave* is not sexually "hyperactive." (*18*) † Even the number of orgasms—on which much of Kinsey's statistics is based—is not indicative of sensuality, since, as R. R. Greenson pointed out in a lecture before the American Psychoanalytic Association (May, 1953), a large number of minor consecutive orgasms in a woman almost always reflect the presence of neurotic mechanisms, which inhibit the occurrence of intense and truly relax-

* The identical inference also forms the gist of an American joke about a French couple . . . which is a neat illustration of the thesis that that which is culturally implemented in one society may be repressed, or expressed only in a humorous form, in another society.

† The entire problem of what represents sexual hypoactivity, be it due to physiological deficiency or to psychological inhibitions, and what represents sexual hyperactivity motivated by neurotic factors, is, by and large, *terra incognita.*

ing and gratifying orgasms. As a young woman patient once expressed it: "Before I found the right man, I used to have a large number of consecutive small orgasms, and was still not satisfied. Now I have one intense orgasm and feel happy and relaxed."

The foregoing considerations do not have a direct bearing upon the problem which we propose to investigate in this section. They simply indicate that neurotic (i.e., originally extrapsychic) motives may influence the number and intensity of sexual experiences. The real problem under study at this juncture is the role which sexual experiences play in the total life-pattern of the primitive.

Since our topic is a rather difficult one, it seems best to approach it in a relatively roundabout way, by means of data which have no direct bearing upon sexual activity *per se*. Hence, we arbitrarily take as our point of departure Kroeber's perspicacious and in many respects deeply moving comments on the *Mohave* Indian's sense of aimlessness in life, which he finds reflected in the fact that, in a narrative concerning an important incident of nineteenth-century *Mohave* history, there is hardly any mention of motivation. (*45*) Apparently the protagonists in that incident did various things, dropped their usual pursuits to undertake trips, etc., almost aimlessly, since the narrative nowhere even hints at their motivation. It could be argued, of course, that we are dealing here not with a true absence of motivation, but with a peculiarity of *Mohave* stylistic convention—perhaps in the sense that, as we pointed out elsewhere (*14*), individualized "psychologizing," as a *distinct* literary device or major theme, is a relatively late and quite sophisticated trait in the history of world literature. Yet, despite the possibility of offering this alternate interpretation, there is something about Kroeber's interpretation which completely convinces the present writer, who is not exactly unfamiliar with *Mohave* attitudes.

If such a sense of aimlessness pervades even the life of the *Mohave,* who are a notoriously ebullient people, with an almost Latin emotional freedom, and totally unlike the Occidental's stereotype of the impassive "cigar-store Indian," it is legitimate to expect that similar traits would also be found among other groups. As regards acculturated groups—among whom the incidence of abortions is, by the way, often on the increase—we described elsewhere (*22*) the "flattened, and emotionally impoverished, personality which is commonly met with in times of social disintegration." Hallowell, too, made similar comments about acculturated natives. (*37*) The total impoverishment and degradation of the acculturated or subjugated native's environment was also discussed elsewhere (*10*) in theoretical terms, and was confirmed, almost point by point, by Kluckhohn and Leighton's *Navaho* data. (*43*)

We must stress most emphatically that whereas this sense of aimlessness is particularly *noticeable* in acculturated tribes, Kroeber's remarks about the *Mohave* pertain to a period in history where the *Mohave* were still far from being destructively or degradingly acculturated. The fact is that life in primitive society is far less thrilling than many travel books seem to indicate. For example, primitive warfare notoriously impresses the Occidental reader as something "utterly thrilling." Yet, except in a few tribes which deliberately made warfare a glamorous business, primitive warfare was often quite dull and almost tame. The *Samoan* data of Count Rodolphe Festetich de Tolna (*30*) are very much to the point in this context. As regards the *Sedang Moi,* the writer once asked them how they felt about the fact that, as a result of their pacification by the French, instead of going on a genuine raid they had to stage a mock combat, so as to be able to hold a certain ceremony. The men shrugged their shoulders and said in effect: "Slave raids were more profitable, but this way, at least, no one from our village is likely to get hurt." It should be added that this remark was made only two years after this particular village—long notorious as the fiercest in that area!—was pacified after a pitched battle.

The simple fact is that the average primitive is no exception to Thoreau's thesis that most men lead lives of quiet desperation. He leads a fairly dull and routine life, which may explain why he is occasionally capable of such sudden—though usually transitory—emotional outbursts. In fact, whereas urban Western man may, in a way, be thought of as being chronically overstimulated, the primitive is often chronically understimulated. Thus, *Sedang Moi* adults have literally neither games nor dances, and, on the whole, very little fun in life. When asked why they had no games, they replied: "If we played, we would have nothing to eat." This statement is not exactly correct, since their economy is relatively adequate; however, the point is that they *believe* it to be true. Their only real nonsexual routine entertainments are occasional sessions of music—at which they excel—gossip, petty backbiting, and the display of skill in certain crafts.* Other entertainments, such as hunting, fishing, and getting drunk at feasts, were distinctly mere intermezzos, because the *Sedang Moi* are agriculturalists rather than hunters or fishermen, and because their ritually consumed rice beer is so weak that it cannot be stored. Under these circumstances, just about the only major "entertainment" available to them at all times was sexual activity: heterosexual activity among married couples, and homosexual or autoerotic activity among the unmarried.

We might add that this situation is far from unique. Holmberg (*38*), in speaking of the *Siriono,* also stresses that sex is one of the few "entertainments" available to them at all times. Premarital sexual freedom in *Muria* society is specifically contrasted, by the *Muria* themselves, with the far less thrilling life led by the married couple.

It should be emphasized that the preceding paragraphs neither justify nor condemn the use of sexual activity for the purposes of "entertainment." They simply describe what does, in fact, take place in many primitive societies.

While circumstances differ from place to place, it is, we feel, fairly correct to state something which brilliant descriptions of South Sea "sexual paradises" have somewhat obscured. We refer to the fact that even in the case of such "paradises" we are dealing less with uninhibited "natural" sexuality than with a socially deeply modified conception and function of sexuality.

In many groups coitus is much more (i.e., ultimately much "less") than an outlet for passion and affection. It is also the primitive's equivalent of the theater, the concert, the novel, the Sunday comics, the TV show, and the Saturday evening "binge." In other words, sexual behavior is but the mouth of a major river, whose tributaries can often be traced back to a goodly number of wholly nonerotic sources . . . witness, e.g., the role of seductions in the prestige-seeking patterns of *Plains Indians*

* Vong, who was the strongest man in the village and also a passive homosexual, excelled in basketry. He explained that his skill in basketry, which was almost comparable in its delicacy to weaving, gratified his desire to compete with the women who, in that tribe, are the weavers.

(22) and of the *Angami Naga* (35). In the latter tribe the sexually active man has three rows of cowries sewn on his breechcloth. He may add a fourth row for the seduction of a married woman, or for having carried on simultaneous affairs with two sisters. We also know that the *Baiga,* who are culturally expected to be sexually very active, experience a good many anxieties over their potency (*28*), while among the *Tanala* some unmarried men who believe their potency to be inadequate become transvestites—though apparently not necessarily homosexuals—in order to avert the danger of their impotency or inadequate potency being revealed by the wives they would be expected to marry if they chose to remain males socially.*

Given this *synthetic function of primitive sexuality,* it is but seldom that cohabitation may be viewed as something truly glamorous, in the romantic ("love") sense of the term. It may, however, be endowed with glamour of a different kind: the glamour of the exploit, of triumph, of humor (*Mohave*), and even of rebellion and defiance, etc. That seems to be the case even among the *Muria,* who, judging by Elwin's description, are an unusually gentle and well-adjusted people. In most other instances, however, sexual activity becomes somewhat dull, as a result of its being the *sole* outlet for so many tensions, and also because it is resorted to so often for purposes *other* than the manifestation of true passion and genuine, individualized love. In fact, it is often little more than a conventional "cultural bromide." Thus, the *Mohave,* who are anything but puritanical, clearly differentiate between two aspects of sex: coitus *per se* is a thrilling and, in a sense, humorous exploit, which they often endeavor to make as comical as possible, and which they discuss rather freely. By contrast, all matters related to the reproductive aspect of coitus, and indeed all matters pertaining to procreation, are viewed as serious problems and are discussed soberly, if at all. (*18*)

We hasten to add that such a degradation of sexuality, such an exploitation of sexuality for essentially nonsexual purposes, is by no means limited to primitives. Even in Occidental society there is much aimless and routine "lovemaking" which is not

* In societies which dispose of a steady, inexpensive, and relatively nonperishable supply of alcohol, drunkenness may also serve as a culturally implemented synthetic outlet for a great variety of tensions, impulses, and wishes.

only far from being truly sensual, but is actually often compulsively neurotic ("sexual addiction") and is more than occasionally inspired by sheer boredom and motivated by the inarticulate person's inability to communicate on the symbolic level. It was reliably reported to the writer that, during World War II, when male dates were hard to get, a group of girls from a women's college managed to arrange a blind group date with some semimilitarized students attending a nearby men's college. As several of the girls expressed it independently, and in almost identical terms: "Those of us who were fortunate enough to get an interesting date had a good time talking and flirting, while the unlucky girls who paired off with dull boys were reduced to necking." This information dovetails with data found in the extensive autobiography of an uneducated *Polish* immigrant, published by Thomas and Znaniecki. (*62*) Whenever this man moved to a new American town, he promptly found himself a mistress . . . this being apparently his only means of initiating human relationships and of achieving social integration.

Given this highly characteristic synthetic function of sexuality in primitive society, it becomes understandable why many primitive spouses are so reluctant to give it up for a period extending anywhere from nine months to several years. The giving up of coitus means far more than mere deprivation of the pleasures of orgasm *per se*. It means, in many ways, a forsaking of one's chief *routinely available* outlet for a variety of tensions, and of the principal "entertainment" and thrill available day after day. In other words, certain types of abortions, which initially seemed to be clearly motivated by extreme "voluptuousness," on closer examination appear to be motivated by an attempt to escape a *pervasive* kind of frustration, by the preservation of one of the chief components of one's psychic security system.

2. *Sexuality in Primitive Marriage.* Many early accounts of the abortions of married women "for the sake of voluptuousness" (the Kamchadal) reflect a great deal of indignation over the fact that primitive marriage should have as its goal sexual gratification rather than the procreation of children. Quite a few of our earlier authorities seem particularly exercised over this matter—almost more so than over the abortion of premaritally conceived children, which probably seemed more understandable

and even "conditionally more acceptable" in terms of Western practices and attitudes.

It is a fact that—until quite recently—respectable Western society did not expect marriage to be erotically pleasurable, nor even romantic. It tolerated and even encouraged a certain amount of romanticism in courting couples, but the idea of finding true sexual fulfillment in marriage is, despite the existence of such a unique item as the old French book on *The Fifteen Joys of Marriage,* a relatively new idea in Western society. The traditional Occidental attitude is neatly reflected in the decision of Provençal Courts of Love that true love cannot obtain in marriage, and also in La Rochefoucauld's celebrated maxim: "There are good marriages, but there are no delightful ones." Such a view of marriage is sharply at variance with primitive attitudes, even where marriage is by purchase or arrangement. We have clear-cut *Konyak Naga* data which reveal the bitter resentment of a man over the fact that, in his childhood, his father had chosen for him a much older wife, who was sexually so unattractive to him that he would never cohabit with her. Yet, even though neurotic inhibitions were clearly at work in this instance, it is equally certain that this man did *expect* to find sexual fulfillment in marriage, since he occasionally dreamed of cohabiting with the very wife whom he would never touch in reality. (35) The *Muria,* too, while admittedly contrasting the delights of sexual freedom in the unmarried age-group's house, the *ghotul,* with the monotony of married sexuality, are quite aware of the delight of cohabiting with a spouse who is truly one's own.

Even Western society once knew that marriage, rather than courtship, is the climactic moment of life. While novels about marriage, as distinct from courtship—the latter ending in the traditional "And they lived happily ever after"—are relative latecomers in the literary landscape of postclassical Europe, the two great Homeric epics both have marriage and its vicissitudes as their central theme. The *Iliad* is fundamentally the projection, on the political and military scene, of Menelaus's domestic difficulties, while the chief motivating element and major plot-component of the *Odyssey* is the *marriage* of Odysseus and Penelope —and *not* the suitors' *courting* of Penelope. In addition, both epics depict in great detail a number of other marriages. The same is largely true also of *Greek* tragedy: it is not the courtship but the marriage of Agamemnon and Clytaemnestra, of Oedipus and Jocasta, of Theseus and Phaedra, etc., which occupies the center of the scene. Courtship as such is simply not one of the chief themes of classical Greek literature, except Attic comedy—and even there only in a limited ritual (5) sense. By contrast (as Herbert and Judith Williams kindly pointed out to the writer) contemporary plays and films about *marriage* are almost always comedies.

3. *The hierarchical superordination of the sex drive to the maternal impulse* is found in many primitive societies, and especially in those where there is a taboo on coitus during pregnancy and lactation, and where monogamy prevails, if not as a social norm, then at least—as is often the case in nominally polygamous societies—as a demographic fact. This hierarchy of values is not very difficult to understand in the light of the role which sexuality plays in primitive society, and also in primitive marriage. Pregnancy represents too great an interference with the habit patterns of the parents, and the prospect of sexual deprivation involves too threatening a breach in their psychic security system, to enable primitive parents to accept pregnancy with equanimity. In truly polygamous households it is, admittedly, only the pregnant or lactating wife who is sexually frustrated—but, in that case, her anxieties are further exacerbated by envy, and by the fear of losing to a rival her privileged position in her husband's home. The same fear may also actuate the abortion of the wife in a society where divorce is easy, so that the pregnant wife may be repudiated for the sake of a non-pregnant new mate. (*Abipones*)

B. COUNTEROEDIPAL FACTORS: The foregoing data clearly indicate that the fetus, or, a fortiori, the newborn, is an intruder in the family, who disturbs the existing relationship between his parents, especially in the sexual sphere—which, in view of the relative rarity of functionally diffuse and highly individualized interpersonal relationships in primitive society (9), is often one of the chief nuclei of the *private and personal—as distinct from the social—relationship* obtaining between the parents.

This distinction is an important one. *Socially,* the focus of many primitive marriages is the establishing of a kinship bond and of a network of reciprocal rights and obligations between two lineages. The *personal* and *private* (idiosyncratic) relationship between the spouses—such as "love" or "sex appeal," etc.—is often entirely ignored, at least from the social point of view. This means that, in a very comprehensive sense, "married love" and even "married companionship" are, socially and culturally, often grossly underimplemented in primitive society. Since people living together do have a need for some kind of *personal* relationship, in instances where society hardly gives them any directives as to how to go about establishing such a relationship they have to develop the private and personal side of their marital bond "from scratch." Obviously, under such circumstances the biologically actuated sexual relationship is as good a starting point for the establishment of a broader private relationship as any. This, needless to say, only serves to increase even further the importance of marital cohabitation in the security system of such individuals. Though such primitive marital relationships may closely resemble, at least externally, purely sexually motivated marriages among ourselves, they are functionally and psychodynamically very different from the latter. Indeed, whereas purely sexual marriages among ourselves reveal simply a state of deficiency and an incomplete compliance with social expectations, the evolving of an intensive sexual relationship in a primitive marriage is a true act of creation, which adds something new and personal to that which society expects from the spouses in the way of a relationship.

We have already specified that a pregnancy not only interferes with the basic sexual rapport between the spouses, but also threatens to undermine a large number of additional functions, meanings, and implications which are significant though latent components of the primitive matrimonial relationship. The tremendous import of conflicts elicited by this intrusion may be judged by the almost obsessive and, indeed, near-paranoid intensity and elaborateness of some taboos insuring abstinence from coitus during lactation and pregnancy. Thus, among the *Chagga,* a husband may oblige his wife to abort if, during her pregnancy, he has an erotic dream, while a pregnant lactating wife may commit suicide from shame. Equally revealing is the hostility and cruelty shown in certain areas to the wife who commits adultery, especially if, as a result of her act, she happens to become pregnant. Since the taboo on coitus would have to be observed by her husband even in this instance, his wrath, and his occasional insistence (*Masai,* etc.) that his adulterously pregnant wife should abort, is quite understandable, even—and perhaps especially—when this compulsory abortion masquerades as a benevolent attempt to save the woman's life, which her adulterous pregnancy is believed to have put in jeopardy. (*Ashanti*) The hostility displayed toward the woman who, during her pregnancy, cohabits with a lover is also significant in this context. One motive for this hostility may be the feeling that if the husband has to renounce sexual relations, the wife should renounce them too. In addition—as suggested in another chapter—there is also the unconscious fear that the adulterous cohabitation of a pregnant woman may cause superfetation or a change in the paternity of the unborn child.

In presenting these arguments we certainly do not seek to minimize the relevance of such facts as the obvious difficulty which the care of several small children entails for a primitive nomad woman. It should be noted, however, that similar lactation taboos also obtain in societies which are economically relatively well situated, and where, despite the absence of such important economic considerations, wives nonetheless have to abort children conceived during lactation . . . if only in order to avoid public disgrace.

At this juncture it may be argued that such economically ill-motivated coital taboos during lactation may represent survivals from some earlier stage of economic marginality and nomadic existence. In other words, tradition, with all its obsolete and even irrational components, may be brought in as an explanatory device.

Nothing could be further from the writer's thought than to deny the force of tradition and of habit. However, as Lowie—one of the most profound and most witty students of man's proneness to persevere in his habits, instead of following the dictates of his reason—pointed out: "Man is not a total abstainer from common sense, even if he indulges with fanatical moderation." (*51*) Customs and habits do become obsolete, and are discarded—often greatly to the relief of all concerned. Thus, we have detailed reports about the manner in which human sacrifice came to an end among the *Skidi Pawnee.* When a certain

Pawnee decided that human sacrifices had become obsolete, and therefore rescued the next intended victim, there was no one to say him nay. In fact, there are ample indications that the tribe as a whole heaved a collective sigh of relief at having gotten rid of this practice, which no longer seemed right to them. (*49*) The writer himself was able to witness the decline of cannibalism among the *Sedang Moi*. Mbra:o, the oldest member of the village, reported that in his time he had attended cannibalistic human sacrifices, but had not actually eaten the flesh of the victims; he had merely touched his lips with a piece of the liver. As regards middle-aged people, they had participated in human sacrifices where not the flesh of the human victim, but that of a simultaneously killed animal, was eaten. In fact, in one case the "human victim" was not even killed; he was merely lightly pricked under the arm. The rites, as practiced in 1934, did not even involve any longer the pretense of having a living human victim present in person. The human victim was simply "impersonated" by little wax figurines, representing slaves . . . of which the village had none, by the way.

In brief, while man is not a model of rationality and adaptability, neither is he a mechanical zombie, chained hand and foot to habit and tradition by his own inertia. In addition, we must also realize that *human inertia is not an irreducible datum. It is quite as dynamically motivated as human spontaneity is.*

Hence, what we have to do in this context is to explain the *persistence* of the taboo on coitus during pregnancy and lactation, despite the many inconveniences it entails. We do know that this taboo can, and does, lapse, as it did in the case of some Christianized *Chagga*. We feel that, in this particular case, the factors responsible for the *persistence* of this taboo are identical with those which are responsible for its genesis. (In other cases the factors responsible for the persistence of a practice may differ from those which brought it into being.)

We have indicated that the child interferes with the relationship between the parents: diverting libido from the father, monopolizing the mother and making her sexually rather inaccessible. In other words, *the child's mere existence brings into being the very state of affairs which its subsequent oedipal hostilities and affections will seek to bring about.* It should be stressed at this point that this state of affairs comes into being long before the child is actually born—long before even a Melanie Klein would impute oedipal impulses to a child, let alone a fetus. The point we seek to make is that the mere existence of the fetus causes the parents to *experience in fact* what they would be *meant* to experience later on, were the child able to implement its oedipal impulses. This explains our view that *parental counteroedipal attitudes necessarily antedate historically the child's oedipal attitudes and may, as suggested elsewhere, actually stimulate their coming into being by a type of parental "expectation" ("chip on the shoulder") which, through the parents' behavioral and attitudinal expression thereof, leads to what Merton (55) calls a "self-fulfilling prophecy."*

It is easy to demonstrate the existence of prenatal hostility toward the unborn child, especially on the part of the father. We already mentioned the belief that coitus with a pregnant woman may cause her to abort. The *Masai* even have a special procedure for punishing men guilty of having aborted a woman by such means. The *Mohave* believe that violent coitus with a pregnant woman may damage the child, that anal cohabitation with a pregnant woman will cause the *child* to have "loose bowels," and that if a pregnant woman performs fellatio her *child* will have no "throat cap" (glottis). (*13*) We interpret these beliefs as culturally implemented expressions of masculine hostility toward the unborn. The further theoretical implications of such fantasied phallic attacks upon the unborn were discussed elsewhere in some detail. (*20*)

It will be pointed out perhaps that, since coitus in advanced pregnancy is, in fact, likely to cause miscarriage or premature birth, this may explain why the *Masai* (Merker) punish also the parents of stillborn or deformed children. However, the *objective fact* that coitus in advanced pregnancy *can* start birth pains does not mean that primitives possess an *objective knowledge* of this fact. Indeed, the primitive—like everyone else—has occasion to *perceive* a good many things without actually *registering* i.e., truly observing, and understanding systematically) that which he has perceived.* Already Malinowski, in seeking to persuade us that the *Trobrianders* were truly unaware of the nexus between coitus and pregnancy, asked why we should im-

* Elsewhere in this work we referred to Ackerknecht's sagacious comments on why cannibals are not expert anatomists. (*1*)

pute to the primitive knowledge in *this* sphere when we do not impute to him also an understanding of *other* observable natural phenomena. While—as Róheim has shown (*58*)—Malinowski's example was ill chosen, his reasoning was quite accurate, and his question a legitimate one.

We therefore postulate that the native who believes that coitus with a pregnant woman may cause abortion is right in his *conclusions;* however, he did not *reach* this conclusion on the basis of observation and induction, but simply through his unconscious hostility toward the unborn. This hypothesis receives partial confirmation from the fact that several of the tribes holding such beliefs force adulterously pregnant wives to abort. This is certainly something which we may legitimately interpret as a sign of hostility toward at least one group of fetuses. Additional unconscious sources of hostility toward unborn children were discussed in other chapters of this section, and need not be referred to further in this context.

As regards the nursing child, our chapter on sibling-rivalry components clearly indicates one set of motives actuating parental hostility toward them. In the present context we simply have to add that the nursing child occupies in the mother's bed the place previously reserved for the husband, and, by its demands for nourishment and care, interferes with marital relations.

In summary, it is felt that counteroedipal attitudes are at the root of many abortions, especially in societies where there is a taboo on coitus during pregnancy and lactation. We must add, however, that such attitudes probably prevail, though perhaps with lesser intensity, also in societies lacking this taboo. The taboo itself must therefore be construed as a *cultural implementation of intrapsychic defenses* against a hostility which is directed primarily toward the child, but, partially at least, also toward the woman who committed the "indiscretion" of getting pregnant. These considerations explain not only the *existence* of the taboos in question and the occurrence of abortions in societies having these taboos, but also the tenacious *persistence* of these highly inconvenient taboos. It furthermore reveals that such abortions, far from being motivated by unbridled sensuality in the conventional sense, are actually striking illustrations of the function and intensity of counteroedipal impulses, which—like all essentially pregenital impulses masquerading as genital ones—are *primarily hostile* and only *secondarily erotic* in the psychoanalytic sense of this term. The real pregenital roots of this hostility are revealed by our examination of the multiple function and role of sexual activity in primitive society. What the parents fear and seek to prevent is not simply basic sexual frustration, but primarily the unavailability of a major source of entertainment, etc.—or, simply stated, of a major item in their psychic security system. "Voluptuousness" as a motivation of abortion exists primarily in the imagination of the biased Western observer, even in the case of girls who abort in order to continue to engage in premarital license (*Ainu*), since such girls know that this period is likely to be the only free and easy one of their lives. The laments of a *Konyak Naga* (35), married to a sexually uninteresting wife, that whenever he began an affair the girl became pregnant at once—which meant that she had to marry immediately the spouse previously chosen for her—are well worth mentioning in this context, as are many of the sayings and songs of the *Muria* extolling the happiness of the carefree life of the *ghotul*. Here too, what is primarily aimed at is not "voluptuousness," but a safeguarding of the right to a "last fling" before settling down to lifelong drudgery.

On the whole, whenever there are taboos on coitus during pregnancy and lactation, one function of polygyny may be the reduction of paternal counteroedipal hostilities toward the unborn. Where (as in many parts of *Melanesia*) nominal polygyny exists side by side with demographic monogamy, and such taboos nonetheless prevail, counteroedipal hostilities become exacerbated. Hence, in contradistinction to *Africa*, fertile women are not esteemed very highly and the men are far less interested in fathering children than they are in *Africa*. They are, consequently, also apparently somewhat less jealous, though even in *Buka* married women abort only the children of their lovers, and never those of their husbands.

9. THE FLIGHT FROM PARENTHOOD

Innumerable reports suggest that an important motivation of abortion is the desire to postpone the effects and duties of parenthood and of social and biological maturity. Roughly speaking, three major types of motivation come under this heading:

1. The preservation of beauty.
2. The continued enjoyment of freedom and irresponsibility.
3. The avoidance of sexual abstinence during pregnancy and lactation.

Actually, we propose to show that all three of these motives, but more particularly the first two, may best be understood not in terms of vanity and shiftlessness but in terms of a neurotic flight from maturity, and from an unavoidable unconscious identification with one's own parents. The third factor, the avoidance of prolonged continence, also comes to a certain extent under this heading, but was, for reasons of expository convenience, discussed in terms of counteroedipal attitudes.

The Preservation of Beauty and Sex Appeal. Abortion is frequently reported to be motivated by the woman's desire to preserve her youthful charms, and especially to protect the shape of her breasts. This motivation is specifically mentioned for *Polynesia,* but also seems to occur in *South America* and in some other areas. As regards the *Marquesans,* Linton specifically informs us that women refuse to lactate what children they do have, lest this should spoil their breasts. Childbearing as a means of enhancing one's charms is mentioned for a few *Orinoco* tribes only, and even there the reference is a rather questionable one. It is however, quite significant that this belief does not seem to obtain among the *Aranda,* even though, according to Strehlow (*60*), they consider pendulous breasts desirable, because they are indicative of maturity. Likewise, and not unexpectedly, *Aranda* women do not seem to abort in order to protect their beauty, though apparently *Australian* women of the Port Jackson (Sydney) area did so. It is also interesting that, even though many primitive women are extremely anxious to have children, and are encouraged to have children by their husbands, who desire offspring quite as much as or even more than the women do, the writer has never found in his anthropological readings a single instance paralleling the Occidental belief that some women look more beautiful when pregnant; and, as stated above, he located only one dubious report of a belief that early childbearing—or childbearing in general—enhances a woman's charms. This is true even of some *African* tribes where female beauty is, for all practical purposes, measured in terms of pounds, and where marriageable girls are literally stuffed with food. In brief, there are indications that the matronly figure—*i.e.,* the figure of a motherly (*matrona* comes from *mater*) woman—is, in general, not deemed to be particularly attractive sexually even in certain *African* groups where men readily marry women who have already proven their fertility.

Without seeking to deny the basic human reality of the urge toward motherhood, it must be recognized that this urge is far less basic than the purely sexual one. Helene Deutsch's assertion that for a truly feminine woman the real culmination of coitus is childbirth is, we feel, somewhat extreme. (*6*) The fact remains that the urge toward motherhood, while real enough, is a relatively plastic and modifiable one, so that in a society where children are desired by the men women will frantically consult oracles and undergo innumerable rites (PB) to become pregnant, while in societies where too many children entail the risk that the woman may be deserted (*Abipones,* etc.) or where pregnancy interferes with marital, or permissible extramarital, relations (*Ainu,* etc.), the women abort quite readily, and apparently with little or no *conscious* psychic turmoil. In fact, anthropological data seem to suggest that, even conservatively speaking, the intensity of the urge toward motherhood is pretty much a function of male attitudes toward fatherhood, the latter being determined, in turn, partly by the economic usefulness or uselessness of children, and, even more profoundly * by the role which the fathering of a child plays in the prestige patterns of a given society.

It is regrettable that even psychoanalytic theory is not altogether free from such culturally determined preconceptions. It is an interesting wissenssociological observation that probably no area of psychoanalytic theory is less adequately elaborated than the problem of feminine psychology, and that no other single *special*—as distinct from general—segment of psychoanalytic theory has led to a distinctive "schism," motivated by a major analyst's reluctance to accept the theory of female penis envy.

Actually, it is not surprising that such a state of affairs should prevail in the psychoanalytic theory of feminine psychology. At present, the status of women is undergoing a rapid change, and, in such a period of turmoil, where traditional expectations are alternatingly disappointed and gratified, *seemingly* without rhyme or reason, it is little wonder that the formulation of a sound theory of feminine psychology should be beset with many difficulties. It is interesting to note in this context that the myth of feminine unpredictability (or evilness) prevails especially, though not exclusively, in times where the status of women is undergoing a change. It prevailed, characteristically, when the rise of Christianity drove the worldly women of classical antiquity into convents and to penance; when, during the early Renaissance, they were liberated for a while from extreme matrimonial shackles; when, during the onset of the baroque period, they were once more expected to be sophisticated and yet easily offended by declarations of love (cf. Molière); and, again, in modern times, when women are increasingly expected to be not only women but also human beings. At other times women do not seem to be considered, a priori or chiefly, either mysterious or capricious, but are felt to be as predictable as anyone else, in terms of an established frame of reference which, while different from that pertaining to men, is as orderly and socially as fully sanctioned as the male code of conduct.

* We wish to stress specifically that we have chosen the term "more profoundly" most carefully, to indicate that, on the one hand, the noneconomic factors are more important than the economic ones, and, on the other hand, to suggest that these noneconomic factors have deeper roots in the unconscious than have economic ones.

In brief, whenever abortion is motivated by the desire to win or to keep a lover or husband, either by remaining sexually available or by safeguarding one's female charms, we are dealing not with "debased and salacious" female sensuality but rather with a predominance of the sexual urge over the reproductive one, this hierarchical ordering of impulses receiving also an additional, but strictly subsidiary, support from social pressures and problems of economic security.

One last word may be said in this context against the allegation that the instinct of motherhood is stronger than the sexual instinct in women. This thesis is untenable in the light of the basic definition of the world of the id, which is characterized by a certain degree of shortsightedness—by an inability to wait, and an incapacity to think in terms of the future. As long as human pregnancy lasts nine months, we will simply have to discard the heartwarming but utterly fallacious masculine myth of woman's primordial maternal urges and will be compelled to assert that the woman who cohabits without love, and *solely* for the purpose of having a child, is acting quite as neurotically as the woman who cohabits *solely* in order to relieve a momentary sexual tension, which, needless to say, is also a neurotic type of activity. The plain fact is that neither the organism nor the id think nine months ahead. Hence, the maternal behavior exhibited by nullipara and female children is due partly to an identification with a maternal model and partly to a complex compensatory mechanism, which cannot rationally be identified with the simple nest-building reflexes of female rats.

Transition to Adulthood. In discussing the age-grading of the people of *Truk,* Gladwin and Sarason specifically differentiate between young and irresponsible, and mature and responsible, persons. Their point is well taken, and aptly underscores the fact that as the individual's range of experiences broadens and deepens he usually becomes increasingly mature. New parents are striking examples of this maturation process. The birth of their first child in particular confronts them with major problems of psychological readaptation, especially as regards a change in their self-definition, and in regard to a required, though often more or less unconscious, identification with their own parents.

Indeed, our data indicate that, on the whole, the least frequently aborted child is the second and, next, the third one. In some tribes (*Guaycuru, Mataco, Formosa,* etc.) nearly all first pregnancies are systematically aborted—for a variety of reasons, such as the preservation of youthful charm, the facilitation of later deliveries, the impropriety of getting pregnant too early in marriage, etc. In some cases, as in *Formosa,* up to the age of thirty-four to thirty-seven, all pregnancies are aborted. It should, however, be noted in this context that one reason why so many first pregnancies are aborted is that illegitimate pregnancies tend to be first ones . . . a point which, in itself, deserves consideration. By contrast, in other areas the children most frequently aborted are those of parents who already have approximately two children.

If we concentrate, for the time being, upon the abortion of the first pregnancy or pregnancies, we are clearly confronted with an attempt to postpone the assumption of the adult parental role, and, in many cases, also the acquisition of a matronly figure, both of which often imply a renunciation of "good times." As all those who have had children—and a good many of those who have deliberately avoided having children—know, childbirth is, for both parents, a surprising and sometimes quite uncomfortable experience, somewhat reminiscent of being discovered by one's parents, presumptuously dressed in their clothing. It is psychologically far from easy suddenly to be a father, after having been up to then a son; to be addressed suddenly as "mother," after having been called "daughter" for a long time. In other words, and speaking on a much broader level, it is often a surprising and even painful experience to discover suddenly that one has irrevocably become an adult. We have specifically described elsewhere (*24*) this surprise and feeling of "impersonation," which sometimes actually amount to that unconscious denial of the fact that one is truly an adult which is so characteristic of many neurotics.*

Thus, the new parents have to adjust themselves to and to identify themselves with, the parental role which, until then, they have viewed as a "privileged" one, to which they may not

* A young married woman, very much under her mother's thumb, systematically, though quite "unintentionally," spoke of her apartment as "the apartment," while speaking of that of her parents as "home." When this was brought to her attention, she conceded that she felt she was "simply playing house" with her husband.

(yet) aspire. The more rigidly the cleavage between adult and child is defined, and the more systematically the child is discouraged to "presume above its age" (*Samoa*) (Mead), the more traumatic this adjustment will be. By contrast, it is legitimate to suppose that where the adult-vs.-child dichotomy is underemphasized, the task of the new parents in adjusting themselves to having become parents will be considerably facilitated. In view of these considerations, it may perhaps not be altogether an accident that some of the chief areas of abortion of first pregnancies (which are often illegitimate ones) are those in which children, though kindly treated if they are permitted to live, are definitely thought of as possessions of their parents: *Africa, Melanesia,* parts of *South America,* etc. While there are numerous exceptions to this rule—if indeed it can be called a rule at all—there is just enough truth to it to deserve mention. Of course, the abortion of first pregnancies also occurs in areas where children are not defined as possessions, but sometimes, as in the case of *Plains Indians,* this *may* be partly a result of social upheavals created by acculturation problems. The implication is, that in this latter type of society the new parents may experience fewer anxieties over the assumption of the parental role than in societies where the transition from child to adult status is a greater one.

Be that as it may (and, in view of the unevenness of the available data, no real certainty is possible in this matter), one thing seems quite probable. Abortions motivated by the desire to retain one's youthful charms are not quite as crudely sensual in their motivation as some well-intentioned, but psychologically naïve, observers would have us believe. Youthful charm is more than an absolute entity. It is something which reveals its true meaning *only by being contrasted with* the concept of the matronly figure. Thus, it is perhaps not altogether an accident that in our own society—where the child-vs.-adult dichotomy is very pronounced—girls are more and more inclined to postpone marriage and motherhood, while middle-aged persons battle desperately to save themselves from "showing their age." * Thus, on being asked whether they thought of themselves as "girls" or as

* Weston La Barre cogently indicates that whereas in our society the social cynosure is the pretty girl, in some *Semitic* groups it is the impressive old patriarch. (*46*)

"women," an entire senior sociology class in a women's college agreed that they were "girls."

Once in a great while a society finds a way out of this impasse, at least partially. Among the *Comanche* (50), old women freed the younger ones from the trouble of taking care of their children, so as to enable them to remain the playmates of the young warriors who were their lovers or husbands. But such solutions are fairly rare and may even be deemed atypical, despite the fact that in a good many societies much of the care of small children devolves upon the grandparents who, one infers, rediscover in such activities their "youth" (childbearing age), which, to the younger women, represents "middle age."

Even the above statements represent a certain amount of oversimplification, in that, even where a strong child-vs.-adult dichotomy prevails, initiation rites may serve to bridge this gap in one sense, but also perhaps to deepen it in another sense. Likewise, we have suggested elsewhere (7) that a change in designation (e.g., "girl" vs. "woman") may take place at three crucial moments in a woman's life: at puberty, at marriage (Miss becoming Mrs.)* and at childbirth (the *Sedang vînjoh* becoming a *kînjae*). An attempt to correlate the tendency to abort first pregnancies (be they legitimate or illegitimate) with a reluctance to change one's age-grade is impossible in the present state of our knowledge, since we simply do not have enough data on psychological attitudes elicited by a change in age-grade in various ethnic groups. For *Alor,* Du Bois has pointed out that whereas paternity is rewarding to the man, maternity means no social advancement for the woman. In other areas, where the sterile woman is an object of pity and contempt, women go from pillar to post in order to conceive and to deliver children. We also know that among the *Masai* it is extraordinarily shameful to impregnate an uninitiated girl, and that a girl impregnated under these conditions is immediately initiated at the expense of her guilty lover. In other words, in these tribes pregnancy is clearly an adult privilege.

What we are seeking to establish here is that, in the abortion of first pregnancies, one of the chief motivating factors appears to be the reluctance to assume the parental role, because of the anxiety which a seemingly "presumptuous" identification with

* The *Aymara* word "to marry" means literally "to become a person."

the "privileged" role of one's own parents entails. (This may, conceivably, be an additional reason why the care of children often devolves upon the grandparents.) In addition, the parental role is also often explicitly viewed as a most onerous one, especially by parents who have never grown up emotionally, and who therefore constantly emphasize the burdens of adulthood to their children, partly in order to blackmail them into "gratitude."

As regards the abortion of later pregnancies, we have suggested that they appear to be largely motivated by an identification of the parents with their older children, and also by a revival of their own early sibling-rivalry conflicts. Needless to say, both of these may be operative at the same time, particularly in the limitation of the absolute number of pregnancies, where it is felt that too many children "spoil the figure entirely," or "are too much trouble."

10. COMPULSORY ABORTION AND THE IMAGINARY FATHER

Precisely because we are culturally conditioned to assume that abortion is an extralegal act, whose purpose it is to conceal the derelictions of a woman, we may hope to overcome our ethnocentric bias and psychological scotomata most effectively by examining in detail those instances of abortion which are imposed upon the woman against her will, and in a more or less *public* and *legal* manner. In so defining our problem we specifically leave out of consideration at this point abortions foisted upon women by anxious lovers, or by husbands not wishing to support additional children or reluctant to renounce cohabitation during pregnancy and lactation, or for (inferentially) dynastic reasons, as in the case of the Prince of *Badong* in *Bali.*

If we disregard the two *African* (*Achewa* and *Tiv*) instances of the surreptitious aborting of a woman for magical purposes and against her will, and the altogether unique *Nukuoro* case of Queen Kauna, who forced pregnant women to abort so that they would share her own maternal bereavement, our data fall into rather simple categories, all of which come under the heading of improper paternity. Women are compelled to abort:

1. Children fathered by demons. (*Truk, Jivaro*)
2. The offspring of incest. (*Gunantuna, Pukapuka*)
3. The children of old, ailing, or weak fathers. (*Masai*)
4. The children of alien fathers. (*Cuna*)
5. Adulterine bastards. (*Masai*)
6. Legitimate children, tainted by the adultery of the pregnant mother. (*Ashanti*)

In each of these instances there is a supposition that the birth of such children would lead to a calamity for the group, or at least for the biological family as a whole, or for some member thereof.

Before we go further, we must stress the "arbitrariness" of some of these concrete decisions, i.e., the fact that, in psychoanalytic parlance, they represent culturally sanctioned equivalents of "acting out."

1. As regards the monstrous children of demons (*Jivaro, Truk*), it hardly needs to be pointed out that such an imputation is, objectively speaking, always arbitrary.

2. As regards allegedly incestuous children, we are specifically informed that in *Pukapuka* this determination is made on the basis of lightning striking or a meteor falling.

3. As regards the children of biologically inadequate fathers, it is fairly obvious that we are dealing here with matters of opinion, since there is no indication that the *Masai* carefully subject all prospective fathers to a general medical examination.

4. The arbitrary element in the abortion of children of alien parentage is particularly conspicuous in the case of the *Cuna,* who aborted all fetuses fathered by aliens, save only those whose fathers were *Frenchmen.*

5. When we come to the case of adulterine bastards, the situation is, if possible, even more striking. We learn that among

the *Azande* the husbands of pregnant women habitually consult the *benget* to ascertain whether or not the fetus had been conceived in wedlock. This *routine* clearly reveals a paranoid attitude, which we shall discuss shortly more in detail.

6. The aborting of legitimate children whose pregnant mothers have committed adultery, is likewise a noteworthy phenomenon, and will be shown to imply a clear suggestion of theories of multiple paternity.*

One thing is certain. Even if we make allowance for the probability that no *Jivaro* or *Trukese* would, without some conscious or unconscious motive, assume that a child was fathered by a demon, and that similar, more or less justified, suspicions may also play a role in the next four types of prescribed abortion, the fact remains that, when suitably motivated, men sometimes consent to close their eyes to what is notoriously an illegitimate pregnancy of their wives, in order, for example, to avoid a public scandal. (*Buka*) Conversely, social pressures may motivate men to repudiate responsibility for any unwelcome pregnancy whatsoever. Thus, in *Wogeo,* we are specifically told that, despite the girl's protestations of fidelity, her lover will usually refuse to recognize her child as his own, because it is held that all premaritally conceived children are, and must be, the result of promiscuousness. By contrast, in *Hungary* for example, there are areas where peasant women believe that promiscuousness is a guarantee of sterility. (*61*). *Homines id quod volunt credunt!* Still other societies strenuously maintain that premarital conception is altogether impossible, and therefore deny that their premaritally completely free girls practice either contraception or abortion. (*Trobriand*) In countless other societies, where complete premarital license prevails, the birth of bastards is, illogically enough, deemed to be utterly shameful. (E.g., many parts of *Melanesia*)

We have stressed elsewhere in this work that female attitudes toward maternity appear to be largely determined by masculine attitudes toward paternity, and that the romanticization of the maternal role—the Madonna complex—is conspicuously absent

* Changes of imputed biological and actual sociological paternity resulting from the cohabitation of a pregnant woman with a man other than the impregnator have been carefully documented for the *Mohave* (*16*) and could, no doubt, be documented also for other groups.

in primitive societies, even where children are ardently desired and where fertile women are much esteemed. We therefore infer—not at all arbitrarily, in our opinion—that even where women abort of their own free will, and including even instances where they abort from spite or as a result of a domestic quarrel, they do so under the impact of a genuine or expected masculine attitude.*

We feel therefore that, if we were able to learn something more about masculine motives for insisting that a woman abort, we might, inferentially at least, be able to develop some not altogether implausible new hypotheses also about the motivation of women who abort of their own free will. In fact, it may well happen that the new hypotheses so obtained will prove to be more faithful representations of the psychodynamics of voluntarily aborting women than are hypotheses which are derived directly from the study of manifest primitive female attitudes, particularly if these latter studies are made by Occidentals, whose culturally determined bias is the (perhaps tacit) supposition that women always abort only in order to conceal their lapses from chastity or fidelity.

We have shown so far that, in every instance in which more or less *public* and *lawful* pressures are brought to bear upon a woman to abort, there is an imputation of improper paternity, which, in most cases, may well be a completely fallacious or at least arbitrary one.†

In simplest terms, the man insisting upon the abortion of a woman simply proclaims: "Not I, but someone else, and, specifically, someone socially improper, is the father of the baby." Sometimes this is done disingenuously, as among ourselves, in

* That this expected attitude sometimes does *not* materialize is shown by the case of Gwaramun of *Wogeo,* who—perhaps because of unconscious incestuous wishes—to the amazement of the whole village, and contrary to the attitude of the rest of his family, joyfully welcomed his sister's premarital pregnancy, because it meant that she would remain by his side a while longer.

† By "arbitrary" we mean that whereas the person alleging that the pregnancy is a socially inappropriate one may be right, he is right *despite,* rather than *because of,* the reason which he cites in support of his opinion—i.e., his right *noema* is the result of a fallacious *noesis,* which (in *Pukapuka* for example) may be based upon certain meteorological occurrences. Needless to say, this *noesis* which is false on the ego-level may be motivated by an unconscious insight into the real facts of the matter. That is often the case where a false *noesis* produces a correct *noema.* That, however, is beside the point at this juncture, where cultural factors are our chief object of study.

order to escape inconvenience and expense. The *Bakongo* settled this problem once and for all by the simple method of forbidding illegitimate children to have any relation whatsoever with their fathers, whereas among the *Ainu* the bastard's nursing mother receives alimony, and the child, once it is past nursing age, lives with its father. At other times cultural belief itself justifies the repudiation of one's inconvenient paternity; it does so inflexibly in *Wogeo,* and more or less elastically among the *Azande* and elsewhere. However, the most convincing argument to be adduced in support of this thesis is the fact that a *Masai* who impregnates an uninitiated girl must wipe out his disgrace by killing an *alien.*

Let us now seek to identify more carefully the alleged improper father, to whom the undesired pregnancy is imputed, by concentrating our attention for the moment only upon the first four categories: demons, blood relations, old or ailing persons, and aliens.

As regards demons, psychoanalysis has shown, conclusively we believe, that they are partly projections of the child's own destructive impulses, and, even more significantly, also extrajections of the "evil" or "nocturnal ogre" half of the child's ambivalently loved-hated father (or father surrogate).* It is therefore not at all surprising that incestuously conceived children are the next ones on the list of fetuses to be aborted by social fiat. Now, although this may be simply an accident, it is nonetheless worth noting that our entire body of data contains only one single specification of the identity of the particular blood relative who happens to have fathered an aborted child: it is a *Sedang* father, who both impregnated and aborted his own daughter, though this happened in a society in which abortion is never enjoined by collective social or legal action.

As regards aliens, it is a psychoanalytically acceptable thesis that the alien, like the demon or ogre, represents the "evil," sensual, or hated half of the child's conception of the father. This thesis has been specifically shown to be tenable for the *Mohave* (*18*), and the writer has little doubt that it could be demonstrated for tribe after tribe. In fact, long before the

* It may be noted in passing that, from the viewpoint of instinct theory and of psychoanalytic metapsychology, this dual origin of demons supports Freud's first, rather than second, theory of the origin of aggressions.

writer knew anything about psychoanalysis, he was impressed by the obvious identity of *Sedang* attitudes toward their (hated) gods and toward the dominant *French.** The imputation of extreme sensuality, sexual potency, and malevolent magical powers to aliens also points in this direction.†

The law that the children of old and ailing *Masai* men must be aborted may, on a very superficial level, be deemed to represent a "sound" racial policy. (PB) However, this imputation of an allegedly "enlightened" policy to the *Masai* (PB) is open to serious doubt, in view of the fact that, like most primitives, they do relatively little—beyond castrating bulls who did not develop well (Merker)—to improve their livestock,‡ and, above all, seem to be singularly unconcerned over the pregnancies of old or ailing *women.* It is hard to escape the conclusion that the "old or ailing and weak men" of the *Masai* are father surrogates—the more so since the *Masai* are but a little distance, the way the range of cultural influences is reckoned, from an area where impotent or ailing or aging kings (father surrogates) are killed. (*Shilluk*) (59) §

The adulterine bastard's problem is likewise closely tied up with the problem of incest. In a great many polygamous African tribes, where the young men have few or no single nubile girls available to them, custom allows them access to the wives of their older brothers or maternal uncles. In addition, they also prey pretty systematically, though illegally, on the wives of older polygamists. In some areas in *Africa* sons inherit all of their father's wives, with the sole exception of their own mothers. By contrast, in this area at least, maternal uncles and

* It should be noted in passing that, according to *Sedang* belief, after a series of *different* metamorphoses, the ghosts of dead Gods and of dead human beings eventually become transformed into *one and the same category* of ghosts.

† It was almost comical to note how the highland *Sedang* dreaded the allegedly malevolent magic of the lowland *Reungao* (*Sedang* borderers), and vice versa.

‡ This argument is far from being a specious one. Already Malinowski, in his study of the *Trobrianders,* supported his assertion of their nescience of physiological paternity by pointing out that they castrated all male pigs, while vehemently denying that the offspring of their sows were fathered by the wild boars of the bush, which are taboo as far as food is concerned. Just as the *Greeks* projected their social structure upon the Olympians, so the *Trobrianders* project theirs on their pigs.

§ We may even tentatively venture to speculate that the *Masai* term for bastard, "child of the fireplace," may have the implicit connotation that the bastard was "home-grown," i.e., incestuously conceived.

older brothers usually have no compensatory access to the wives of young men, when the latter finally do get married. Under these conditions it is far from implausible psychoanalytically to suggest that the now married ex-adulterer unconsciously expects retaliation from these father surrogates or from the father himself.

This view is indirectly supported by the fact that, in certain other areas of the world, where the taboo of virginity (*32*) prevails, the exact opposite of this situation takes place. In the latter group of tribes the bridegroom has no access to his bride until she has been publicly or officially deflowered by some ruler or lord (*ius primae noctis*), by the deity (represented by a phallic statue, by a priest, or by pilgrims to whom the virgin must, for a period, ritually prostitute herself), by her future father-in-law, by a senior relative of her own, by the entire village, or by a hired alien.* The two sets of data complement each other psychologically.

The problem of unborn legitimate children tainted by the adultery of the mother is, in a sense, the clinching argument in support of our thesis that the social and/or legally acceptable masculine demand that the woman abort is ultimately rooted in the convenient—though often unconscious—assumption or wish that the child be not that of its real legal father. The women themselves readily adapt themselves to this pattern, as when, for example, the women of *Buka* abort the children of their lovers, but never those of their husbands. Since this statement appears to refer not only to faithful wives, but also to occasionally adulterous ones (or, at least, there is nothing in the text about the *Buka* to make us think otherwise) one may well ask precisely what *objective* criteria enable an occasionally adulterous woman to decide whether the child she happens to be carrying at a given time is that of her husband or that of her lover. Obviously not only logical factors are at work in the shaping of such decisions. (Although our concrete data do not mention any tribe in which there is the practice of aborting both the children of one's adulterous lovers, and one's legitimate children because of a domestic quarrel, the two practices do occur

* The material pertaining to the taboo of virginity has been fairly well surveyed, and brilliantly analyzed by Freud (*32*) as well as by Yates (*67*), and therefore does not require detailed discussion.

in not too widely separated culture areas—e.g., in *Australia.* We may be confronted here more with incomplete reporting than with a true mutual exclusiveness of these two culture traits).

Returning to the problem of legitimate children tainted by maternal adultery, two factors seem to be operative. The most obvious one is the principle: "Once unfaithful, always unfaithful." Even in our society one finds examples of fathers who repudiate—or at least reject—their own children on discovering their wives' subsequent adultery, or, what is worse, that their last child is an adulterine bastard. The second belief seems to be that the identity of the child may be changed as a result of adultery during pregnancy. Indeed, in some societies, in which coitus during pregnancy is not necessarily taboo, it is often held either that repeated intercourse is necessary to father a child (or, in a more limited sense, to father a *healthy* child), or else that the fetus benefits in some manner by the semen which the copulating pregnant woman receives. (*13*). Conversely, where coitus during pregnancy is taboo—which is not at all gladly accepted by either wife or husband—the wife's adultery during pregnancy adds insult to injury. Interestingly enough, the notion, which is physiologically far from being altogether inaccurate, that coitus with a pregnant woman may cause her to abort (*Ashanti, Masai*), or even to die (*Ashanti*), prevails precisely in an area where coitus with pregnant women is taboo; whereas the belief that violent or perverted coitus with the pregnant woman may harm the *fetus* is reported from a tribe—the *Mohave* (*13*)—where postimpregnation coitus is thought to feed the fetus, and is supposed to be able even to change its biological and sociological identity, if the man cohabiting with the pregnant woman does not happen to be the impregnator. (*16*)

It is therefore suggested that the taboo on coitus with a pregnant woman may, tentatively speaking, have at its root a more or less unconscious fantastic fear of superfetation. This is suggested by the fact that in the selfsame groups where such taboos prevail (*Chagga,* etc.) there is also a very elaborate taboo on coitus during lactation, and also by the fact that in numerous areas (*Aranda*) where this taboo does not exist, the proper spacing of children is insured by aborting a pregnancy which follows too closely upon a previous one. (This point was further elaborated in connection with sibling rivalry as a motive of abortion). We may legitimately stress here that the fantasy of superfetation is so deeply rooted in the unconscious that, despite biological evidence to the contrary, it keeps on troubling even modern man. What is more important for us in this context is, however, the fact that in many areas twins are automatically believed to be the result of superfetation, and often specifically of adulterine or ghostly superfetation. This fantasy may provide the unconscious—that is, the real—reason for the killing of one or both twins, which many anthropologists have hitherto arbitrarily "explained" by references to economic factors, in utter disregard of the fact that if twins are considered a calamity in many low-subsistence level groups, there are other, economically equally marginal, tribes where twins are, officially at least, considered highly welcome supernatural beings (*Yuman* tribes), though even for such tribes it was possible to demonstrate (*8*), side by side with the official attitude of delight, the existence of a second set of beliefs which points in exactly the opposite direction, both on the cultural level and in terms of psychological attitudes.

Given the fact that twins are often believed to derive from ghostly, or divine superfetation, the tainting of the legitimate child by the mother's adultery acquires a new meaning, especially since both beliefs occasionally occur in one and the same area. At the risk of stating something which direct inquiry has not as yet demonstrated, the present writer—who, like many of his colleagues, has had numerous personal experiences with the possibility of making valid "predictions" of this type—would venture to predict that further field work will demonstrate that this tainting of legitimate children by maternal adultery is actually a consequence of an implicit or explicit belief in superfetation, and of a fear of twins. In fact, it may even be suggested that further field work may eventually reveal that the taboo on coitus during pregnancy may represent chiefly an attempt to prevent the birth of twins, one of whom may be a monster. (*Dayak*) Indeed, the taboo on coitus during pregnancy is frequently co-areal with a fear of twins, and even with the killing of one or both twins.*

* Unfortunately, this inference was formulated too close to the publisher's deadline to permit of statistical verification, but the author is reasonably certain that it will be found tenable.

The recurrent theme of the supernatural *origin* of twins, which seems independent of either a positive or a negative attitude toward twins themselves, once more brings us back to the notion that the intervening impregnator is ultimately the father or paternal *imago*. This inference may possibly have to be extended also to superfetation in general and may, therefore, serve to explain the tainting of legitimate children by their pregnant mother's adultery.

This hypothesis gains unexpected support from the *Ashanti* belief that the adulterous (though not necessarily adulterous*ly*) pregnant woman may miscarry, or may even die.

Indeed, it is a well-known anxiety of little girls in the throes of the Oedipus complex that they would be killed by the "huge" paternal penis while cohabiting with him. We may remark in passing that this anxiety may be one of the sources both of feminine masochism and of the maturing girl's motivation for resolving some of her oedipal impulses.

The foregoing considerations may now be summed up in what is admittedly simply a working hypothesis, albeit an unusually plausible one: Compulsory abortion, especially of the more or less public and legal kind, suggests that the fetus is unconsciously believed to be, or is in fact, the child of a socially improper father, and that, on further analysis, one may tentatively assume that this improper impregnator is fantasied to be the man's, or, occasionally, the woman's, father (or at least father surrogate or father *imago*).

Whether or not these considerations should be extended to include also the case of women who are asked or forced by their husbands or lovers to abort for purportedly practical reasons (poverty, among many groups; avoidance of the coitus taboo during pregnancy, in many *African* tribes; the desire to acquire wealth, in *Malekula;* the concealment of a love affair, almost everywhere; the limitation of the number of royal uterine nephews, in *Uganda;* etc.) is not a problem which we can settle in the present state of our knowledge with any degree of certainty, especially since there is more than a suspicion that—because of the cultural bias of field investigators—our data are distinctly skewed in the direction of an overemphasis on abortion for the concealment of illicit relationships. Fortunately this matter is not of too great importance, even from the psychoanalytic point of view. The psychoanalyst is not totally absorbed in a contemplation of the unconscious, and is ready to recognize that conscious reasons—especially when they have the support of practical social reality—are far from inoperative. At the most, he will, in such cases, seek to determine what unconscious motives underlie man's (usually rather halfhearted) readiness to behave realistically. The analyst will certainly recognize that in a society where the adulterer suffers severe penalties, he is chiefly motivated in urging his paramour to abort by the very realistic and practical wish to avoid pain; and the analyst will therefore inquire only incidentally into the motives which impelled the adulterer to act practically in this particular situation. The analyst may, or may not, find that in such cases the adulterer also conveniently fantasied that, in the last resort, the child was not his own but that of another personage, who may or may not be a father *imago*. This, however, would be something relatively secondary from the point of view of a psychoanalytic study of *culture,* though it may be of great importance in the analysis of an actual *patient* for therapeutic purposes. We might also add that if an adulterer, on finding himself in such a predicament, did *not* urge his mistress to abort, this would likewise be something which the analyst would be interested in, but again only from the clinical rather than from the cultural point of view.

POSTSCRIPT

In the preceding chapter we suggested that whenever pressure is put on the woman to abort, this is indicative of a (possibly unconscious) belief that the child is both illegitimate and incestuous, and specifically that it is the child of the woman's own father. This conclusion was reached on the basis of a psychoanalytic interpretation of primarily indirect evidence. After the manuscript had gone to press, the writer came across the following data, which unequivocally confirm the fact that such fantasies not only exist, but are occasionally even enunciated in the form of fundamental social tenets. Not at all unexpectedly, this belief managed to penetrate into the conscious mind, and even to find a cultural implementation, in a tribe where premaritally conceived children, whose (sociological?) paternity is attributed to the girl's father, are not only not aborted but are highly prized.

Father H. Trilles, in his work "Le Totemisme chez les Fan," *Collection Internationale de Monographies Ethnographiques,* Bibliothèque Anthropos, Vol. I, No. 4, 1912, writes: "It happens frequently even nowadays that young girls bear a child. Far from this being a disgrace, it is, on the contrary, an honor which increases the [bride] price of the young girl, by proving her fecundity. However, when she marries, her child does not follow her; it continues to belong to the tribe of her father, who is then considered to be the real father of the child. When there is no known father, it is the maternal uncle who shall own the child, and such is the case for [the culture hero] Ngurangurane." (p. 196, fn. 1)

This paragraph speaks for itself. We need only underscore that Trilles specifically states that the girl's father is considered the child's *true* ("vrai") father, which suggests that more than a mere socially convenient imputation of *sociological* paternity is meant, since the sole purpose of the latter would be to place the child within the kinship structure. Our strict interpretation of the paternity imputed to the girl's own father is supported by Trilles' explicit reference to the culture hero Ngurangurane, whose actual "father" was a magical man-eating crocodile, to whom the hero's mother had been offered as a sacrifice. Later on, in order to protect his human kin from the exactions of this crocodile, the hero killed his father, the crocodile. However, in the best Freudian tradition of the "primal horde," he then proceeded to preserve the corpse of this monster animal, and established human sacrifices in its honor—despite, or rather because of, the fact that he had killed the crocodile in the first place so as to put an end to its insatiable demands for human victims. In conclusion, we only have to add that the human person who, throughout this period, functioned toward Ngurangurane in the capacity of a father was the father of his mother, the chief of the Fan tribe.

Although this episode could have been incorporated into the main text of this chapter, even after the galleys had arrived, we preferred to cite it in the form of a postscript, so as to underscore once more a point already made in connection with the discovery that actual data could be found to substantiate the inference that a deliberate violation of pregnancy taboos may be an attempt to procure an abortion. The methodological point we seek to make is that a suitable psychoanalytic interpretation of available *indirect* evidence can usually be confirmed subsequently by newly discovered direct and unequivocal data.

11. CASTRATION OF THE FATHER

Anthropological literature is replete with examples of two major types of abortion motivated by revenge against the father, or by the desire to harm him in some way.

1. Voluntary abortion and infanticide may occur as a result of a domestic quarrel (*Australians of Victoria*), or in order to take revenge on a faithless lover (*Araucanians*), or husband (*Dusun*).

2. Compulsory abortion may be required of the woman, so that she would not bear a halfbreed (*Cuna*), the offspring of an enemy of the tribe (*Jivaro*), or the child of an outsider to whom she is married, and who may inherit some of her real estate which is part and parcel of the total holdings of her ingroup (*Fiji*).

In each of these cases, the intention is clearly that of damaging the child's father. As regards voluntary spiteful abortions, the husbands are so well aware of the aggression against them which this act implies that they will severely punish their wives for aborting. Among the *Riff*, the men specifically suspect a wife who bore them no child of having aborted. Hence such attempts are severely penalized. (*Azande*, etc.) The hostility against the father implicit in the aborting of a halfbreed offspring, of the child of a tribal alien, and of a potential outside heir, is likewise clearly manifest in the *Tupinamba* practice of deliberately causing a *Tupinamba* girl to be impregnated by a prisoner of war, whose offspring is then cannibalized, in order to hurt his feelings. (It might be mentioned in this context that the *Caribs* (HDBK) castrated the prisoners of war intended for a cannibalistic meal, in order to fatten them up.) The fact that many a *Tupinamba* girl forestalled this dire contingency by prematurely aborting her half-alien child is, in a sense, a two-edged weapon, since its ultimate result is likewise the depriving of the prisoner of war of his offspring.

We do not even have to refer to psychoanalytic experience to show that the spiteful abortion of a child—be it voluntary or compulsory—represents an attempt to castrate the father, though this element is clear enough when we are dealing with tribes where paternity is either a means of social advancement, or a proud public token of one's potency. (Compare in this context the fact that the fathering of children by old men is deemed "newsworthy" in our society.) We can demonstrate this point much more simply by reference to concrete *Araucanian* data. There the deserted girl not only aborts or kills the offspring of her faithless lover, but, in addition, roasts the child's testicles, for the explicit purpose of making its erring father impotent.

In other words, the spiteful abortion of a child is tantamount to a depreciation of the potency of the impregnator, and to a frustrating of his sexual and social aspirations. This feminine attitude of depreciation and of doubt toward masculine potency is quite clear in the case of *Efik* women, who "test the quality of their pregnancy" by taking, in small quantities, a drug which, if taken in larger ones, causes an abortion.

In brief, our anthropological data obviously match the findings of psychoanalysts that abortion is indicative of a spiteful feminine aggression against the male, and represents a degradation and depreciation of his potency, and, more specifically, an attempt to castrate him and to render him impotent. Thus, the psychoanalytic thesis that the baby is unconsciously equated with the penis also receives indirect confirmation from the findings of anthropologists.

12. ABORTION, FEMALE INITIATION, AND SELF-CASTRATION

In the previous section we indicated that abortion is sometimes an attempt to castrate the father, and in our analysis of the flight from parenthood we have correlated, at least tentatively, the abortion of the first child with a reluctance to grow up.

There are, however, also many indications that we may—speculatively at least—envisage the possibility that the abortion (or killing) of the first-born in particular may also represent a kind of initiation into adulthood and be an equivalent of female castration, "circumcision," or excision.

There are, as we have already shown, many beliefs suggesting that pregnancy is viewed as a privilege of adults. We spoke of the fact that, if a noninitiated *Masai* girl is impregnated, this is deemed to be such a scandal that the impregnator can redeem himself only by killing an alien, and must bear the cost of the girl's immediate initiation, which involves also the African type of female circumcision. Among the *Chagga,* mother and daughter may not simultaneously function in a procreative capacity. Hence, some *Chagga* mothers use an amulet to delay the advent of their daughters' puberty. In numerous areas of the world the pregnancies of very young girls are aborted, as being harmful to their health or beauty. *Bafiote* women who led a loose life dread a first delivery in their later years, and abort the fetus in order to forestall a delivery on term. Among the *Mataco,* women abort their first pregnancy so as to facilitate the delivery of future pregnancies. The *Tiv* elders secretly, and without her knowledge or consent, abort for ritual reasons the first pregnancy of some woman, who will then be a special favorite of the deity and will soon conceive again and bear a healthy child. A somewhat related fact was told to the writer by the R. P. André Dupeyrat, who reports that in some tribes of *Papua* the woman must cast her first-born into a ravine, in front of the village's sows. One of the sows will then devour the small corpse, whereupon the woman will take one of that sow's piglets and nurse it in place of her baby.

Before we seek to draw even tentative inferences from these data, we once more wish to state that they will be admittedly speculative, though not implausible. Hence, they are offered not as concrete findings, but as attempts to *define a new problem,* which may well be worth further investigation.

We find three sets of facts:

1. The denial of the right to be pregnant to uninitiated or very young girls.
2. The immediate initiation of pregnant uninitiated girls, which, in the area in question, involves circumcision, and the excision of the clitoris.
3. The belief that the abortion of the first pregnancy will facilitate a more adequate and successful maternal functioning later on: easier deliveries; bearing—by special favor of the deity—a healthy child; replacement of the child surrendered to a sow by a piglet of that sow; etc.

In view of the equation baby = penis, the abortion of the first pregnancy may thus conceivably be thought of as a form of female castration, corresponding to female circumcision and excision rites practiced in parts of *Africa.* However, this is a problem which we have only raised but are not able to answer with any degree of certainty.

It is also necessary to point out here, at least in passing, that Bettelheim (*3*) recently questioned the legitimacy of equating initiatory male or female circumcision with castration in the analytic sense. He asserts that no actual primitive data confirm such an interpretation. This is a rather startling statement, since Bettelheim himself, in the very work which contains his *caveat,* cited Merker's work on the *Masai,* and Merker specifically reports that a man whose son groaned while being circumcised was taunted with the remark that his son *behaved like a bull bellowing with pain while being castrated.**

It should also be mentioned that in a good many areas (*Melanesia, Chagga,* etc.) suicide is an alternative to abortion, and is resorted to especially where attempts at abortion were unsuccessful. In fact, the technique of procuring an abortion by jumping off some elevated place has been reported predominently—though not exclusively (*Ainu,* etc.)—from *Melanesia,* where the same procedure is also one of most prevalent and areally most characteristic techniques of *suicide.* The *Ila* woman who wishes to abort is asked by the abortionist whether she wishes to kill herself, and replies that she does not care! † In this sense, then, suicide may be considered as an alternative for abortion. It is wholly unnecessary to point out that the foregoing conclusion does not refute the perfectly sound thesis that such a suicide is also an attempt to escape social ostracism. On the other hand, it would be wrong indeed to disregard the fact that, in the unconscious, dying is often conceived of as castration, and suicide as self-castration. The loss of a tooth is interpreted in psychoanalysis as a castration symbol, while many primitives interpret dreams about loss of teeth sometimes as symbols of old age (*Crow*) (52) but more often as tokens of impending death. It is therefore very significant that, according to Karsten, several *South American* tribes consider abortion on a par with the pulling of a tooth. And it is precisely this latter unconscious meaning of suicide which links it with abortion which—both in view of its dangerous and painful character, and in view of the penis

* It should be specifically noted that Merker's text says "bull" and not "bull *calf,*" though Merker always carefully distinguishes between the two. Now, it so happens that whereas the *Masai* do *not* castrate goats, rams, and donkeys *before they reach maturity,* they castrate bull *calves* at fourteen days. They castrate adult bulls only if they do not develop adequately and seem unsuitable for stud service. Furthermore, whereas bull calves are castrated by a surgical opening up of the scrotum and a manual tearing out of the testes and seminal cords, goats, rams, and jackasses—but apparently not the aforementioned type of inadequate adult bulls—are castrated by entirely different and apparently bloodless means; i.e., without a surgical opening of the scrotum. Instead, they crush the seminal cords with a club, while the scrotum is held between the string and the wood of a bow.

† The *Ila* data, which are our best argument in favor of this thesis, came to our notice only the day *after* the completion of this chapter—which once more indicates that correct inductive inferences from either psychoanalytic considerations or the comparative study of cultures can usually be verified by objective data.

= baby fantasy—often represents self-castration in the unconscious.

This latter observation leads us to one special aspect of the eating of babies (*Tupinamba*) or of fetuses (*Ngali*), and to the problem of autophagy. The concept of autophagy is a relatively unexplored one, although it plays a considerable role, e.g., in *Sedang Moi* beliefs regarding a certain ghost whose liver aches because he eats it himself, and also in matters related to fines. We know that, on giving birth, many female animals eat the afterbirth (and sometimes even their offspring) and that they lick the newborn clean. The human custom of licking the newborn clean was specifically reported for one group of *Eskimo* (*Inuit*) and may also occur elsewhere. Sterile *Kamchadal* women eat umbilical cords in order to become fertile. Furthermore, in his analysis of *Mohave* postpartum practices (*17*), the present writer suggested that the meat taboos imposed on recently delivered mothers may be *culturally provided defenses* against such mothers' cannibalistic impulses, which, in our society, express themselves in the form of pretending to devour the baby from sheer love, because it "looks good enough to eat." This impulse may well be partly biochemically motivated, as it appears to be in the case of animals devouring the afterbirth. However, in the human mother, it may also be retaliatory, since the baby is, in fact, "eating up" its mother. (Cf. in this context the remark of a native of *Papua,* that their children "destroy them.")

In other words, there is enough cultural material available to induce us at least to ask the question whether abortion may not symbolize also initiatory or noninitiatory self-castration. To do more than just *ask* the question, and suggest that it *deserves being asked,* would be little short of wanton speculation. On the other hand, a failure at least to ask this question would mean "playing safe" in the most objectionable sense of this term. Science progresses because scholars are occasionally willing to "stick out their necks."

APPENDIX I. ILLEGITIMACY AND ABORTION

One of the most surprising results of our survey of data on abortion was that the material pertaining to the relationship between illegitimacy and abortion was distinctly scanty—and, in some ways, also quite unreliable.

In many instances the ethnocentric bias of observers was responsible for an undue emphasis on illegitimacy as the major cause of abortion, simply because it is one of the chief conscious motives for abortion in our own society. In some instances this led to a neglect of other conscious motives, while in a surprisingly large number of cases (e.g., as regards the tribes covered by the University of California *Culture Element Distribution Study)* there is information on techniques of abortion, but none on the motivation of abortion, as though the latter were self-evident.

In addition, many statements on illegitimacy as a cause for abortion assign an unusually important role to abortion as a consequence of premarital *sex freedom,* as distinct from premarital *pregnancy.* This emphasis can again be understood in terms of ethnocentric bias, since in our own thinking (and, a fortiori, in the thinking of our Victorian forebears) pregnancy is a well-deserved punishment for sexual freedom, which is defined as a form of delinquency or sin. We need only recall in this context the monotonous regularity wherewith erring Victorian heroines became pregnant in the novels of that period.

Yet, abundant data indicate that many primitive girls do not abort their premaritally conceived children in order to conceal their sexual activities. Expressing this in somewhat grotesque terms, we may say that they do not abort because they are premaritally *promiscuous* but because they are premaritally *pregnant*—which is an entirely different matter in their own opinion.

Indeed, one of our most striking and most consistently reported—and also hitherto altogether inadequately explained—facts is that in many societies where girls are not only permitted, but are actually *expected* and even institutionally *induced*, to cohabit before marriage, pregnancy is nonetheless deemed to be wholly scandalous. To a certain extent this is true of much of the area in which there are the kind of special dormitories for youths in which premarital experimentation can, and is *expected* to, take place on a large scale.* This extraordinary "paradox" (which, as we propose to show, is actually a pseudoparadox) has not been adequately explained, save in terms of various native theories regarding the causes of pregnancy, which, however, fail to explain why such premarital pregnancies should be shameful. In one area, *Wogeo*, the objection to premarital pregnancies is very conveniently justified by the assertion that such pregnancies always result from promiscuousness. This explanation is the more startling since, in many other primitive and folk cultures, as well as in some serious scientific circles, it is believed that—even without disease—promiscuousness may be an obstacle to conception. (It is hardly necessary to add that this latter belief arises chiefly in societies which place a premium on monogamy and on childbearing.)

By contrast, there are a good many societies where premarital sexual relations are not institutionalized nor specifically expected and demanded from the young, but which take a "large view" about such matters and accept *informal* premarital relations as something inescapably human. In such societies there is much less pressure on the premaritally pregnant girl to abort, and, in fact, in a good many such areas the bearing of illegitimate children is not something anyone gets unduly disturbed about. This is exemplified, e.g., by the *Mohave* attitude toward premarital sexuality *and reproduction*. When, in such an area, the unwed mother wishes to get rid of her child, she does so

* The overlap is most striking in some parts of *Melanesia*. In other areas there are noteworthy exceptions. Among the *Sedang Moi* the bachelors' quarters are not a trysting place and, after puberty, sexual relations between the unmarried must be atoned for by the payment of a fine.

usually either by *postnatal* exposure or infanticide, or else by making it available for adoption, including informal "adoption" by her own relatives or kin group. In both cases she is apparently motivated not so much by shame as by the inconvenience which an illegitimate child may cause her.

On the whole, it is fairly safe to state that in many areas where *institutionalized* premarital relations prevail, premarital *pregnancy* is viewed as *shameful*, and the unwed mother *aborts*. By contrast, in numerous other areas, where premarital sexual relations are more or less *informally taken for granted*, without being institutionalized, premarital *pregnancy* is *not* viewed as *an outrage*, and the child is either not gotten rid of at all, or else it is *disposed of after its birth*. It would be idle pedantry to quote figures in support of this statement, since—as we repeatedly point out—our data are far too spotty and nonhomogeneous to permit us to make a meaningful statistical analysis. Besides, a glance at our tabulation will prove this point.

In a sense, this observation further underscores the "paradox" that premarital pregnancy should be deemed shameful *precisely* in those areas where premarital coitus is actually *institutionalized*. If the thesis of a postpubertal period of sterility were proven (and, in our opinion, this thesis has not yet been proven *to the point* where it can be made the *fulcrum* of a complex argument) it might be argued that premarital pregnancy is shameful because it indicates that the girl has stayed too long in the courting-house, being more interested in having fun than in being a wife and mother. However, there is little or no evidence to indicate that such a view prevails in the area in question.*

In brief, speaking in terms of Occidental logic and ethics, we are confronted with the "paradox" that in some islands the sexually "liberal" *Melanesian*, etc., is quite as puritanical as a Victorian clergyman when it comes to premarital *pregnancy*, though only in a few places, such as in *Wogeo*, is such a pregnancy definitely attributed to promiscuousness.

Now, it is a cornerstone of both the Durkheim-Mauss concept of functionality, and of psychoanalytic theory as well, that any custom must make some kind of sense in terms of the other cus-

* It is known that, e.g., in *Yap* the rule that a pregnant girl must marry motivated some abortions. However, we lack specific reports that even in *Yap* the postponing of marriage is, *per se*, regarded as objectionable.

toms of the same society. One's first impulse might therefore be to relate this condemnatory attitude toward unwed pregnancy to a particularly strong emphasis on paternal descent or on kin membership. However, the *Trobrianders,* and many other groups in the area under consideration, are matrilineal, and, furthermore, there is nothing to indicate that they are more passionately interested in kin membership than, e. g., the *Mohave.* Nor is it possible to say that the birth of an illegitimate child necessarily represents a great burden for the girl's family, since, in matrilineal society, it is anyhow up to the family to support even its married female descendants and their offspring. Thus, we saw that in *Dobu* Kopu beat his niece for aborting her child, who was his legal heir.

Under these circumstances it may be possible to find an answer only by appealing to one of the most basic concepts of anthropology, developed by the school of Durkheim, and, in particular, by Mauss: the concept of reciprocity. In parts of this area the ritual exchange of goods is one of the cornerstones of the social system, so that an unwed mother is, by that very fact, placed in an asymmetrical position within this economic-ritual system: that is to say, she occupies an anomalous position in the network of reciprocal gifts and services. Since in parts of *Melanesia*—e.g., in *Manus*—even aborted fetuses and stillborn children are inserted into the network of reciprocal services and gifts (and one infers from Mead's text that these fetuses and stillborn children are legitimate ones) it may be possible to suggest, at least tentatively, that *the odium of premarital pregnancy is primarily connected with the disturbances which the birth of an illegitimate child would create in this network of reciprocities.* A full documentation of this hypothesis would, however, require a monograph in itself, and is, hence, beyond the scope of the present work.

The argument just presented dovetails logically with the well-known fact that in patrilineal societies premarital pregnancy is strenuously objected to because the illegitimate child is in a wholly anomalous social position, in that it has no kin and "no name," and therefore, as among the *Rwala,* no one to support it and to back it. Hence, in a sense, institutionalized premarital cohabitation, combined with the view that premarital pregnancy is shameful, is, sociologically at least, more comparable to the puritanism of patrilineal societies than to the sexual liberalism of societies which do not institutionalize premarital cohabitation.

We may also add that so extremely "paradoxical" a position as that of some *Melanesians,* who institutionalize premarital cohabitation but penalize premarital pregnancy, must be very powerfully motivated indeed. This supposition is confirmed by the objective fact that in some *Melanesian* societies the wealth quest related to the cycle of reciprocities is perhaps the single most powerful social factor and motivation. Indeed, as we had occasion to stress in various portions of this work, though man is not exactly the most rational of creatures, neither is he utterly devoid of reason. Hence, if we meet with a situation in which the triggering mechanism (coitus) is institutionalized and the consequence of the action (pregnancy) thus triggered off is penalized, one must assume that very powerful social forces are at work to make such "irrationality" palatable to man—even *Melanesian* man.

This hypothesis is equally plausible from the psychoanalytic point of view. Although psychoanalytic jargon should not be bandied about as loosely as it often is, we can state with some measure of confidence that in their obsessive preoccupation with wealth, many *Melanesian* cultures are distinctly rooted in anal interests, and encourage the nonsublimation and the acting-out (institutionalization) of the derivatives of anal eroticism. Such a fixation could not take place without a certain amount of puritanism resulting from it. Superficially, this inferential puritanism appears to be contradicted by the existence of "free" premarital cohabitation in that area . . . or would be contradicted by it, *were these Melanesians actually engaged in the practice of "free love," in the Occidental sense.* However, that is exactly what they are *not* engaged in. They are engaged in the practice of *institutionalized*—and very highly institutionalized!—premarital cohabitation. Hence, as in *Dobu,* they can also be quite prudish at the same time.

Now, as we pointed out in *Reality and Dream* (22) the very fact that some impulse is institutionalized sheds a great deal of light on the conflicts and anxieties related to that impulse: "Indeed, at the risk of laboring the obvious, it seems necessary to make an almost self-evident theoretical point: No basic and strong impulse, acted out in an undisguised and socially approved form, needs a high degree of institutionalization. Only attitudes and impulses which are reaction formations against, or sublimations of, the repressed opposite drives need such institutional crutches. If the socially sanctioned impulses and attitudes expressed in such reaction formations are *overinstitutionalized*—i.e., if they make excessive demands upon the individual—the repressed basic impulse will also be given relatively minor institutional outlets which—and this is most significant—will usually be *peripheral* to the most fully institutionalized reaction formations." (p. 73)

We therefore suspect that the high degree of institutionalization to which various derivatives of anal eroticism are subjected in some *Melanesian* societies brought in its train the aforementioned type of peripheral institutionalization of sexuality as well. In fact, the simple observation that this culture has *institutionalized* premarital cohabitation, instead of leaving it to chance, as, e.g., the *Mohave* did, suggests that we are confronted here with an anal-obsessive attempt to systematize and to regulate positively, and not only prohibitively, something fundamentally very private and individualistic, namely, premarital sexuality. Thus, in *Eddystone Island* even premarital coitus in the bush is an institutionalized "deal."

The point we seek to make is a rather simple one: the very fact that in some of this area men sought to institutionalize premarital cohabitation suggests that they experienced the need to make it ego-syntonic, and that they felt compelled to comply, at least in a roundabout way, with the demands of their rather puritanical superegos. Since sex could not be altogether sidestepped, nor premarital cohabitation altogether prevented, a social seal of approval "had" to be placed on it. In this manner, premarital sexuality could—as some humorous wartime posters expressed it—be "coordinated," in the sense that "disorderly confusion was replaced with regimented chaos." In a sense, this procedure resembled an allegedly standard Chinese military strategy, proverbially inspired by the principle: "If you can't lick 'em, join 'em."

In brief, our "paradox" turned out to be a pseudoparadox. The condemnation of premarital pregnancy is not only not incompatible, either sociologically or psychoanalytically, with an institutionalization of premarital cohabitation, but, in a sense, is almost an inevitable derivate and consequence of the former, at least in a society which emphasizes wealth and has to impress its obsessive, institution-minded mold on anything and everything within its scope. Hence, it seems permissible to express the hypothesis that the condemnation of premarital pregnancy in this area is sociologically motivated by the complications and asymmetries resulting from illegitimate births in a system based on involved reciprocal services, gifts, and "potlatches." In addition, speaking now psychoanalytically, the *institutionalization* of premarital cohabitation is, *per se,* an expression of a basic "puritanism" rooted in anality, which finds a concentrated outlet in a "paradoxical" condemnation of premarital pregnancy resulting from institutionalized premarital cohabitation. In turn, premarital pregnancy was chosen as the focal object of social disapproval, because this contumely could be justified in terms of the major preoccupation of that group of societies.

We repeat that our hypothesis, and especially its sociological phase, is set forth simply as a working hypothesis to be tested, rather than as a conclusion established beyond reasonable doubt. However, we are confident that it will be possible to verify it either in this form, or else in a closely related one . . . provided only that we are not blinded by the theories of natives but look at the facts themselves, and always remember that the native, as a theorist, is sometimes no better than some Occidental ones,* if for no other reason than because, as Elizabeth de Gramont pointed out long ago: "One cannot be in the landscape and also have a view of it."

* The writer is indebted for this valuable methodological point to Claude Levi-Strauss's introduction to Marcel Mauss's book: *Anthropologie et Sociologie,* Paris, 1950.

APPENDIX II. NEGATIVE EVIDENCE

Under the present heading we propose to discuss:

1. Nonreporting of abortion.
2. Denials that abortion occurs.
3. Emotional defensive maneuvers of the informant.
4. Evasions of the informant.
5. Positive lies.
6. Affirmation by denial.

1. *The nonreporting of abortion* is very common in anthropological monographs. For nearly 40% of the tribes on whom there are data in HRAF, we find no mention, affirmative or negative, regarding abortion. This fact suggests that abortion was hitherto of little interest to anthropologists and that, therefore, many reported denials may be due to a lack of effort on the part of the field-worker to inquire intensively into this matter. It also suggests, by implication, that most of our positive data on abortion are likely to be fragmentary.

2. *Positive denials* that abortion occurs in a given group are often flatly contradicted by positive data reported by other authors, and in some instances the author reporting the denial is himself uncertain of the validity of his negative data. A few examples will serve to illustrate reported instances of denials of abortion:

a. As regards *Islamic Persia,* Polak denies the occurrence of abortion, while Chardin gives concrete details about such practices. In such a case one obviously has to believe the positive evidence.

b. Concerning *Samoa,* C. S. Ford, in a theoretical paper, implicitly denies the occurrence of abortion, whereas Mead gives positive evidence, and our data on *Nukuoro* specify that abortion was introduced there by *Samoan* immigrants.

c. Malinowski was unable to secure data on abortion among the *Trobriand* Islanders. However, he himself was not fully satisfied that his negative data were reliable, and neither can we be, since the *Trobrianders* live in an area notoriously addicted to abortion. Montagu's argument that *Trobriand* girls, who live in complete premarital freedom, do not conceive in the first place, because they are sterile for a certain period after the onset of their menses *(56)* may be valid as a general law, but would necessarily involve numerous individual exceptions, as do all biological laws.

d. Morice Vanoverbergh's *Isneg* data are the only ones which appear to be rather credible, not only because of the inherent excellence of his work, but because, as a missionary, he was interested in this topic and was, furthermore, in a position—i.e., during confessions—to learn the truth. Perplexing as this single apparently reliable denial may seem, we have to accept it, for the time being at least. Yet, even in this case it is conceivable that Father Vanoverbergh did not hear of abortions simply because the Christianized *Isneg* had given up this practice. *(63)*

3. *The Emotional Defensive Reactions* of the informant will always seem suspect to the psychologically sophisticated field worker. The following is a good example of such a maneuver.

Mooney's *Cherokee* informant "did not understand" at first what the anthropologist's questions were aiming at. When he "finally" understood what was meant, he was horrified. This seems to be a telling argument, until one recalls that one third of Bailey's *Navaho* informants denied the practice of abortion. Much more detailed proof would be needed before we can be persuaded that the *Cherokee* in question did not simply *refuse* to understand Mooney's questions, but had actually never heard of such acts. Also, Mooney's informant may well have been a representative of a "see no evil, hear no evil, speak no evil" group which exists everywhere (cf. also Nela of *Dobu.*) Finally, we may well ask how many American "*men* in the street" would know what an investigator was talking about if he were asked about female masochism.

4. *Evasions* of the informant are quite common, and often succeed in discouraging the field worker, though apparently the evasions of an *Aleut* abortionist, Jenny of Nikolski, who switched an attempted discussion about abortion to a conversation about basketry (i.e., about female genital symbols) did not succeed in persuading Shade that she was not an abortionist, though they frustrated his attempts to get concrete details.

5. *Constructive lies* uttered by informants, or reported by them as having been uttered by certain persons seeking to cover up their attempts to abort, are, needless to say, direct confirmations of the occurrence of abortion in a given society. They are, furthermore, of great psychological interest to the field worker, and to the scholar seeking to interpret such data psychologically. Indeed, we have already indicated that, in the interpretation of concrete data pertaining to one tribe, the practices of other tribes, as well as various other data from the same tribe, may be treated as if they were the equivalents of the "free associations" of some member of that tribe to the *latent* content of the practice under study. The following example of a constructive lie will illustrate this methodological thesis: When a *Sedang Moi* girl, who had just aborted, was asked why she had blood on her skirt and legs, she pretended that she had been bitten by leeches, which happens to be one of the means used in *Islamic Persia* (PB) to produce an abortion. Hence, we may safely state that constructive lies (23) not only confirm the existence of abortion in a given society, but—like the *Aleut* example of an evasion (diverting conversation from abortion to basketry, i.e., to uterine symbols)—also provide valuable psychological clues for an understanding of the psychodynamics of abortion in general.

6. *Affirmation by denial.* Very interesting examples of seeming denials amounting to affirmation are instances in which the *practice* of abortion is denied, but a *word* meaning abortion is known to occur in that language. (*Persia*) In other cases abortion is denied for the informant's own tribe (*Mam*) but is said to occur among neighboring groups. (*Ladinos*) The presence of an explicit prohibition, with penalties, must also be considered prima facie evidence of the occurrence of such practices. Men do not legislate against the nonexistent.

Of an entire different order are denials regarding the occurrence of certain special *forms* of motivation or techniques of abortion. An interesting example is that of a difference between the *Pima* and the *Mohave*.

Even though the *Pima* and the *Mohave* are practically neighbors, and even though both destroy the property of a man at his death, the pregnant *Pima* widow, who already has several children, aborts her posthumous child from fear of being left destitute, while the *Mohave* widow, who can always count on the boundless generosity of every *Mohave*, does not abort hers. This does not mean, however, that the *Pima* data cannot be treated as "associations" to the *latent* thoughts of the pregnant *Mohave* widow, or vice versa. It suggests that the *Mohave* widow too may *wish* to abort, but that she refrains from doing so because of certain reality factors and because of certain conscious motivations on the level of ego functions. This inference is supported by the finding that halfbreeds, whom usually no *Mohave* wishes to support, are often killed at birth.

In conclusion, for various reasons not one explicit denial seemed entirely convincing to the present writer, who feels that *there is every indication that abortion is an absolutely universal phenomenon, and that it is impossible even to construct an imaginary social system in which no woman would ever feel at least impelled to abort.*

APPENDIX III. A NOTE ON DEMOGRAPHY

The Actual Occurrence of Abortions. The fact that no abortion has been known to occur in some small tribe for one or two generations has sometimes been held to indicate that abortion was absent in that group. Such views represent a radical confusion between *culture* and *vital statistics.* It is quite conceivable that in some small tribe, where the abortion of, e.g., incestuously conceived children may actually be mandatory, decades may elapse before some girl not only commits incest, but is actually impregnated thereby. Thus, while eyewitness accounts and case histories are highly desirable, their nonavailability is certainly no proof that abortion is not part of the official or clandestine cultural tradition of a given group. It is also certain that social usage (as distinct from custom) may change. Thus, we reported that the fatal outcome of a *Koyukuk Eskimo* girl's abortion discouraged all abortions for quite some time. Even social custom may change, as when, in parts of *Polynesia,* the conquering white's laws against infanticide led to an increase in abortion.

The Incidence of Abortion in Mankind as a Whole is a problem which the cultural anthropologist cannot discuss with any degree of assurance, since, for his purposes, the unit of study is a culture—be it that of 160 million Americans, or that of the half-dozen survivors of a near-extinct tribe. Hence, our data provide no more than the skimpiest scraps of information for a demographic study of mankind in relation to abortion. All we do know is that abortion and infanticide have decimated some demoralized tribes, chiefly in *Melanesia,* but also elsewhere. A general demographic study of abortion was, therefore, not attempted.

PART THREE

SOURCE MATERIAL

1. INTRODUCTION

Purpose. The present section is intended to serve as a sourcebook on abortion in *primitive* society. This definition of our objective explains why, even though the typological section also dealt with 20 European and other nontribal groups, the present section contains only data pertaining to non-European primitive tribes. This limitation of our objective can be justified fairly easily. Time and again, even in regard to data pertaining to primitive tribes only, it was found that the statements of a reputable author were flatly contradicted—often with ample documentation—by an equally reputable scholar. In many other instances, the data of one author supplemented those of another author. If this is the state of affairs which prevails even in regard to data on fairly simple societies, described by only one or two authors, one can well imagine the difficulties of seeking to offer a representative picture of abortion in a complex society. For example, it is to be doubted whether anyone who is not a professional expert on classical *Greece* could hope to cull, from the tremendous corpus of *Greek* sources, all representative material pertaining to abortion in ancient *Greece,* and to synthesize it in a meaningful manner. Under these circumstances, it seemed advisable to limit the sourcebook section to primitive societies. The one or two exceptions to this rule concern either states that have disappeared (*Aztec, Inca*) or groups whose "primitiveness" is a matter of personal opinion regarding the meaning of the term "primitive."

Provenience of the Material. The data presented hereinbelow were culled from a variety of sources, both primary and secondary, and are highly variable in quality. It is therefore very necessary to state their provenience, and to appraise their reliability, at least in general terms.

1. *The Yale University Human Relations Area Files*—henceforth referred to as HRAF—contain verbatim typewritten copies of primary published or manuscript sources on some 200 tribes, and in some 60% of cases (approximately 125 tribes) contain data on abortion. Most of these sources are at least moderately reliable, and it is one of the chief merits of the HRAF that the latest additions also assess the quality of the cited sources. Thus, for all practical purposes, the material found in HRAF can be treated as the strict equivalent of the printed source itself. Slips pertaining to the same topic, but derived from various sources, are grouped together for each tribe, and the original source from which any particular slip was copied is always indicated. For some tribes all known sources have been copied on slips, while for others only the most important primary sources have been so transcribed. For example, we found it desirable to supplement our HRAF data on *Bali* by data derived from PB.* Thus, the completeness vs. incompleteness of the HRAF files on any tribe has a direct bearing upon the completeness or incompleteness of our data pertaining to that tribe. Where the HRAF data included all sources, our data may be considered more or less complete—but only in the sense that they represent all that has been *published* on abortion for a given tribe. Even this does not mean, however, that in such cases we know all that *might* be known on this topic were an anthropologist especially interested in abortion to investigate this topic anew in the field. In fact, it is best to assume that our information on even the most carefully described tribes' abortion practices is incomplete. In particular, we note the singular scarcity of case histories.

It would have been highly desirable to copy verbatim all relevant slips found in the HRAF. However, the holders of copyright to the sources reproduced in HRAF gave permission to have them copied for HRAF only on condition that HRAF would not allow their being *further* reproduced verbatim by any means other than the typewriter or handwriting. We could, of course, have simply taken bibliographic notes on the HRAF files, enabling us to locate the original source and to copy it,

* See the section on bibliographic abbreviations in Part One: Typology (Introduction.)

thus circumventing the copyright holders' agreement with HRAF. This subterfuge was, however, deemed to be unethical, at least by implication. For this reason the writer personally abstracted and reworded the HRAF slips on abortion, and, when there were several sources, he blended these separate sets of data into a continuous account, indicating each time the particular source from which a given statement was derived. A block of material derived from HRAF is, therefore, *never in quotes,* and, in most cases, can be recognized by two signs: The text is *not* in quotes, and a bibliography of several items *precedes* the text. We should mention, however, that in a few instances material also found in HRAF has been reproduced verbatim. This was done only when the primary source was a book or periodical which the author had located either in his own library or in some other library to which he had access, or by means of a secondary source, *previous to* the time at which he consulted for this purpose the HRAF (e.g., Fortune's material on *Dobu*). While this mode of proceeding may seem overscrupulous to some, HRAF is simply too valuable to all students of man for anyone to jeopardize its further expansion by giving holders of copyright cause to deny permission to include additional material in HRAF.

2. *Original Published Data.* The majority of such data were located in the author's own library, or in the libraries of institutions with which he was associated during the writing of this work. Additional data on *Polynesia* were located in the personal library of Professor E. W. Gifford of the University of California at Berkeley, who kindly permitted the writer to browse in it for this purpose. Such data are always preceded by a detailed bibliographic reference, are reproduced verbatim, and, invariably, *in quotes,* which serve to distinguish them from material located through HRAF—the HRAF data, as indicated, being presented in reworded and abstracted form. On rare occasions, one such source (original published data) is reproduced partly in quotes and partly in the form of a summary which is *not* in quotation marks; such abstracts and summaries were resorted to whenever a verbatim reproduction would have taken up more space than the nature of the material seemed to warrant. In other instances (e.g., as regards the *Kgatla* material), it was found necessary to organize the many scattered references found in the same work

into a continuous narrative. In such cases the text has been largely reworded, and each statement is followed, in parentheses, by a reference to the page on which it is found.

3. *Original Unpublished Material.* The writer is indebted to Dr. E. M. Loeb for permission to reproduce verbatim his data on *Kuanyama Ambo* abortion, to Miss Marianne L. Stoller for writing up her data on abortion in *Tahiti,* and for a brief comment on Ellis's data on abortion among the *Polynesian Areoi,* and to Mr. Herbert H. Williams for obtaining permission from Mr. R. K. Lewis to reproduce the latter's data on abortion among the *Maronites.* In addition, the present section also includes the author's own unpublished data on abortion among the *Sedang.* Unpublished data found in HRAF (cf. *Achewa, Kwakiutl, Truk,* etc.) were usually, but not always, treated like the rest of HRAF data, i.e., they were usually abstracted and reworded.

4. *Secondary Sources.* No undertaking of this magnitude could dispense with secondary sources. Unfortunately, it was found that these secondary sources were highly variable in quality. At the lower end of the scale, some specific quotes either could not be traced back to the primary source allegedly used, or else somewhat distorted the meaning which the present writer would read into the original source. PB was found to be particularly open to criticism on this score, which is not surprising since this work represents the collective efforts of four scholars over a period of decades, and is world-wide in scope. Under such circumstances some errors were bound to slip in. At the upper end of the scale a very high reliability coefficient may be assigned to HDBK, each of whose chapters was written by a specialist on a particular area, so that, e.g., the *Chaco* section, compiled and interpreted by Métraux, can be treated as a primary source, and as an original contribution. On the whole, data derived from such secondary sources as HDBK, NH, GPM, and—with one exception—WGS may be treated as the equivalents of primary data, since they were invariably found to be accurate when the primary source referred to could be located. This does not mean, however, that the authors of these three primary sources surveyed *all* material pertaining to the tribes which they mention. Thus, GPM, whose reliability score in the quotation of primary sources is 100%, states—on good authority—that the

Haida do not abort, whereas it was possible to locate in Bancroft (who, be it said, often fails to give an authority for *his* assertions) a statement that the *Haida do* abort. Nonetheless, in this case at least, we are tentatively inclined to accept Bancroft's statement, because the *Haida* live in an area where abortion is known to have been fairly frequent. At the middle range of the scale, HK was found adequately reliable in its summary of those primary sources which could be located. HA, CS, and NM also usually come close enough in their summary of primary sources to the meaning which the present author would assign to them, to enable one to state that the difference is usually simply a matter of nuance, and of a debatable one at that. As regards PB the situation is—as we said before—somewhat different. PB contains many quotations or summaries which are definitely accurate, side by side with what we cannot but describe as gross distortions, and even, as we could occasionally ascertain, outright errors of fact. Hence, it would have been desirable to track down to its original source all material located through secondary sources, and especially through PB. However, even with the resources of Philadelphia libraries at our disposal, this was not always possible. For this reason, whenever the original source was not seen, the text of the secondary source is cited verbatim, *in quotes,* and is followed by a page reference to the secondary source (whose name appears in abbreviated form at the head of the text). In addition, this page reference is then often followed by a reference to the primary source allegedly used by the author of the secondary source. This device was adopted after considerable thought, simply because even PB was overwhelmingly more often right than wrong, and, because, in numerous instances, even PB quoted verbatim the original source—as we ascertained by collating some of these quotations with the original text. Under these circumstances, to omit (for example) all PB material, which is probably 90% correct, in order to eliminate some 10% of inaccurate material, seemed an inexcusable waste; particularly since the interested reader, by referring to the secondary sources, could always track these data down to their primary sources and check their accuracy—assuming, of course, that he had unlimited time and first-rate library facilities at his disposal. It should also be mentioned that secondary sources often quote only one or two salient items from the *total* material contained in the original source. The last point to be made is that, even though in our typology chapter we quoted preferably *secondary* sources, so as to eliminate footnotes, the material cited is invariably one which was either also located in a primary source, or else is so extremely plausible as to arouse no suspicion of possible inaccuracy.

5. *Combined Data.* In some instances the material on one and the same tribe is made up of reworded HRAF data, of data copied verbatim from available original sources, and of data culled from secondary sources. Such groups of data have been presented in such a manner that the reader can easily identify the provenience of each individual statement.

6. *Abbreviations.* A list of the abbreviations of references to secondary sources will be found in the Introduction to Part One: Typology.

On the whole, it is reasonably safe to say, at least as a guess, that practically all the relevant published material pertaining to some 300 tribes has been located, the material on the other 100 tribes being admittedly fragmentary. It is therefore felt that the sourcebook represents a "reliable sample" of abortion in primitive society, save only in its relative lack of case histories and of truly detailed psychological material. Above all, it presents to the reader all the material used by the writer in reaching his conclusions, and should therefore facilitate a constructive criticism and creative reappraisal of the writer's formulations and findings. This fact alone justifies the inclusion, *in extenso,* of material of so variable a quality and compendiousness into this work. As it stands, our set of data is believed to represent the largest single body of material pertaining to a particular cultural practice which has ever been assembled.

Arrangement of the Material. After considerable thought, and bearing in mind the true purpose of this section—which is to enable the reader of the theoretical sections to locate, with a minimum of effort, the actual material referred to—it was decided to arrange the tribes alphabetically. We suspect that, regardless of how erudite an anthropologist is and regardless of how familiar he may be with some established scheme of arranging tribes in a certain order—by linguistic affiliation, by position in a culture-area, or by type of economy—even he will find it easier to locate the *Cheyenne* under the letter "C" than under

"Northern Plains," where personal opinion alone will determine whether the *Cheyenne* are to be listed before or after the *Arapaho* or the *Sioux*. The adoption of some theoretically justifiable system of arranging the tribes in a certain order, when the most efficient and simplest way, for our present purposes at least, is an alphabetical listing, would have been a rather gratuitous bit of scientific complication-mongering. As regards African tribal names, we followed no strict policy, except the policy of using what, in our opinion, was the most common way of referring to a given tribe. Hence, we write *Pedi, Uganda,* and *Bakongo,* though each represents a different form of designation. This policy will, it is felt, help the nonanthropologist. As to anthropological readers, as a colleague expressed it: "He who knows enough about African tribal names to object to this policy—or lack of policy—is the very person who will be least confused by it."

2. ETHNIC GROUPS ALPHABETICALLY LISTED

ABABUA (Magbwanda and Bokiba)

HUTEREAU, ARMAND. *Notes sur la vie familiale et juridique de quelques populations du Congo Belge.* Musée du Congo Belge, Annales, I, #1, 1909.

"Abortifacient plants are known and used by the women, but if the husband hears that his wife has used them, he deems this maneuver as a token of contempt for his person, sends the woman back to her parents and demands another daughter as wife, or else an integral refund of the bride price." (p. 101)

ABIPONES

DOBRIZHOFFER, MARTIN. *An account of the Abipones, an Equestrian People of Paraguay,* Vol. II. London, 1822.

"Like the other American savages, some of the Abipones practise polygamy and divorce. Yet they are by no means numerous; the whole nation consisting of no more than five thousand people. Intestine skirmishes, excursions against the enemy, the deadly contagion of the measles and small-pox, and the cruelty of the mothers towards their offspring, have combined to render their number so small. Now learn the cause of this inhumanity in the women. The mothers suckle their children for three years, during which time they have no conjugal intercourse with their husbands, who, tired of this long delay, often marry another wife. The women, therefore, kill their unborn babes through fear of repudiation, sometimes getting rid of them by violent arts, without waiting for their birth. Afraid of being widows in the lifetime of their husbands, they blush not to become more savage than tigresses. Mothers spare their female offspring more frequently than the males, because the sons, when grown up, are obliged to purchase a wife, whereas daughters, at an age to be married, may be sold to the bridegroom at almost any price.

"From all this you may easily guess that the Abiponian nations abound more in women than in men, both because female infants are seldomer killed by their mothers, because the women never fall in battle as is the case with the men, and because women are naturally longer lived than men. Many writers make the mistake of attributing the present scanty population of America to the cruelty of the Spaniards, when they should rather accuse that of the infanticide mothers. We, who have grown old amongst the Abipones, should pronounce her a singularly good woman who brings up two or three sons. But the whole Abiponian nation contains so few such mothers, that their names might all be inscribed on a ring. I have known some who killed all the children they bore, no one either preventing or avenging these murders. Such is the impunity with which crimes are committed when they become common, as if custom could excuse their impiety. The mothers bewail their children, who die of disease, with sincere tears; yet they dash their newborn babes against the ground, or destroy them in some other way, with calm countenances. Europeans will scarce believe that such affection for their dead children can co-exist with such cruelty towards them while they are alive, but to us it is certain and indubitable. After our instructions, however, had engrafted a reverence for the divine law in the minds of the Abipones, the barbarity of the mothers gradually disappeared, and husbands, with joyful eyes, beheld their hands no longer stained with the blood of their offspring, but their arms laden with those dear pledges. These are the fruits and the triumphs of religion, which fills not only Heaven but earth with inhabitants. When polygamy and divorce, the iniquitous murdering of infants, and the liberty of spontaneous abortion were at length, by means of Christian discipline, abolished, the nation of the Abipones, within a few years, rejoiced to see itself enriched with incredible accessions of both sexes." (pp. 96–99)

(See also *Chaco*.)

ABYSSINIA

PB

"Wood and the resin of the cedar and of the Sabe tree are used in order to produce an abortion." (2:531, quoting Hartmann)

ACHEWA

STEYTLER, J. G. "Ethnographic Report on the Achewa Tribe of Nyasaland." Unpublished MS in the possession of Professor G. P. Murdock of Yale University.

Achewa women abort voluntarily if they conceive a child before weaning their last baby, and if they wish to dispose of an adulterously conceived fetus, because, if such children are born, they cause sickness in the community. In addition, the women also fear the results of being found out. They abort by drinking various decoctions of roots. Even though the birth of children of the type usually aborted is calamitous, neither such children, nor deformed ones, nor twins are ever killed once they are born. (pp. 81–82) Achewa women are also made to abort involuntarily. If a man wishes to make a furnace, he first consults a medicine man, who puts medicine into a stripped corn cob and instructs a small boy to throw it at a pregnant woman, who will then miscarry the same evening. The abortus will be buried in the refuse heap, in the usual manner. The medicine man then digs it up at night, mixes it up with medicines and buries it in a hole in the ground. Next, the furnace is made, by working the clay into a wall rising above this hole. When the hoes are made, some are given as compensation to the woman who miscarried, but she is not supposed to know the reason for this gift. (pp. 19-20)

ACHOMAWI

STEWART, O. C. *Culture Element Distributions : XIV, Northern Paiute.* Anthropological Records, 4, #3, 1941.

"Abortion [is] by pressure [or] by lying on rock." (p. 409)

ADMIRALTY ISLANDS (in general)

PARKINSON, R. *Dreissig Jahre in der Südsee.* Stuttgart, 1907.

"When getting married, the men make sure that the bride is of good repute. If she has become delinquent before her marriage, the damaged bridegroom takes bloody revenge on the man who cohabited with her or on the relatives of that man. Men who have trespassed against propriety with single girls are, hence, interested in having the girls keep quiet and therefore sometimes kill them. The girls know how to abort the fetus; usually this is done by jumping off some high object." (p. 395)

(See also *Manus.*)

AFRICA (unspecified; probably West Africa)

HARLEY, G. W. *Native African Medicine.* Cambridge, Massachusetts, 1941.

"The use of abortifacients is probably much more general than the literature would lead one to suspect. Adams, however, says: 'The practice of procuring abortion is very common.' Adams was informed that in cases of pregnancy from illicit intercourse, where the woman would not submit to this alternative, it was not an unusual thing for the father secretly to poison her." (p. 215)

AGARIA

ELWIN, VERRIER. *The Agaria.* Oxford University Press [Calcutta], 1942.

". . . In case of an abortion, a drink of the water in which the iron has been washed is useful, and a similar drink, made by washing Virgin Iron five or six years old, is useful in a case of difficult labour." (p. 162) *

AINU

PILSUDSKI, BRONISLAW. Schwangerschaft, Entbindung und Fehlgeburt auf Sachalin, *Anthropos* 5:756–74, 1910.

GPM

Abortion is more frequent among the Ainu than among the Gilyak, whose life is more normal and traditional, whereas the Ainu have been strongly under Japanese influence for some 200 years. Some of their women have almost turned into prostitutes, cohabiting with Japanese and other foreign men. Some of these girls seek to avoid becoming pregnant and if they do become pregnant, they abort. (Pilsudski, p. 769) The girls enjoy absolute sex freedom, but either refuse or are ashamed to bear children before marriage. [Yet, according to Scheube, it is no shame to have a bastard child. While nursing it, the mother receives alimony, and, at the end of the nursing period, i.e., at 4–5 years of age, the child goes to his father's house. G.D.]. The girls use a variety of means in order to abort:

(1) The most frequently used technique consists in the girl pressing her abdomen with her hands or with a heavy object. It is an old technique, but a dangerous one, and nearly always entails deleterious consequences. Some old informants witnessed cases of death resulting from abortion. The author himself saw a worn-out invalid woman who was barely able to hold herself upright. She had aborted a few years earlier, and this had caused her illness; she died in the author's presence. Some women, however, are so skillful at aborting that they can abort repeatedly.

(2) During the first months of pregnancy they tie their body above the waist, in order to produce a premature birth. The

* The text is ambiguous. It may refer to an attempt to prevent a miscarriage, or to a remedy administered to alleviate the aftereffects of an abortion or of a miscarriage.

consequences of resorting to this technique are severe pains in the sides. It is very uncomfortable to be thus laced up tightly; it hampers work and even interferes with the casual love affairs, although the abortion was undertaken in order to continue indulging in such affairs.

(3) They jump off high places, e.g., from the stairs of the storehouse.

4. A "sympathetic magic" technique consists in the lower garment being cut in two as far up as the belt. It is worn in this state until the woman aborts. This technique is so little known, and, in fact, may possibly be so new, that only one woman mentioned it. The other women were amazed when it was mentioned to them, and were unable to confirm it.

(5) Old rust is used in the northern and southern portions of the eastern part of the island. In the north certain herbs are added to the rust. The men did not know the name of these herbs. (Pilsudski, p. 769–770)

Other means may also be used. (Pilsudski, p. 770)

Nowadays they chiefly use Japanese "medicines," introduced by Japanese whalers and fishery officials. It was difficult to find out about these drugs, because, due to the drop in the birth rate, Japanese laws are severe in regard to such matters. A Japanese informant said that these drugs contained saffron, which grows wild on Hokkaido, and is a very safe abortifacient. Ainu women have great faith in Japanese abortifacients, but seldom betray their secret, because they receive these drugs under conditions of secrecy. (Pilsudski, p. 770)

"Ainus greatly desire children and regard childlessness as a manifestation of divine displeasure. They never practice infanticide except possibly to slay one of a pair of twins, and abortions are performed only by unmarried mothers." (GPM, p. 178)

AKAMBA

HOBLEY, C. W. *Ethnology of A-Kamba and other East African Tribes.* Cambridge, 1910.

"Abortion is known among this tribe. It is sometimes practised by young unmarried girls who find themselves pregnant. They drink a cupful of hot butter which is said to produce the desired effect; a person who does this is called *Ekuvuna.*" (p. 58)

LINDBLOM, GERHARD. *The Akamba in British East Africa.* Uppsala, 1916.

"In connection with birth, a few words may be said on abortion, which is at times practiced by young girls. Free intercourse is permitted between youths and girls, but it is considered a disgrace for a young girl to be with child, and she will have difficulty in getting a young lover, often being obliged to content herself with an older man. When the dances of young people are at their height, the desire to take part in this recreation will by itself be sufficient to induce a pregnant girl to try to free herself of the unwelcome burden, which begins to weigh down her body. In the earlier stages of pregnancy, she consumes quantities of melted butter or soot from the roof of the hut (*mwae*). At the more advanced stages, a decoction is prepared from the roots, leaves, and fruit, of several well-known plants, which are considered to be highly poisonous, namely *kilia mbiti* (Jatropha species), *mutanda-mbo,* or *iua-mbumbu* (Phytolaccae). The decoction is drunk. It is considered very poisonous, and if the desired result is not obtained, the woman seems in most cases to pay the penalty with her life." (p. 38)

ALASKA INDIANS (unspecified)

PB

"The Indian women of Alaska also occasionally obtain an abortion in the fourth month of pregnancy. This is done by means of a manual kneading and compressing of the uterus through the wall of the abdomen." (2:524)

ALEUT

SHADE, C. I. "Ethnological Notes on the Aleuts." Unpublished MS submitted in accordance with requirements for the degree of A.B. with distinction, Harvard University Department of Anthropology, 1949.

Shade is sure that Jenny of Nikolski practiced abortion, and felt there are indications that the technique involved magic, but Jenny refused to speak and she and the author ended up by discussing basketry techniques. (p. 21) [According to other authors girls sometimes kill their illegitimate babies in this tribe, but the ghost of the baby will haunt the place in the shape of a bird and must be captured by the mother, who lures it to her exposed breast, and then rips the bird apart, thus ending the haunting. If this is not done, dreadful disasters befall, first the kin, then the village, and then other villages, which will be damaged by floods.]

ALOR

DU BOIS, CORA. *The People of Alor.* Minneapolis, 1944.*

"Further, mechanical abortions are practiced, and a pregnant girl would probably attempt to avoid difficulties by a deliberate and early miscarriage. Although the society does not approve, married women, particularly older ones, make no very great secret of the fact that they avoid unwanted children by very vigorous labor or by even more deliberate attempts, like jumping repeatedly from a tree or rock or by jolting themselves in a squatting position against a stone. It is felt that these practices are most efficacious in the first two or three months, when the child is still in liquid form. Probably the accuracy of ideas on fetal development can be attributed in part to the practice of abortions.

". . . The care of infants by men and boys and their affectionate attitudes toward babies have already been mentioned. Supporting the thesis that women are often less eager for children than men, were frank statements by two older women that they had committed abortions during their first pregnancies to spite their husbands, who were buying other wives.

". . . A further sociological point that may have considerable weight is that neither men nor women are considered fully adult until they have children. Adulthood for men means financial status and a role in the prestige system, whereas for women it carries no such social premium, their life pattern is set in childhood and continues through life with only marriage as a break, and marriage per se does not confer adult status.

". . . For instance, if women are generally reluctant to bear children, it is unlikely that questions on vital statistics put to sixteen women past the menopause would give 7.5 pregnancies per woman, and that miscarriages and abortions were only 10.5 per cent of one hundred and twenty-one recorded conceptions for these sixteen women. Here, of course, social disapproval of contraception and abortion may have acted as a deterrent.

* Reprinted by permission of the University of Minnesota Press.

". . . Her wish to abandon herself sexually to the man is filled with internal resistance. Likewise there is resentment at bearing children and caring for them, a fact that leads to two consequences, frequency of abortions and maternal neglect of children." (pp. 108–109, 186)

AMAZON RIVER, Tribes of the Middle and Upper (Cocama, Omagua, perhaps also Xibitaona and Omagua-yeté)

HDBK

"Infanticide occurred among the Omagua when the mother was already nursing or when the parents had desired a child of the opposite sex. The Cocama killed the crippled and deformed children (thought to be the children of spirits) as well as illegitimate or unwanted children. In such cases, unless one of the parents or some relative lifted it from the ground the infant was buried alive with the placenta. Abortion was widely practiced. (Cruz 1900, p. 97; Figueroa, 1904, p. 111; Maroni, 1889–92, 29:82)" (3:698)

AMBON

PB

"Abortifacients are extensively used." (2:513)

ANGAMI NAGA

HUTTON, J. H. *The Angami Nagas.* London, 1921.

" . . . Illegitimate children are very rare, and Mr. Davis remarks that 'it is impossible to resist the conclusion that they are made away with immediately after birth, or that abortion is procured before birth of the child.' The practice of infanticide is denied by Angami men, but they admit that some method of procuring abortion may be known to and practised by the women, although they, the men, do not know about it. In Kohima illegitimate children were born in private and killed by their mothers; in the Eastern Angami country illegitimate children were forbidden by the village to be reared. Girls about to become mothers used to, and probably still do, though, of course, it is denied, procure abortion by twisting and squeezing the abdomen." (p. 171)

AO NAGA

HUTTON, J. H. *The Angami Nagas.* London, 1921.

" . . . The Aos undoubtedly procure the abortion* of illegitimate children, and, as Mr. Davis suggests, it is only fair to assume that for every case of abortion or infanticide that comes to light 'many happen of which nothing is heard. The custom being one that is approved of by all Nagas, it is impossible to expect them to give information of the occurrence of such cases.' " (p. 172)

SMITH, W. C. *The Ao Naga Tribe of Assam.* London, 1925.

(Cites verbatim on p. 57 the same passage from Davis.)

APACHE (Jicarilla)

AH

"Among the Jicarillas, according to Mr. Johnson, the agent, and Doctor Murphy, the physician of the tribe, abortion is but seldom practised, and only in the case of unmarried women. For this purpose certain herbs and plants found in that part of the country are used; what they are is a secret with the old women of the tribe. It is very probable that the herbs are aided by physical means." (p. 164)

APACHE (Mescalero)

AH

"Among the Mescaleros, according to information given to the writer by Dr. W. McM. Luttrell (in 1900 the agent of the tribe), as well as by others, abortion was not very rare. For this purpose the women swallowed certain vegetal subtances, particularly large doses of the fermented acid juice of the inner bark of the pine; or they tried to destroy the fetus by violent pressure upon the abdomen. In a few instances a stick or a bent wire was said to have been used, being introduced by another woman into the uterus; this practice was not heard of elsewhere, and it is possible that it did not originate with the Indians." (p. 164)

* A method used in the Ao village of Nankam is to feel from the outside for the child's head a few days before birth and catching hold of that part of the mother's body together with the head of the child inside to give a sharp rap on it with a stone, which causes the child to be born dead. This method is said to be known to certain old women who practise it in privacy.

APACHE (San Carlos)

AH

"Among the San Carlos Apache the means for induction of abortion are mainly mechanical (e.g., pressure, as over an edge of a box or a rock). Some of the old people are said to know a strong medicine which produces the desired result. The attempt is always made in secrecy." (pp. 163–164)

APACHE (White Mountain)

AH

"Among the White Mountain Apache abortion is usually produced by leaning on a rock or a stout stick, or by manual pressure applied to the fundus of the uterus." (p. 164)

APINAYE′

NIMUENDAJÚ, CURT. *The Apinaye′*. Catholic University of America Anthropological Series, 8, Washington, D. C., 1939.

"In general an Apinaye′ primipara greatly dreads pregnancy and parturition, hence has recourse to all sorts of remedies for hindering conception or producing an abortion. For the former purpose the pounded-up bark of the tinguy shrub (kalō′n) is mixed with urucú and smeared on the navel and abdomen; or pulverized rocks are substituted. Not so harmless are the abortives, which are also sometimes employed when a pregnant woman is deserted by her husband. They include first of all, the decoction or infusion of a shrub called kalą′-gandę′ (deer medicine) of unquestionably poisonous character. And one Amdyi′ told me she had successfully used the root of a plant called teb-gande′ (fish medicine) for the same purpose." (p. 98)

ARANDA

BASEDOW, HERBERT. *The Australian Aboriginal.* Adelaide, 1925.

"Abortion is a rare occurrence among natives untouched by European influence, and rather frequent among those living near civilization. At Fowler's Bay the woman collects a certain kind of black beetles, called yarralyi, roasts them, reduces them to powder and rubs some of this powder in her armpits and on her breasts and pubes." (p. 64) [Almost all authors mention that infanticide among the Aranda is common, especially in times of famine, when the killed child is fed to the other children, in order to enable them to survive. They also kill children who are born too soon after the preceding child, as well as the younger twin if both are of the same sex, or else the female twin, if they belong to different sexes. G.D.]

GPM

"Women occasionally produce an abortion by tying a belt very tightly about the abdomen." (p. 34)

ARAPAHO

HILGER, M. I. *Arapaho Child Life, and its Cultural Background.* Bureau of American Ethnology, Bulletin 148, Washington, 1952.

"All informants were agreed that abortions were not induced in the early days. A midwife in her eighties was emphatic in her statements. 'Arapaho had no means of killing an unborn baby or of getting rid of it. On the contrary they did have, and still have, medicines that prevent mothers from having miscarriages which may occur when they work too hard, or when they get hurt. I know the plants to use, but I can't give you any. When I need them I get them over there,' she concluded, pointing in the direction with her chin.

"Other informants remarked:

"No voluntary abortions were ever committed by our people. . . . I never heard of intentional abortions. If an expectant mother feared an abortion, she was given a decoction of medicine so that she wouldn't lose the baby. This might happen if she got hurt. . . . I know of one woman who had one pregnancy after another, but never gave birth to her children. The Indians believed that such a woman would eventually be killed by her own babies. They would come back to kill such a mother. Such a woman ought to get help so she would not lose her babies. . . . The Arapaho women knew that they could have something done to themselves so that they would not bear children; but once a child was conceived, it was always given birth. Nothing was ever done to get rid of the unborn child; but they really never lost them. Today there are people around here, some of them White doctors, who tell the Indians how to abort children. I don't think it is right to do that, but I think it is all right for a woman to have treatments so that she will not have any children." (pp. 11–12)

"Prenatal Period.—Arapaho believe that speaking of prenatal life or of birth will cause a relative to become pregnant. Some informants believed that the fetus was human from the time of conception; others, only from the time of quickening. Some gave an aborted fetus adult burial; others disposed of it in the same manner as the placenta." (p. 217)

ARAUCANIANS

HDBK

"Both abortion and infanticide occurred, but how commonly is not clear. Gusinde (1936, passim) lists about a dozen different plant abortifacients. . . . Félix José (1916, 1:91) lists the verb koftun, meaning to kill an infant and roast its testicles in a heated pot, as done sometimes by an unmarried mother to avenge herself on her unfaithful lover—so making him impotent (Guevara Silva, 1908, p. 222; 1929, 2:242). The present writer [J. M. Cooper] has come across no specific mention of contraceptive practices; apparently in recent times they were disapproved, to judge from a somewhat vague reference in Housse (1939, p. 249)." (2:733–734)

ARAWAK of the Antilles

PESCHEL, O. *Geschichte des Zeitalters der Entdeckungen.* 1877.

"[Due to Spanish oppression] the women promised to themselves not to bear further children, and instead aborted them by means of well-known plant poisons." (p. 431)

[This epidemic of abortions was connected with mass suicides. For similar data see *Chontal, Haiti, Marianas.* G.D.]

ARU ISLANDS

PB

"According to Ribbe: 'One seldom finds more than three children per couple; as in all of India, so here also, abortion is permissible, which, in view of the overpopulation of India, and in view of its sad internal political condition, which is due to the present administration, is a blessing.' " (2:513) (Quoting Ribbe, Carl, *Die Aru Inseln,* Dresden, 1888.)

ASHANTI

RATTRAY, R. S. *Religion and Art in Ashanti.* Oxford, 1927.

Abortion seems only to be done incidental to saving the life of a mother in consequence of a particular kind of adultery. Adultery with a pregnant married woman is considered an offense against the community as well as the husband, and in the past was a capital offense. If the woman in such a case confesses, she will prevent the miscarriage and danger to her own life that is considered likely to result. "That confession is deemed good for the soul is clear, for when we have a case of the wife's infidelity coming to light by an accident or otherwise than by her own confession, it is legitimate (at any rate at the present day) to endeavor to bring about abortion in order to save the mother's life, which is supposed to be endangered should nature be allowed to take her course. The means employed would be 'the drinking of medicine,' a decoction of the leaves of the plant called in Ashanti *abini buru* (Alternanthera repens), mixed with salt (conversely there is a medicine to counteract the attempts of *abayifo,* witches, or supernatural powers to bring about abortion). For this purpose the pounded bark of the *opam* tree, mixed with eggs and cold water is used." (p. 55)

[At present, an abortion is tantamount to a confession of adultery while pregnant. (*Ibid,* passim) An involuntary miscarriage can also be caused by a malicious co-wife, for example. (*Ibid.,* passim)]

ASSINIBOINE

CURRIER, A. F. "A Study Relative to the Functions of the Reproductive Apparatus in American Indian Women," *Transactions of the American Gynecological Society,* 16:264–94, 1891.

"Among the Crows and Assiniboines criminal abortion is very common, being performed or superintended by specially trained women. In some cases a pointed stick is introduced into the uterus, the ovum being ruptured. In others a stake is driven into the ground, the patient rests her belly upon the upper end of it, which is about two feet from the ground, and whirls around until the foetus is expelled.

"Another method is for the patient to lie upon her back, a wide board being laid across her belly. Upon this board two or three of her female friends, in turn, stand or jump until the blood gushes from the vagina; or the belly is kneaded or tramped upon until the foetus is expelled. Severe as this treatment is, it is said that death seldom results." (p. 279)

DENIG, E. T. *Indian Tribes of the Upper Missouri.* Bureau of American Ethnology, Annual Report, 46, Washington, D. C., 1930.

"Cases of infanticide are very common among the Sioux, Crows, and Assiniboin, perhaps most so among the Crow women. It is not far from the correct number if we state that one-eighth of the children are destroyed in utero or after birth by the Crow women. The same also often is done by the Assinboin, particularly if the father of the child has abandoned the woman before its birth. A quarrel with the husband or even unwillingness to be at the trouble of raising them are the causes for these actions. We think and have strong reason to believe that in some instances, they are destroyed at the instigation of their husbands, although they will not acknowledge this to be the case.

"At all events no punishment is inflicted on the woman for the crime but frequently the means and time they use to produce abortions are the cause of death of the mother. To produce its death in the womb they use violent pressure and blows upon the abdomen. Frequently they retire to the woods, bring forth the child alone, strangle it and throw it into the water, snow, or bushes. The whole of these measures are publicly talked of among them, and no great degree of repugnance is attached either to the act or to the woman, but the circumstance is laughed at as something ludicrous." (p. 521)

ATJEH

HURGRONJE, C. S. *De Atjehers.* Leiden, 1894–96.

[The people of Atjeh] "themselves admit that both in marriage and outside of marriage they often use devices to produce contraception or abortion." (1:73)

PB

"The women of Atjeh also abort occasionally. But this always happens only if the husband consents." (2:513) (Quoting Jacobs, Julius: *Het Familie-, en Kampongleven op Groot-Atjeh,* Leiden, 1894.)

(See also *Kling.*)

AUSTRALIA (in general)

CURR, E. M. *The Australian Race.* Melbourne and London, 1886–87, 4 vols.

"Abortion is practiced occasionally throughout the continent." (I:76)

AUSTRALIANS (Melville Island)
COON, C. S. *Personal Communications,* 1954.

"A Melville Island woman died recently as a result of having aborted."

AUSTRALIANS (New South Wales)
PB
"According to von Scherzer the natives disappear more and more rapidly because in that area abortion is beginning to predominate. The activity of the mission is also a factor in this, because it is absolutely unsuitable for the mode of living of these people." (2:511)

AUSTRALIANS (probably Portland Bay, Victoria)
PB
"It has allegedly been observed in Australia that 'due to the difficulties connected with the rearing of children' native mothers often cause themselves to abort." (2:511, quoting Oberländer, Richard, and, secondarily, Klemm, G.)

AUSTRALIANS (Queensland, North-West-Central)
ROTH, W. E. *Ethnological Studies Among the North-West-Central Queensland Aborigines.* London, 1897.

"329. Abortion appears to be a common practice in the later months among the aboriginals of the Boulia, Upper Georgina and Leichhardt-Selwyn Districts. It is performed by the fixation of thick twine wound very tightly round and round the abdominal walls, combined with the 'punching' by hand or stick upon the more palpable and apparently firmer portions of the unborn child as recognized through the abdominal walls. I can find no traces of other methods being used." (p. 183)

AUSTRALIANS (Sydney Area)
BONWICK, JAMES. *Daily Life and Origin of the Tasmanians.* London, 1870.

(Data identical with *Tasmanian* data.)

AUSTRALIANS (Victoria)
PB
"Abortion through pressure is by no means rare, especially after

a quarrel between husband and wife." (2:527, quoting Oberländer)

AUSTRALIANS (Western Arnhem Land)

BERNDT, R. M. AND BERNDT, C. H. *Sexual Behavior in Western Arnhem Land.* Viking Fund Publication in Anthropology, No. 16, New York, 1951.

"On the other hand, this society practises a certain amount of abortion and contraception, and a woman consciously pregnant by a man other than her actual husband or husband's brother, her *ma:mam,* might resort to these. Native authorities insist that too much promiscuous or extra-marital coitus stops conception; while a woman having relations with a man who is not 'straight' (i.e., marriageable) to her, will not conceive." (p. 84)

AYMARA

LA BARRE, WESTON. *The Aymara Indians of the Lake Titicaca Plateau, Bolivia.* American Anthropological Association, Memoir 68, 1948.

"The Aymara women know how to procure an abortion by drinking an infusion of the orange flowers of a murderously spiny nettle, *Urtica magellanica* Jussieu et Poiret (*Urticaceae*), called *q'ač u itapalu,* 'female nettle,' *nina* or *ninanina,* 'fire fire'; this is probably the same plant as Forbes' 'itapalu . . . a decoction . . . used for cutting short the menses.' " (p. 119)

HDBK

"Although disapproved, abortion is occasionally practiced by unmarried women, who drink a strong laxative tea or roll a heavy stone on the abdomen." (2:548)

AZANDE

REYNOLDS, HAROLD. "Notes on the Azande Tribe of the Congo," *Journal of the African Society,* 3:238–46, London, 1904.

HUTEREAU, ARMAND. *Notes sur la vie familiale et juridique de quelques populations du Congo Belge.* Musée du Congo Belge, Annales, I, #1, 1909.

CZEKANOWSKI, JAN. "Forschungen im Nil-Kongo Zwischengebiet." *Wissenschaftliche Ergebnisse der Deutschen Zentral Afrika Expedition, 1907–1908, unter Führung Adolf Friedrichs, Herzogs zu Mecklenburg,* Vol. 6, Pt. 2, pp. 21–110, Leipzig, 1924.

LAGAE, C. R. "Les Azande ou Niam-Niam: L'Organisation Zande, Croyances Religieuses et Magiques, Coûtumes Familiales," *Bibliothèque-Congo,* Vol. 18, Bruxelles, 1926.

EVANS-PRITCHARD, E. E. "Heredity and Gestation, as the Azande see Them," *Sociologus,* 8:400–414, 1932.

Abortion is rather common. Some women never rear children, due to frequent miscarriages. Native medicines are used but are kept secret. (Reynolds, pp. 240–41) Abortion is very prevalent among the Southern Azande, who use the leaves of a secret plant for this purpose. The knowledge of the technique is not restricted to a few experts as is so often the case in other groups. (Czekanowski, p. 89) Abortifacient plants are known to the Azande. (Hutereau, p. 34) If an abortion takes place for other reasons than adultery, the husband asks his wife's father for an indemnity in the value of twenty knives. If he refuses to comply with this demand, and if the abortion is well established, the husband will complain to the chief. (Lagae, pp. 164–65) If the husband learns that his wife has used an abortifacient plant, he considers this tantamount to the assassination of his child. He therefore asks his father-in-law for a second wife, or else, in vengeance, he kills the wife of his father-in-law or one of his father-in-law's children. Often he also chases his wife away. (Hutereau, p. 34) If the father of a married woman learns that his daughter has used contraception, he punishes her severely (Lagae, pp. 164–65)

When a wife is pregnant, the husband consults the *benget* to find out if it is his own child that his wife is carrying. If he "learns" that it is not his child, he will first oblige his wife to abort and then will proceed as in other cases of adultery. (Hutereau, p. 34) A man sometimes kills his wife's male child whom he has not fathered himself, but does not always kill his wife's adulterine daughter because he wants the marriage spears which he can get for her eventually. (Evans-Pritchard, p. 410)

AZIMBA (?)

ANGUS, H. CRAWFORD. "A Year in Azimba and Chipitaland: The Customs and Superstitions of the People," *Journal of the Anthropological Institute,* 27:316–25, 1898.

"Another much used drug is that for procuring abortion, and I have collected a small quantity of it. The action is quite harmless, and it generally takes effect in the course of two or three days; the effect is said to be lasting, inasmuch as a woman, having taken this drug and at some future period desiring to become a mother, will go to the medicine man and obtain another drug which will counteract the effect of the one taken perhaps years before." (p. 324)

AZTEC

BANCROFT, H. H. *The Native Races of the Pacific States.* London, 1875.
GPM

Bancroft states that various authorities said that Montezuma had from one to three thousand women in his harem and that of these, he had one hundred and fifty pregnant at one time, all of whom killed their offspring in the womb. In spite of this wholesale abortion, he was said to have had more than fifty children. (Bancroft, I:183)

"Abortion was not unusual, and was procured by taking a decoction of certain herbs; the crime was nevertheless punished with death." (*Ibid.*, I:269)

"Abortion, produced by a herb decoction, was forbidden on pain of death, unless to save the life of the mother. Infanticide was similarly prohibited, except that one of a pair of twins was invariably killed." (GPM, p. 383)

AZTEC (Modern)

(See *Nahua* and *Southwest U. S. Indians.*)

BABAR

PB

"Abortifacients are extensively used. . . . The pregnant women resort to artificial abortion, so as not to be deprived of coitus which is most severely prohibited during pregnancy. (2:513) They start the process of abortion by drinking Spanish pepper in arak. In addition, the man who impregnated her each day carefully steps on her abdomen, either in the house or in the forest, so as to eliminate the foetus." (2:526, quoting Riedel, J. G. F.)

BAFIOTE

PB

"It would seem that only single women, and especially those who for a prolonged period have led an all too free life and in their riper years are afraid of childbirth, seek in secret to produce an abortion by means of a kneading and pressing of the body as well as by an excessive use of red pepper." (2:516, quoting Pechuel-Loesche)

BAHOLOHOLO

HA

Women who have had stillbirths and also slave women take medicine, the latter in order to prevent the bearing of children who will become slaves. (p. 42) They sterilize themselves by herbs recommended to them by medicine men or else drink water into which a blacksmith has just plunged a red-hot iron. (pp. 62–63)

The smithy's fire bucket contains iron sulphate, which is an emmenagogue. (p. 120, quoting Schmidt, Robert, "Les Baholoholo," in van Overbergh, Cyril, *Collection de Monographies Ethnographiques,* Vol. 9, 1912, p. 146)

BAHUANA

TORDAY, E., AND JOYCE, T. A. "Notes on the Ethnography of the Ba-Huana," *Journal of the Anthropological Institute,* 36:272–301, 1906.

"Abortion . . . is common, the reason being that women are obliged to abstain from sexual intercourse during the long period of lactation." (p. 288) "[For the above reason] artificial abortion is very frequent, either by drinking very hot water or the infusion of a certain root, the identity of which is known only by the women." (p. 292)

BAKAIRI

VON DEN STEINEN, KARL. *Durch Central-Brasilien.* Leipzig, 1886.

"The use of abortifacient means is felt to be common and to explain the small number of children. The end of this community can be clearly foreseen." (p. 123) (The author also gives the results of a population count, which shows that most couples are childless or have but one offspring.)

BAKONGO

WEEKS, J. H. *Among the Primitive Bakongo.* Philadelphia, 1914.

"After the above remarks it may seem strange that there should be various methods of procuring abortion; yet there are times when a woman does not wish to be a mother, as when her hatred towards her husband more than counterbalances her longing for children; or, when she is desirous of shielding an illicit lover. It must be remembered that in a country where polygamy is recognized a large number of virile young women are often tied to an old man, hence when such wives stray from the paths of native virtue they will submit to such means as will hide their shame, protect the child from scorn, and save their lover from the payment of a heavy fine. They may go to a medicine-man, but this is not very probable, as such visits are soon noised abroad, and will in time reach the ears of the husband. They resort mostly to the juice of manioc leaves, or to a large dose of common salt, or to a small piece of *nsele-nsele* root, powdered and drunk with water or palm wine, or to eating manioc leaves that have been soaked in water for many days. The leaves are astringent, and the root causes severe diarrhoea.

"When an unmarried woman has a child, no fine is paid by the man, but the child is never allowed to call him father, although they may both be living in the same town. The child belongs to the woman's family, is known to all as a 'child of adultery' (*mwan' a zumba*), and is spoken of as such. The other children taunt him by saying, 'You have no father, you came from a tree.' In the Ngombe Lutete district the man has now to pay a fine for adultery." (p. 108)

BALI

PB

WECK, WOLFGANG. *Heilkunde und Volkstum auf Bali.* Stuttgart, 1937.
COVARRUBIAS, MIGUEL. *Bali.* New York, 1937.

"Every Balinese woman knows a quantity of abortifacients and there is no doubt that much use is made of them. This explains why so few extra-maritally conceived children are born, despite the fact that most daughters of this voluptuous people also engage in prostitution. Not only the unmarried women resort to these means. One of the panjeroan, i.e. one of the slave women of the Prince of Badong, Bali, told Jacobs that as soon as one of them becomes pregnant she must report to the Prince, who immediately gives her a Chinese obat named 'pengeret.' [Obat in Malay means simply "medicament." G.D.] This compound, which is black in color and has a harsh taste, produces, after it is ingested, a sensation of warmth and almost always has the desired result." (PB 2:514, quoting Jacobs, Julius, *Eenige tijd onder de Baliërs,* Batavia, 1883)

"According to Jacobs the women of Bali used as an abortifacient the chopped fibers of the Kepoh (Sterculia foetida L.); and also a cold extract of the Manga kawini (Magnifera foetida)." (PB 2:526, quoting Jacobs, *ibid.*)

The female babyan mandak, as a less reputable part of her work, is active as an abortionist. This is also done by male babyan mandaks. (Weck, pp. 17–18)

"With children generally welcome, birth control is rarely practiced, although it is not unknown to unmarried girls who do not want to become pregnant. Apparently the only method of prevention they know is for the woman to stand up after intercourse and free herself of the seminal fluid. There are medicines to cause abortion and to make a woman sterile, but both ideas are criminal and fall within the category of black magic." (Covarrubias, p. 123)

BANGALA

WEEKS, J. H. "Anthropological Notes on the Bangala of the Upper Congo River. Part II," *Journal of the Anthropological Institute,* 39:416–59, 1909.

". . . Illicit intercourse . . . has madc abortion common in order to hide their condition from the husbands, and save the lovers heavy fines." (p. 449)

BAROTSE

KAMMER, V. M. "The Custom Observed as Regards Miscarriage Among the Barotse," *East African Medical Journal,* 18:56–59, 1941.

"When I attended a case of miscarriage in a nearby village I took the patient to my hospital on account of a rather heavy haemorrhage. After a few days her position had improved, but there was still some bleeding. Despite that, she asked to be allowed to go home. I questioned her why she wanted to go home, annoyed because I had had a difficult time to get her all right again, and wanted her to stay on until I thought her fit for discharge. The reply I got was she had to go because the new moon was coming. At the moment I did not know that there was truth behind that explanation, but thought she had wanted to attend some village feast. So, despite my advising her against leaving the hospital, she left. I made some inquiries as I still could not believe the 'new moon' to be the reason and found the following custom out.

"As soon as a pregnant woman feels the first pains indicating a premature end of her pregnancy, she has to leave her hut. She has to go to an old female relative, a woman that has already passed the menopause. To her she confides her position.

"Thereafter both of them leave the village and select a place about 200 yards away where they build a temporary grass-hut in which the pregnant woman has to stay. The hut is built with the help of other women of the village, but no man is allowed to help nor even to come near.

"The woman stays there now, not only until the abortion has been completed, but lives in this hut until the new moon comes. During all this time she is looked after by some female of her relations. But none of them is allowed to touch her or any of her belongings, e.g., her mat or her hut, or her dishes, etc. This can only be done by women already past the menopause. Should a woman below this age disregard this rule and touch something, she is threatened to have a miscarriage herself the next time she becomes pregnant.

"The husband is not permitted to visit his wife and talk to her while she is living in this hut. Should he do it, he is in danger of getting consumption.

"When the new moon has been seen, a native doctor (*naka*) who must be a woman in this case is called. She brings some roots and leaves of certain plants and soaks them in cold water. Then she washes with this water the woman that had had the miscarriage outside the hut where she is now living. After the washing, the woman is not permitted to enter the hut any more.

"The hut is now burnt, the calabashes she ate from are broken (these women do not eat from dishes, as they would have to be broken and this would be regarded as waste. For the same reason the women take off the good clothes they wear when they feel they have to leave their house on account of an approaching miscarriage, and take only their oldest rugs [sic]), the clothes she wore are burnt, and only the mat she slept on may be taken by one of the old women, if it is still good. But usually the mat is burnt too.

"Now, the woman dresses in fresh clothes brought from her home and is led back to her village. But she has still not to enter her own house. She must stay with an old woman. There she can be visited by her husband but he must not touch her.

"The next day is a holiday. Nobody goes to work. But this is not a holiday on account of the coming back of the woman, but the day following the first appearance of the new moon is in Barotseland the day on which the people bring a sacrifice to Nyambe their god. The woman is brought back on this day only in order that every villager should be at home.

"On this day all the villagers have time to be sorry for the stillborn child, but they do not mourn aloud. No sacrifices are brought on this day, because it is observed as a day of mourning. (There are never sacrifices being brought when during the month somebody has died. Always the first new moon after a death has occurred is let pass, and only on the second are the sacrifices resumed again.)

"Early in the morning the woman goes and brings water, this being the first time since she fell ill that she may bring the water herself. (If somebody brings the water for her, she may use it too.) Then she takes mealie meal and prepares a porridge after she has added some powder made from roots, given to her now by the female native doctor.

"The porridge ready, all the villagers gather round the fire, women and men sitting in two separate groups. The woman now gives to each of them a little porridge in their hands, serving it out with the stick she stirred the porridge with. She must not touch the porridge with her own hands.

"All the villagers who have eaten of this porridge are now thought to be immune against consumption.

"After this, the woman may go home to her own hut and resume her ordinary way of life.

"There is but one restriction still imposed on her husband. He must not resume marital relations, until his wife has menstruated. Should he disregard it, he is still liable to get consumption. It is thought that there is still some poisonous blood in her, which is left over from her miscarriage. This leaves her with her menstrual blood.

"Should a woman try to keep it secret, the fact that she had an abortion is soon found out. She is then taken by old women (no young one is permitted to touch her) to the river and beaten, afterwards thrown in the water and her head kept under water until she is nearly suffocated. The hair is torn out and sometimes she is laid for some time under an upturned canoe there to contemplate how bad it is to treat with contempt the laws taught to her by old women when she was still a child. Then she is taken to a hut outside the village and has to stay there, as told above.

"The Mambowe tribe has almost identical customs the difference being that the hut need not be outside the village, and is not burned. They do not think that a woman still young, that touches the sick one or any of her belongings will have a miscarriage herself, but that she will get the falling disease.

"The husband himself is during all the time his wife spends in exile, confined to his own hut. He may not do any work in the cattle kraal, else the cattle would die. He may be visited by his friends and talked to, but must not be touched. Those who touch him are also threatened with consumption.

"A reference to the custom I described is to be found in the book *On the Threshold of Central Africa,* by François Coillard, page 399, and reads as follows: 'In case of an abortion, a woman is also left in the fields under a miserable shelter, where she lives in complete isolation, eating the meagre fare brought to her every day. She is thus sequestrated till the new moon. For the same reason, her husband is confined to the court of his house; all communications with his neighbours is forbidden, and all visits to his cattle-fold or fields. They fear he may exercise some evil influence over men, cattle, and things. Consequently, the whole community watches to see that the custom is rigorously observed. At the new moon, he and his wife will be made to pass through certain purifications, and only after having cleansed themselves in the river will they return to their ordinary course of life.' "

BARU (Papua)
MURRAY, J. H. P. *Papua, or British New Guinea.* New York, 1912

". . . The women smother any children born after the first child, should the practice of abortion fail to prevent the birth." (p. 194)

BATAK

PB

"More rational than these [Lampong and Kroë] methods may be the one which is used among the Batak who also inhabit Sumatra, and which is performed by the guru, or magician-priest. According to Roemer he pierces the fetal membranes 'by means of a bamboo sliver or the rib of a leaf, but uses for this purpose a kind of popgun, wherewith he fires a small bamboo arrow at the uterus.' (!) The sad consequences seldom fail to take place." (2:527, quoting Roemer, R., "Die Heilkunde der Batak auf Sumatra," *Janus,* 12:382–392, 467–474, 572–589, 1907) "The Batak, being a fighting people, are consistent in their attitude toward abortion." (2:537)

BERGDAMA

LÜBBERT, A. "Über die Heilmethoden und Heilmittel der Eingeborenen in Deutsch-Südwestafrika," *Mittheilungen aus den Deutschen Schutzgebieten,* 14:77–90, 1901.

(Data identical with *Herero* data.)

BONTOC IGOROT

JENKS, A. E. *The Bontoc Igorot.* Philippine Islands Department of the Interior Ethnological Survey Publications, 1905.

"Both married and unmarried women practice abortion when for any reason the prospective child is not desired. It is usual, however, for the mother of a pregnant girl to object to her aborting, saying that soon she will become 'pó-ta'—the common mate of several men, rather than the faithful wife of one. Abortion is accomplished without the use of drugs and is successful only during the first eight or ten weeks of pregnancy. The abdomen is bathed for several days in hot water, and the body is pressed and stroked downward with the hands. The foetus is buried by the woman. Only the woman herself or her mother or other near female friend is present at the abortion, though no effort is made at secrecy and its practice is no disgrace." (I:60)

BORNEO, NORTH (Tampassuk River)

ROTH, H. L. *The Natives of Sarawak and British North Borneo,* Vol. II. New York, 1896.

[Quotes Witt:] "If an ordinary slave woman becomes *enceinte* by her owner, she and her offspring are henceforth free, and she may remain as one of her late master's wives. But the jealousy of the inmates of the harem often causes abortion to be procured." (p. 214)

BRAZILIAN AMAZONAS TRIBES (in general)

WOODROFFE, J. F. *The Upper Reaches of the Amazon.* London, 1914.

(1) TASTEVIN, CONSTANT. "Le Fleuve Muru. Ses habitants. Croyances et moeurs Kachinaua," *La Géographie,* 43:403–22, 44:14–35, 1925.

(2) TASTEVIN, CONSTANT. "Le Haut Tarauacá," *La Géographie,* 45:34–54, 158–75, 1926.

In order to abort, they use the nuts of the mirity, which look like elongated red golfballs. When baked and ground, they are abortifacients. (Woodroffe, p. 290) Among the Kachinaua Indians of the Muru river, in the Brazilian Amazonas area, the average woman does not want many children and feels that three are usually enough. She therefore drinks a permanently sterilizing decoction, made of a root which exudes a very bitter juice. It is drunk at one draught, after which the woman vigorously rubs her stomach. Then she is no longer afraid of conceiving. (Tastevin 1, p. 32) Brazilian Amazonas women do not want more than one or two children, because it would make them get old quick, and their husbands would scorn them. They therefore take the *imi ráu* (remedy of the blood). This is a decoction of the leaf of a small forest shrub mixed, "like all Indian remedies," with the juice of another plant which serves as a corrective or auxiliary for the first one. Throughout the period during which this remedy is taken, the woman observes a very rigorous diet, barely nourishing herself with fruits and tubers. They assume that this drug is efficacious, since it was found that 114 women only had a total of 110 children between them. (Tastevin 2, p. 52)

BRUNEI (North Borneo)

PB

". . . The only reason infanticide is so rare is that this is forestalled by means of abortions, at which the natives are so skilled that they can attain their objective without endangering the patient. Since prominent men are in the habit of pensioning off their concubines after they had one or two deliveries, the women shrink from no device which would permit them to retain longer their favored position. In addition, half of the noble girls remain single; hence timely precautions are taken to prevent them from giving birth as a result of a prohibited relationship." (2:513–14, quoting St. John, Spencer, in *Das Ausland,* No. 31, p. 727, 1862)

BUIN (Bougainville)

THURNWALD, HILDE. "Woman's Status in Buin Society," *Oceania,* 5:142–70, 1934.

"Some women . . . do not like to be troubled with the upbringing of children, and confess it candidly. Even girls say that children would cause them too much worry, and that they prefer to preserve their good looks. . . . Girls and married women who do not want to become barren on account of taking *uále* apply hot stones to induce abortion." (p. 163) [Uále is a native Buin medicine used to cause permanent sterility—taken by many Buin women, either before marriage, shortly thereafter, or after the first or second child.]

BUKA

BLACKWOOD, BEATRICE. *Both Sides of Buka Passage.* Oxford, 1935.

"There are a number of plants (see pp. 134–8) believed to possess contraceptive properties, which are generally known and widely used by the women in their intrigues. Whatever the reason, it is certain that these affairs are followed by pregnancy less often than might be expected. When conception does occur, the matter begins to be taken seriously. Sometimes the woman will pretend that the child is her husband's, and this will be tacitly accepted, even though other people besides the couple and the woman's husband know it to be false. This I have on hearsay evidence only. In other cases—this also I have only through informants, but from more than one, and these reasonably reliable—attempts are made to produce an abortion in order to avoid discovery. One account given to me runs as follows: 'If a woman has been with her lover in the bush and finds she is pregnant, she says to him: "My blood is not flowing, I think I am going to have a child, I have had no flow for one moon." They are ashamed, and talk about it for a long time. Then the man gets the leaves of the *karēb* plant (a tough creeper, of the *Rutaceae* order, whose stems are used for making string), and chews them with lime, and rubs the mixture on the woman's abdomen. She swallows some of it, and it causes the flow to begin again. Then the man says to all the people who laughed at the woman because they thought she was pregnant: "Look, she is menstruating, she is not pregnant." ' It may be that the massaging of the abdomen is sufficiently violent to produce the desired effect, without presupposing any actual result of chewing the *karēb* leaves. They say that a woman will never bring about an abortion in the case of a child by her own husband, however many she may have. But they do it for the children of their lovers, because if a woman has a child by a man other than her husband she is ashamed. Cases have occurred in the past of women pregnant by their lovers committing suicide by jumping from the top of a tree." (p. 117)

BUKAUA

LEHNER, S. "Bukaua," in Neuhauss, R., *Deutsch Neu-Guinea,* Vol. 3, Berlin, 1911.

"Childbirth in young women is not viewed with favor; first they should become strong and vigorous—hence they hand to the girl reaching sexual maturity many prophylactic drugs. One of these is a kind of onion (mum) which is also used in the preparation of foods. It is fried, stripped of its leaves and husk, and is then eaten by the girl. Another means is a kind of tree bark (asuka) which is mixed with grated nutmeat. If a woman wants to have no children at all, in order to be free of the bother which they cause, she brews a beverage from the juice of the hung sama—a kind of banana—which is mixed with *susa ngatequi* (fern tree), to which is added a decoction of asala and amasa which are two large leafy trees. This brew is supposed to make the woman sterile (auwi kabo). If all these means fail and if an undesired pregnancy occurs, an attempt is made to get rid of the foetus: (a) by an artificial loss of blood; they make incisions on the body, elbows, knuckles, finger tips and the heels with *balim muli,* which is a tall, sharp-edged kind of grass—as a result of the loss of blood, a miscarriage is supposed to occur; (b) by means of rubbing of the abdomen with tapa cloth and by kneading it, which is done by old women; (c) by means of a certainly very painful procedure which consists in the pregnant woman being pulled back and forth through a tree fork in the forest by two other women until the desired abortion occurs.

"The men know nothing of this activity of the women and do not even want to know anything about it since, in such matters, they leave complete freedom to the women." (p. 425)

BUNA

BASU, M. N. "Bunas of Bengal," *Journal of the* [Calcutta University] *Department of Letters,* Vol. 32, 1939.

"Infanticide is never practised. Abortion is practised generally with the root of a plant called 'Rakta-chita' to save the widows and the unmarried from shame. Raw juice of the 'Royel' bark is also largely used for bringing about abortion. The community extensively practise contraception, owing to the low morality of the females, with the juice of the betel plants along with powdered black pepper, during menstruation in three or four successive periods. It gives immunity for four or five years." (p. 44)

BURU (Malay Archipelago)

PB

"Emmenagogues are extensively used to avoid having children and, likewise, artificial abortion is generally tolerated and often performed upon girls and women. The secret means used for this purpose do not seem to cause the body of the woman any lasting damage." (2:513)

BUSHMEN (German Southwest Africa)

LÜBBERT, A. "Über die Heilmethoden und Heilmittel der Eingeborenen in Deutsch-Südwestafrika," *Mittheilungen aus den Deutschen Schutzgebieten,* 14:77–90, 1901.

(Data identical with *Herero* data.)

CADUVEO (Guaycuru)

WGS

"The Kadiveo are perishing largely through abortion by the women who will not bear more than one child each.[1] They are a subdivision of the Guykurus who were reported sixty or seventy years ago to be decreasing in number from this cause.

1 *Globus,* 88:164, after Joly.

The women, 'until they are thirty, procure abortion, to free themselves from the privation of pregnancy and the trouble of bringing up children.' "[2] (2:77)

(See also *Guaycuru*, *Mbaya*, and *Chaco*.)

CAHITA (Yaqui)

WAGNER, C. J. "Medical Practices of the Yaquis, Studies of the Yaqui Indians of Sonora, Mexico." *Texas Technological College Bulletin,* 12:79–90, 1936.

The Cahita abort by drinking a tea made by boiling corcho (a corklike pine) in water. A lump of sugar is put into a cupful of [this] water which is drunk once daily for three days. This makes the woman deathly sick. She has spasms, and occasionally becomes perfectly rigid. Another abortifacient tea is made from the roots of the immortal plant. Sometimes they cause abortion by mixing resin in the brea tea with tallow and making a paste out of it, which is rubbed on the belly. When this is effective, it is probably due to the severe rubbing, and not to the paste. Another abortifacient technique is for the woman to press her belly across a tree or rock. (pp. 84–85)

CANARY ISLANDS

PB

"On the Canary Islands the fertility of women is very great and even prostitutes often give birth, because they use no means in order to abort. However, one often has recourse to abortifacients and this is the more easy to do since certain plants and herbs which cause an abortion are well known in the countryside while in the cities there is no lack of expert female abortionists." (2:515)

CARAYA (Rio Araguaya)

EHRENREICH, PAUL. *Beiträge zur Völkerkunde Brasiliens,* Königliches Museum zu Berlin, Vol. I, 1891.

"Artificially induced abortion occurs, but only at the request of the husband. It is produced by a manual compression of the

2 Spix, J. B. von, and Martius, K. F. P. von. *Reise in Brasilien,* 3 vols. and atlas, München, 1823-31.

uterus and is thought to cause death more than just occasionally." (p. 27)

CATAWBA

PB

"According to Smith, the Catawba Indian women frequently abort, especially when they become pregnant extramaritally. It is, therefore, easy to understand why Smith seldom found women who had more than two children." (2:517)

CELEBES (Central) (Toradja?)

RIEDEL, J. G. F. "De Topantunuasu of Oorspronkelijke Volkstammen van Centraal Selebes." *Bijdragen tot de Taal-, Land-, en Volkenkunde van Nederlandsch Indië,* 35:76–95, 1886.

"The women don't care about premarital intercourse; once they are married they use varied means of abortion. Roots or leaves cooked in lemon juice and lime water are used. The reason is not to have children, for in doing so they would rip their perineum, which is considered to be the greatest dishonor." (Free translation by Mr. Thomas Maretzki)

(See also *Toradja.*)

CHACO

(Mbayá, Abipón, Mocoví, Toba, Cocolot, Aguilot, Pilagá, Payaguá, Guachi, Mahoma; Mascoi, Kaskihá, Sapukí and Sanapá, Angaité, Lengua, and some other Mascoians; Lule, Vilela; Malbalá, Matará; Mataco, Agoyá, Taini, and Teuta, Ojota and Taño, Palomo, Hueshuos and Pesatupe, Choroti, Ashluslay, Lengua-Enimagá and the so-called Cochaboth family, Máca; Tapieté; some tribes of the Arawakan family; Guarañoca, Moro, Chamacoco, Tsirakua, Poturero; some unidentified tribes on the Upper Paraguay)

HDBK

"The rapid decline of so many Chaco tribes has often been explained by the deeply rooted practice of infanticide so general throughout the Chaco. The vehement accusations of infanticide made by early missionaries have, in fact, been borne out by modern evidence. When an unmarried Mataco, Choroti or Toba girl is pregnant, she commits abortion or kills her baby without the slightest hesitation. The Mbayá women did the same in order to postpone becoming mothers as long as possible. It is reported that even married Mataco women provoke miscarriage at their first pregnancy to facilitate the delivery of the next child. Many legends circulating in the Chaco extol marvelous drugs used by the native women to cause abortion. Actually, the method is purely mechanical: in the third or fourth month of pregnancy a friend presses the woman's abdomen with her thumbs or fists or beats it until the foetus is dead. A deserted woman always kills her newborn offspring. . . .

"Many theories attempt to explain the widespread practice of infanticide in the Chaco. One holds that the seminomadism of these Indians makes many children an excessive burden for the woman, who has to carry and care for them. Moreover, in several tribes where the nursing woman abstains from sexual intercourse with her husband, and the children are suckled 3 or even 4 years, she often prefers to kill her child rather than be deserted. (Abipón) The Jesuit Baucke (1870, p. 247) states that the Moví killed their newborn babies when there was the slightest suspicion of illegitimacy, when they had too many children, when they were on a journey, or when there was scarcity of food." (1:319–20)

CHAGGA

DUNDAS, CHARLES. *Kilima-Njaro and its People.* London, 1924.
GUTMANN, BRUNO. "Die Frau bei den Wadschagga," *Globus,* 92:1–4, 1907.
RAUM, O. F. *Chaga Childhood, A Description of Indigenous Education in an East African Tribe.* Oxford, 1940.

Premarital contraceptive practices include intrafemoral coitus, coitus interruptus and complete coitus, but with a rag inserted in the vagina. (Raum, pp. 67–68) Coitus interruptus is also practiced by (pagan) Chagga husbands while the wife is lactating. (Raum, p. 88) "It is the greatest shame when a woman who is still nursing a two-year-old boy becomes again pregnant; hence abortion occurs not only before marriage but also, one has to admit, quite as frequently in marital relations." (Gutmann, p. 3) Illegitimate and adulterous pregnancies are terminated by abortion, if it is possible to do it in secret. When the pregnancy is known, the unborn child's guardian prevents the abortion. The father will curse anyone who causes the betrothed girl to miscarry, as his title to an indemnity disappears if she dies. Chagga women also abort if they get pregnant while still nursing. If the attempt fails, they sometimes commit suicide if they become pregnant within three years from the date of their last delivery, because they are sensitive, through training, to the rule which prohibits coitus for three years after childbirth, and fear the severe criticism of their companions. They also abort if they conceive within two months after the death of a child, or else if they conceive after their daughter has married. (Raum, pp. 87–88) If a woman wishes to keep on having babies, she uses an amulet to delay her daughter's puberty, which would make the girl eligible for marriage. (Raum, p. 68) If a woman is pregnant and yet menstruates, or if her husband has a voluptuous dream, he demands that she abort the foetus, because pregnancy requires the suspension of the sexual aspects of marriage. (Raum, p. 88) If a lactating woman gets pregnant, she has to abort, so as not to interrupt the lactation, since only a child's own mother should nurse it. (Dundas, p. 21) If premarital contraception fails, the pregnant girl's mother will ask her to abort, because her daughter's pregnancy shames her too. Abortion is procured either by a violent massage of the abdomen, requiring expert skill, or else by inserting the midrib of a leaf into the uterus. The girl can also abort without assistance, by drinking the juices of any of some thirty herbs. C. Ittameier believes that neither of these herbs is a genuine, specific abortifacient, but simply something which produces a general poisoning of the system. This herb-knowledge is general, and is passed on from mother to daughter. (Raum, pp. 67–68)

CHEROKEE

CURRIER, A. F. "A Study Relative to the Functions of the Reproductive Apparatus in American Indian Women," *Transactions of the American Gynecological Society,* 16:264–294, 1891.

"Criminal abortion is an occasional occurrence among the Cherokees." (p. 279)

MOONEY, JAMES, AND OLBRECHTS, F. M. *The Swimmer Manuscript: Cherokee Sacred Formulas and Medical Prescriptions.* Bureau of American Ethnology, Bulletin 99, Washington, D. C., 1932.

"Abortus is totally unknown; even my best informant (a man of 56, prominent medicine man, holding a leading position in the tribal organization, twice married, high school graduate), had never heard of it, and I had a good deal of difficulty in making him understand what I meant. He was horrified at the idea, and I am afraid his esteem for the white people and the ways of some of them was not improved, when he finally grasped the idea.

"It does not seem to have dawned on them that the foetus can be tampered with at all, and to do so, W. thought, would be outright murder. As he put it: 'You might as well cut a 5-year-old child's head off.' " (p. 117)

CHEYENNE

WGS

"They were driven to abortion by their mode of living. 'It has long been a custom that a woman should not have a second child until her first is ten years old.' " (p. 315) (Cf. Grinnell, G. C., "Cheyenne Woman Customs," *American Anthropologist,* n. s. 4:13, 1902 *)

HOEBEL, E. A. "Associations and the State in the Plains," *American Anthropologist,* n. s., 38:433–48, 1936.

"Calf Woman brought out a crucial case which tests the position of the soldier police in the murder situation. An aborted foetus was found in the vicinity of the Cheyenne camp. The discovery was made known to the chiefs. The presumption was entertained that the foetus was that of a Cheyenne. Yet nothing was known about it. The soldier chiefs were consulted; by them a plan of investigation was produced. The two head chiefs of a society convened their group and the society announcer was sent out to broadcast the order of the soldiers for all women to assemble in public. When it was ascertained that all were at hand, the women were ordered to expose their breasts for inspection. Each was then scrutinized by the soldier chiefs to note lactation enlargements of the breasts as a sign of recent pregnancy. One girl showed symptoms and was charged with the crime, judged guilty, and banished from the tribe until after the arrows had been renewed. Calf Woman claims to have been present, but to have escaped the inquisition because she was too young to have been pregnant. This would place the event in the 1860's.

* A check of Grinnell's text shows that abortion is *not* mentioned on the page cited by WGS.

"Three salient points are to be noted here. First, that the unborn child had tribal status and insofar a legal personality. Abortion, too, was murder which tainted the tribal medicine. Second, this was a situation wholly criminal, for the violence had been done within the most intimate family unit possible. Blood feud was precluded. Third, the murder was a secret crime demanding detection of the criminal. The technique was ingeniously invented to meet the situation.

"Clearly, the military associations were well along towards establishment as a civil power." (p. 436)

(Cf. for a briefer version Llewellyn, K. N., and Hoebel, E. A., *The Cheyenne Way,* Norman, Oklahoma, 1941, p. 119)

CHICHICASTENANGO

BUNZEL, RUTH. *Chichicastenango.* American Ethnological Society Publications, 22, Locust Valley, New York, 1952.

"He also told me that they knew of no abortifacients, but seemed somewhat less sure of that, suggesting that although men knew nothing of this, it was barely possible that women might." (p. 99)

CHIMARIKO

DRIVER, H. E. *Culture Element Distributions: X, Northwest California.* Anthropological Records, 1, #6, Berkeley, 1939.

"Husband would kill wife if he knew she had attempted abortion." (p. 407) [Abortion denied, p. 350]

CHINOOK

MOSES, I. "On the Medical Topography of Astoria, Oregon," *American Journal of the Medical Sciences,* n. s. 29:32–46, 1855.

"Abortion is common, and not infrequently brought about intentionally." (p. 39)

BANCROFT, H. H. *The Native Races of the Pacific States.* London, 1875.

"Barrenness is common, the births of twins rare, and families do not usually exceed two children. . . . Although attaching no honor to chastity, the Chinook woman [of Oregon] feels something like shame at becoming the mother of an illegitimate child, and it is supposed to be partly from this instinct that infanticide and abortion are of frequent occurrence." (I:242)

GIBBS, GEORGE. *Tribes of Western Washington and Northwestern Oregon.* U.S. Geographical and Geological Survey, Washington, D. C., 1877.

"Cohabitation of unmarried females among their own peoples brings no disgrace if unaccompanied by childbirth, which they take care to prevent. This commences at a very early age, perhaps ten or twelve years. The practice of abortion is to be considered in this connection. This is almost universal, and is produced both by violence and by medicines. Certain plants are known to them which effect it, and it is generally believed by the whites, that they know of others which will produce sterility at will." (I:199) (Columbia and Kowlitz River groups)

PB

"In the Oregon area the average number of children per woman was two. It is not improbable that natural and artificial abortions are responsible for this seeming sterility. According to Hunter, in some North American native tribes some families only have three to four children, while the rest are aborted." (2:517)

(See also *Nesqually.*)

CHIPPEWA (Ojibwa)

PB

"Some North American Indian tribes abominate artificial abortion, e.g. the Ojibwa." (2:517) [The abhorrence of abortion indicates at least a knowledge of this practice and probably also its occasional occurrence. G. D.]

"Among the Winnepeg [Chippewa?], for example, in the year of 1842 a woman had on the average only one child. It is not improbable that natural and artificial abortion are responsible for this seeming sterility." (2:517)

STONE, ERIC. *Medicine among the American Indians,* New York, 1932.

The Chippewa abortifacient was a decoction of Seneca snakeroot, polygala senega. (p. 77)

HILGER, M. L. *Chippewa Child Life and Its Cultural Background.* Bureau of American Ethnology, Bulletin 146, Washington, 1951.

"' . . . I had an aunt who knew her baby was 2 or 3 months along when she lost it. (She lost it because she carried too heavy a load of wood on her back.) You could tell that it was beginning to form. They cleaned it just like a child that is born and wrapped it. They gave a feast just like for a dead person and buried it in the same way. They believe that a child is human when it is conceived.' " (p. 5)

"*Abortions.* Both induced and spontaneous abortions occurred among the Chippewa. Induced abortions, however, were not looked upon with favor on any reservation and were, therefore, of rare occurrence. Judging from the number of children born to older informants, one is led to believe that among them there were few abortions, but a rather high rate of infant mortality. One informant's story is typical of those told by many of the older women: 'I had six children, all of whom are dead: One died as a mere baby; two were 1 week old; one was 3 years old; tuberculosis took one boy at 19, and my last girl at 21.'

"Several of the oldest informants had heard, when younger, of women who had aborted children voluntarily; these instances, however, were spoken of in whispers. Most informants had never been acquainted with such a woman. 'No, I never knew any woman who did that. An Indian doesn't like to do that. My grandmother said that years ago they suspected a woman of having done that but couldn't prove it.' 'Mothers never induced abortions in old times; they took good care so that their babies would be born right.' 'Indians are proud to be able to conceive and do not think much of abortions.'

"Abortions, however, did occur in the olden days, and they occur today.

" 'In old days, I heard of one woman that was not married, but that had babies; and she caused abortions. They said she used to go where there was a fallen tree and hang over that, and so cause the abortion. But after she was married, every baby died just as it was born. That was long ago. I knew of her; but I was not acquainted with her.'

" 'I know that there is medicine that women take and I know of some women way back that did that, but I don't think that is right. Sometimes the woman never gets over it, and sometimes it kills her. Some try to hurt themselves, too, and cause abortions in that way.'

"A very old informant knew of persons who had drunk decoctions to induce abortions: 'I was brought up by my great-grandmother who had such knowledge. I never heard of abortions due to lying across a log or carrying a heavy weight. The only way I heard of was by means of tea. I don't think there was much of this since Indians liked children too well.' 'I do not know of any full-bloods on the reservation today who cause abortions; but some of the others do that.' 'I know that abortions are being committed on the reservation today, for I know several persons myself who did it. They drink Indian medicine which is made by steeping some roots or herbs; that is all they have to do. Those who know what to use do not tell.' One informant had aborted seven times 'because I'm not rightly married to my man and I don't want to have his kids around. I have enough to do to take care of two—the ones my right husband does not take care of. Some woman here in the village gives me tea to drink. It works every time.' On the same reservation two informants told of four old women who were dispensing decoctions to expectant mothers. A woman 26 years of age—a mother of four small children—said she had been told repeatedly by older women 'to get medicine from Old Lady So-and-So the next time a kid was on the way.' A 30-year-old mother of 7 children had been offered information regarding artificial limitation by a white woman on one of the reservations, and added, 'If I don't want any more children, I'll go to Old Lady So-and-So and get some drink to get rid of the baby; I don't need her, that white woman, to advise me.' Informants noted that induced abortions, in old days, as well as today, were performed either because husbands were mean to their wives and did not support them, or because some women did not like children. Although decoctions were the ordinary means used, women also induced abortions by lifting or straining themselves or by jumping off high places.

"In old times the fetus of an induced abortion was buried either under the floor of the wigwam in which the mother lived or under the roots of the tree from which roots had been taken for making the potion that caused the abortion, or anywhere under the ground. It was never buried with funeral rites. Spontaneous abortions were buried in the same manner as adults." (pp. 10–11)

"Although methods for induced abortions were known, they were seldom resorted to; they were viewed with great disfavor. Old informants today speak of them in whispers. An induced aborted fetus was not given burial rites; a spontaneously aborted one was given burial the same as an adult person. When a spontaneous abortion was feared, the mother submitted to fumigation as a preventive." (p. 163)

CHONTAL

PESCHEL, O. *Geschte des Zeitalters der Entdeckungen.* 1877.

[Due to Spanish oppression] "All Indians agreed to avoid all contact with their women, to use all means to prevent births and to abort any possible pregnancy." (pp. 431–432)

(For similar data see *Arawak, Haiti, Marianas.*)

CHOROTI

ROSEN, COUNT ERIC VON. *Ethnographical Research Work during the Swedish Chaco-Cordillera Expedition.* Stockholm, 1924.

KARSTEN, RAPHAEL. "Indian Tribes of the Argentine and Bolivian Chaco," *Societas Scientiarum Fennica, Commentiationes Humanarum Litterarum,* Vol. 4, No. 1, pp. 1–236, 1932.

"Single girls abort. (Rosen, pp. 159–160) The woman beats her abdomen and then presses out the foetus with her thumbs. She aborts either alone or with the aid of an old woman, in the third or fourth month of pregnancy. There is some pain, but the abortion does not seriously affect her health. No drugs are used. There is no moral opposition to abortion and infanticide, which are strictly private family matters. They have no more remorse over feticide than over a tooth extraction. 'Custom is very strict on this point, not only among the Chaco tribes but among all South American Indians.' (Karsten, p. 79) The abortion of a premaritally conceived foetus, which was licentiously conceived, is approved by social morality." (Karsten, p. 52)

CHUKCHEE

BOGORAZ-TAN, V. G. [Waldemar Bogoras]. *The Chukchee: Material Culture (Part 1), Religion (Part 2), Social Organization (Part 3). Memoirs of the American Museum of Natural History,* Vol. 11. Leiden and New York, 1904–1907.

The Kamchadal [Chukchee?] are decreasing in numbers, despite a lack of drop in the birth rate. Taking three women as examples:

A.	had 5	live	2 dead	and 5	aborted children			
B.	"	7 "	3 "	" 3	"	"		
C.	"	6 "	2 "	" 2	"	"	(Bogoras, p. 35) *	

Among the Chukchee infanticide is frequent. (Bogoras)

COMANCHE

HOEBEL, E. A. *The Political Organization and Law-ways of the Comanche Indians,* American Anthropological Association, Memoir 54, Menasha, Wisconsin, 1940.

"Premarital sex relations were common enough, and abortion was not unusual, but in case of childbirth it is asserted that the father married the mother willingly." (p. 107)

CONGO (in general)

JOHNSTON, H. H. *George Grenfell and the Congo,* Vol. II, London, 1908.

"Of *Birth* customs there are not many notes in the diaries or collections of missionaries which form the staple of this book. From other sources of information it is obvious that the practice of provoking abortion is a very common one throughout Congoland (though ignored, for example, by the Ba-yaka), but most of all in the north and centre. This is brought about at the third or at the fifth month by drinking very hot water, by the use of mechanical means of injuring the foetus, or by swallowing certain drugs known to the medicine-men and to the old women." (p. 671)

COOTCH (India)

PB

"Macmurdo found the women to be very dissolute and abortion a general practice. A mother boasted of having aborted five times." (2:514, quoting Macmurdo, in Ritter, *Erdkunde,* 6:1054)

CORA

(See *Southwest U. S. Indians.*)

CREEK

FOREMAN, GRANT. *The Five Civilized Tribes.* Norman, 1934.

[The text is obscure and may just conceivably refer to infanticide.] There was a nineteenth-century Creek law stating that it

* Other passages suggest that Bogoras may refer here to miscarriages only. G. D.

was unlawful for a woman to use medicine calculated to "cause infanticide." The penalty was fifty lashes. (p. 214)

CROW

VOGET, FRED. *Field Notes.* MS, HRAF.

Yellow-Woman did not know of any infanticide among the Crow—just abortion.

(See also *Assiniboine.*)

CUNA

NORDENSKIÖLD, ERLAND. *An Historical and Ethnological Survey of the Cuna Indians.* Comparative Ethnographical Studies, Vol. 10, Göteborg, Sweden, 1938.

A widow pregnant with a nonposthumous child takes abortifacient medicine. If a woman is pregnant by an alien—for example by a Negro—she is forced to abort. In the eighteenth century the children of French fathers were allowed to live although the Cuna killed the Frenchmen themselves. (p. 33)

DAHOMEIANS

HAZOUMÉ, PAUL. "Le Pact du Sang au Dahomey," *Travaux et Mémoires de l'Institut d'Ethnologie,* 25, Paris, 1937.

HERSKOVITS, M. J. *Dahomey: An Ancient West African Kingdom.* New York, 1938, Vol. I.

Contraception is not practiced. Abortion (xodide) occurs and is procured in the following manner: When the woman is one or two months pregnant, the juice of limes (kelekele), into which a piece of akămŭ, a substance like yellowish stone, has been put, is brought to the boiling point, at which time this "stone" dissolves and makes the boiling juice foamy. The usual quantity is one cup of lime juice made with a "stone" as large as a lime. The woman takes one drink daily, for two or three days—or even more frequently, if she is greatly distraught. This will start her menstruating again. After three months of pregnancy the abortifacient is no longer effective. The woman may try this preparation two or three times, and when it produces no results, she gives up. Abortifacients are taken in secret by girls, and by women who have committed adultery while their husbands were absent. These precautions against detection are seldom successful, however, since someone always reveals the secret to the husband.

A woman's face is said to change after she is one month pregnant, and the old women notice this. If, despite this change in the woman's appearance, no signs of advanced pregnancy become evident, they assume that the woman drank lime juice. "People always find out." This drink is also taken secretly by women who, though lactating, wish their husband to cohabit with them. This happens more frequently nowadays, because husbands are at present less willing to wait for the end of the period during which cohabitation is taboo. (Herskovits, pp. 268–69) If a gestating woman is ill, they "try" the foetus, and, if it is found guilty, it is aborted, in order to cure the woman. If, after labor and delivery, the woman is in trouble, everyone takes care of her only, neglecting the infant and cursing it for having caused trouble to its mother. (Hazoumé, pp. 142–43)

DAYAK (Northern Borneo)

ROTH, H. L. *The Natives of Sarawak and British North Borneo.* New York, 1896, Vol. I.

"Among the Dyaks wilful miscarriage is never resorted to under any circumstances. (Low, Brooke–MS, p. 309)" (p. 101)

DAYAK (Southeast Borneo)

GRABOWSKY, F. "Gebräuche der Dajaken Südost-Borneos bei der Geburt," *Globus* 72:269–273, 1897.

"The Dayak woman is reluctant to bear twins. If the abdomen of a pregnant woman is unusually large—so that there is a possibility that there may be twins—this in the opinion of the Dayaks is due to the fact that snakes, monkeys, leguane, etc., enter the belly of the pregnant woman. One therefore seeks to abort the fetus (*kelus*) which has something beside it; *ngan-doang* or *mangan-doang*. Various means are used for aborting the fetus. For example one eats the lemon-like fruits of the *kabuau*-tree mixed with burnt lime and gunpowder, or the roots and fruits of the *kamunah*-tree, etc." (p. 270)

D'ENTRECASTEAUX ARCHIPELAGO

JENNESS, D., AND BALLANTYNE, A. *The Northern D'Entrecasteaux.* Oxford, 1920.

"Most women desire to have two or three children. Abortion is practised, though it is hard to discover to what extent. They use a mixture called *kobu* for this purpose, but we failed to learn the ingredients from which it is compounded. At Dobu the leaves of the purple convolvulus, which the Mud Bay natives use for burns, are crushed and mixed with water; the woman is given the potion to drink and in one case that we know of it certainly succeeded. Most of our knowledge on this subject came from a few old men, who told us also that pressure of the hands upon the stomach walls was sometimes resorted to; however, they were not certain of this, they made haste to add, since the old women who practised it always kept their knowledge to themselves." (p. 106)

(See also *Dobu*.)

DJUKA (Bush Negroes of Suriname)

NH

"Abortion is also practiced." (p. 18, quoting Kahn, M. C., *Djuka, the Bush Negroes of Dutch Guiana,* New York, 1931)

DOBU

BROMILOW, W. E. "Some Manners and Customs of the Dobuans of S. E. Papua," [Report of the] *Australian Association for the Advancement of Science* (twelfth meeting, held at Brisbane), 12:470–85, 1909.

FORTUNE, REO. *Sorcerers of Dobu.* New York, 1932.

"It is a fact that intercourse between husband and wife is not thought fitting after childbirth until the infant is weaned. The wife and mother is kept apart from her husband for a month after she gives birth—in her own village of birth; the husband meanwhile stays in his own village. At the end of the month apart there is still supposed to be no intercourse before weaning. From this *tabu* comes the motive for such action as a man holding his infant over the fire to die from shock, also a motive for the use of abortifacients. I had the greatest difficulty in discovering that this *tabu* was observed. Those I questioned were so utterly prudish that they declined to discuss the matter. At last I got two or three ashamed admissions that the case was so.

"When I first broached the subject of abortifacients to Nela, with her husband's, Kopu's, connivance, an extremely prudish attitude was also shown. Nela, seated on top of a large flat rock outside my hut, literally bristled at the mention of the matter like a wildcat in defense of its young. Kopu's bringing her to hear such improper suggestions made the matter grave. Eventually it went through well, however. Once it was agreed to, Nela lost her initial horror." (Fortune, p. 246)

"It may be noted that in Dobu as in the Trobriands there is complete freedom for sex intercourse before marriage, and this freedom is used freely. Nevertheless, unmarried girls rarely bear bastards. In the community I know well enough to be certain of my facts, one child in about twelve in all was a bastard. This is partly related to the fact that a pregnant girl may become married before child-birth. Furthermore, means of securing abortion are effective, and are in general practiced both by the married and by the unmarried. For a girl to bear a child out of wedlock is a great disgrace, easily as great a disgrace as it was amongst ourselves in Mid-Victorian days or in old Puritan New England. It may be true that conception is less frequent where a girl has many different lovers and mixes them freely and frequently. Nevertheless, sometimes the unmarried girls of Dobu become pregnant; I was told of definite cases. In these cases abortion is resorted to. One of the abortifacients is the dried root of the *ketomatasekera* tree ('entering-eye-squirting' tree). From this tree I preserved dried specimens which were identified by Kew Botanical Gardens as *Excoercaria Agallocha.* This tree is called River Poison Tree in Southern Asia. It is feared by wood cutters in Malaysia, in Cambodia, and in Southern India because if the tree is cut the sap is liable to squirt into the eyes of the wood cutter and blind them permanently. Hence comes the botanical term *Excoecaria,* and also the Dobuan term 'entering-eye-squirting'-tree. The sap of *Excoecaria* is known to be a poison in Dobu. I was warned from snapping off a branch as I once made to do unwittingly, the warning coming from Alo. For use as an abortifacient a section of the root of this tree, about eight or nine inches long, is smoked over the fire until it is shrivelled to about a two-inch length. It is then chewed and eaten. It is said to be a good abortifacient without any conspicuous weakening effect upon the woman. For using it once, Kadi, Alo's daughter, was severely beaten about the body with a club by her mother's brother, Kopu. A man feels that he has a right to a male heir from the womb of his sister's daughter. His right is socially recognized, and may be corporally enforced.

"There are also other abortifacients. One root I was initiated into the secret of by Kopu and his wife, Nela; Nela chewed and swallowed its thick outer layer, chewed and threw away its inner core, under my inspection inside my hut in the presence of her mother and her husband. At the time of chewing she was full breasted. Twenty-four hours later I noticed that she was absolutely flat breasted, her breasts like small flat plates. I called Kopu aside and commented on this. 'That is the way of its evil—always,' he said carelessly. Nela was not pregnant at the time. She had had one child which died. In all the rest of her ten or twelve years of married life she had secured abortion for all her pregnancies—I could not discover their number as I was on very ticklish ground. She chewed the root in my presence, since it is the custom to do so in giving a secret herb. The giver chews to show that the gift is no treacherous poison. The gift was for reward in this case. Unfortunately, my specimens of this plant were not identified.

"These roots are used to procure abortion without the use of any magical incantation. As in the case of the *budobudo* poison (*Cerbera Manghas* or *Odallam*) they are believed to be naturally efficient. The idea of using magic with them is scorned." (Fortune, pp. 239–240)

Dobuan women abort by jumping off heights, by massage, by lifting heavy objects, by playing games so boisterously as to fall down heavily, and by other means. (Bromilow, p. 483) [Infanticide also exists in Dobu, and especially the sons of dead parents are so disposed of.]

(See also *d'Entrecasteaux Archipelago.*)

DOREH BAY (New Guinea)

VAN HASSELT, J. L. "Aenteekening aangaande de gewoonten der Papoeas in de Dorehbaai ten opzichte van zwangerschap en geboorte," *Tijdschrift voor Indische Taal-, Land-, en Volkenkunde,* 43:566–68, 1901.

"He does not have large broods. Six to eight children are, among the Papuans, a good sized family. If the women are too tired to bear further children, they abort the foetus. This happens, above all, in extramarital pregnancies, and is probably one of the reasons for the considerable paucity of the population. The abortion is procured by manipulations, such as pinching the belly and treading on it, which they call 'making the belly dead.' They also make use of internal means, made of a certain plant species called '*papier.*' " (p. 566)

DUSUN

STAAL, J. "The Dusuns of North Borneo (cont.)," *Anthropos,* 20:120–138, 929–51, 1925.
RUTTER, OWEN. *The Pagans of North Borneo.* London, 1929.

They abort only after a repetition of a bad dream. For example, if a woman dreams twice that she died in childbirth or that her babe was deformed—and happens to know also that her husband does not fulfill his duties—she consults a priestess, who will first pray over her. If, despite this, the bad dream recurs, the woman asks a midwife to abort her. The midwife will smear the woman's abdomen with oil, and will then rub it, seeking to expel the foetus. Such attempts become common knowledge. (Staal, p. 121) Pagan women practice abortion by means of a concoction made of the poisonous derris elliptica root. This practice is not prevalent. Papar women abort if they have unlucky dreams during their pregnancy. (Rutter, p. 73)

EDDYSTONE ISLAND

RIVERS, W. H. R. *Psychology and Ethnology.* London, 1926.

"It is quite certain that births before marriage were very rare, and two causes were given to account for this, abortion and a process resembling the other magico-religious rites of the island, called *egoro,* meaning 'barrenness,' which is believed to prevent conception. Abortion is called *junjui,* and may be produced by mechanical means, such as striking the abdomen with a stone, or by a process called *tambu njunjui.* In this rite a leaf called *meka* is heated and rubbed (*pua*) on the belly and four *tingi* leaves are held under the vulva, when, it is said, the child will come out. A girdle is put around the waist, consisting of a creeper of *boto na Vionona,* which has been lying across a path. The formula used when putting on the leaves is

> '*Manjui pania na kumburu pini, ai ke tinoni.*'
> 'Take away the child here, may it not become a man.' "
> (pp. 76–77)

EETAR ISLAND

PB

"The women use abortifacients, but only in great secrecy." (2:513)

EFATE (New Hebrides)

MACDONALD, REV. D. "Efate, New Hebrides," *Australian Association for the Advancement of Science, Report of the Fourth Meeting* (Hobart, Tasmania, 1892), Sidney, 1892, pp. 720–35.

Infanticide exists and abortion occurs frequently. Violence was applied to the child in the womb by the mother or by the matemauri, this latter accompanying the manipulations with the koro. Nakasu tabu, a plant, was sometimes eaten by the woman who just gave birth, to sterilize herself temporarily while bringing up her child. The reason for infanticide [and abortion?] is that they wish to avoid the need for self-denial, as well as expense and trouble. (p. 721)

PB

"Abortion is also common in the New Hebrides (Island of Efate) and is attempted partly by means of plants and partly by mechanical means. They have a special name for each of these two techniques. The plant used is not known; it is called among them simply "the plant of abortion" (plant of the Saibirien).

"The mechanical technique consists in the pressing and kneading of the body by midwives whereby the child is killed. A certain proportion of women die of this treatment." (2:527, quoting Jamieson, in *Australian Medical Journal,* 7:51, 1885)

EFIK (Old Calabar)

HEWAN, ARCHIBALD. "On Some Customs of the People of Old Calabar Relative to Pregnancy and Parturition," *Edinburgh Medical Journal,* 10:219–24, 1864.

"At the third month they administer medicines, to *prove,* as they say, the *value* of the conception. They regard three kinds of conceptions as disastrous: 1st, conception of twins; 2nd, conception of an embryo that will die before birth; and 3rd, conception of one that will die soon after birth; and so for the purpose of voiding these at as early a period as they think that the conception has fully taken place, they administer medicines.

"These medicines are administered by the mouth, *per anum,* and *per vaginam.* By the way of the mouth, and by enemata, first. If a bloody discharge from the vagina follows, it is assisted by an application direct to the *os uteri.* For this purpose they employ one of three herbs, one a euphorbia, another a leguminosa, and another an amomum. The steminal end of the leaf stalk of the euphorbia, with its exuding juices, is pushed up the vagina. On the same part of the leguminous one is placed a small quantity of guinea pepper, chewed into a mass with the saliva. This *guinea pepper* is a species of the amomums. In the course of a few days the abortion may take place. But it is not the abortion *pure and simple* that is desired; it is conditional, as I have already said. It is only to procure it in the case of one of three conceptions, either of which being, in their estimation, unnatural, they consider to have little or no hold upon the uterus. But it not unfrequently happens that the measures employed are too severe; serious constitutional disturbance and organic lesions take place, and death ensues." (pp. 222–23)

ENGANO

PB

"According to Modigliani, abortions are frequent because many girls who have become pregnant abort not from fear of punishment but in order to avoid the inconvenience and to become free again more rapidly." (2:513, quoting Modigliani, Elio, *L'Isola delle Donne,* Milan, 1894)

ESKIMO (Baffinland and Hudson Bay)

ALDRICH, C. R. *The Primitive Mind and Modern Civilization.* London, 1931.

"Dr. Franz Boas, writing of Eskimos of Baffinland and Hudson Bay, says: 'Cases of premature birth require particularly careful treatment. The event must be announced publicly, else dire results will follow. If a woman should conceal from the other people that she has had a premature birth, they might come near her, or even eat in her hut of the seals procured by her husband. The vapour arising from her would thus affect them and they would be avoided by the seals. The transgression would also be attached to the seal, which would take it down to Sedna. Sedna is the mother of the sea mammals. She lives under the sea and the seals are her cut-off fingers. So, when, in the words of an epileptic boy described by Jung, "a guilt is handed to" a seal, Sedna gets a sore finger.' " (p. 215)

ESKIMO (Copper)

(1) JENNESS, DIAMOND. "The Life of the Copper Eskimos," *Report of the Canadian Arctic Expedition, 1913–18,* Vol. XII, Pt. A. Ottawa, 1922.

(2) JENNESS, DIAMOND. "The Copper Eskimos," *The Geographical Review,* 4:81–99, 1917.

Abortion is unknown. One native quarrelled with his pregnant wife, threw her on the snow and rolled his foot on her stomach. (1, pp. 166–67) Abortion is unknown. (2, p. 89) [Infanticide is known. They give away or expose one of two twins, but the exposed twin is sometimes rescued.]

ESKIMO (Hudson Bay?)

ELLIS, HENRY, in MAVOR, W. *Voyages.* London, 1796.

". . . For this reason, they cruelly oblige their women to procure abortions, when they consider their family is likely to be numerous." (p. 45)

ESKIMO (of Koyukuk)

MARSHALL, ROBERT. *Arctic Village.* New York, 1933.

"Although there is a high proportion of sterility among Eskimo women, some of them are exceedingly fertile. Several methods to avoid the responsibility of children have been tried. One of these is abortion. However, on the frontier with its crude surgical equipment and training, this is a hazardous matter. One young Eskimo girl nearly lost her life in this manner about ten years ago, and she received permanent internal injuries. Her experience was taken so seriously that no abortions have since been attempted." (pp. 261–62)

ESKIMO (Polar)

GPM

"Though greatly desiring offspring, parents are sometimes forced by circumstances to destroy them, and women occasionally produce abortions by crude physical means." (p. 211)

ESKIMO (Smith Sound Inuit)

BESSELS, EMIL. "Einige Worte über die Inuit (Eskimo) des Smith Sundes, nebst Bemerkungen über Inuit Schädel," *Archiv für Anthropologie,* 8:107–122, 1875.

"However, children are not only murdered after their birth; there is also abortion. This is most strange, since infanticide is neither punished nor is it thought of as something unusual. Just as the pregnant girls in missionized Greenland use the *Kamiut* stick (a piece of wood used for stretching wet footwear) for this purpose, so Itanian women use either the stock of the whip or some other object and pound or press with it their abdomen, repeating this procedure several times a day. Another technique of aborting the fetus consists in the perforation of the fetal membranes; an operation which rather amazed us. The thinned down rib of a walrus or seal is ground at one of its ends like the blade of a knife, while its opposite end is blunt and rounded. The sharp end has a cylindrical sheath of sewed tanned sealskin. This sheath is open at both ends and its length corresponds to that of the cutting portion of the aforementioned piece of bone. A fifteen to eighteen inch long thread, made out of reindeer sinew, is attached to each end of this sheath. When this probe is introduced into the vagina, its cutting portion is covered by this leather sheath. When the woman, who performs the operation on herself, believes that she has penetrated deeply enough into her vagina, she gently tugs at the thread attached to the lower end of the sheath. This, naturally, exposes the knife edge, whereupon she gives the probe a half twist, while simultaneously thrusting it upward and inward. After the fetal membranes are ruptured, the instrument is once more withdrawn, but not before one tugs at the upper thread of the sheath, in order to cover the sharp portion of the probe so as to prevent injury to the vagina. I was told that this operation is performed by the pregnant woman herself." (p. 112)

ESPIRITU SANTO (New Hebrides)

BAKER, J. R. "Depopulation in Espiritu Santo, New Hebrides," *Journal of the Royal Anthropological Institute,* 58:279–303, 1928.

"*Apathy Due to Loss of Old Customs.* Rivers * considers this

* Rivers, W.H.R., ed., *Essays on the Depopulation of Melanesia.* Cambridge, England, 1922.

the most important cause of depopulation in Melanesia. He supposed that owing to the apathy due to loss of old customs, the natives' resistance to disease, at all times small owing to their suggestibility, was even further decreased; and that having lost interest in life and the incentive to have large families, they extended the practice of abortion, which formerly they had used mainly to prevent illegitimacy." (p. 284)

"*Ill-Treatment of Women.* It is true that women do nearly all of the carrying of food from gardens to villages, even when pregnant; but I do not think that abortion is often thus caused." (p. 288)

"*Abortion.* Here, without a doubt, we have one of the most important causes of depopulation in both heathen and Christian villages. It is obtained by drinking infusions of the leaves of Dracaena and other plants, usually on instructions from the husbands.* As a result, the number of children per 100 adult females is only 128 in Sakau and 126 in the parts of the rest of Santo studied, although more than 93 percent of those of the rest of Santo are, or have been married.† Why should the people of Santo want to have smaller families than formerly? Is it that the loss of old customs has caused them, as Rivers supposed, to consider it useless to bring up children to live as dull lives as they?" (p. 288)

". . . I think their reason must be the appalling number of deaths caused by diseases brought in by Europeans. The people think it useless to produce children, who will only die in epidemics. In this sense there is apathy. The state of affairs was very clearly put to me by a native woman on another Island. When I questioned her about the recent deaths in her village, she indicated all the children who were sitting around about her, and said: 'Close up all piccaninny here 'e die finish' (all these children will die soon). This feeling, that it is useless to produce children who will only die, is, I believe, the cause of the small families in Santo. Probably it is on account of the medical aid given by missionaries that the people in Christian villages do not feel quite so hopeless, and therefore, by procuring abortion less often, have rather larger families." (pp. 291–92)

* Information from Mr. J. T. Thomas and Mr. W. Anderson.
† See Table 1, Note 2.

HARRISON, TOM. *Savage Civilization.* New York, 1937.

"Our women know no method of procuring abortion except by mechanical means. They are ignorant of the concoctions for this and for the preventing of any growth of child within them, which are said to be known in some of the isles to the north. We trace descent through the father to son, and the need of the one for the other in death would make it go ill with a woman who killed unborn children, unless it was the wish of the man." (pp. 42–43)

FIJI

WILKES, CHARLES. *Narrative of the United States Exploring Expedition During the Years 1838, 1839, 1840, 1841, 1842.* New York, 1856.

"Midwifery is a distinct profession, exercised by women in all the towns, and they are said to be very skilful, performing operations which are among us considered as surgical. Abortion is prevalent, and nearly half of those conceived are supposed to be destroyed in this manner, usually by the command of the father, at whose instance the wife takes herbs which are known to produce this effect. If this does not succeed, the accoucheur is employed to strangle the child, and bring it forth dead." (3:93)

WILLIAMS, T., AND CALVERT, J. *Fiji and the Fijians.* New York, 1859.

"Murder, in various forms, is the result of this vicious system. [of polygyny.] Great numbers produce sterility by drinking medicated waters prepared for that purpose, and many more kill their unborn children by mechanical means; while, in the case of others, death follows immediately on birth. Scarcity and war, when they prevail, are often urged in excuse for these crimes. Perhaps the parents belong to two tribes which are at enmity, in which case the mother, rather than multiply the foes of her tribe, will destroy her progeny. In 1850, the Mbua Chief took a principal wife to his home, whereupon another of his wives, in a fit of jealousy, disappointed him by destroying the child which he expected shortly to be born. Nandi, one of whose wives was pregnant, left her to dwell with a second. The forsaken one awaited his return some months, and at last the child disappeared. This practice seemed to be universal on Vanua Levu—quite a matter of course—so that few women could be found who had not, in some way, been murderers. The extent of infanticide in some parts of this island reaches nearer to two-thirds than half. Abominable as it is, it is reduced to a system, the professors of which are to be found in every village. I know of no case after the child is one or two days old; and all destroyed after birth are females, because they are useless in war, or, as some say, because they give so much trouble. But that the former is the prevailing opinion appears from such questions as these, put to persons who may plead for the little ones' life: 'Why live? Will she wield a club? Will she poise a spear?' When a professed murderess is not near, the mother does not hesitate to kill her own babe. With two fingers she compresses its nostrils, while, with the thumb, she keeps the jaw up close; a few convulsive struggles follow, and the cruel hand of the mother is unloosed, to dig a grave close by where she lies, in which the dead child is placed. Unlike the infanticide of the Hindus, that of Fiji is done from motives in which there is no admixture of anything like religious feeling or fear, but merely whim, expediency, anger, or indolence." (p. 142)

PB

"The native midwives assured Blyth that accidental miscarriage is completely unknown among the women of Fiji and when premature delivery occurs it is certain to have been intentional. Various motives are responsible for obtaining an abortion. The women of Fiji have a pronounced dislike of large families and feel humiliated when they get pregnant too often, because they believe that a woman who brings into the world a large number of children is ridiculed by the community. They therefore seek to reduce the number of births by means of abortion or else seek to avoid thereby that a new pregnancy should follow too rapidly on the heels of a previous one. Frequently they also produce deliberate abortions in order to annoy their husbands, if they are jealous of them because they believe them to be unfaithful. They also abort in cases of illegitimate pregnancy, in order not to have to suffer shame." (2:512, quoting Blyth, David, "Notes on the Traditions and Customs of the Natives of Fiji in Relation to Conception, Pregnancy, and Parturition," *Glasgow Medical Journal* 28: 176–86, 1887).

"Blyth learned from native midwives that on the Fiji Islands the sole method of abortion consists of partaking of vegetable concoctions which are used when life is first perceived. Five plants are used. Two Malvaceae (Kalakalauaisoni: Hibiscus diversifolius and Wakiwaki: Hibiscus abelmoschus), one Tiliacee (Siti: Grewia prunifolia), one Convolvulacee (Wa Wuti: Pharbitis insularis), one Liliacee (Ti Kula: Dracaena ferrea). One used the juice and the leaves and, of the third and fifth group, also the surface layer of the stem. This latter is deemed to be the more effective and is used when the others fail." (2:529, quoting Blyth, David, *op. cit.*)

DANKS, BENJAMIN. "Marriage Customs of the New Britain Group," *Journal of the Anthropological Institute,* 18:281–94, 1889.

"In a note from the Rev. L. Fison, M.A., he tells me that in Fiji the same thing (abortion by use of a pointed stick) existed in the former heathen days, only that two sticks were used. Some say that there is an herb which is used for the same purpose. This custom was also in vogue in Fiji." (p. 291)

THOMSON, SIR BASIL. *The Fijians.* London, 1908.

"Procuring abortion in the old days appears to have been limited to women of high rank who, for reasons of policy, were not allowed to have children. When it is remembered that every lady of rank who married into another tribe might bear children, who as *vasu* would have a lien upon every kind of property belonging to their mother's tribe, it is not surprising that means were taken to limit the number of her offspring. In a polygamous society every wife has an interest in preventing her rivals from bearing sons who might dispute the succession with her own offspring, and the chief wife wielded an authority over the inferior wives that enabled her to carry her wishes into effect. Waterhouse mentions that professional abortionists were sent in the train of every lady who married out of the tribe, with instructions to procure the miscarriage of her mistress. The Rev. Walter Fawsy, who visited Mbau in 1847, declares on the authority of all the resident missionaries, that the practice was reduced to a system. But these motives did not operate with the common people who were seldom in a position to pay the practitioners a fee, although, no doubt, dislike of the long abstinence enjoined during suckling and disinclination to bear children to a man they hated were motives strong enough to induce a few women in every class to rid themselves of their children. The abortionist craft was then in the hands of a few professional experts, who made a good thing of their trade and refused to trust their secrets to any but their daughters who were to succeed to their practice.

"All this is now changed. Both the motive and the means have spread far and wide. The secrets of the trade are common property, and the act is unskilfully attempted by the mother or older female relation of every pregnant woman who cares to take the risk of the operation. By a strange irony the rapid increase in the practice of abortion in recent years is to some extent the doing of the missionaries. With the decay of the custom of separating the sexes at night intrigues with unmarried women increased, and to fight this growing vice the missionaries visited the breach of the Seventh Commandment with expulsion from Church membership. The girls have come to prize highly their *thurusinga* (lit. entrance into daylight), as communion with the Wesleyan Church is called, and, when they find themselves pregnant the dread of exposure, expulsion, and disgrace, drive them to the usual expedients for destroying the evidence of their frailty. Although by suppressing the usual feasts and presentations in the case of illegitimate births, and by refusing the sacrament of baptism to illegitimate children, the Mission authorities may have given some impetus to the practice of abortion, there can be little doubt that an illegitimate birth brought even more shame upon families of every rank but the lowest in heathen times than at present—unless the putative father was of high rank. There still exists enough of the stern customary law that punished incontinency to cast a social stigma upon the mother of an illegitimate child; there still survives enough of the ethical code that refused to regard the procurement of abortion as a criminal act to warrant women in choosing what is to them the lesser of two evils. Moreover the tendency to the practice of abortion is cumulative. A girl induces miscarriage to escape the shame of her first pregnancy; to the natural tendency of women who have once miscarried to repeat the accident is added the temptation to undergo for the second time an operation that has already been successful. If Fijian women dislike the burden of tending children born in wedlock, much more do they shrink from maternity coupled with the disgrace of illegitimacy. The natives themselves quote instances of a number of minor motives such as the dread of the pains of childbirth, and the determination of the wife not to bear children to a man she hates or quarrels with—motives which have influenced women of every race from the beginning of time and which will continue to do so until the end.

"A high birth-rate is not incompatible with the extensive practice of abortion. Where the proportion of stillbirths is also high, and the women are so careful to conceal their practices . . . it is highly probable that they conspire to represent to the native registrars as post-natal deaths, miscarriages that have been caused artificially. The natives of Vanualevu are reputed to be the most adept in procuring abortion, and the three provinces included in that island show an abnormal stillbirth-rate of 10 per cent of the total births, while their general birth-rate is the lowest in the colony. It must be remembered that, since procuring abortion is regarded as a criminal act, the practice is now concealed, not from any sense of shame but from fear of criminal prosecution. The practice is veiled with so much secrecy that very few prosecutions have taken place.

"The methods of the Fijians are, as in other countries, both toxic and mechanical. Certain herbs, called collectively *wai ni yàva* (medicines for causing barrenness), are taken with the intention of preventing conception, but the belief in their efficacy is not general. Some midwives, however, say that when taken by nursing mothers with a view of preventing a second conception, they result in the death of the child. Another midwife—one of the class to which the professional abortionists belong—assured us that miscarriage resulted more frequently from distress of mind at the discovery of pregnancy than from the drugs that were taken. The abortives vary with the district and the practitioner, but they are all the leaves, bark, or root of herbs chewed or grated, and infused in water, and there is no reason why some of them should not be as effective as the medicines employed for the purpose by civilized people, though the method of preparation is more crude, and the doses more nauseous and copious than the extracts known to modern pharmacy. The 'wise women' appear to know that drugs which irritate the bowel have an indirect effect upon the pelvic viscera. Andi Ama of Namata stated that old women caution young married women against drinking *wai vuso* (frothy drinks) meaning a certain class of native medicine made from the stems of climbing plants whose sap imparts a frothy or soapy quality to the infusion, which are taken under various pretexts, but generally as cathartics. . . .

"I do not think that many miscarriages are caused by the taking of infusions alone. . . . Nevertheless even though it be extremely difficult to procure abortion by administering herbs, as stated by one midwife, it is certain that every determined interference with the course of nature must be attended with danger.

"Foremost among mechanical means is the *sau,* which is a skewer made of *losilosi* wood, or a reed. It is used of course to pierce the membranes, and in unskillful hands it must be a death dealing weapon. . . . There are, however, well-attested cases of persons living who bear the mark of the *sau* on their heads. In 1893 there was a man living in Toveuni who bore the scar of such a wound on his right temple, and the fact that the right parietal bone would be the part wounded by an instrument used shortly before the commencement of labour in normal presentation gives a strong colour of truth to the story of Andi Qupiaua and other trustworthy natives who know the young man and the circumstances of his birth.

"The various methods of inducing miscarriage by violence such as one practiced by the Gilbert Islanders, who pound the abdomen of pregnant women with stones, or force the foetus downwards by winding a cord tightly about her body, are not resorted to by the Fijians, but the practice of *vakasikiua* (lit. bathing), a manual operation which midwives are in the habit of performing with the object of alleviating the ailment of pregnancy, do either by accident or design sometimes result in a radical cure of causing expulsion of the foetus. The patient is taken into the river or the sea, and squats waist-deep in the water with the 'wise woman,' who subjects her to a vaginal examination to enable her to ascertain the condition of the *os uteri,* and, through the digital diagnosis, to determine the particular herb to be used locally or internally. Some women assert that the examination under water is adopted for cleanliness only, but most seem to believe that there is virtue in the operation by itself without any subsequent herbal treatment. As there are many practitioners who devote themselves exclusively to this branch of practice, it is more than likely that it is often used as a pretext for an attempt to procure abortion, for a rough manipulation of the *os uteri* may excite uterine contraction, and so bring about expulsion of the foetus. Treatment by *vakasikiua* is used in every form of disease in the abdominal region to which women are subject, and the manipulation of the fundus and vagina is so rough that the patient cries out with the pain.

"*Bombo* (massage) is sometimes practiced upon pregnant women with the result, if not the intention, of producing miscarriage. A few years ago a notorious instance occurred at Rewa. A pregnant woman who suffered pain and discomfort, was received into the Colonial Hospital. After a week's detention the surgeon advised her to go home, and await the term of her gestation, since she was suffering from some functional derangement common to her condition. She fell into the hands of a noted amateur 'wise woman' who diagnosed her complaint as possession by a malignant spirit, and proceeded to exorcise it by the usual means of forcible expulsion by massage. The pinching and kneading began at the solid parts of the trunk, and when the evil spirit fled for refuge into the limbs, they were continued toward the extremities, and the apertures of the body, which are the natural avenues of escape for the afflicting spirit. But the only spirit which the masseuse succeeded in exorcising was the patient's own, for she died of the operation, and the facts were concealed from the authorities for some weeks. The magisterial inquiry did not elicit whether the object was abortion or merely the alleviation of pain.

"A census taken in 1893 of the families of twelve villages showed that out of 448 mothers of existing families 55 had been subject to abortion or miscarriage. If these villages were representative of the people at large, 12.7 per cent, rather more than one-eighth, of the child-bearing women of the Fijians have to contend with this adverse condition, and as has been said, the provinces that have abnormally low and decreasing birth-rates—Mathuata, Mbua, and Thakaundrove—are the very parts where the 'wise women' are noted for their skill as abortionists. These facts would almost suffice in themselves to account for the decrease of the race." (pp. 221–26)

SPENCER, D. M. *Disease, Religion and Society in the Fiji Islands.* American Ethnological Society, Monograph 2, New York, 1941.

FIJIAN PHARMACOLOGICAL THERAPY

Plant Drug Employed as Abortifacients		*Part of Plant Used and Method of Preparation and Use*	*Source*	*Remarks*
SCIENTIFIC NAME	FIJI NAME			
Cerbera manglias Linn.	rewa	Inner bark of root is soaked in cold water; drink liquid until desired results are obtained	Field notes	This turns foetus to liquid which is passed out as blood, according to native theory
Hibiscus (Abelmoschus) diversifolius	kalani soni	Juice of leaves used	Seeman [1]	
Hibiscus (Abelmoschus) Abelmoschus	waki waki	Juice of leaves used	" "	

1 Seemann, Berthold. *Flora Vitiensis.* London, 1865–73.

QUAIN, BUELL. *Fijian Village.* Chicago, 1948.

". . . Any stopping of the menstrual flow suggests disease; the cervix must be artificially opened. Thus many witless abortions are produced among young girls. But menstruation, which is called 'sickness of the month,' inaugurates a period of mild but constant worry. When it fails to appear, there is uncertainty as to the cause of failure: unless a woman has been cohabiting regularly with one man and therefore knows that she is pregnant, she believes that a disease which is peculiarly fatal to women has fallen upon her; she may travel long distances to some famous wise woman who will insert a twig in her cervix and draw forth the blood." * (p. 317)

FLATHEAD

TURNEY-HIGH, H. H. *The Flathead Indians of Montana.* American Anthropological Association, Memoir 48, 1937.

"Abortion was known and universally condemned. All the words meaning abortion contain the verbal root indicating murder. Informants say that abortion refers only to unmarried girls who feared their relatives, since until the introduction of white ideas no married woman would have sufficient motivation to do such a socially disapproved deed. Contraception in all its forms was unknown." (p. 84)

FORMOSA (Aborigines)

CAMPBELL, WILLIAM. *Formosa under the Dutch Described from Contemporary Records.* London [1836].

JOEST, W. "Beiträge sur Kenntniss der Eingebornen der Inseln Formosa und Ceram," *Verhandlungen der Berliner Gesellschraft für Anthropologie, Ethnographie und Urgeschichte,* 14:53–76, 1882.

WIEDFELDT, O. "Wirtschaftliche, rechtliche und soziale Grundtatsachen und Grundformen der Atayalen auf Formosa," *Mitteilungen der Deutschen Gesellschaft für Natur- und Völkerkunde Ostasiens,* 15 (Part C), 7–55, 1914.

PB

As regards the Atayal, the father has the right to have a child

* "This is not considered abortion unless they believe that pregnancy has been previously established. Abortion is in disrepute, but the disease warrants pity. One girl, who was very active sexually, resorted frequently to this treatment. Though her prestige suffered because of her indiscreet promiscuity, the village sympathized with her in her diseased condition. This practice could account for a period of sterility which might seem to follow first menstruation at Nakoroka."

killed. Infanticide occurs for eugenic reasons. There is no punishment for the killing of an as yet nameless—i.e., less than two- or three-year-old—child. (Wiedfeldt, p. 23) The prevailing sexual freedom troubles no one. The girl's father kills the bastard infant, despite the high value placed on children. (Wiedfeldt) [They also abandoned or killed baby girls as well as one of a pair of twins. Most tribes killed all bastards. (HRAF)] It is an ancient practice among the people of Chin hoan to abort all pregnancies until the woman is between thirty-four and thirty-seven years of age. The pregnant woman goes to the soothsayer who beats and massages her belly, to induce an abortion. (Joest, p. 62)

In ancient times the natives of Formosa aborted all pregnancies until they were thirty-five, thirty-six, or thirty-seven years of age. They called in a priestess, and when she arrived the pregnant woman lay down on a couch, or on the floor, prone on her back. She was then pushed and pinched and roughly handled, until she aborted. This caused more pain than would a normal childbirth. This type of abortion was not performed from lack of love for children, but for religious reasons. If a woman had a child before she had reached the socially defined age of childbearing, it was deemed to be a "great shame, great sin." Some women aborted fifteen or sixteen times. One particular woman allowed only her seventeenth embryo to mature. (Campbell-Candidius, pp. 19–20) [This practice appears to be obsolete, and some authorities even doubt its validity, though apparently not on particularly convincing grounds. One thing is certain, nowadays young mothers are commonly seen.]

"The belly of the pregnant woman is stepped upon in order to cause an abortion." (PB, 2:526)

FUTUNA

BURROWS, E. G. *Ethnology of Futuna.* B. P. Bishop Museum, Bulletin 138, 1936.

"Early missionaries said that abortion and infanticide were common. Native tradition bears this out; witness *Tamole's* statement that a restless baby, which would not stay on its back so that its head would become flat, might be designated for killing. Chevron (1, Vol. 15, p. 43) wrote in 1841: 'The infanticides which are committed in this country are endless. It is even no disgrace for a mother to take the life of her children. There are those who have killed as many as six infants; some crush them in their own bodies by pressing them with large stones; others strangle them as soon as they are born, and bury them alive in the sand. . . . For a mother to decide to commit such a barbarity, it is enough that the father of the child is not pleased with it or that her husband has abandoned her. In either of these cases, if she has not the fortitude to strangle the voice of nature, the women of the neighborhood assemble and together vote the death of the child, and take it upon themselves to execute the sentence even if the mother is not willing.' " (pp. 57–58)

GALELA (Gilolo)

PB

"The Galela make great use of abortifacients." (2:513)

"They often use abortifacients made of oil of Kalapa, the juice of lemons and various treeroots." (2:526, quoting Riedel, J. G. F., *De Sluik- en Kroesharige Rassen tusschen Selebes en Papœa,* s'Gravenhage, 1886)

GAUA (New Hebrides)

HARRISON, TOM. *Savage Civilization.* New York, 1937.

"The women of Gaua and Pentecost are expert in contraception, abortion and permanent sterilization, by several methods—tangled chemistry, mechanics and magic." (p. 362)

GILBERT ISLANDS

MEINICKE, C. E. *Die Inseln des Stillen Oceans,* Vol. II: *Polynesien und Mikronesien.* Leipzig, 1876.

FINSCH, OTTO. *Ethnologische Erfahrungen und Belegstücke aus der Südsee.* Wien, 1893.

At certain periods women practice abortion (Meinicke, p. 342). There is no infanticide, but abortion is practiced by women who have more than two children. The operation is performed by old women who crudely maltreat the abdomen. This seldom has evil consequences. Single girls also abort. Wood disputes this statement for Makin, and the accounts do require reliable confirmation. Illegitimacy is no dishonor. (Finsch, p. 31)

THOMSON, BASIL. *The Fijians.* London, 1908.

"[On Tamana Island] . . . about four or five children are considered enough, and any above that number are not allowed to come to maturity. All the women practise abortion because they are so prolific. If they did not they would have from ten to twenty children apiece. But neither medicine nor instruments are used. The common method is to pound the abdomen with a billet of wood, and this is not fatal to the mother. Now, however, the practise is being abandoned, because the missionaries have persuaded the people that it is dangerous." (p. 211)

"The Gilbert Islanders . . . pound the abdomen of pregnant women with stones, or force the foetus downward by winding a cord tightly about her body." (p. 224)

PB

"In the Gilbert Islands artificial abortion was very common, due to the infertility of the soil and the anxieties over food resulting therefrom." (2:512)

GILYAK

PILSUDSKI, BRONISLAW. "Schwangerschaft, Entbindung und Fehlegburt auf Sachalin," *Anthropos,* 5:756–774, 1910.

The Gilyak abort less frequently than the Ainu, because they have been less disturbed by foreign contacts. (p. 769)

GUAYCURU (in general)

PB

[Guaycuru women often abort their early pregnancies]. "However, if Guaycuru women become pregnant also after the age of 30, then they do raise their children. The probable cause of abortion among these people [Lengua, Guaycuru, Abipon] is thought to be the taboos on cohabitation with the husband during pregnancy and during the long period of lactation." (2:516)

(See also *Chaco, Caduveo, Mbaya.*)

GUAYCURU (Pampas, Brazil)

VON MARTIUS, C. F. P. *Beitrage zur Ethnographie und Sprachenkunde Amerikas zumal Brasiliens.* Leipzig, 1867.

". . . In their youth the women are in the habit of aborting by unnatural means the fruits of their womb.* . . . In order to

* Dobrizhoffer remarks that the women of all cavalry people give birth with great difficulty and explains this fact, not unconvincingly, by means of a malformation and hardening of the coccyx as a result of premature and incessant riding without clothes or saddle, which more often makes the horses rather than the riders sore.

support more easily the wear and tear of life on horseback, and in order not to be deserted by their husbands, only when they reach the approximate age of 25 years, do they exercise their maternal duties." (p. 231)

"Their great dependence on the husband forces them to be always compliant toward the men; hence the vice, widespread in many tribes, of aborting. Among the Guaycurús it is very common for women to start bearing and raising children only after the age of 30.* Although this is not a dominant national custom, one nevertheless frequently notes this unnatural act, and the organic ailments resulting from it, among the women of several tribes on the Amazon and Yupurá: the Juri, Uainumá, and Coëruna." (1:121)

GUAYCURU (Paraguay)

SANCHEZ LABRADOR, P. JOSÉ. *El Paraguay Católico.* Buenos Aires, 1910.

Abortion is widespread. It is done secretly by single girls, and more openly by married women. There is no social disapproval. The husband does not repudiate his wife, and the single girl has no trouble finding a new suitor. (2:305)

GUIANAS (in general)

HDBK

"Mechanical abortion is probably known among all tribes, most of whom claim vegetable abortifacients although these have not been scientifically identified." (3:851)

GUNANTUNA

MEIER, JOSEPH. *Illegitimate Birth Among the Gunantuna.* Catholic Anthropological Conference Publication, Vol. II, No. 1, Washington, D. C., 1938.

"*Illegitimate Children Regularly Done Away with by the Mother.* Among a people who so strongly condemn illegitimate birth, there is, generally, but one course open to a single woman who becomes pregnant. Ordinarily she will endeavor to make away with the child while she is still in the early stages of pregnancy, for the aversion which she has to exposing herself and

* Prado, *op. cit.* According to Azara, *Voyage* II: 116, they kill all their children but two, and the Lingoas and Machicuyo are said only to let the last child live (?). (Azara, *op. cit.* 152, 156)

her offspring to public disgrace, and the fear of being unmercifully and unremittingly rebuked by her relatives, urge her to such action as soon as she is aware of her condition. She will, first, try to bring about abortion or, as the Gunantuna say, to 'kava vue ra kom,' or 'ra paka na bul'—bear forth the piece (or rudiment) of child (that is, 'to expel the embryo or fetus').* If she is unsuccessful in this attempt she will do away with the child after its birth.

"That this is the usual procedure in such a case is indicated in the reproach which the relatives address to a woman who fails to make away with her illegitimate child:

" 'Ari na ra vavina / a urivavet, ave ruva tana / ma ave kankan utna / ma ave biti utana: Pa u ga valeke vue † / na ra bul dave? Ba upi natu i Iia?'

" 'If that the woman (that is, the mother of a bastard) / a bone-(of)-we others, we-others feel-ashamed-of-her / and we-others be-angry with-her / and we-others say to her: 'Not thou have lay low / that the child why? He-shall-pass as offspring of Who?'

" 'If a woman who gives birth to a bastard is of our flesh and blood, we feel ashamed of her, get angry with her, and say to her: 'Why did you not do away with that child? Who is his father?'

"The above text denotes clearly that the woman's relatives do not want their moiety membership increased by a bastard, any more than they want it increased by an incestuous child. However, they do not consider an illegitimate child as disreputable an issue as an incestuous one, for the bastard has at least one redeeming feature: he is the offspring of a man and a woman of different moieties. But, whether the child be illegitimate or incestuous, the Gunantuna code prescribes that it be made away with.

"The law of doing away with a bastard is not so rigorously enforced by the Gunantuna as that referring to incestuous off-

* Father Otto Meyer, M.S.C., mentions another expression for 'committing abortion,' namely, 'di papa vue ra bul'—one opens away the child, that is, 'one loosens or expels the unborn child.'

† Valeke vue, used in its proper sense, means 'lay low, prostrate, overturn,' and so on. In its figurative sense, as used here, it means primarily 'to rid oneself of, to do away with, to bring about the death of' in an indirect manner, that is, without using any weapon.

spring. If it were, we would find no bastards among the tribe, as in actuality no persons of incestuous extraction are found in those districts which have adopted the dichotomic division.

"We do, however, find some illegitimate children among the Gunantuna, although not many. Illegitimate children, at least in some instances, are spared and reared by their mother, while such is never the case, to our knowledge, with incestuous children. Why this distinction since the relatives are opposed on principle to an increase of their moiety by either bastards or incestuous offspring?

"One reason, already given, is that the disgrace which the birth of a bastard brings upon mother, child and relatives is not as deep as that resulting from the birth of incestuous progeny. Another reason why occasionally an illegitimate child is spared is that if the mother herself should fail to do away with such offspring, the kin would not play the executioner in her stead as they would most certainly do in the case of an incestuous issue. This attitude of the relatives is implied in our text above, for although it indicates that the kin expect the bastard's mother to make away with him and reprimand her severely for having failed to do so, at the same time it does not give the slightest intimation that they intend to make up for her omission.

"The Gunantuna have in mind, however, only an 'indirect killing' of such a child. They do not expect the mother to murder her bastard in a direct way by striking him with a stone, or a piece of wood, or by hitting his head against a tree or rock, for it is the tribal law that no member shall kill a close relative (computed in accordance with matrilineal descent) in direct assault by using a weapon or something equivalent (ubu vamat ia—strike make dead him). This prohibition, based upon native feeling, is still further inculcated by the moiety system. In fact, to murder directly one's mother, brother, or sister is considered as abominable as to perpetrate incest with one's mother or sister. In other words, 'thou shalt not slaughter directly thy close kin nor eat them' is a moral principle of this tribe. . . .

"However, direct killing, as I have stated, is not allowed by the Gunantuna in the case of a woman who wants to rid herself of her bastard. The very fact that the phrase 'valeke vue' is used in our text instead of 'ubi vamat,' indicates that the relatives of the woman have in mind only an 'indirect killing' of her illegitimate child. For, 'valeke vue' applied to a human being, primarily means to 'rid one's self of or to do away with in an indirect manner,' while 'ubi vamat' means to 'put to death in a direct manner' by using a weapon.

"Abortion, a common method resorted to by the guilty woman, is looked upon as an 'indirect' method. Abortion was known to the women of this tribe before the influence of the whites. Here are some of the methods used to induce abortion in the case. The woman eats certain herbs or drugs handed down from one generation of women to another and believed to cause abortion. These drugs are made even more effective, in Gunantuna belief, by a magic ritual likewise known only to the female sex. If the drugs are not effective, the woman resorts to massage and in addition ties the upper part of her abdomen tightly so as to expel the fetus. Again, she lies down on a mat and presses her abdomen against the ground or stands erect and presses against a solid object. Another procedure is to climb a low tree and then to jump down. If the woman lives on the shore, she takes dives from an overhanging tree, from a cliff, or from the protruding edge of a reef. Surgical operations to abort are unknown.

"Such methods may endanger the life of the mother, and are not always successful. If, in spite of them, the woman gives birth to a bastard she will endeavor to make away with him immediately after birth by other methods considered as only an indirect killing of one's kin. For instance, the mother will not nurse the babe and thus starve him to death, or she will expose him, or will bury him alive in the forest. Indirect killing is also resorted to when twins of a different sex are born, even if they be legitimate, for fear that if spared they might later commit incest.

"However, not all Gunantuna women who become pregnant out of wedlock go to the extremes just mentioned. Some of them spare their bastards, notwithstanding the consequent dishonor and rebukes. And what are the motives in such cases?

"The first motive is motherly love, common to 'savage' and civilized woman. Secondly, a Gunantuna woman may be loath to do away with a bastard who is well favored at birth and may spare him on account of his looks. . . .

"In concluding this chapter I submit some data relative to a number of illegitimate Gunantuna children. The statistics refer only to one district, and a few minor countrysides which I include in that district. The district is Rakunai and the minor countrysides are Rakadakada lying south of it, Rakotop and Kikitabu to the west, and Vunalaka to the north.

"In the district proper of Rakunai, with a population of 237, I found only two bastard children, a boy and a girl born of the same mother. In Rakadakada with 222 people, in Rakotop with 106, Kikitabu with 137, and Vunalaka with 63, I found no bastards. Among all the people living in these districts I learned of no adults whose extraction was illegitimate.

"We must not infer from these statistics, however, that in the districts mentioned, during a period of thirty years or more, only two illegitimate children were conceived or born. Others may have been simply done away with either by abortion or infanticide. Then, too, the statistics, if taken up in other districts, might show a larger percentage of illegitimacy. However, all informants with whom I have conferred agree that there are few bastards among the Gunantuna.

"We may conclude then that illegitimate children do not play an important role among the Gunantuna, and there is no evidence that conditions were any different in the past. So far as our knowledge goes, there is no ground for attributing the origin of matrilineal descent among the Gunantuna to illegitimacy." (pp. 35–37, 41–43)

HAIDA

BANCROFT, H. H. *The Native Races of the Pacific States,* Vol. I: *The Wild Tribes.* London, 1875.

GPM

"Abortion and infanticide are not uncommon. Twin births are unusual, and the number of children is not large, although the age of bearing extends to forty or forty-six years." (Bancroft, 1:169)

"They never practice abortion or infanticide, even in the case of weaklings, twins, and illegitimate children." (GPM, p. 248)

HAITI, Arawak of

WISSE, JAKOB. *Selbstmord und Todesfurcht bei den Naturvölkern.* Zutphen [1933].

[Due to Spanish oppression] "Here too women sought to prevent the birth of their children by means of vegetable poisons, and then followed the example of their men and hung themselves." (p. 211)

(For similar data see *Arawak, Chontal, Marianas* in general.)

HAWAII

PB

"It is reported of the women of Hawaii that they abort so that their breasts would not become flaccid and wilted. . . . In the Hawaiian Islands infanticide was formerly very prevalent. At present, according to information received from missionaries, only one-half of the marriages are fertile. Andrew found that twenty-three out of ninety-six married women, i.e. one-fourth of them, lived in childless marriages. According to Wilkes voluntary abortion is very frequent." (2:512, quoting Wilkes, Charles, *Narrative of the United States Exploring Expedition 1838–42*, Philadelphia, 1845)

Arning obtained in Hawaii an object which is now in the Berlin Museum für Volkerkunde, and was reproduced in PB, Vol. II, Fig. 667. It is a dagger-shaped object named Kapo, made of brown wood, whose "handle" is a grotesque head with a cock's comb like crest, and whose "blade" is a prolongation of the head. The "blade" is shaped like a slightly conical ream, about as thick as a medium-sized index finger. The point is rough, unevenly chipped and much worn down. M. Bartels concludes from this that the original length of this object was greater than its present length of twenty-two centimeters, and that it was worn down as a result of having been repeatedly used for the purpose of procuring an abortion by instrumentation. (One infers that Bartels means that the point was repeatedly sharpened, and, thus, also shortened.)

According to M. Bartels, this object is an "idol," i.e., the image of a deity who causes women to abort, and whose image was actually used as an instrument for procuring an abortion. Bartels considers this deity—as well as the idol itself—quite unique, because, whereas many groups worship deities for the purpose of protecting women against miscarriage, this seems to be the only deity known to him whose task it is to cause abortions and/or miscarriages.

It is stated that this dagger-shaped idol's point was thrust into the uterus for the purpose of rupturing the fetal membranes. However, M. Bartels believes that it was also used for exactly the opposite purpose, i.e., as a means of dilating the os uteri of women who desired to become pregnant, so as to facilitate the entry of the semen into the uterus. This latter inference was challenged by F. v. Reitzenstein, who edited the last edition of PB. (2:529–30)

HANDY, E. S. C., PUKUI, M. K., AND LIVERMORE, KATHERINE. *Outline of Hawaiian Physical Therapeutics.* B. P. Bishop Museum, Bulletin 26, Honolulu, 1934.

"I have accounts, however, of physical and ceremonial measures resorted to after the birth of a first child, believed to be effective in preventing subsequent conceptions (*e ho'opa i ke punao,* "to close the womb"). And in the recipes at hand there are several which purport to induce embryonic abortion.

"Abortion (Hoene). There is no evidence that fetal abortion and infanticide existed as a social institution in Hawaii as it did in Tahiti, where it was obligatory for the noble who married a commoner to kill the offspring before or immediately after birth in order to maintain the purity of the aristocracy, and where all women who joined the Arioi order of minstrels took oath to kill their offspring. The fact that in Hawaii those born out of misalliances between alii and low-caste people were not killed at birth, but were permitted to grow up as outcasts, argues against any widespread acceptance or practice of abortion or infanticide. Several medicinal agents in the native pharmacopoeia, compounded in *apu* and drunk, or applied externally or internally in late pregnancy, are said to act as abortives. In the Museum collection is a pointed stick that was found with the body of a young Hawaiian girl in a cave; it had evidently served for piercing the skull of the fetus in inducing abortion. This find may, however, only indicate an effort to save the mother in a case of obstructed delivery." (pp. 7–8)

PUKUI, M. K. Hawaiian Beliefs and Customs During Birth, Infancy and Childhood. *B. P. Bishop Museum, Occasional Papers.* 16 #17, 1942.

"Miscarriage (He'ewale). Induced miscarriage was called *'omilomilo'* (twisting). It was rarely practiced among my people and I have never heard of any drastic measures used other than the giving of herbs, the prescription of which was kept secret by the *kahumas.* I heard of the piercing of the foetus with a sharp pointed instrument called the *koholua* and the rolling of weights on the abdomen after I had grown up and travelled among other people. Miscarriage was induced only when a girl of high birth became involved in an affair with a man far beneath her rank. Often the foetus was allowed to develop normally and at birth the midwife or helper snuffed out the life of the new-born baby so that there would be no child with the blood of the low in his veins to claim kinship with one of high rank.

"A natural miscarriage was called *he'ewale.* There were many superstitions in connection with the foetus in a natural miscarriage or abortion. The foetus, born long before it was due or had fully developed, was called a *pu'u-koko.* It was believed to acquire mana when properly disposed of and to grow in the care of a family *'aumakua* or ancestral god. So far as I know the foetus was not buried in the ground but was taken to a fresh-water stream, a pond, the sea, or wherever it would be in the care of the gods to whom it properly belonged. If the family was related to the god of thunder, *Kanehekili,* and to the god of lightning, *Kauilanuimakehaikalani,* a clap of thunder and a flash of lightning would appear at the time of birth and take it away. It then became a lightning spirit. It was usually the nearest male relative, preferably the father or grandfather, whose duty it was to dispose of the foetus. The color of the foetus was often examined to determine the sex; if bright red, it was a male and if of a lighter shade, a female.

"These *pu'u-koko* were believed to develop and grow in the care of the family god and to assume an animal or a human form at will. The animal form depended upon the class to which it belonged, whether reptile, fowl, or fish. There were times when a spirit was said to possess a medium (*haka*), usually a member of the family through whom it spoke, telling its name, how it fared, and what it wished them to do. Such spirits were sometimes worshipped by calling upon them to partake of *'awa* whenever the keeper or *kahu* took his drink. The spirit never partook of the *'awa* itself but of the essence (*aka*). In the prayer the *kahu* always said: *'Ke aka ka oukou, o ka i'o ka makou'* (The essence is yours, the substance ours). The *'awa* was believed to give the spirit great strength and there are legends that tell of persons born in the shape of roots or rope and others developing into powerful fighters.

"The nature of these spirits depended largely upon the keeper. If the keeper was a person who was kind and thoughtful of others, the spirit he worshipped became helpful and friendly, but if he was quick to anger and sent the spirit to punish (the object of) his wrath, that spirit became malignant and was known at times to destroy its keeper when he failed to keep a promise. When that happened, the spirit was called an *akua 'al kahu* or a god who ate his keeper.

"A certain deified spirit in *ka'u* who took the form of a shark was said to have caused his keepers to become insane because they had sworn that all of the fruit of a certain banana grove was his, but had given some to guests who came to their house.

"I was told a story about a *Kona* woman who was on her way from *Keauhou* to *Kahalu'u* to visit a relative. She had not gone far when she had a miscarriage. The foetus was partly developed and she could see that it was a male child. She wrapped it in a calico *mu'umu'u* (a loose, long-sleeved undergarment) and placed it under some convolvulus vines, intending to carry it home to her husband when she returned from her visit. Late that afternoon she returned with her brother and found that the bundle was gone. A few weeks later while she was fishing at *Keauhou,* the nipple of her breast was seized by a small shark which began to nurse.* The markings of its body were exactly like the design of the *mu'umu'u* in which she wrapped the foetus. She knew then that the gods of the sea had come for him themselves and had given him the form of a shark. This shark is said to be still seen at *Keauhou.*

"Hundreds of such stories are told and retold in Hawaiian families, but they are rarely ever told to outsiders for fear of ridicule and of being accused of idolatry (*ho'omanamana*)." (pp. 378–80)

HEHE

PB

"Nigmann states that among the Wahehe abortion is practiced on a very large scale and even the killing of small children im-

* [Cf. the similar role of birds among the *Aleut.* G. D.]

mediately after birth is not punishable. The enormous prevalence of abortion, which among the Wahehe allows few women to have more than two children, is related to the custom that sexual relations are forbidden to women while they are lactating. Since the colored people in general, and consequently also the Wahehe, nurse for a long time and since both spouses dislike a long continence, the obstacle to intercourse is simply gotten out of the way." (2:515–16), quoting Nigmann, E., *Die Wahehe,* Berlin, 1908)

HERERO

BÜTTNER, C. G. "Aus Natur- und Völkerleben Südwest Afrikas," *Das Ausland,* pp. 852–58, 1882.

"The abortion of the fruit of the body, for various reasons,* occurs not infrequently among the Herero. On the other hand, I do not know of a single case, in which a living child has willingly been abandoned to death. At any rate, the latter happens only rarely." (p. 852)

[In a later article "Ärztliches aus Damaraland," *Das Ausland,* 1884 (pp. 693–97), Büttner describes the obstetrical procedures used by the Herero and other tribesmen at some length. He states that they are so skillful at this art that they are able to manipulate a malpositioned fetus within the womb by external massage. In this light it seems probable that such skills would also play a part in bringing about abortion, although Büttner does not say so explicitly. G. D.]

LÜBBERT, A. "Über die Heilmethoden und Heilmittel der Eingeborenen in Deutsch-Südwestafrika," *Mittheilungen aus den Deutschen Schutzgebieten,* 14:77–90, 1901.

"Miscarriages occur often enough and probably artificially induced ones at that. Laziness may well be the chief motive for this. The operation is a very simple one. Beginning with the third or fourth month the pregnant woman causes her abdomen to be trodden on by some stranger or by a woman friend. In ad-

* Thus I know of one woman who had been betrayed in the most shameful way and cast away by her husband and who out of anger tried to kill the child that she carried under her heart. Abortions are done most frequently by means of external force, through beating or pushing of the abdomen with fists or stones.

dition, the abdomen, just above the uterus, is constricted as tightly as possible with a rope, in order to prevent the growth of the foetus.

"Internally they take saltpeter or an excess of kitchen salt. These measures apparently cause special damage only in the rarest of cases. If the woman wishes to prevent a threatening miscarriage, she lies down very quietly on her back and covers herself with a fresh hide." (p. 88)

PB

Pepper is believed to be an abortifacient. (2:531)

HOPI

AH

"Among the Navaho, Hopi, and other tribes manual or bandage (sash) pressure is applied to the woman's abdomen with the object of crushing or expelling the fetus." (p. 164)

BEAGLEHOLE, PEARL. *Notes on Personal Development in Two Hopi Villages.* American Anthropological Association, Memoir 44 (pp. 25–65) 1935.

"Most informants know nothing about abortion. One old man said that single girls used manual pressure, in order to abort so as to avoid gossip. Another old man said that pregnant girls get a medicine man to abort them, because otherwise it would be hard for them to get a husband afterwards. . . . Girls can cause themselves to miscarry or to have stillborn children, simply by wishing it. If they do it repeatedly, the souls of their dead babies will conspire against them and kill them, so that they can have no further stillbirths. When a normal but undersized birth takes place, the girl may squeeze the neonate to death with her legs, during the delivery." (pp. 25–26)

(See also *Southwest U. S. Indians.*)

HOTTENTOT (German Southwest Africa)

LÜBBERT, A. "Über die Heilmethoden und Heilmittel der Eingeborenen in Deutsch-Südwestafrika," *Mittheilungen aus den Deutschen Schutzgebieten,* 14:77–90, 1901.

(Data identical with *Herero* data.)

HOTTENTOT (Nama)

LAIDLER, P. W. "The Magic Medicine of the Hottentots," *South African Journal of Science,* 25:433–47, 1928.

"Klipsweet, boiled and strained, is given in large doses as an abortifacient tea. In regular-size doses it is administered for the treatment of an inadequate flow of the birth waters and for unhealthy menses. Still smaller doses are given for back pains. Today this tea is considered an ideal medicine for children." (p. 446)

HUICHOL

(See *Southwest U. S. Indians.*)

ILA

SMITH, E. W., AND DALE, A. M. *The Ila-speaking Peoples of Northern Rhodesia.* London, 1920.

"*Feticide.* Here is a native account given to us: Should a woman become pregnant she is taboo; she is not to be slept with by any man but her husband. Should another sleep with her the child will not be; it will be born the day following. But the woman is not delivered in peace (*chitela*), but in a state of unconsciousness (*mu chiu*) not knowing what is taking place, and the child comes from the womb dead. Why? Because she slept with a man other than the one she always sleeps with. Now that also is a case for *lwembe.* The man is in fault against the woman's clan who are bereft of a child, and also against the husband of the woman. They all take it up, saying, 'This is a great matter. Why is our child killed by this man? Let him die also!' But the elders who have seen these things before say, 'No, he is not to die; let him pay the *lwembe.*' So he has to pay what they decide upon. Sometimes in addition to the child being born dead, the mother also dies, and then there are two *lwembe* faults. The *lwembe* for the mother is paid first, and then that for the child. The greater is for the mother's death, and this is not paid, as is the *lwembe* for the child, to both the husband and the wife's clan, but only to the latter.

"If a pregnant woman is vexed at being in that condition and desires that the child shall not be, she goes to somebody, an old woman maybe, who she is informed has an abortifacient (*musamo wa kuyazha mafu*). The old woman asks her,'Do you wish to kill yourself?' and she replies, 'I don't care.' 'Bring me a gift,' says the hag, and the woman gives her something big, because she knows that to procure abortion is the death of a person. Then the old woman hands her the medicine with directions how to take it at home. Having drunk it, the woman feels pains in her abdomen, and whether there be a child formed, or not, she aborts. Maybe somebody has observed her drinking the medicine and tells the husband. He puts the question to her, 'Wife, is it true that you got and drank medicine, and that is the reason of this effusion?' The woman begins to deny it, saying, 'No, no, the abortion came of itself.' Then the person who witnessed her is sent for and the wife convicted. She is silent and hangs her head in shame. Thereupon the husband and his clansmen rise in indignation, and addressing the woman's people say fiercely, 'Pay *lwembe* for killing our child.' The others have nothing to say, but pay up. And the woman who dispensed the medicine is not overlooked; they are in the mess together (literally, *Balabila ibia diomwinana,* 'they boil as one pot'), and she will have to pay. Twenty head of cattle is the amount paid, and it is divided among the man's clansmen." (pp. 418–19)

INCA
HDBK
"Professional midwives got their power either through a . . . vision or by bearing twins and going through an elaborate series of fasts and ceremonies. They massaged pregnant women to straighten out the foetus, and could produce abortion for a price." (2:312)

INDIA (Aboriginal Tribes)
PB
"Shortt reports on the enormous proportions which abortion has assumed in India. It is practiced for religious reasons among the Hindu living in the British Presidencies, as well as among the wild tribes." (2:514, quoting Shortt, J., (presumably), "On Criminal Abortion in India," *Obstetrical Society, Transactions,* 9, #6, 1868)

IROQUOIS of Canada
PB
"Frank reports of the Iroquois women of Canada that [the men urge the women to abort their children by the use of a certain

herb which grows everywhere in that area, in order to avoid the inconveniences of rearing children.]" (2:525, quoting a not further identified authority named Frank)

JAKUN

SKEAT, W. W., AND BLAGDEN, C. O. *Pagan Races of the Malay Peninsula.* London, 1906.

"The practise of abortion was well understood by the Jakun women. It was procured in order to avoid the labour which the bringing-up of a child would entail. It was, however, very seldom practised, for if it was discovered by the husband, he had the right of giving his wife a sound drubbing with a club, and if in such a case he accidentally killed her, he was not brought to justice for doing so. In the case of a premature delivery, a sort of council of sage-femmes or elderly women might be called to try whether the woman had procured abortion. If she were found guilty, she was delivered over to her husband for punishment. He was not, however, compelled to punish her, and if he forebore, she escaped without a penalty.

"When an unmarried Jakun girl had recourse to abortion, she entirely lost all position and status in the clan. She was despised by all the other women, and scorned as a bride by the men; and finally she exposed herself to the disgrace of being chastised by her parents." (pp. 23–24)

JAVA

NH

"Abortion is frequent." (quoting van der Burg, C. L., *De Geneesheer in Nederlandsch Indië,* Batavia 1884–1887, 3 vols., 1:104) (p. 36 fn.)

PB

"[In Java abortions occur frequently.]" (2:514, quoting Jacobs, Julius, *Eenige tijd onder de Baliërs,* Batavia, 1883) " 'In Java (Banjoewangi) the unripe fruits of the [Manga Kawini, Magnifera foetida] tree are used for this purpose. Among mechanical means they chiefly resort to the rubbing and pinching of the abdomen, which they call ngoe-oet (in Malay: oeroet).' " * (2:526–27, quoting Jacobs, *ibid.*)

* Oeroet means "to rub" or "to massage" (Favre, P., *Dictionnaire Malais-Français,* Vienna, 1875. 1:37 [G. D.]

JIVARO

(1) KARSTEN, RAFAEL. "Contributions to the Sociology of the Indian Tribes of Ecuador," *Acta Academiae Aboensis, Humaniora,* 1, #3, 1920.

(2) KARSTEN, RAFAEL. "The Head-Hunters of Western Amazonas; The Life and Culture of the Jivaro Indians of Eastern Ecuador and Peru," *Societas Scientiarum Fennica: Commentationes Humanarum Litterarum,* 7, #1. Helsingfors, 1935.

TESSMAN, GÜNTER. *Die Indianer Nordost-Perus: Grundlegende Forschungen für eine Systematische Kulturkunde.* Hamburg, 1930.

VIGNA, JUAN. "Bosquejo sobre los Indios Shuaras o Jibaros," *America Indigena,* 5:35–49, 1945.

Women abort mostly if they believe that the pregnancy is due to a demon. Canelos women use a decoction of the vine shigshi huasca or the rind pétun cara. The Canelos practice contraception by means of drugs. Then they observe a special diet and, if they violate these dietary rules, they will be especially susceptible to the risk of pregnancy. If a woman goes bathing in the river a demon, in the form of a small fish or water insect, will enter her and she will sicken and die, or get pregnant and give birth to a monster. (Karsten, 2, p. 221) Single women are especially inclined to abortion. Normally Jivaro husbands do not allow their wives to abort, except under special circumstances, e.g., when a woman is made pregnant by a member of an enemy tribe, or if the marriage is unlawful in some way so that there is a risk of a monster being born. Abortion is usually mechanical, and is apparently done in the third or fourth month of pregnancy. An older woman grasps the girl from behind and gradually expresses the foetus. Another technique consists in a medicine man causing the girl to swallow a raw egg poured directly in her mouth. They use no poisonous drugs. (Karsten 2, p. 233) Jivaro women know vegetable abortifacients. (Karsten, 1) The Canelos do use poisonous drugs, however. They crush and boil the stem of the vine shigshi huasca and the rind of the shrub pétun cara, and give this decoction to drink to the girl who wishes to abort an extramaritally conceived baby. (Karsten 2, p. 233) The newborn is the absolute property of the parents, and they can therefore kill it. They view monsters as not being human at all, and believe that their birth is unlucky for the tribe, causing epidemics and general misfortune. The Canela kill the second twin, which is deemed "the son of a demon."

Yet there is no lack of parental feelings; they are very fond of children and take good care of them. The parent sometimes subjects himself to long privations for the sake of a newborn son. (Karsten 2, pp. 251–52) Midwives know herbs and serve infusions to check the menses or to cause an abortion. (Vigna, p. 47) Abortions occur when the parents are too lazy to take care of the child. It is never done just because the woman does not love the child's father. To cause abortion they use Lecythidacee Grias grandifolia Pilger (sacha-mangue L.). The fruit is cut and thrown into water and the whole is drunk. They also use for this purpose the leaves of verbena. (Tessman, p. 363)

JUKUN

MEEK, C. K. *A Sudanese Kingdom.* London, 1931.

An adulterously pregnant woman will either automatically abort, or else she will have twins. (pp. 356–7)

KABYLES

HA

[Quoting Frazer's *Golden Bough,* this author states that] if a Kabyle woman procures an abortion under her husband's roof, she is killed. (p. 134)

KAFFIR

KROPF, ALBERT. *Kaffir-English Dictionary.* Lovedale, South Africa, 1899.

"isi-Qǒmfo An abortion (applied to women only, not to animals).
uku-Qǒmfa To abort, procure abortion
(It was looked upon as a crime, for which payment had to be made to the chief, who had lost by this practice one of his subjects.)" (p. 339)

MACLEAN, JOHN, ed. *A Compendium of Kaffir Laws and Customs.* Grahamstown, 1906.

"The procuring of abortion, although almost universally practised by all classes of females in Kaffir society, is nevertheless a crime of considerable magnitude in the eye of the Law; and when brought to the notice of the chief, a fine of four or five head of cattle is inflicted. The accomplices are equally guilty with the female herself." (p. 64)

KAGORO (Nigeria)

TREMEARNE, A. J. N. "Notes on the Kagoro and Other Nigerian Head-Hunters," *Journal of the Anthropological Institute,* 42:136–99, 1912.

"There are medicines for producing abortions . . ." p. 171)

KAI

KEYSSER, CH. "Aus dem Leben der Kaileute," Neuhauss, Richard, *Deutsch Neu-Guinea,* Vol. 3. Berlin, 1911.

"Papuan women are greatly afraid of the pains of childbirth. Hence, when pregnancy occurs, they seek to get out of the difficulty by aborting the fetus. This happens in two ways—either they eat the very sharp roots of a grass species (Zamang) whereby the germinating life is supposed to be killed and expelled, or else the child developing in the maternal womb is killed by smiting it repeatedly with a stone. Since this kind of abortion is dreaded—and not without reason—if Zamang has been taken and has produced no effect, many women allow birth to take place, and comfort themselves with the thought that they too will survive that which many others have survived before them." (p. 26)

"Abortion is not deemed here a wrongful act, because nobody is harmed thereby, and the woman is permitted to do with her own body as she pleases." (p. 91)

"No Papuan woman deems a large brood a desirable goal of her marriage. Naturally it would be different if no pains were involved, if a nursemaid took care of the children, and a governess took care of raising them! But all such wishes must remain unfulfilled. As a result, the Papuan woman seeks help elsewhere and believes that she will find this succor. In their belief, a formula uttered into the palm of the hand, with which she then smites her abdomen, has the desired effect. All kinds of tree and herb roots which must be ingested perform the same service, by expelling the fetus. An interesting abortifacient is a fruit kernel, taken from the excrement of the cassowary bird. This kernel is cooked together with some legumes, which the woman must then eat. The kernel itself is left uneaten, since all they seek to accomplish is that the soul-substance, which resides in the kernel expelled from the abdomen of the cassowary should communicate itself to the herbs. This soul-substance then initiates in the body of the woman the expulsion of the fetus. If all 'natural' animistic medicine fails, one has to take recourse to ghosts. Two ghost women, Godewa and Laulabu, are thought to have at their disposal abortifacient powers; therefore, one solicits their help by means of a magic formula, although, as the women themselves now concede, this is done in vain." (p. 121)

"Such ghost women as Bombong and Soiga are begged by pregnant women to restore their missing menses: 'Belabor my abdomen with your club so that the coagulating blood shall come apart again and flow out.' While saying this one compresses, as strongly as possible, one's abdomen by placing one's hands on one's hips." (p. 153)

KAINGANG (Eastern Brazil)

SANTIN DE PRADE, BENJAMINO. "Una Spedizione ai 'Coroados' nello Stato di S. Paolo nel Brasile," *Anthropos,* 1:35–48, 1906.

This writer found in an abandoned village a woman—wife of the chief—who was too ill from a miscarriage to flee. (p. 45)

KALMUCKS

PB

"Among the Kalmucks undesired pregnancies are gotten rid of with the help of old women, who are said to achieve this by a prolonged rubbing of the abdomen, by placing on the region of the uterus a glowing piece of coal wrapped in an old shoesole and by other skin-irritating devices, all of which the girls are said to endure with the greatest patience." (2:525, quoting Pallas, P. S., *Voyages*)

(See also *Mongol-Oirat.*)

KAMCHADAL

STELLER, G. W. *Beschreibung von dem Lande Kamtschatka.* Frankfurt and Leipzig, 1774.

PB

"If the women do not wish to give birth, they elicit sterility in themselves or, with inhuman cruelty and without compassion they break in two the arms and legs of children in the maternal womb. Such female murderers often had to pay with their lives for their cruelty in aborting, in that they died while giving birth.

In former times special women were trained for such a crushing of the children and they performed this office at will." (Steller, p. 294)

"It may be said of the Itälmen that they marry more out of voluptuousness than for the purpose of having children, since they frustrate pregnancy by means of various drugs, and seek to abort by means of herbs as well as by external attempts. They have various means for aborting their children, which, up till now, I know only by name, but have not seen as yet personally. The most cruel one is the practice of crushing the child to death inside the mother's body and of causing old women to break and to crush their arms and legs. If, after such attempts, they abort the whole fetus, or if the fetus putrefies and comes out in pieces, and if this happens several times, then the mother too may have to die of it." (PB, 2:525, quoting verbatim from Steller, G. W., *passim*)

CZAPLICKA, M. A. *Aboriginal Siberia.* Oxford, 1914.

"A woman who wished to become pregnant had to eat spiders; some of them also for this purpose would eat the umbilical cord together with a grass called *kiprei*. On the other hand, if a child was not desired, there was a widespread custom of causing abortion by shock or by killing the child in the womb. Old women specialists in these matters were found, but they frequently caused the death of the mother. If the undesired infant did not die before birth, the mother strangled it or gave it, living, to the dogs to eat. In order to induce sterility, a drink made from a grass called *konlakhion* was taken." (p. 129)

KASAI

MASTERS, WALTER E. "The Prevention of Conception Amongst the Natives of the Kasai Basin, Central Africa," *Journal of Tropical Medicine and Hygiene,* 19:90–91, 1916.

"The patient was a chief's daughter, aged about 17, who had been 'given to a white man.' Conception was not desired. Several decoctions were prepared from native plants and given by the mouth but without success, for the girl became pregnant. The natives then administered a black powder to her which 'was sure to bring the child away prematurely.' The dose was followed by severe vomiting, acute abdominal pain, diarrhoea, and exhaustion for two days. In a month another dose was given with the same result. One month later a third dose was given and the contents of the uterus were expelled, which contained an embryo of about six months. The girl was seen by me for the first time three days after this latter incident, when I found her suffering from a foul vaginal discharge. Temperature 104.6° F., pulse 140, retained secondaries, left salpingitis and localized pelvic peritonitis. The vomiting and diarrhoea had ceased. After twenty days in hospital she was discharged cured.

"This latter case is one more of criminal abortion than an attempt to prevent conception, but it indicates what drastic measures the natives will adopt in order to prevent childbirth." (pp. 90–91)

KATO

DRIVER, H. E. *Culture Element Distributions: X, Northwest California.* Anthropological Records, 1, #6, Berkeley, 1939.

"Medicine eaten or drunk. Blows or pressure on abdomen." (p. 350) "Mother tramps on pregnant daughter's abdomen." (p. 407)

KAZAK

GPM

"Parents welcome offspring; infanticide is unknown and abortion is practiced only by unmarried girls." (p. 155)

KEISAR

PB

"Abortifacients are extensively . . . used. The women do this against the will of their husbands so as not to have more than a maximum of two children." (2:513)

KGATLA

SCHAPERA, ISAAC. *Married Life in an African Tribe.* New York, 1941.

Engagements are long and a girl's fiancé may often be away for long periods, working. If in his absence the girl gets pregnant, she sometimes tries to abort. Dikiledi had several lovers during this period and tried to abort using croton oil, washing blue, epsom salts, castor oil, several local herbs (p. 68) and bleeding the veins of her foot (p. 224), without result. Then she fled to

Transvaal. When her parents told her prospective parents-in-law what had happened, the boy's mother burst into tears, saying that, being a Christian, she had been warned not to let her son marry the daughter of a witch. She expressed surprise that the girl ran away, and declared herself ready to accept Dikiledi as daughter-in-law, although she doubted that her son would consent to this, since he had already previously complained of the girl's looseness. The son wrote back, however, that he loved the girl and would marry her. The girl gave birth in Transvaal and then came home to await the arrival of the fiancé for the wedding. (p. 68) Some women seek to expel the semen after coitus, or drink certain medicines immediately after coitus. The most common of these is prepared from the Phukutsa shrub, which yields a well-known purgative. If such measures fail, or are not taken, abortion is attempted. Married women seldom do this, except when they are particularly anxious to conceal adultery. Single girls practice it frequently. Of a group of forty-four, eight had had abortions. The reasons are as follows: Sometimes the girl is engaged and fears that her fiancé may break with her. In other cases her lover urges her to do it, to avoid trouble for having seduced her. In still other cases the girl wishes to pass as 'unspoiled,' so as to make a good marriage. The usual abortifacients are ordinary writing ink, sometimes mixed with pulverized match-heads, and strong solutions of washing blue or potassium permanganate, all of which are obtained from traders. Various native drugs, mostly purgatives, are also used, but do not seem too efficient, witness the Kgatla preference for European products. Abortions are kept secret and few come to light. Only when the girl's appearance changes suddenly is inquiry made, and even then the people of her ward seek to hush it up, partly through pity, and partly to avoid trouble. Yet she is condemned, because the local saying is: 'To force out the womb is grievous, the knot of the cradle-skin is a flower,' (i.e., one should let even a bastard live, because motherhood is joyful). Publicity seldom occurs, as the women stick together. When an abortion does become known, the girl is reported to the Chief, who causes her—and her lover, if he is known—to be thrashed severely. Her body is also smeared with the irritating juice of the mogaga bush, which is used for ritual cleansing. This is done because her blood is 'hot,' so that, wherever she goes, she will 'scorch' the land, and keep away rain. If an aborted fetus is found lying around, the girls in that vicinity are summoned, and their breasts are examined for traces of milk. The culprit is then punished and purified as described above. In addition, the tribal rain-maker is sent to the place the fetus was found in order to 'cool' the land again. The fetus is then put in a small pot and is buried inside the girl's hut, or in another shady place, where it will always be 'cool.' When unmarried girls fail to abort, they sometimes commit infanticide. If detected, they are punished as if they had aborted. Women who have once aborted sometimes become sterile, because, by aborting they have 'spoiled their blood' permanently. (pp. 223–31)

KIOWA APACHE

MC ALLISTER, J. G. "Kiowa-Apache Social Organization," in Eggan, Fred, ed., *Social Anthropology of North American Tribes.* Chicago, 1937.

Abortion is practiced especially by married women still nursing their last baby. (p. 138)

KIWAI

LANDTMAN, GUNNAR. *The Kiwai Papuans of British New Guinea.* London, 1927.

They place a rope tightly around the waist, both as a contraceptive and as an abortifacient. They also heat a coconut-husk or a stone on the fire and lie down on top of it. "The heat goes inside" and kills the foetus. Some old women are expert abortionists and warn young women not to dabble alone with such matters, as they would risk their lives in doing it unassisted. (p. 229)

KLIKITA

STONE, ERIC. *Medicine among the American Indians.* New York, 1932.

"The Klikita used as an abortifacient the powdered rattles of the rattlesnake." (p. 77)

KLING (Atjeh, Sumatra)

JACOBS, JULIUS. *Het Familie- en Kampongleven op Groot-Atjeh.* Leiden, 1894.

The people of Atjeh have several abortifacient methods (oebat bĕh anék [drugs to abort the child]. Jacobs was unable, however, to find out exact details as to their nature. Some of these drugs are said to have been obtained from the Klings, who compound and sell them to the people of Atjeh. [Summary of data, G. D.]

KNISTENEAUX

MACKENZIE, ALEXANDER. *Voyages from Montreal.* New York, 1902.

The author mentions female infanticide and then goes on to say: "They also have a ready way, by the use of certain simples, of procuring abortions, which they sometimes practice, from their hatred of the father, or to save themselves the trouble which children occasion and, as I have been credibly informed, this unnatural act is repeated without any injury to the health of the women who perpetuate it." (I:148)

KOITA

SELIGMANN, C. G. *The Melanesians of British New Guinea.* Cambridge, 1910.

". . . Although abortion is undoubtedly still brought about, it seems that even in the old days it was less common than might have been expected." (p. 134) "Abortion was formerly produced without any feeling of doing wrong." (p. 135)

KPELLE

WELMERS, W. E. "Secret Medicines, Magic and Rites of the Kpelle Tribe in Liberia," *Southwestern Journal of Anthropology,* 5:208–243, 1949.

"A special type of poison or related drug is koo-kpaaŋ-kula, literally 'abdomen-fence-put-out,' an abortifacient. It is not known whether there are more kinds than one. Abortifacients are rarely used, since great value is attached to any potential child, and any woman normally desires childbirth and a living child desperately, even if she is unmarried. In Kpelle customary law, penalties for injuring an expectant mother, an unborn child, a nursing mother, or a baby are extremely severe. With an infant mortality rate estimated at as high as 90 percent, prospective and actual infant life is considered most precious. However, the author knows of one case of attempted abortion; in this case the attempt was unsuccessful." (p. 215)

KROË (Sumatra)

PB

"The procuring of abortions is frequent." (2:514, quoting Helfrich, O. L., "Bijdrage tot de geographische, geologische en ethnologische kennis der Afdeeling Kroë: S. W. Sumatra," *Bijdragen tot de Taal-, Land-, en Volkenkunde van Nederlandsch Indië,* 5th series, 4th part: part 38 of whole, 1889)

". . . Midwives procure an abortion by giving the pregnant woman arak or brandy beaten with eggyolk, and by placing on their bellies warm ashes or a warm stone and by massaging the abdomen." (2:527, quoting Helfrich, *ibid.*)

KUANYAMA AMBO

LOEB, E. M. "Kuanyama Ambo Field Notes" (Unpublished MS).

"Omulondaxuxua (omilondaxuxua pl.) not identified. *Omu* means big, *londa* means climb, *xuxua* means chicken. The plant comes from southeast Angola and serves to prevent conception. The scraped root is mixed with water and is secretly drunk by a woman who has had sexual intercourse.

"This remedy does not seem very effective, for the Kuanyama unmarried women frequently practice abortion (ongadji). The pregnant girl makes a mixture of gunpowder and water, puts some in her vagina by a clyster, and drinks some. The foetus is thereby dislodged. Still more frequently the girl goes to a female abortion doctor, whose practices are unknown."

KUSAIE

SARFERT, P. "Kusae." *Ergebnisse der Südsee-Expedition 1908–1910* (G. Thilenius, ed.) IX, B, XV. Hamburg, 1919, 2 vols.

Abortion is an old custom in Kusae. (p. 56) It is practiced both by girls and by women. The girls do it because having a bastard reduces their value. Abortion is practiced even at present [1908–1910] and is performed by older women, whose only technique is massage. (p. 309) The rubbing of the belly is done both to alleviate stomach-aches and to produce abortions. (p. 534)

KWAKIUTL

GRANT, W. C. "Description of Vancouver Island," *Journal of the Royal Geographical Society,* 27:268–320, 1857.

WOLDT, A. *Kapitän Jacobsens Reise an der Nordwestküste Amerikas.* Leipzig, 1884 (quoted in PB, 2:524).

PB

BOAS, FRANZ. "Current Beliefs of the Kwakiutl Indians," *Journal of American Folklore,* 45:177–260, 1932.

FORD, C. S. "Manuscript Field Notes." Yale University, Human Relations Area Files [1940].

"Not less horrible is the custom, very prevalent among the women, of endeavouring to extinguish life in the womb; from this and other causes premature births occur with great frequency. The object of the creatures would seem to be partly to save themselves from the pains of child-birth, and partly to avoid the trouble of bringing up a large family . . ." (Grant, p. 304)

Among the Queka [a Kwakiutl subgroup] "Jacobsen saw how medicine men knelt on the bellies of girls and women in order to extinguish germinating life." (PB, 2:524; cf. Woldt)

"31. Internal Pains . . . In cases of internal pain, the juice of the hellebore or devil's club is drunk. The root is rubbed on a sandstone and the scrapings are mixed with cold water. This is left standing until the fine particles of the root have settled. Then the liquid is poured off, and one horse-clam-shell full is drunk. It is so poisonous, that a larger dose would kill the patient. When the stomach feels hard (*ϵmEgwī's*) they believe that there is something in it which is killed by the potion. The patient vomits, and is thus relieved from it. It is also used by women to produce abortion." (Boas, p. 183)

"To have a baby without being married is a bad disgrace when I was young. It isn't so much now. I never knew of any when I was young. They say that they used to kill the babies they was carrying. I never saw this done but they say that they lay the girl on the floor and begin to step on the small of her back so that she don't go on with carrying the baby and the thing that is going to form into a baby is busted. And sometimes they lift heavy things to spoil the forming of the baby. And if they are too late when the baby comes at birth they say that they get the baby; they take the afterbirth and put that on the face of the baby and that smothers it. It will be only the girl and her mother and perhaps some near relation attends to her and sometimes they just squeeze the neck of the baby and bury the baby secretly in the ground. They try to hide it from everybody but maybe the relations tell somebody and it spreads. I don't know of any cases in the days when I was young." (C. S. Ford, MS pp. 33–34)

"Abortion is effected by manual pressure alone. If a girl becomes pregnant before marriage, an unusual occurrence in the old days but relatively common today, the mother will abort the child of her daughter. She gets behind the girl and squeezes her abdomen with both hands. This is still done today if the parent feels deeply the disgrace which would be attached to illegitimate birth. Aborting is done as soon as the baby is noticeable. If it fails, infanticide will be resorted to. In the old days making the man marry the girl would only make public the disgrace and would not be thought of. Today, however, this is often done because the Dominion government imposes such a heavy penalty upon abortion. The idea of an abortion in the old days was to keep the disgrace as private and as quiet as possible." (C. S. Ford)

Adulterine bastards are usually claimed by the woman's husband, so as to conceal the scandal. (HRAF). [An understandable trait in an extremely "face"-conscious society. G. D.]

LAMBA

DOKE, C. M. *The Lambas of Northern Rhodesia.* London, 1931.

Infanticide is practiced for "ominous" (bad omen) reasons. If a pregnant woman dies, her husband is forced to participate in the funeral rites. If he is afraid to do so, he may pay as much as a gun to some village elder to substitute for him. Before they arrive at the burial place they prepare a sharp stake and, when they reach the burial site, the husband (or his substitute) rips open his wife's corpse, pierces the child with the stake, holds it up in the air and shouts: "God has eaten two!" Then he throws down the foetus and runs back to the village alone. The headman, Kalimbata, had to perform this rite for his younger brother's dead wife, because the husband ran away. After this rite is completed, the woman is buried in the normal way, with the child laid against her front. The stake has to be pulled out of the foetus and is used to prop up the screen. If the ritual was performed by a substitute, the substitute goes that evening to a public gathering, where the husband joins him and gives him a gun, saying: "You have helped me in a difficult task!" If the husband is unwilling to perform this rite and if no substitute can be found, the husband is actually forced to go along and do his ritual duty, because the Lamba are afraid that, if this rite is omitted, other women of the clan might die while pregnant. This rite is only performed when the pregnancy is well advanced and is known to anyone. In Doke's opinion this rite is related to sympathetic magic. (pp. 184–185)

LAMPONG

PB

". . . The procuring of abortions is frequent." (2:514, quoting Harrebomée, G. J., "Eene bijdrage over den feitelyken toestand der bevolking in de Lampongsche Districten: Lampong," *Bijdragen tot de Taal-, Land-, en Volkenkunde van Nederlandsch Indië,* 4th series, 10th part, 1885) "A girl goes to the healing woman (doekoen) if she believes herself to be pregnant, and asks her to procure her an abortion. Then her initials are spoken into a lemon, and the girl is bathed while prayers are being uttered. Every time the doekoen causes, by squeezing the lemon, a few drops [of lemon juice] to fall on the head of the moeli, the following formula is uttered:

Child, who are not yet born, and have not even assumed a shape as yet,

Emerge before your time, lest you bring shame upon your mother.

"The girl is then given nauseating drinks which have to be ingested at certain specified times, with the face turned eastward. Then the squeezed lemon must be stuffed, with certain rites, into the hollow of a tree, into the rimba. In the end, however, it is mostly the pidjet (massage) which achieves the desired result, when the strongly astringent beverages are not successful fast enough." (2:527, quoting Harrebomée, *ibid.*)

LENGUA

PB

"The families are raising not more than a maximum of two, and many of them only one child, and . . . they interrupt additional pregnancies by artificial means." (2:516)

[Probable cause: Taboo on coitus during pregnancy and lactation. Cf. PB, 2:516, for context.]

LEPCHA

GORER, GEOFFREY. *Himalayan Village.* London, 1938.
MORRIS, JOHN. *Living with Lepchas.* London, 1938.

Morris denies the occurrence of contraception and of abortion, but states that if a woman should miscarry a bastard, the matter will be kept quiet. (Morris, p. 215–216) After an aborted or still-born child is thrown in the river, the priest waves (*pek*) thorny or stinging plants over the parents and a live animal, which will be sacrificed so as to prevent the devil, who had caused this particular death, from also causing others. (Gorer, p. 230)

LESU

POWDERMAKER, HORTENSE. *Life in Lesu.* New York, 1933.

[In Lesu, there is no true concept or function of "illegitimacy," though it is deemed unfortunate not to have a father.]

Some leaves can sterilize a woman, while others can cause her to abort. In order to abort, they take several leaves in succession, chew them, swallow their juice and spit out the pulp. They have great confidence in the effectiveness of their abortifacient drugs. No physical means of inducing an abortion were reported. The knowledge of sterilizing and abortifacient drugs is carefully and jealously guarded by those who possess this knowledge. Those who know abortifacients are usually men, who obtain their knowledge from their maternal uncles. (pp. 242–43) Seven specimens of abortifacients were obtained. Rubus moluccanus is used for this purpose also in India. Four specimens were also used in India, but for different purposes. Three specimens were not known in India. Of the drugs used, two are useful emmenagogues: The acanthaceous one contains a bitter alkaloid, and curcuma contains a volatile oil. The author is not at all certain that the leaves contain *enough* of the effective drug to produce the desired result. She also doubts that seven plants in the same area could all be emmenagogues, and suspects that if one went thirty miles from the village she studied one would be shown different specimens. She stresses that native drugs are, as a rule, not very efficient. (p. 294) The knowledge of these drugs is a source of income, since the women pay for the leaves. (p. 243) It is certain that the people of Lesu think of these substances as drugs, rather than as magic. Indeed, in order to have magic performed, one has to pay in advance, whereas one pays for medicaments, including abortifacient drugs, only after they take effect. An abortion costs one tsera—i.e., shell money to the value of five shillings—and it might be mentioned here that the people of Lesu take pride in paying too much for the doctor's services.

This desire to overpay is related to their pride in pig-trading. (p. 206–207)

LKUNGEN (or Songish)

HA

They eat the leaves of a plant of a Carex species if they wish to abort, or if the menses are irregular. The sharp leaves are supposed to kill or cut the embryo, thus restoring the menses. (p. 140, quoting Boas, Franz, "The Lkungen or Songish," in Hale, Horatio, *Northwestern Tribes of Canada,* p. 25)

LOANGO

PB

"Among the Negroes of Loango abortion is rare." (2:516)

LOYALTY ISLANDS

PB

"According to Samuel Ella, the women of the Loyalty Islands drink the water of a hot sulphur spring in order to abort their fetuses. (2:512, quoting Ella, Samuel, "Native Medicine and Surgery in the South Sea Islands, [The London] *Medical Times and Gazette,* Vol. I for 1874, p. 50)

MACHIGUENGA

HDBK

"Possibly because of demoralization through extended White contacts . . . Machiguenga women practice much abortion (Fernandez Moro 1926–27, pp. 154–155)." (3:546)

MACUSI

SCHOMBURGK, R. M. *Reisen in Britisch Guiana in den Jahren 1840-1844.* Leipzig, 1847–48, Vol. II.

FARABEE, W. C. "The Central Caribs," *University of Pennsylvania, The University Museum, Anthropological Publications,* 10:1–152, Philadelphia, 1924.

The piazong can produce abortion if children are not desired. The woman is given a drug whose composition is a great secret. The person who gives this drug prevents conception by blowing on the drink and repeating a formula. (Farabee, pp. 73–74) Small families and childless ones "almost lend testimony to the view" that contraception and abortion are used. (Schomburgk, p. 247) Contraception [and abortion? The text is unclear here] is practiced because women feel they have too much work, and also from vanity, as pregnancies and childbirth make them homely. Infanticide is unknown, and those who heard of such a case among the Pirara were horrified. (Schomburgk, p. 248)

ROTH, W. E. (translator and editor). *Richard Schomburgk's Travels in British Guiana 1840–1844*. Georgetown, 1923, Vol. II.

"If polygamy is indigenous among almost all remaining tribes of Guiana, it is only very rarely met with amongst the Macusis, and it was on this account surprising to me to meet among them not alone generally small families but also many couples without any children at all, so as almost to lend testimony to the view that in many cases women seek artificial means to prevent the progress of pregnancy." (2:247)

"However reluctantly I might accept the assertion made against my will that pregnancy is often prevented by artificial means, it appears to me that still further ground for this detestable practice may lie in the burden of the labour imposed upon the woman, as well as in the vanity so universally peculiar to her sex, because her work and trouble is increased with each newborn child and all traces of her former beauty which her first child may have left will completely disappear after repeated confinements." (2:248)

[Note: This was checked against the German edition. The passages quoted appear in Schomburgk, Richard, *Reisen in Britisch Guiana in den Jahren 1840–1844,* Leipzig, 1848, Vol. II, pp. 312–13. G. D.]

ROTH, W. E. *An Introductory Study of the Arts, Crafts, and Customs of the Guiana Indians.* Bureau of American Ethnology, Annual Report 38, Washington, 1924.

"There is the authority of Gumilla that the practice of making themselves barren by taking herbs and drinks existed among the women of the Orinoco tribes. . . . (G, ii, 294, 318), a statement which would seem to have been subsequently confirmed by Von Humboldt, who mentions this custom of preventing pregnancy by the use of deleterious herbs as among the causes tending to depopulate the Christian settlements on the river in question

(AVH, II, 248). Schomburgk makes similar remarks of the Macusi women when he says that we must almost accept as true that the females in many cases seek, by artificial means, to prevent pregnancy (SR, II, 312). My own opinion, however, is that these statements are based rather on hearsay than on fact." (p. 697)

MAFULU

WILLIAMSON, R. W. *The Mafulu: Mountain People of British New Guinea.* London, 1912.

"Abortion and infanticide are exceedingly common, the more usual practice being that of procuring abortion. Although sexual immorality so largely exists, and young unmarried women and girls are known to indulge in it so freely, and it is not seriously reprobated, it is a disgrace for one to give birth to a child; and if she gets into trouble, she will procure abortion or kill the child. The same thing is also common among married women, on the ground that they do not wish to have more children. There is another cause for this among married women, which is peculiar. A woman must not give birth to a child until she has given a pig to a village feast; and if she does so it will be a matter of reproach to her. If, therefore, she finds herself about to have a child, and there is no festal opportunity for her to give a pig, or if, though there be a feast, she cannot afford to give a pig, she will probably procure abortion or kill the child when born. . . . Abortion is induced by taking the heavy stone mallet used for bark cloth beating, and striking the woman on the front of the body over the womb. It is also assisted by the wearing of the tight cane belt already mentioned. I could not hear of any system of using drugs or herbs to procure abortion; but herbs are used to produce general sterility, which they are believed to be effective in doing." (pp. 176–77)

MAILU, SOUTHEAST (Papua)

MALINOWSKI, BRONISLAW. "The Natives of Mailu," *Royal Society of South Australia, Transactions,* 39:493–706, 1915.

As among the Massim, abortion is not frequent. Whether or not contraception is practiced is uncertain. Abortion may explain the rarity of bastards. (p. 563)

MAIRAPA AREA (New Guinea, East Central Highlands)
BERNDT, R. M. "A Cargo Movement in the East Central Highlands of New Guinea," *Oceania,* 23:40–65, 137–158, 202–34, 1952–53.

"A rumour spread down from the northern Kamano . . . to the effect that now that the Europeans had come all pregnant women would die—killed by snakes which, sent by the Europeans, would enter their vulvae.* To prevent this, the husbands of such women made skin 'bibs' or aprons, which they hung round their necks to hide their dilated bellies and so deceive the snakes. To make doubly sure, they prepared beaten bark 'cloth,' which they fastened firmly around their pubes, passing between their legs and attached to a waist band at front and back. This was apparently done to all women, pregnant or not. But some women (it is not possible to estimate the number) were apparently so frightened that they practised abortion, killing their unborn children in order to save themselves.

"We can perhaps gauge the relative importance of such a reaction by the examples that followed. Abortion had not, as far as could be ascertained, been practised to any extent; children were always desired and never deliberately killed except in warfare. Here, however, under these new conditions abortion seems to have been socially sanctioned.

"Thus the next message that snakes would come, with a special spirit called Katokatoveifa:ni, following as it did on the first threat, caused much consternation. The case given in Appendix Five is an elaboration of this first reaction. Fear was expressed that this spirit (or spirits), with two snakes, would come from the north and enter the vulvae of all women, particularly pregnant women, when the snakes would eat the unborn children. Then men built a large round house, big enough to hold all members of the parallel patri-lineages and their wives and children inhabiting one small village; some villages had two or three such houses. Each house, with special latrines for men and women, was enclosed by a stockade. Firewood was collected and stacked within, with lengths of bamboo for holding water, and bark 'cloth' was prepared. From their gardens people dug

* This rumour possibly had its origin in a warning by native leaders that the natives should guard their women folk and not allow them to have promiscuous intercourse with the aliens. Europeans, like the native officials they brought with them, in and near Kainantu, were perhaps beginning to cast their eyes in the direction of native women as sexual partners.

sweet potatoes and yams, and cut bunches of bananas, which they stored in the house, and from the men's house they brought all their spare weapons and sacred objects.

"When everything was ready, all the men, women and children entered this house, closing its door; bark cloth was fastened between the women's legs; the ɔ:g'gɔ:na flower was plucked and chewed by the men, and sprayed by mouth over the bodies of pregnant women, to counteract the power of the snakes. At night the women slept while their menfolk kept guard. On the first morning they killed pigs and prepared an oven. Over the green leaves of a special variety of croton they had collected, over the door-posts of the house, and over all the pregnant women they sprinkled pigs' blood; this was in the form of a sacrifice to the spirits of the dead, the blood negativizing any harmful effect the Katokatoveifa:ni and snakes might have. The croton is of great significance here, for in this case it represents the ancestors; the sprinkling of blood is thus a form of libation.

"When the pork was removed from the oven presents of choice pieces were made to the women, and all feasted; then some slept, while others kept watch. They continued in this way for ten days, not moving beyond the stockade. By that time all the firewood was finished. On the eleventh day, after much talking, the men decided to abandon the house and return to normal living: they declared that again they had been deceived by the Kamano, for neither the spirit nor the snakes had appeared. Emerging, they killed more pigs and sprinkled blood around the house as well as on all the women; then they removed the bark coverings and threw them away." (pp. 53–54)

[Note: The native text recording these events is found in this same article on pp. 206–209. G. D.]

MALAGASY

ELLIS, WILLIAM. *History of Madagascar,* Vol. I. London, 1838.

"It is not, however, after birth alone that destruction of life takes place. This species of murder is effected at times for the purpose of avoiding the disgrace to which the violation of moral propriety would expose the guilty parties, and in some instances from the same shameful motives which occasionally operated formerly among the natives of the South Sea islands . . . the fear of having too large a family: the destruction of life before birth, from the latter consideration, occurs, however, but rarely, and in general a numerous offspring is a source of much satisfaction." (pp. 154–55)

MALAY

FAVRE, P. *Dictionnaire Malais-Français.* Vienna, 1875, 2 vols.

"*Gugur* means to fall, to spill, to decline. *Gugur anak* means to abort [i.e., to drop a child]." (I:410)

"The word *babang* means the stillbirth of a not fully developed child, i.e., a miscarriage. In Javanese the identical word means 'to escape' or to 'pass unobserved.' " (II:167)

(See also *Semang.*)

MALEKULA (New Hebrides)

LEGGATT, T. W. "Malekula, New Hebrides," *Australian Association for the Advancement of Science, Report of the Fourth Meeting* (held at Hobart, Tasmania, in January 1892). 4:697–708, 1893.

"I know of only one case of infanticide. A woman gave birth to a female child and immediately buried it under the floor of her hut. She had sons previously, but this was her first daughter. . . . Abortion is often practiced by the women, as they do not wish to be troubled with the rearing of children; it is also caused by the carrying of heavy loads, climbing coconut trees, or eating certain herbs." (p. 704)

DEACON, A. B. *Malekula, a Vanishing People in the New Hebrides.* London, 1934.

"Nevertheless, although most people wish to have some children, infanticide and abortion (*ivihiva* in Seniang, *isanmbör* in Lagalag = 'she aborts') were formerly common, and to-day the changed conditions appear to have made the natives even less anxious to have offspring. Even before the advent of the white man the principal reason for these practices appears to have been an economic one, for it was said that the constant tending of children prevented a woman from giving sufficient attention to her garden work, and thus from helping her husband to acquire wealth and, through wealth, social eminence. Another reason of perhaps equal importance is the desire of both husband and wife for constant sexual intercourse, which is prohibited while the woman is pregnant and perhaps during lactation. Although the people of Malekula are, in theory, polygynous, it is only a few men who can afford to have more than one wife, unless another has been inherited from the maternal uncle or elder brother; most of the adult male population are perforce monogamous. It is clear, therefore, that the long period of continence enforced upon a man as a result of his wife's being with child would be disliked and that attempts at abortion would not uncommonly result.

"There are no details to tell us how this was effected or attempted in Seniang, but it seems that the woman drank an infusion made from a certain leaf. In Lagalag two methods were practised; in one the pregnant woman jumped from a tree; in the other she drank large quantities of very hot coco-nut milk. Should the unwanted child be born despite these efforts, it was, both in Seniang and in the north-west, buried alive in the ground without any ceremony. In this event no distinction was made between male and female infants." (pp. 232–33)

(See also *New Hebrides.*)

MAM INDIANS (Guatemala)

WAGLEY, CHARLES. *Economics of a Guatemalan Village.* American Anthropological Association, Memoir 58, 1941.

"The desire for a large family of sons would be more in keeping with the older land system than with the present one. Formerly more sons meant that a man could rent more land from the community. Today, it would seem advisable for a family to want only one son to keep from dividing the land among many. Thus, Diego Martin felt sorry for a man with five sons, yet two or three sons in a family is thought ideal. I know of no attempts in Chimaltenango to limit the number of children—the number of male heirs. Even among poor families with meager land holdings, abortion and contraception were never practiced although Chimaltecos have heard of *ladino* contraceptives and abortions. In the Quiche village of Chichicastenango, there was an extreme interest in means of contraception because of the land problem. (Bunzel, Ruth, "Chichicastenango," in MS) In a Peruvian Indian group with a more intensified land shortage families resorted to infanticide usually after the third child to limit the number of heirs. (Mishkin, B., in MS)" (p. 80, fn.)

WAGLEY, CHARLES. *The Social and Religious Life of a Guatemalan Village.* American Anthropological Association, Memoir 71, 1949.

". . . Diego Martin told me that he felt sorry for one man with five sons because there would not be enough land for each of them. Yet, I know of no attempts in Chimaltenango to limit families. Although Chimaltecos have heard of *ladino* contraceptives and abortions, they do not make use of these practices. Instead, people want children." (p. 20)

[Statements that only one's neighbors engage in certain common deviant actions imply knowledge of that type of action and the denial is therefore to be accepted only with reservations. G. D.]

MAMBOWE

(Data identical with *Barotse.*)

MANGAREVA

HIROA, TE RANGI (P. H. BUCK). *Ethnology of Mangareva.* B. P. Bishop Museum, Bulletin 157, Honolulu, 1938.

TABLE 7. FAMILIES OF THREE RULERS[1]

1. *Te Oa*

Purura (1st wife)	Piroeke (2nd wife)	Toa-tamakai (3rd wife)
Te Ma-teoa, m.	*Te Paru-taitoko, m.	*Te Verokura, m.
†Toa-teoa, f.		Marama
Teiti-a-purure, f.		Toupiri
†Toa-pakia, f.		*Te Agai-a-tuhorokava, m.
†Te Akarotu-iti, f.		

2. *Te Mahuru*

Te Akatua (1st wife)	Toa-tokiama (2nd wife)
*Te Tuaiga, m.	Mataira, m.
Toa-huru, f.	Toa-mahuru, f.
	Rima-repo
	Teiti-houiti, m.

3. *Te Ma-tetama*

Omotu (1st wife)	Maiti (2nd wife)	Papariga
*Te Ma-omotu, m.	Toa-matetama, f.	†Toa-papariga, f.
	Te Ma-matetama, m.	†Toa-kopiroeke, f.

[1] Table from p. 85.
* Abortions which were deified
† Suicides

"In the above table two remarkable features are illustrated. The first is that children born dead (*'anau ero*), either as abortions or stillbirths, were given names, and later were deified (*etua mota'v*). The family of Te Oa provided three such deities, those of Te Mahuru and of Te Ma-tetama produced one each. The immature son of Te Ma-tetama was given the name of Te Ma-omotu, and when deified was named Te Agu." (p. 85)

MANGBETU

HANOLET ET LAPLUME in VAN OVERBERGH, CYR, Les Mangbetu. *Collection de Monographies Ethnographiques,* Vol. 4, Bruxelles, 1909.

"Among the Mangbetu sterile women are rare and the women are prolific. The children are devotedly nurtured. Abortion is rarely practiced; sometimes as a result of an agreement between the husband and the wife; but ordinarily upon the decision of the woman only." (Hanolet, p. 298)

"Separation occurs either because of sterility or because of incompatibility of temperament, or because of infidelity chiefly on the part of the woman. Abortion is practiced. The following is one of the methods employed: The woman thrusts an iron or ivory needle into the uterus." (Laplume, p. 298)

MANJA

VERGIAT, A. M. *Moeurs et Coutumes des Manja.* Paris, 1937.

"Manja women are prolific. Induced abortion is not rare. After having taken the 'medicine' the woman goes to a plantation and it is generally there that she makes the fetus disappear. However, sometimes it happens that, having taken too strong a dose of 'medicine,' she pays for her crime with her life. The abortifacients are very numerous and we shall only mention some of them. During the first month of pregnancy it suffices to eat the honey of a kind of bee, which is gathered in the forest. (The action of this honey may perhaps be due to the nectar of certain flowers which this species of bee drinks in preference to others). The decoction of the root of an under-shrub of the forest undergrowth, goéba or garkanzi, Acanthacea, Acanthus sp. is very effective. The grains of *schindou,* Cucurbitacea, Cucumis melo, either of the sweet or of the bitter variety, are impregnated with water, are made to germinate, are dried in the sun, and are then crushed with a pestle and reduced to flour. This flour is thrown into cold water, and is drunk in the form of a porridge by the pregnant woman. Grains of *maize,* prepared and drunk in the same manner, have the same effect. The pregnant woman also makes a big fire and, when the earth is very hot, cleans the fire-place, sprinkles it with water and lies down on it on her belly. She delivers a few seconds afterwards. (p. 51) *Damam,* Amplediacea, cissus species: The dried and crushed tubers provide a flour which, if consumed as a porridge, causes abortion. [The root is an aphrodisiac.] (pp. 51–52) *Dokoen,* Anonacea, Artabotrys olivoeformis: A decoction of this root is an abortifacient as well as an aphrodisiac. (p. 52) *Dop,* Leguminosa, mimosea, Albizzia zygia: If a young girl sits down on this, her future children will be stillborn. (p. 53) *Ina batoua* Leg. pap. Indigofera simplicifolia: A decoction of the root is abortifacient. (p. 54) *Ndandalida* Nyctaginea. Boerrhavia diffusa L.: The leaves have abortifacient properties, while the root is aphrodisiacal." (p. 55)

MANO and MANDINGO

HARLEY, G. W. *Native African Medicine.* Cambridge, Massachusetts, 1941.

"Abortifacients are very generally used with apparent safety to the mother, but the native realizes that after three months one is no longer entirely free from danger. One abortifacient used is the root of the cotton, *yue.* That which seems most often resorted to is the shrub called 'corset leaf,' or *wana* (Mareya spicata). Its use as a cathartic has been described above. The Mandingo leech warned us that a pot in which the *wana* cathartic had been prepared should not be used afterward for cooking food for a pregnant woman, because even a small amount of *wana* remaining in the pot might cause abortion. Even the fumes from the boiling leaves are thought to be dangerous. A pregnant woman will not eat with her neighbors or with her fellow wives for fear some jealous woman will put a little of the leaf in the food and cause her to abort. When an abortion is desired, one leaf is put into the food, or an infusion prepared from three leaves. It acts within a day. It is used by the midwife if the afterbirth does not come away naturally, and it is used during the postpartum period." (pp. 61–62)

MANUS

MEAD, MARGARET. *Growing up in New Guinea.* New York, 1930.

"Miscarriages, *ndranirol,* are treated as real births; the child is named and all the economic ceremonies are gone through. The women distinguish the time when they first feel life: 'It has become a human being. Its soul is there.' " (p. 324)

"26. Pondramet's house. His wife is very sick. Paleao says it's because she tried to tie a string around her belly. (Attempted abortion from which she died afterwards)." (p. 358)

MEAD, MARGARET. *Male and Female.* New York, 1949.

"The products of the body become identified as non-personal, and the orientation of the individual to the outside world is made more predominant as the relationship to the own body shrinks. . . . This externalization shows up vividly in the Manus's handling of miscarriages and abortions, all of which are named, and treated as if they had been full individuals. Years afterwards the mother will not distinguish in retrospect between a miscarriage at three months, a stillborn infant, and a child who died several days after birth. All have been seized upon by the outside world, property was exchanged in their names, and they are equated in her expressed memories about them." (pp. 154–155)

MAORI

DIEFFENBACH, ERNEST. *Travels in New Zealand with Contributions to the Geography, Geology, Botany and Natural History of That Country,* Vol. II. London, 1843.

"Early intercourse with the other sex, which their customs permit, frequent abortions, and the long nursing of the children, often for three years, contribute to cause the early decay of their youth and beauty, and are prejudicial to the full development of their frame." (p. 12)

"They have other modes of killing the child: the head of the infant not yet fully born is compressed, and thus its existence is terminated; and sometimes abortion is effected by pressing violently on the abdomen with a belt. Many children are stillborn; but I suspect that in almost all cases death was caused by the mother." (p. 26)

GOLDIE, W. H. "Maori Medical Lore," *New Zealand Institute, Transactions,* 37:1–120, 1904.

"Premature labour and miscarriages were not uncommon; in fact, one well-informed medical man states that the latter were of frequent occurrence, many females suffering as often as from two or three to ten to twelve times. Whether this was the result of procuration or simply accidental, he was unable to say; but he had strong suspicions that the former was frequently put into practice. The native woman, however, was subject to many accidental causes of such a condition. Dr. Dieffenbach stated that many children were still-born; but he suspected that in almost all of these cases death was caused by the mother.

"Various methods were resorted to to bring about the unnatural condition which was termed *whaka tahe, mate roto* (to die within), or *tutae atua* (lit., 'excrement of the gods'). In some instances herbs were taken, such as a decoction of *kareao* (*Rhipogonum scandens*); in others the desired end was obtained by pressing violently upon the abdomen with a belt; and in addition they had some instrumental method, but its precise nature is unknown. It does not seem to have been in very general use.

"According to Maori belief premature birth was usually caused by some infringement of the laws of the *tapu* on the part of the mother and for which she would thus be punished by the Gods. When a woman in former times, desired to procure abortion on herself she would proceed to *taiki* the foetus—that is, she would pollute a *tapu* person, as a *tohunga,* or one of her elders, by passing some cooked food over his garment or his resting place. Or she might take a portion of cooked food to some sacred place and there eat it. Such acts would, to the native mind be deemed quite sufficient to cause a miscarriage. Generally when a woman noticed that she was *papuni*—i.e. that menstruation had stopped, and she was pregnant—and desired to procure abortion, she would proceed to some sacred place, as the *tuahu,* where the priests performed various religious rites, and she would pluck some herb growing there, and, applying it to her mouth, would then cast it away. This would be quite sufficient: she has eaten, or polluted a sacred place. The gods will attend to her case." (p. 110)

[The last paragraph refers specifically to the Tuhoe tribe. G. D.]

HIROA, TE RANGI (P. H. Buck). *The Coming of the Maori.* Wellington, 1950.

"Another rationalization is that the *hei tiki* 'was made, wholly, or partially, in the form of the human embryo.' Skinner * disproved this statement by showing that the tiki did not conform to the anatomical details of the human embryo, except for the large head, which however, is characteristic of Maori art. It is more feasible to believe that the *hei tiki* was developed as an art form following established conventions in wood and bone carving but influenced by the character of the material and the initial form of the pieces cut out for working. It is evident that what was originally a valuable ornament in itself was later converted into an amulet. Thus, the small compact figure was likened to a human embryo and endowed with the magic power of promoting the growth of a viable embryo in the womb of the woman who wore it. To embellish the complex, the myth was composed that the first *tiki* was made for Hineteiwaiwa, the goddess of childbirth. The fact that some of the early European visitors saw men wearing the tiki would seem to indicate that the 'fructifying' properties of the *tiki* were a comparatively late addition to the ornament." (pp. 295–96)

MARIANAS (in general)

KOTZEBUE, O. VON. *Entdeckungsreise in die Südsee and nach der Behringstrasse,* Vol. III. 1821.

"[Due to Spanish oppression] women made themselves deliberately sterile and threw their own infants into the water, convinced that by means of such a premature death, which saved them from being overworked and from grief, they made them [the infants] happy and fortunate." (III:78, quoting Fray Juan de la Concepción) [There were also many suicides for the same reason. G. D.]

(For similar data see also *Arawak, Chontal, Haiti.*)

FREYCINET, LOUIS DE. *Voyage autour du monde.* Vol. II. Paris, 1829–39.

MATSUOKA, SHIZUO. *Mikuronesha minzoku-shi.* [An Ethnographical Study of Micronesia]. Tokyo, 1927.

THOMPSON, LAURA. *Guam and its People.* San Francisco, New York, Honolulu, 1941.

* Skinner, H. D. "Maori Amulets in Stone, Bone, and Shell," *Journal of the Polynesian Society,* 41:206, 1932.

The people of Guam do not practice infanticide. (Thompson, *passim*) The women of Guam give birth easily, but the lack of medical knowledge caused many accidents. Formerly the women of these islands practiced abortion and some even abort nowadays [1817–20], either because they do not want the child, or because they wish to prevent the birth of a bastard. (Freycinet, p. 280) In Spanish times suicide, abortion, and infanticide had decreased the aboriginal population. Juan de la Concepción wrote that the Chamorro [people of Guam] so resent the yoke of the alien [Spaniard] that some women either purposely sterilize themselves or cast into the waters their newborn infants. (Thompson, p. 167) In Saipan, abortion is widespread. The Chamorros drink *Ephedra vulgaris,* pinebark, and the root of abas (a tree) which they soak in water. They do this within three months after conception. (Matsuoka, p. 367) In Guam abortion is procured by using one of the following four recipes: (1) They boil in aguardiente a small piece of ironwood (*Casuarina equisetifolia*), using the trunk with the bark removed. They drink one cup of this decoction three times. "This is the most effective dose." (2) They boil the roots and leaves of the *Cyperus kyllingia* grass and drink a dose three or four times. (3) They mix ground plementa pepper with aguardiente and drink one small glassful. (4) They grind kapok (*Ceiba pentandra*) root, then boil it and drink it. (Thompson, p. 164)

MARICOPA

SPIER, LESLIE. *Yunan Tribes of the Gila River.* Chicago, 1933.

"It is difficult to tell how frequently abortion was practiced in the old days: it is common enough today. A cloth was tied tightly around the abdomen, draughts of a boiling hot tea made of iciu' (a plant growing near the river) were taken, and the constricting process repeated until the embryo was killed. (My informant had never heard of pressing the abdomen on a rock.)" (p. 314)

(See also *Southwest U. S. Indians.*)

MARONITES (Northern Lebanon)

LEWIS, R. K. "Unpublished Field Notes." 1950.

"The women here don't take any medicine before having the child nor none to make it easier. They eat the same food they always ate, both before and after. They keep on working right up to the last hour. A lot of women would rather have a miscarriage than have a child because they are poor. Some of them are working again right after they have had the child.

"They do not take any medicines to cause a miscarriage, they just carry heavy loads to help the process of having a miscarriage."

MARQUESAS

NH

This work contains a statement by Ralph Linton to the effect that the Marquesans aborted fairly often even after marriage. Indeed, many women refused to bear children, because they did not want to have their children taken from them and given to someone else to rear. Linton also states that the Marquesans used abortifacient herb remedies, whose nature he did not learn, as well as instrumentation, which consisted in inserting a sliver of bamboo into the uterus. Linton was of the opinion that, since the Marquesans were cannibals, they knew quite a bit of anatomy, so that few casualties resulted from instrumentation. (p. 23) [In 1952, in a personal conversation, the late Professor Linton reconfirmed these data. G. D.]

LINTON, RALPH. "Marquesan Culture," in Kardiner, Abram, *The Individual and his Society*. New York, 1939.

"The *fanaua* attacked other women at the bidding of his woman and also protected her from attacks from other *fanaua*. The techniques of *fanaua* attack were primarily connected with pregnancy. The *fanaua* might destroy the child in the womb (cases of neurotic symptoms of imaginary pregnancy were, as has been said, a fairly common phenomenon here) or cause the woman to die, during either pregnancy or childbirth. Practically all such deaths were explained on this basis.

"The woman knew she had a *fanaua* by the fact that a spirit came to her in dreams, frequently of an erotic nature. Other people knew that she had a *fanaua* by observing what happened to women who antagonized her. Although the woman herself never announced the fact, the knowledge that she was being aided by a spirit spread around the community. . . . The women were very reticent about the whole *fanaua* belief,probably because it was a source of great anxiety and mutual suspicion . . . . The woman's familiar never operated against her husbands and could even be invoked to help them indirectly by attacking women of other households whose men had wronged them. In one instance, a chief had expropriated a garden which belonged to a household of low rank. The wife sent her familiar to make the chief's wife sick and give her the appearance of pregnancy. When the chief's wife realized that her illness was due to magic, a ritual was performed to discover what *fanaua* was causing her trouble. As soon as she and her husband, the chief, learned the name of the *fanaua,* they knew who had sent it and why. The chief thereupon returned the garden, the spirit was called off, and his wife was well again. In cases where restitution was not made, however, the attack continued until the woman died.

"Occasionally women who had *fanaua* were killed by the irate relatives of women whom their spirits had attacked. This was the only case in which men killed women, and even this seems to have been somewhat unusual and to have resulted in a blood feud.

"The incidence of *fanaua* was about one to every three women. The *fanaua* themselves were graded in power, a *fanaua* who was a relative being considered more effective for defense than for offense. He protected his women against the attacks of other *fanaua* but would not act as a strong or constant aggressor against her enemies." (pp. 190–91)

MARSHALL ISLANDS

ERDLAND, A. *Die Marshall-Insulaner.* Munster i. W., 1914.

"If, despite all precautions, the woman gets pregnant, depending on the disposition of the couple, the child is either spared or is gotten rid of by massage. Abortion does not rate as murder because the undeveloped fetus is not deemed to be a human being. However, since couples do greatly desire to have at least one child, and since they know that the expulsion of fetuses weakens the female organs and often makes them sterile, abortion is not very common among married couples. It is common among single girls, since the child is a 'child procreated on the roadside' (*ajeri iturin ial*). The massage is executed with the hands or with bottles and is further promoted by hot baths." (p. 124)

MASAI

MERKER, F. *Die Masai.* Berlin, 1904.
(1) HOLLIS, A. C. *The Masai—Their Language and Folklore.* Oxford, 1905.
WEISS, MAX. *Die Völkerstämme im Norden Deutsch-Ostafrikas.* Berlin, 1910.
(2) HOLLIS, A. C. "A Note on the Masai System of Relationship and other Matters Connected Therewith," *Journal of the Royal Anthropological Institute,* 40:473–482, 1910.
MAGUIRE, R. A. J. "The Masai Penal Code." *Journal of the African Society,* 28:12–18, London, 1929.
LEAKEY, L. S. B. "Some Notes on the Masai of Kenya Colony," *Journal of the Royal Anthropological Institute,* 40:185–210, 1930.
FOX, D. S. "Further Notes on the Masai of Kenya Colony," *Journal of the Royal Anthropological Institute,* 60:447–465, 1930.
BRYK, FELIX. *Dark Rapture.* New York, 1939.

Abortion is rare. In three and one-half years of residence among the Masai the author saw one case only: A husband caused his wife to abort, because he was jealous of the child's father, a warrior of his own age-group. If a woman aborts on her own initiative, the matter is left for the women of the kraal to handle, who usually beat her. If the husband or another man causes the woman to get an abortion, the man is handed over to the women of the kraal, who sometimes beat him, but, more frequently, seize one of the man's oxen, take the beast to some quiet place and beat it to death with sticks. The women then eat the ox, and no man or pregnant woman may be present while they do so. (A related practice is the fact that women may not see the meat for the warriors' meal before it has been cooked.) (Maguire, p. 17) If a girl finds herself pregnant, she sends for the father of the unborn child and tells him of her predicament. He must then help her. If her parents do not know that she is pregnant, she might try to abort. If they know of it, they will not allow her to do so. The abortion is procured with a special stick, which can only be obtained from medicine men. This stick is inserted into the vaginal passage and is said to be absolutely effective. It is the only method used. (Leakey, p. 198) "In order to produce an abortion, the woman drinks a decoction of dried goat dung or a strong decoction of *os segi* (*Cordia quarensis*) or of *ol durgó* roots. During the next two or three days of convalescence she partakes of a weak decoction of the *ol mokoton* bark or of the *ol oilale* (*Colubrina asiatica*) bark." (Merker, p. 191) "The pregnant girl chews four finger-sized pieces of the root of *os segi* (*Cordia quarensis Gürke*) in order to obtain an abortion, whereupon the foetus allegedly dies and is expelled very rapidly." (Merker, p. 348) "Approximately three finger-sized pieces of the root of *ol durgó* are chewed, in order to induce an abortion." (Merker, p. 342) If a man cohabits with a pregnant woman and thereby causes her to abort, he is punished. All the neighborhood women collect and, having stripped him, seize the guilty person and flog him, after which they slaughter as many of his cattle as they can, strangling and suffocating the animals with their garments. (Hollis, 2, p. 40) "The immature foetus is expelled, against nature, when the woman is pregnant by an outsider or by an ailing or old person. They use as a remedy a certain potion which is said to be harmless during the first two months of pregnancy. After two months of pregnancy they wait until birth and then kill the neonate." (Merker, p. 50, fn.) They also practice eugenic infanticide. (Weiss, p. 385) While "rape, abortion, and unnatural perversion, which is said to occur in the form of sodomy, are not punished" * (Merker, p. 208), it is a great disgrace for a warrior to impregnate an uninitiated girl, and he must kill an enemy to wipe out the disgrace. This is the usual reason for the murder of people of other tribes, although such murders have been erroneously attributed to the desire to blood one's spear. (Fox, p. 451) A pregnant uninitiated girl is initiated at once, the burden of her rite being on her seducer. (Leakey, pp. 198–99) The Masai shame unmarried pregnant girls. The bastard is called "child of seduction" or "child of the fireplace." (Hollis, pp. 310–311) ". . . A [Masai] woman who had a grown daughter, but was a harlot, told me that she paid a woman one hundred shillings, for a medicine that was excellent. This decoction (*skyomeryat*) was taken only once, and then one did not get any more children. If one did want a child, an antidote must be taken. A white farmer who had much to do with uncircumcised girls, doubted the value of these mediums for abortion. The thorough washing after coitus probably really serves this purpose among the prostitutes." (Bryk, p. 113)

* It should be noted, however, that according to Merker (p. 159) bulls and billy-goats with unnatural sexual impulses are slaughtered as soon as their vice is noted, because it is deemed to bring misfortune. It is believed that by their conduct they bring upon the herds divine punishment in the form of a pestilence.

MASSAWA (Arabian Gulf)

PB

"In Massawa, on the Arabian Gulf, abortion is very frequent because fathers are obliged to hang their daughters (! ! !) if they become pregnant without being married." (2:515, quoting Brehm, A. E., *Reiseskizzen aus Nord Ost Afrika,* Jena, 1855, Part I, p. 169) "They use a decoction of a Thuja species." (2:531, quoting Brehm, *ibid.*)

MASSIM, SOUTHERN

SELIGMAN, C. G. *The Melanesians of British New Guinea.* Cambridge, 1910.

"Foeticide and infanticide are, or were, common. . . ." (p. 568)

MATACO

KARSTEN, RAFAEL. "Indian Tribes of the Argentine and Bolivian Chaco," *Societas Scientiarum Fennica, Commentationes Humanarum Litterararum,* Vol. 4, No. 1, Helsingfors, 1932.

MÉTRAUX, ALFRED. *Myths and Tales of the Matako Indians.* Ethnological Studies, 9, Göteborg, 1939.

If, as a result of license, a single girl gets pregnant, she aborts. This is all right, since social morality does not oppose it. (Karsten, p. 53) Since single girls abort, the writer never saw an illegitimate baby. Married women abort or commit infanticide if they are deserted by their husbands. They beat the abdomen with their hands, and press out the fetus with their thumbs, either alone, or assisted by an old woman. There is some pain, but it has no serious effects. No drugs are used. Such abortions are socially approved and are emotionally on a par with the extraction of a tooth. (Karsten, p. 79) They abort by means of a plant which looks like manioc. The root is ground and is taken in water. It has sterilizing effects which last one, two, four, or even eight years. Infanticide is not disapproved, since children are not independent persons, but the absolute property of their parents. (Métraux, p. 115)

MATTOLE

DRIVER, H. E. *Culture Element Distributions: X, Northwest California.* Anthropological Records, 1, #6, Berkeley, 1939.

"Medicine eaten or drunk." (p. 350)

MBAYA

PB

"The Mbaya in Paraguay abort their children because the women dread to age prematurely if they carry their children to term, and because the raising of children represents too much trouble for them, in view of the hardships which they have to endure." (2:516)

"Azara once asked the Mbaya women in Paraguay by what means they brought about abortions. They replied: 'You will see it right away.' Thereupon one of the women lay down, entirely naked, on the ground, and two old women began to rain the heaviest blows of their fists upon her abdomen, until blood ran from her genitals. This was for them a sign that the foetus was in the process of being expelled, and Azara did, in fact, learn after a few hours that the foetus had, indeed, been expelled. At the same time he was also informed, however, that quite a few of these women suffer the most deleterious consequences from this act, and that many die either in the course of the operation itself, or, partly, as a consequence thereof." (2:524, quoting Azara, Félix de, *Voyages dans l'Amérique Méridionale,* Paris, 1809, 4 vols.)

MBUNDU

HAMBLY, W. D. "The Ovimbundu of Angola." *Field Museum of Natural History, Anthropological Series,* 21:89–362, 1934.

In this tribe bastards are a disgrace. (p. 189) They kill deformed neonates, but this has to be done before the infant has lived a few days. (p. 187) Since they procure abortion by means of a bitter drug, Mbundu women refuse to take quinine, because they think it might cause them to abort. (p. 185) Abortion is never performed by mechanical means. They use the ihemba drug, made of the root of a plant, which they boil in water and then drink. It is called: "Medicine to take away the belly." (pp. 186–87)

MELANESIA (in general)

CODRINGTON, R. H. *The Melanesians.* Oxford, 1891.

"Abortion and infanticide were very common. If a woman did not want the trouble of bringing up a child, desired to appear young, was afraid the husband might think the birth before its time, or wished to spite her husband, she would find someone to procure abortion either by the juice of certain plants taken in drink or by twisting and squeezing the foetus." (p. 229)

BROWN, GEORGE. *Melanesians and Polynesians.* London, 1910.

"I was not able to get any trustworthy information as to the extent to which abortion is practiced, beyond the statement that it is frequently done."

[In a further discussion the author points out that in all of the Polynesian and Melanesian islands the natives believe that a certain plant, a long creeper, that grows commonly on beaches there, is the specific for abortion. He says,] "In practice, however, the administration of the 'specific' is generally accompanied by vigorous kneading or shampooing [sic] which probably effects the desired results. . . . The same plant is used for suppressed menstruation." (pp. 33–34)

DURRAD, REV. J. W., in RIVERS, W. H. R., ed. *Essays on the Depopulation of Melanesia.* Cambridge, 1922.

"Abortion is and always was practised and unfortunately is not regarded as a great crime. It is not considered on a par with infanticide. It is not reckoned as anything approaching the crime of murder." (p. 15)

MENOMINI

HOFFMAN, W. J. "The Menomini Indians," *Bureau of American Ethnology, Annual Report 14,* 1893.

"The hair of the tail of the blacktail deer has been used in a manner similar to that in which cactus spines are used, for producing abortion. The hair is chopped fine, then mixed with the fat of a bear's paw, and administered. Gastric irritation follows, leading, possibly, to uterine contraction, and the ultimate expulsion of the foetus. The Indian's explanation is, however, that the fine spicules of hair act like magic arrows, dart forward in the body in pursuit of the life of that which it is desirable to overcome, with the result indicated." (p. 286)

MERIR (Western Caroline Islands)

FRITZ, G. "Eine Reise nach Palau, Sonsol und Tobi," *Deutsches Kolonialblatt,* 18:659–668, 1907.

In Sonsol, Merir, and Pulo Anna women procure abortion by means of a decoction of pandanus roots. (p. 666)

MEXICAN INDIANS, N. W. (in general)
AH

"Among the Mexican Indians the writer heard more about 'medicines' and less about violence as a means of inducing abortion; but among most of the Mexican tribes observed, on account of their contact with whites and their adoption of Christianity, investigation of subjects of this nature is usually unsatisfactory." (p. 165)

(See also *Southwest U. S. Indians.*)

MICRONESIA (especially Caroline Islands)

FINSCH, OTTO. *Ethnologische Erfahrungen und Belegstücke aus der Südsee.* Wien, 1895.

MATSUOKA, SHIZUO. *Mikuronesha minzoku-shi* [An Ethnographical Study of Micronesia]. Tokyo, 1927.

Deane blames the decline of population in the Caroline Islands on abortion. (Finsch, p. 124) They sometimes use for this purpose bathing and massage. (Matsuoka, p. 367)

MIRIAM

HUNT, A. E. "Ethnographical Notes on the Murray Islands, Torres Straits," *Journal of the Anthropological Institute,* n.s. I: 5–19 (o.s. Vol. 28), 1899.

"Abortion was very common, for various reasons: sometimes (as in the case of a single girl) from shame, sometimes to save the mother the trouble of child rearing. For the purposes of abortion the leaves of certain trees were chewed. The leaves of the *sesepot, mad leuer, ariari,* and *ap* were sometimes mixed with coconut milk and drunk. This caused little or no pain. Failing that, the leaves of the *tim, mikir, sorbe, bok, sem* and *argerarger* were chewed together. This medicine caused great pain, but killed the child. When medicine failed harsher measures were resorted to. Sometimes the abdomen would be beaten with big stones, or the woman would be placed with her back against a tree, when two men would take a long pole, and, taking either end, would place it against her abdomen and by sheer pressure crush the foetus. It need scarcely be added that such treatment frequently killed the woman as well." (pp. 11–12)

(1) HADDON, A. C. *Reports of the Cambridge Anthropological Expedition to Torres Straits,* Vol. VI: *Sociology, Magic, and Religion of the Eastern Islanders.* Cambridge, 1908.
(2) HADDON, A. C. *Reports of the Cambridge Anthropological Expedition to Torres Straits,* Vol. I: *General Ethnography.* Cambridge, 1935.

They abort both by means of drugs and by mechanical means. The drugs are derived from the shore Convolvulus, Ipoemoea biloba. Abortion is very common. Single girls abort from a sense of shame. Others abort because raising children is too much trouble. They chew such leaves as Clerodendron sp., Poulzolzia microphylla, and Macaranga tanarius. Sometimes this is mixed with coconut milk and drunk. Abortion so induced causes little or no pain. If this remedy fails, Terminalia catappa, Eugenia, Hibiscus tiliaceus, argerarger and Callicarpa are chewed together. This medicine causes a great deal of pain, but it kills the fetus. They also beat the belly with big stones, or a woman will stand with her back to a tree, while two men take a big pole and apply pressure on her abdomen, crushing the fetus. This technique often kills the woman as well. The women may also tie a vine or a rope of coconut fiber around her belly or else climb a coconut tree, and bump her abdomen against the tree trunk both in ascending and descending. Or else, while in the garden, she may fill a big basket with yams and sweet potatoes, and place it on her abdomen. She may also press a bamboo on her belly or strike it with a heavy and hard object. Old women also advise the carrying of heavy loads from the garden. (Haddon 1:107) If a parturient woman dies before delivering the child, the women attending her press her belly with a bamboo and extract the child. (Haddon 2:178) The leaves of a plant, tentatively identified as Ipomoea biloba, are chewed both as a contraceptive and as an abortifacient. (Haddon 2:110) These leaves are also heated and applied to relieve pain, as well as for purposes of contraception and abortion. (Haddon 2:116)

MOHAVE

DEVEREUX, GEORGE. "Mohave Indian Infanticide," *The Psychoanalytic Review,* Vol. 35:126–38, 1948.

"The Mohave knew of no means of contraception in aboriginal times, and never used either coitus interruptus or sexual perversions for contraceptive reasons. The only modern device known to them is the condom, mistakenly called 'French tickler.' It is never used as a contraceptive or as a prophylactic device. To the Mohave the condom is merely a funny toy, purchased by some wags for the purpose of injecting an element of comedy into the sexual act.

"In aboriginal times abortion was a means of getting rid of an illegitimate child, whose father did not wish to recognize it. The psychological causes of abortions which occurred in aboriginal times are obscured by the motivation of present-day abortions, which are frequently a result of acculturation. Most contemporary abortions are performed on young school girls, partly for the purpose of concealing their sexual activities from school officials, and partly for the purpose of protecting their lovers from being prosecuted for contributing to the delinquency of minors. As a result Mohave girls now abort children which would have been permitted to live in aboriginal times, and whose conception might have led to a marriage. This is a disastrous situation. Since coitus in Mohave society does not seem to be accompanied by any sense of guilt, and since they are fond of children, the external, though indirect, pressure which compels them to perform abortions is likely to lead to an increase in promiscuousness. Even more deleterious perhaps are the psychological effects of pressures and punishments which are endured without a sense of guilt. Situations of this type are, unfortunately, quite characteristic of contemporary reservation life.

"Abortion was never performed without the consent of the girl herself, though it is quite possible that external pressures were sometimes instrumental in causing her to agree to have an abortion performed. This is particularly true of present-day schoolgirls.

"The exact number of abortions is difficult to ascertain, because they are performed in secret. It is furthermore quite important to realize that a normal pregnancy is hard to terminate. Many pregnancies can be interrupted only because, due to venereal diseases, they were already doomed to end in miscarriages or stillbirths. The fact that the Mohave know a great deal about the appearance of foeti at various stages of foetal development suggests that abortions occurred rather frequently, even in aboriginal times.

"Abortions and miscarriages can be induced in three ways:

"(1) Pregnancies could be terminated by means of witchcraft. This technique was never resorted to by the woman herself, partly because of the Mohave Indian's generalized fear of witchcraft, and partly because witchcraft of this type often killed both the mother and the child. Witchcraft causing abortions was used only by persons who had grievances against the girl or her family. If the aggrieved person had the necessary supernatural powers he bewitched the girl himself. If not, he obtained the services of a venal black magician. This type of witchcraft is no longer practiced at present, and the very art of inducing miscarriage by means of witchcraft is said to have been forgotten.

"(2) It is theoretically possible to induce an abortion by violating some of the pregnancy taboos. There is, however, no evidence to suggest that any Mohave woman ever resorted to this expedient for the purpose of terminating her pregnancy.

"(3) Mechanical abortion can be induced in two ways:

"(a) The woman who wished to produce an abortion lay flat on her back, on the ground, and caused another woman to step on her abdomen, or to jump up and down on it. After a while the patient rolled over and the abortionist stepped, or jumped, on the small of her back, where the pelvic bones are attached to the spinal column. Sometimes several assistants relayed each other.

"An abortion of this type was described by Dr. Nettle: 'We had a fourteen-year-old girl in the school some years ago, who became pregnant during the summer vacation and miscarried after four and a half months, while at the school. She confessed that she had some older schoolgirls jump on her stomach in relays. The infant's arm was broken and had begun to heal. The girl herself suffered no ill effects.'

"Attempts at inducing abortion by these means frequently resulted only in the crippling of the child. Whenever an obviously unwanted child was born in a crippled state, the community assumed that an attempt had been made to abort it.

"(b) Another means of inducing abortion required a certain amount of technical skill and was therefore used on a somewhat smaller scale. During the third lunar month of pregnancy a skilled woman put her 'hand inside' and 'choked the child.' (Since this is an impossibility, I presume that the abortionist merely manipulated the cervix in a rather violent manner.) This operation was usually performed either by a girl's mother, or else by a skilled older female relative.

"The two mechanical means of inducing an abortion could be used either separately or in succession.

"In aboriginal times the abortionist was usually the girl's own mother. At present it is frequently a schoolmate.

"As soon as the foetus emerged from the maternal body it was picked up either by one of the assistants, or, if need be, by the mother herself, and was buried in a wholly informal manner. Stillborn children were disposed of in the same way.

"Mohave society did not penalize abortion and the lover had no claim either against his mistress or against the abortionists.

"Though abortion was by no means an exceptional act, its marginal character is clearly indicated by the fact that it is not mentioned in any Mohave myth. In reply to a direct question the Mohave merely remarked that abortion, like everything else pertaining to human life, had been provided for at the time of creation.

"The Mohave are disinclined to talk about abortion, partly because they do not like to discuss matters pertaining to actual procreation, and partly because they know that abortion is illegal." (pp. 137–39)

(See also *Southwest U. S. Indians*)

MOJO and BAURE

HDBK

"Those who suffered a miscarriage were immediately drowned lest dysentery epidemics spread through the village. (Cf. Orellana, Antonio de, *Carta de Padre Orellana sobre el origen de las misiones de Mojo,* Madrid, 1906, p. 12)" (3:419)

MONGOL (Yuan Dynasty)

RIASANOVSKY, V. A. *Fundamental Principles of Mongol Law.* Tientsin, 1937.

"Abortion was forbidden." (p. 287)

MONGOL-OIRAT (Kalmuck)

RIASANOVSKY, V. A. *Fundamental Principles of Mongol Law.* Tientsin, 1937.

"Anyone causing the abortion (a miscarriage) of a child was fined as many nines of animals as the child was old." (p. 98)

MONTANA and BOLIVIAN EAST ANDES TRIBES

HDBK

"Abortion and infanticide were once fairly common, probably resulting from disturbances of the Contact Period" [with the Spanish]. (3:529)

MONUMBO (Potsdamhafen)

NEUHAUSS, RICHARD. *Deutsch Neu-Guinea,* Vol. I. Berlin, 1911.

"The women use as an abortifacient the juice of a plant. They also know how to provoke premature birth by working unusually energetically with the hoe or adze, whereby the body sustains intense shocks. The premature birth so initiated is further promoted by an intensive constriction of the abdomen." (p. 150)

MORIORI

SKINNER, H. D. AND BAUCKE, WILLIAM. "The Morioris," B. P. Bishop Museum, Memoirs 9, #5, Honolulu, 1928.

"When his daughter felt the urge of motherhood, she calmed it in the only way she knew; and unless motherhood ensued, the parents saw no harm in the manner of that calming so long as the calmer bore a status of which they need feel no shame. In the older days when the 'unwanted' made its presence known, she knew of means to stay its growth. Should this happening reach the tribal ear it altered no jot her status or value in the marriage mart." (p. 369)

MOUNT HAGEN, NEW GUINEA

GITLOW, A. L. *Economics of the Mount Hagen Tribes, New Guinea.* American Ethnological Society, Monograph 12, New York, 1947.

"Although large families are desirable to men of chiefly rank, children are not desired by the average young male who has just married, at least not for several years, probably due to the prohibition of sex relations while nursing. Consequently, children are not produced usually until several years after a man has acquired his first wife, although this does not hold for older men who already have multiple wives. In the case of the young monogamous couple abortion will be employed to avoid the birth of children until the parents desire them. The process of aborting a pregnant woman is generally undertaken by one of the older, experienced women of the group. The method employed is one involving massage, by pressing around the womb with crooked thumbs over a period of time in such a manner as to induce miscarriage. However, this will be done only in the early stages of pregnancy, prior to the formation of any extensive bone structure in the foetus. The extent of this practice is such that many women are ruined by it, and are thereafter incapable of bearing children. In this last respect, it is interesting to note that sterility in the female is not a ground for divorce, and it is reported that the husband will sympathize with a sterile wife, and console her with the assurance that they will be able to obtain a child eventually by another wife." (pp. 39–40)

MUNDA KOLH (Chota Nagpore)

JELLINGHAUS, TH. "Sagen, Sitten und Gebräuche der Munda-Kolhs in Chota Nagpore," *Zeitschrift für Ethnologie,* Vol. 3:326–337, 365–380, 1871.

"It happens, however, now and then, that married women of the poorer classes, whose pregnancies succeed each other too rapidly, go to evil old women and use abortifacients. They even allow their uterus to be compressed and displaced without the knowledge of their husbands, so as to be rid of the plague of pregnancy. It seems that they have learned this contemptible aberration from the lower caste Hindus. It may be remarked that the better kind of public opinion among them definitely condemns such acts. They say: 'The maternal body is the farmland of Singbonga and one is not permitted to destroy it. What a longing for children is there in the hearts of childless parents who have no children or whose children have died—and you kill the child of your own womb!' This indignation, however, is much smaller when the violent abortion takes place shortly after conception." (p. 365)

MU'Ò'NG

CUISINIER, JEANNE. *Les Mu'ò'ng.* Travaux et Mémoires de l'Institut d'Ethnologie, Paris, 1948.

"The Mu'ò'ng know abortifacient manipulations but seem to take recourse to them only seldom. Naturally one does not publicize either illegitimate births or the means employed to avoid them. Without having made an attempt to inquire into this matter systematically, in the course of ten months in the same village we learned, by means of gossip so useful to the ethnographer, of one single case of abortion and of three clandestine births." (p. 68)

MURIA

ELWIN, VERRIER. *The Muria and their Ghotul.* Bombay, 1947.

". . . To prevent conception, says Roy, an Uraon girl 'either reverses her loin-cloth for the nonce by wearing it with its front side to the back or ties to her loin-cloth just over the abdomen the false plait of hair sometimes worn as a coiffure.' If this fails, recourse is made, as in Bastar, to abortifacients." (p. 296)

"But if there is a pregnancy it is a serious matter. In such a case, I was told at Kabonga, the members of the ghotul assemble and pass judgment. 'Look, brother, look, sister, you are both of the same clan; you are brother-sister to each other, yet you have done this evil. If the elders hear of it, we can give them no answer. We ourselves do not think it sin; it was the lust of youth, you were made with love; but the elders will think it sin.' And they insist that the boy should bring an abortifacient. In Munjmeta when a Katlami boy fell in love with a girl of the Wadder-clan—these are forbidden to one another—the ghotul members held a meeting, and solemnly warned them that they would be fined if they continued to sleep together and that if the girl became pregnant it would be most serious for them both. But I heard that they took no notice." (p. 415)

"But when all precautions fail, and a girl finds herself pregnant, what happens? Directly she finds that 'the moon has come again, but the stream of blood is dry,' she tells her chelik. There is no difficulty in the old type of ghotul; her ghotul-husband will look after her. In the newer type, where during the course of the month the girl may have been sleeping with a dozen different boys, she chooses either the one she likes best or the one with whom she first had congress after her last period. His immediate duty is to bring abortifacients.

"Abortions are probably fairly common. In one village I was told that they mixed gur, ashes and the strongest mahua spirit available and gave it to the girl to drink. In another place the Muria said that they used gunpowder mixed with mahua spirit. In Kokori, the Gaita recommended the obviously magical remedy of taking a bit of bark from a mahua tree which had been struck by lightning. This was burnt and the ashes mixed with liquor. In Burma, an eighty-year-old Muria recalled how when he was Nengi of the ghotul he made the Nirosa pregnant. He first dosed her with *keksa* root, but without success, apparently because he did not know the correct ritual of obtaining it, and then on a Monday he bought a bottle of *phuli* liquor. 'On that day we both fasted and in the evening, after bathing, I offered an egg and some liquor to Lingo Pen saying, O Mahapurub Lingo, if you are a true god, let this girl abort; if you don't, the sin is yours and not mine. You founded the ghotul and if you truly live there till this day, show proof of it and I will offer you another egg. I then made the girl drink the rest of the liquor and in her drunkenness she aborted. As I had promised I gave the second egg to Lingo Pen.'

"In one ghotul, about which I believe I have entirely authentic information, six of the girls had procured abortions; one had achieved it three times, twice in the third month and once in the fourth; another girl had achieved it twice. But the motiari do not like using abortifacients, for they believe that they lead to sterility later on, and this ghotul was probably exceptional. There were a number of older girls there; in other places, where only a few motiari exceed three years from the menarche, such large-scale abortifacient practices appear to be unnecessary. In any case the practice is not approved by the elders of the tribe. In Hathipakna, the Malko was made pregnant by the Jamadar, both being of the same clan. An older man tried to procure an abortion, but failed; the matter became known and he was fined five rupees by the clan panchayat.

"If all their efforts fail, the chelik and motiari report the matter to the ghotul leaders, who keep it dark as long as possible. There is no greater ghotul crime than to reveal such a secret in the village." (pp. 465–66)

"Yet few cases come to the courts, and even Hutton with his great experience was unable to find examples. For the Muria I have described an attempt at abortion as a routine measure in cases of ghotul pregnancy, but its ineffectiveness is shown not only by definite statements to that effect, but also by the number of children actually born." (p. 469)

"A few years ago in Hathipakna there was a scandal when the Malko, 'a daughter of Naitami,' was made pregnant by the Jamadar, also a Naitami. They attempted an abortion, without success, but after the boy's father had paid twelve rupees, the Malko was married, by the reduced ceremonies, to a boy at Sodma." (p. 416)

MURNGIN

WARNER, W. L. "Morphology and Functions of the Australian Murngin Type of Kinship," *American Anthropologist,* n. s. 32:207–256, 1930.

"Abortion, practised for the same reason as infanticide, is not infrequent. The pregnant woman's sisters exert pressure with the knees and hands on her abdomen.

"Sometimes a mother kills her newborn babe because it has followed too closely to the others, and she has not enough milk to feed it. This would be done without the knowledge of the father, who would be most angry if he knew about it."

WARNER, W. L. *A Black Civilization.* New York, 1937.

Sometimes they kill the newborn which follows too closely upon the previous one, if the mother does not have enough milk. It is done without the father's knowledge, because he would be angry. If the child dies at birth, the father suspects his wife of having smothered it. Abortion is not frequent, and has the same motivation as infanticide. The woman's sister exerts pressure on the belly of the pregnant woman with her knees and hands. (p. 96)

MYTHUGGADI (Queensland)

PALMER, EDWARD. "Notes on Some Australian Tribes," *Journal of the Anthropological Institute,* 13:277–334, 1884.

"Infanticide is not so common as supposed, though a girl's first child is often sacrificed. Abortion can effect the same purpose, and they have no hesitation in having recourse to it, effecting their object by blows. One girl was known to have thrown herself across a log to produce the death and the speedy delivery of the child." (p. 280)

NAHUA

LEÓN, NICOLAS. *La Obstetrica en Mexico,* Mexico, D.F., 1910.

"It seems evident to Gomara that many pregnant females 'abort in secret,' and to Sahagun that there are women who 'give herbs for abortion,' a crime which is punished by death.

"Brother Juan Batista . . . tells us: 'There are other sorcerers, who are called *Tetlatlaxilique,* who give charms to women who became pregnant in secret, so as to expel the infant."

NAVAHO

AH

(See AH's data on the *Hopi.*)

BAILEY, F. L. *Some Sex Beliefs and Practices in a Navaho Community.* Peabody Museum of American Archaelogy and Ethnology Papers, 40, #2, Cambridge, Massachusetts, 1950.

"The existence of abortion as a method for disposing of an unwanted child was confirmed by twice as many informants as denied it. Those who said abortion was practised gave examples of methods used.

"Sometimes they carry a log right on top of the baby, or put something heavy on their belly to kill the baby. It comes out dead. Maybe they don't like to have the baby. I never knew of a case around here.—jtw

"There's a lot of it (abortion) around here. The girls use pressure to destroy their (illegitimate) children.—ern

"They carry something heavy on their back. It makes the baby come right away.—cw

"Only one man gave a first-hand account of an abortion. He relates as follows:

"I've heard that Navahos use it. When a girl feels the baby move the first time she kills it with her hands. It is born dead and they hide it away. It happened around here. A girl over at Ramon's did it about a year ago. She killed it and threw it away. The Navahos all kept quiet about it. She had another about two months ago. It was born dead, and they hid it, too. People worried about it at first. Said she shouldn't do this. If she wants a man why not marry a man and do like other women, have a baby the right way. Then people like it better. The way she's acting is not good at all. They might talk about it. It might be (incest) or she might have done it with a dog or something. People talk this way.—I

"The reason for abortion is that the child is unwanted or is illegitimate. Three people also discussed the reaction of the community to an action of this sort. They said:

"People won't ever like a woman who does that. The father and mother will give them lots of talk afterwards. It's the worst thing to do. Better let it be born. The woman can be very sick from this (abortion).—cw

"Maybe the people would hate a woman who does this. I don't know.—jtw

"The foetus is said to be disposed of by hiding it, throwing it away, or putting it in a cave.

"Hill tells in his notes that in order to have an abortion a woman would lie on a round rock or log. These would usually be girls who were pregnant or women who became pregnant through adulterous relationships. One woman told him:

"Abortion is caused by a woman going out and lying face down with her stomach on a rock. Sometimes the woman will die. This method is not always effective. . . .

"An account of another illegitimate child, attempted infanticide and the resulting interfamily tensions centering around the same woman discussed above has been recorded:

"At the time of the Big Snow, Mrs. Gregorio had a baby by a truck driver from Tohachi. Her mother had chased her, made her fall off a cliff, and baby came early. Then her mother talked nice to her and made her expose the baby. Found by a white man, taken to a missionary, and died ten minutes later. Mrs. Gregorio said if she had really wanted the baby to die, she could have hid it in a canyon. She purposely put it near a white man's ranch so he could find it." (pp. 98–99)

". . . The practice of abortion was admitted by twice as many informants as denied it. Methods mentioned were pressure and carrying heavy loads. The foetus could be hidden or placed in a cave. Reasons offered were that the child was illegitimate, or was unwanted." (p. 102)

(See also *Southwest U. S. Indians.*)

NAVAHO (Northwestern)

STEWART, O. C. *Culture Element Distributions: XVIII, Ute–Southern Paiute.* Anthropological Records, 6, #4, Berkeley, 1942.

"Northern Navaho women abort." (p. 303) "They prepare also a contraceptive concoction from boiled mule rectum and various plants." (p. 346)

NEGRITOS of Malaya

EVANS, I. H. N. *The Negritos of Malaya.* Cambridge, 1937.

". . . The Kintak Bong, according to Schebesta, know, and use, various kinds of aphrodisiacs and means of producing abortion." (p. 215)

NESQUALLY

LORD, JOHN KEAST. *The Naturalist in Vancouver Island and British Columbia,* Vol. II. London, 1866.

"Q. Does infanticide occur to any extent; if so, what are the probable causes?"

"A. (Anderson)—No.

"A. (Tolmie)—Amongst the Chenooks and the Indians of Puget's Sound, as well as the Chimsians or Fort Simpson Indians, infanticide and causing of abortion are not uncommon. Certain old women at Nesqually I knew were reputed experts at the last mentioned business. The causes are at first shame at having a child without an acknowledged father; latterly the desire of unmarried women not to be hampered with children." (pp.231–32)

[The two informants were men in the Hudson Bay Company service. Tolmie was a doctor.]

NEW BRITAIN and DUKE OF YORK ISLANDS

DANKS, BENJAMIN. "Marriage Customs of the New Britain Group," *Journal of the Anthropological Institute,* 18:281–94, 1889.

"After marriage children arc not borne by the women for a period of from two to four years. I am informed that this is the result of a popular dislike to speedily becoming mothers on the part of the women, who use various means of procuring abortion and use them successfully. The favorite method is that of clasping the waist between the thumb and fingers on both sides, pressing and working the fingers strongly into the stomach and so compressing it. Others insert a sharp pointed stick into the womb thereby destroying the foetus. The latter operation I give merely as hearsay, and for what it is worth. . . . Some say there is a herb which is used for the same purpose." (p. 291)

[The usual interval between babies is three years, though Danks knew of one or two exceptions. (p. 292)]

NEW BRITAIN (Gazelle Peninsula, Northeastern Tribes)
PARKINSON, R. *Dreissig Jahre in der Südsee.* Stuttgart, 1907.

"Girls who become pregnant without being married attempt first to destroy their fetus. If they are unsuccessful in this undertaking they go, at the time of delivery, into the forest, where they give birth without any help whatsoever. The newborn child is killed and buried immediately after birth." (pp. 71–72)

NEW BRITAIN (Western Tribes)
PARKINSON, R. *Dreissig Jahre in der Südsee.* Stuttgart, 1907.

"Not quite as devastating as pestilences but also harmful is the custom, as widespread there as in Western New Britain, that, at the death of a native, his wives are strangled and that perhaps nowhere else in the archipelago does the abortion of fetuses and the killing of children prevail to the same extent as here." (p. 209)

NEW CALEDONIA
ROCHAS, H. V. "Sittliche und Materielle Zustände der Neu-Caledonier," *Das Ausland,* 1862 (pp. 1087–94).

"They have an infernal readiness with abortions and a very customary method is called the banana cure. It apparently consists of the pregnant woman eating boiling hot cooked bananas. Since bananas are completely harmless, they serve as the disguise for the real, as yet undiscovered, abortion remedy. Only too frequently one hears from one of the natives: 'There goes one who also took bananas.' This shameful custom is not only made use of by unmarried girls, but also by women who want to avoid the trouble of nursing and wish to preserve certain bodily charms." (p. 1092)

PB

"This information is also confirmed by Moncelon." (2:512, quoting Moncelon, Léon, in *Bulletin de la Société d'Anthropologie de Paris,* 9:345 ff., 1886) [Not verified by checking this article. G. D.]

"They also do it to save their breasts from becoming flaccid and wilted." (2:512) Moncelon likewise indicates that the abortifacient drugs are unknown but are of a vegetable origin. He believes that they use for this purpose the bark of certain trees." (2:527, quoting von Rochas, *ibid.,* and Moncelon, *ibid.*)

NEW GUINEA (Territory of, in general)
NH

"Abortion . . . is practiced." (p. 20, quoting Krieger, Maximilian, *Neu-Guinea,* Berlin, 1899, p. 165)

NEUHAUSS, RICHARD. *Deutsch Neu-Guinea,* Vol. I. Berlin, 1911.

"The germinating life is far from secure in the womb and the newborn is subject to a series of threats from the mother herself. Not only do they seek to get rid of an extramarital pregnancy, but even the young married woman, who wishes to safeguard as long as possible her rounded figure and bodily strength, may induce abortion. For this reason, the first years of marriage are frequently childless. In addition, one has the impression that the young Papuan woman finds it rather difficult to conceive: were it not so, the girls would get more often pregnant, as a result of frequent premarital intercourse, than seems to be the case.

"Abortion is also resorted to in the later years of marriage in order to limit the number of children, because too large a family would represent too much agricultural work for the parents." (p. 150)

NEW HEBRIDES (in general)

HAGEN, A., AND PINEAU, A. "Les Nouvelles Hebrides: Etudes Ethnographiques," *Revue de l'Ethnographie,* 7:302–62, 1888.

"Abortion is rather frequent and is practiced by means of certain special herbs and by a rubbing of the abdomen." (p. 332)

[JOLY, P. R.] "Kleine Nachrichten," *Globus,* 88:164, September 14, 1905.

"A French research worker, Dr. P. R. Joly, publishes in the *Bulletins de la Société d'Anthropologie* 1904, p. 356, various new data upon the New Hebrides whose interior is still so little known, and where he has traveled and whose inhabitants he describes as very barbaric and wild. However, they are everywhere rapidly decreasing in numbers; on the Coast they disappear more and more because they retire from the whites into the mountains and the forests. Some ten years ago, when Catholic missionaries settled in Port Sandwich on Malekula, the local tribe still numbered 600 persons while today there are only half as many. Artificial abortion is widespread and when a deformed child is born they not only kill the baby but also the mother." (p. 164)

(See also *Efate, Espiritu Santo, Gaua, Malekula, Pentecost.*)

NEW IRELAND

PARKINSON, R. *Dreissig Jahre in der Südsee.* Stuttgart, 1907.

"In the north marriage is not very stable. The spouses can separate at will and the woman returns to her own sib accompanied by such children as may have been born to her in the course of her marriage. An exchange of wives also occurs frequently; however, this happens only between two members of one and the same totemic group. The tribe and the people suffer a great deal as a result of this very loose relationship, because the women consider children as inconvenient appendages and use the most variegated means in order to abort their fetuses. These are partly mechanical, such as an intensive kneading of the abdomen, jumping from a high rock or tree trunk, a strong constriction of the belly, etc., and partly involve drugs, which are prepared from various plants known to them. Through this aberration the women weaken themselves so much that they die young and do not contribute to the increase of the tribe, so that the latter is increasingly diminishing in numbers." (pp. 267–68)

NGALI

RÓHEIM, GÉZA. *Psychoanalysis and Anthropology.* New York, 1950.

"A unique aspect of Central Australian cannibalism is that of procuring an abortion for the purpose of eating the embryo. Patjili, a Ngali woman, told us that the Ngalis and Yumus eat their own children or procure an abortion out of 'meat hunger.' They pull the child out by the head. Then they burn the placenta, roast the child, and eat it. The infant is eaten by the mother and the older siblings. The older children are supposed to eat it so that they may grow bigger, the mother does it because she is hungry." (p. 61)

NIAS

CHAMBERLAIN, A. F. *The Child and Childhood in Folk-Thought.* New York, 1896.

The ghosts of women who die in childbirth torment the living, plague women who are with child, and kill the embryo in the womb, thus causing abortion. [This information was apparently derived by Chamberlain from Modigliani, Elio, *Un Viaggio a Nias,* Milan, 1890, pp. 553–54.]

NIGERIA

TREMEARNE, A. J. N. *The Ban of the Bori.* London, 1914.

"Should an unmarried girl become pregnant, she will take drugs to restore her regularity but this is said to be very uncommon and it seems certain that some regular drink is taken before and after each act to prevent trouble arising, so abortion and child-murder must happen but seldom." (Quoted in Harley, G. W., *Native African Medicine,* Cambridge, Massachusetts, 1941, p. 215)

HARLEY, G. W. *Native African Medicine.* Cambridge, Massachusetts, 1941.

"Compare C. K. Meek, "Deathbed Confessions of Witches," in *Law and Authority in a Nigerian Tribe,* London, 1936, p. 84. One confessed that she had 'caused hundreds of women to abort by devouring their babies in their wombs.' Compare also Field, *Religion and Medicine of the Gā People,* pp. 128 and 139." (p. 27, fn.)

NIGERIA (Southern)

HARLEY, G. W. *Native African Medicine.* Cambridge, Massachusetts, 1941.

"Talbot says that cases of abortion have occurred over and over again after the taking of medicines prescribed by the leech. These medicines are usually known by all the midwives and used promptly by a woman as soon as she has missed her first period so that she does not think of them as abortifacients but as medicines to restore the function of menstruation. Gilkes says that the midwives use these same drugs to aid in removing the placenta." (pp. 215–16, quoting Talbot, P. A., *Life in Southern Nigeria,* London, 1923, p. 210, and Gilkes, H. A., "Native Customs in Africa and the Medical Officer," *Royal Society of Imperial Medicine and Hygiene, Transactions,* 1933–34, p. 315)

NIUE

THOMSON, BASIL. "Notes Upon the Natives of Savage Island, or Niue," *Journal of the Anthropological Institute,* 31:137–145, 1901.

"Infanticide used to be common in the cases of illegitimate children and children born in time of war. In the latter case the child was disposed of by Fakafolau, that is to say, it was put into an ornamented cradle, and, with many tears, set adrift upon the sea. Mothers are very affectionate to their children. . . .

"Abortion was formerly common, because if a couple did not come together with the consent of the girl's relations, they were punished. Drugs and trampling on the abdomen were the usual methods employed. Abortion seems to be less common now since the law against seduction is administered with caprice, and influence can generally be brought to screen those who offend against it. An illegitimate child has no disabilities, and its parents do not suffer in public estimation. The absence of so many of the men, and the consequent predominance of women, are sufficient to account for a large increase in illegitimacy." (p. 141)

NONGATL (of Van Duzen River)

DRIVER, H. E. *Culture Element Distributions: X, Northwest California.* Anthropological Records, 1, #6, Berkeley, 1939.

"Lifting, hard work." (p. 350)

NOOTKA

BANCROFT, H. H. *The Native Races of the Pacific States,* Vol. I: *The Wild Tribes.* London, 1875.

"Women rarely have more than two or three children, and cease bearing at about twenty-five, frequently preventing the increase of their family by abortions." (1:197)

WELLS, R. AND KELLY, J. W. *English-Eskimo and Eskimo-English Vocabularies,* U. S. Bureau of Education, Washington, D.C., 1890.

"Women are kept in the huts a month after confinement, and are not allowed to enter any other house than their own till the season, summer or winter, is over. Maternal cares and drudgery make their lives such a burden that they often destroy their unborn offspring. Some of them do this secretly, and if this is found out by their husbands, they are beaten till insensible, then thrown out of the house." (p. 19)

NORTH AMERICAN INDIANS (in general)

HA

The reluctance to bear children is characteristic of the American Indian's decline. (p. 52)

STONE, ERIC. *Medicine among the American Indians.* New York, 1932.

"Slippery elm sticks were inserted in the cervical canal." (p. 76)

NH

"American tribes . . . relied for the regulation of family size more upon abortion, infanticide and periods of tabued intercourse than on methods preventing conception." (p. 16)

NUFOR ISLAND (near New Guinea) *

PB

"According to van Hasselt, the women use [as an abortifacient] a certain beverage; but, in addition, they also cause their bellies to be tightly constricted by means of a reed sash, and then to be stepped upon." (2:528, supposedly quoting Hasselt, J. L. van, "Volksbeschrijving van Midden-Sumatra," in Veth, P. J., *Midden-Sumatra* [sic!], III-i-1, Leiden, 1882) *

NUKUORO

MEINICKE, C. E. *Die Inseln des Stillen Oceans,* Vol. II: *Polynesien und Mikronesien, Leipzig,* 1876.

KUBARY, J. S. *Beiträge zur Kenntnis der Nukuoro—oder Monteverd—Inseln (Karolinen-Archipel).* Reprinted from *Mitteilungen der Geographischen Gesellschaft in Hamburg,* Hamburg, 1900.

EILERS, ANNELIESE. "Inseln um Ponape (Kapingamarangi, Nukuor, Ngatik, Mokil, Pingelap)," *Ergebnisse der Südsee-Expedition 1908–1910,* G. Thilenius, ed., II, B, VIII, 1–464, Hamburg, 1934.

Infanticide does not occur anywhere in the Caroline Islands except among the Samoan inhabitants of Nukuoro. (Meinicke, p. 383) Premaritally conceived or illegitimate children are equated with legitimate children. (Eilers, pp. 63–64) The Nukuoro population is small, due to abortion and infanticide. (Kubary, p. 14) If, because of poverty, they decide to dispose of a child, they try to abort it first by pressing and maltreating the abdomen. (Kubary, p. 36) Queen Kauna lost her son after birth.

* [Nufor Island also appears on maps under other names: Noefor, Mefor (French Admiralty map), Noemfor ("Atlas Universel").] G. D.

To cause her subjects to share her mourning, she ordered all small boys to be killed. Then, still not satisfied, she ordered all pregnant women to abort. (Eilers, pp. 217–89)

OMAHA

DORSEY, J. O. "Omaha Sociology," *Bureau of American Ethnology, Annual Report 3,* Washington, D. C., 1881.

"Foeticide is uncommon. About twenty-two years ago, Standing Hawk's wife became *enceinte.* He said to her, 'It is bad for you to have a child. Kill it.' She asked her mother for medicine. The mother made it, and gave it to her. The child was stillborn. The daughter of Wacka^{n}ma^{n}¢i^{n} used to be very dissolute, and whenever she was pregnant she killed the child before birth. These are exceptional cases; for they are very fond of their children, and are anxious to have them. Infanticide is not known among them." (p. 263)

ONA

COOPER, J. M. *Analytical and Critical Bibliography of the Tribes of Tierra del Fuego.* Bureau of American Ethnology, Bulletin 63, Washington, D. C., 1917.

HDBK

"Infanticide does not occur at all among the Onas, nor does intentional abortion except occasionally in fits of violent rage (Gallardo, 136, 227–228, 233)." (Cooper, p. 171)

"No contraceptives or abortives were known or used, and there is no clear evidence of infanticide." (HDBK 1:119–20)

OPATA

AH

"Among the Opata, according to Doctor Alderman, abortion is sometimes attempted, principally from two causes—first, the rapidly increasing family without corresponding means of support, and second, the shame that comes to unmarried women from having children. The old women give various roots and herbs which they claim are infallible. One is a tea made of rosemary and the 'ocean artemisia.' They administer these, then place the woman on her back and knead her abdomen until pains are brought on. Then they place her on her knees, take a position before her, and holding her by the hips, shake her back and forth with all their force, as in normal labor. If this is not successful the first time the whole process is repeated." (p. 165)

LEÓN, NICOLAS. *La Obstetrica en Mexico.* Mexico, D.F., 1910.

"Abortion is practiced among them for two reasons: (1) a rapid increase in the family and few means of taking care of it, (2) when the single woman finds herself pregnant, old women or midwives give her certain roots and some herbs among which we shall mention *artemisia oceanica.* To this is added the massage of the abdomen, strong shaking and other illtreatments." (p. 90)

(See also *Southwest U. S. Indians.*)

ORINOCO TRIBES (Some)

PB

"The Abbé Gilij reports that some of the Indian women of the Orinoco believe that feminine beauty is best preserved through bearing children at a very early age. Others, however, believe that it is precisely through this that they wilt prematurely, and therefore seek to get rid of their pregnancies." (2:516)

[Cf. Gilij, F. S., *Saggio di Storia Americana,* Rome, 1780–84, 4 vols.]

OTOMI

(See *Southwest U. S. Indians.*)

OTTAWA

STONE, ERIC. *Medicine among the American Indians.* New York, 1932.

The Ottawa abortifacient was a decoction of Seneca snakeroot, polygala senega. (p. 77)

OWAMBO

PB

"It appears from the report of Wulfhorst that the Owambo tribes of German Southwest Africa are familiar with the arts of abortion. 'A girl may not, however, give birth before the efundula (puberty rite). If she does become pregnant, the baby is aborted by manipulation or else by a beverage which causes many of them to die. (The ground for this is the falsification of the fetus [sic!].)' " (2:516, quoting Wulfhorst, A., in Brinckner, P. H., Charakter, Sitten und Gebräuche speziell der Bantu Deutsch-Süd-West-Afrikas: *Mitteilungen des Seminars für orientalische Sprachen,* Vol. III, Part 3, Afrikanische Studien, pp. 69–70)

PACIFIC ISLANDS (in general)
ROBERTS, STEPHEN H. *Population Problems of the Pacific.* London, 1927.

"In particular this ill-nurture (epidemic and endemic disease, malnutrition, etc.) caused an abnormal infant mortality, which combined with the artificial restriction of births to bring about a decline in the population. Abortion and infanticide were prevalent everywhere." (p. 61)

PAIUTE (Harney Valley)
WHITING, B. B. *Paiute Sorcery.* Viking Fund Publication in Anthropology, 15, New York, 1950.

"Although abortion is practiced, it is somewhat disapproved of. The only cases reported were of husbands who beat their pregnant wives' stomachs to induce miscarriage and prevent the birth of an unwanted child. The informants who described these cases felt that a husband must be pretty mean to do this, but there was no immediate sanction against such behavior.

"Infanticide by abandonment is sometimes practiced, but is considered bad. In two cases reported, mothers 'threw away' their newborn infants to express hostility against their husbands." (p. 102)

PAIUTE (Northern)
STEWART, O. C. *Culture Element Distributions: XIV, Northern Paiute.* Anthropological Records, 4, #3, 1941.

[In the Pakwi dökadö band] "abortion [is] by pressure." (p. 409)

[In the Tagö-töka band] "abortion [is] by pressure [or] by lying on rock." (p. 409)

[Kuyui dökadö and Küpa dökadö bands informants] "both said modern Indian girls are bad. If someone gives them a little whiskey, they lie down any place so that they often get pregnant before they are married. The girls have an abortion or kill the baby. Old-time Indians did not do this. They never chased around before they got married." (p. 442)

PAIUTE (Surprise Valley)

KELLY, I. T. *Ethnography of the Surprise Valley Paiute.* University of California Publications in American Archaeology and Ethnology, Vol. 31, #3, Berkeley, 1932.

"Abortion is procured by hitting the belly with a stone." (p. 160) [They have magical techniques involving the use of the placenta or of parts of a dead baby to cause sterility.]

PALAU (Western Caroline Islands)

BORN. "Die Palau-Inseln," *Deutsches Kolonialblatt,* 18:286–289, 1907.

KRÄMER, AUGUSTIN. "Palau." *Ergebnisse der Südsee-Expedition 1908–1910,* G. Thilenius, ed., II, B, III, iii, 1–362, Hamburg, 1926.

Abortion occurs during the second or third month of pregnancy, generally by recourse to poisonous plants. (Kramer, p. 269) Formerly girls used to abort extensively by means of drugs, when the custom of keeping girls in the men's house promised the long maintenance of youthful charm. (Born, p. 287)

[There was male infanticide because girls were hard workers and therefore valuable. Uncertain paternity—often a problem when women are promiscuous—was perhaps responsible for matrilineal descent. (Born, *passim*)]

PALAUNG

MILNE, L. *The Home of an Eastern Clan: A Study of the Palaungs of the Shan States.* Oxford, 1924.

Abortion is held to be contemptible. It is produced by eating the seed and flesh of the papaya. There is also a medicine, compounded of wild herbs, garlic and the slough of a snake, all of which are pounded together and are then mixed with vinegar. A small dose is taken twice a day. (p. 254–55) Abortion is a "wicked act" which is severely punished in the next incarnation. (p. 284) Infanticide is unknown. (p. 25)

PAPAGO

(1) UNDERHILL, R. M. *The Autobiography of a Papago Woman.* American Anthropological Association, Memoir 46, 1936.

(2) UNDERHILL, R. M. *Social Organization of the Papago Indians.* Columbia University Contributions to Anthropology, 30, New York, 1939.

Contraception is practiced as follows: If a baby dies and the mother does not want others, the baby will be buried deep. Abortion was denied by women, who said: "There is no need for it, since there is no stigma on the unwed mother." There was infanticide of deformed children and of the children of promiscuous women, who exposed their offspring. (2, p. 158) Some babies were dropped into arroyos and no one knew anything about it. This technique of infanticide was standard. (1, p. 30) Not sexual lightness or the birth of bastards prevented a girl from finding a husband, but laziness. If she stopped being lazy, she soon found a husband. (2, pp. 183–84) If a married woman bears no child, she would soon die of this unnatural condition. (2, p. 158)

(But cf. *Southwest U. S. Indians.*)

PAPUANS (Geelvink Bay)

WGS

"Papuans [of Geelvink Bay] say 'Children are a burden. We become tired of them. They destroy us.' The women practice abortion to such an extent that the rate of increase in the population is very small and in some places there is a lack of women." (p. 314, quoting von Rosenberg, S. B. H., *Reistochten naar de Geelvinkbaai op Nieuw Guinea,* 1869–1870. C's Gravenhage, 1875, p. 91)

PAPUANS (New Guinea Territory)

PFEIL, JOACHIM, GRAF. *Studien und Beobachtungen aus der Südsee.* Braunschweig, 1899.

"It is but seldom that women bear children during the first year of marriage. Mostly two or three years elapse before they give birth to their first child. The women dread having children, since this makes more work for them. It is true, of course, that the girls are eventually of assistance to their mothers, but many years elapse before they can really be of help to them. Hence, intentional abortion is often resorted to. The women leap off from some high place, or cause themselves to be massaged by certain persons, so as to expel the fetus." (pp. 30–31) [Cf. PB, 2:528]

PAYAGUA

RENGGER, J. R. *Reise nach Paraguay.* Aarau, 1835.

PB

"The Payagua, who abort frequently, are greatly reduced in numbers." (PB, 2:516)

"If a woman already has several children, on the occasion of her next pregnancy she causes her abdomen to be kneaded with fists, so as to produce a premature delivery—a procedure which was imitated even by white girls in Paraguay." (Rengger, quoted verbatim in PB, 2:524)

PEDI

FRAZER, SIR J. G. "Taboo and the Perils of the Soul," in *The Golden Bough.*

"The secretion of a childbed is particularly terrible when it is the product of a miscarriage, particularly a concealed miscarriage. In this case it is not merely the man who is threatened or killed, it is the whole country, it is the sky itself which suffers. By a curious association of ideas a physiological fact causes cosmic troubles. (Cf. H. A. Junod, "Les Conceptions physiologiques des Bantu sud-africains et leurs tabous," *Revue d'Ethnographie et de Sociologie,* i (1910), p. 19.) Thus, for example, the Ba-Pedi believe that a woman who has procured abortion can kill a man merely by lying with him; her victim is poisoned, shrivels up, and dies within a week. As for the disastrous effect which a miscarriage may have on the whole country I will quote the words of a medicine man and rain-maker of the Ba-Pedi tribe: 'When a woman has had a miscarriage, when she has allowed her blood to flow, and has hidden the child, it is enough to cause the burning winds to blow and to parch the country with heat. The rain no longer falls, for the country is no longer in order. When the rain approaches the place where the blood is, it will not dare to approach. It will fear and remain at a distance. That woman has committed a great fault. She has spoiled the country of the chief, for she has hidden blood which had not yet been well congealed to fashion a man. That blood is taboo (yila). It should never drip on the road! The chief will assemble his men and say to them, "Are you in order in your villages?" Someone will answer, "Such and such a woman was pregnant and we have not yet seen the child which she has given birth to." Then they go and arrest the woman. They say to her, "Shew us where you have hidden it." They go and dig at the spot, they sprinkle the hole with a decoction of "mb endoula" and "hyangale" (two sorts of roots) prepared in a special pot. They take a little of the earth of this grave, they throw it into the river, then they bring back water from the river and sprinkle it where she shed her blood. She herself must wash every day with the medicine. Then the country will be moistened again (by rain). Further, we (medicine men) summon the women of the country; we tell them to prepare a ball of the earth which contains the blood. They bring it to us one morning. If we wish to prepare medicine with which to sprinkle the whole country, we crumble this earth to powder; at the end of the five days we send little boys and little girls, girls that yet know nothing of women's affairs and have not yet had relations with men. We put the medicine in the horns of oxen, and these children go to all the fords, to all the entrances of the country. A little girl turns up the soil with her mattock, the others dip a branch in the horn and sprinkle the inside of the hole saying, "Rain, rain!" So we remove the misfortune which the women have brought on the roads; the rain will be able to come. The country is purified!' (Cf. H. A. Junod, *op cit.*, pp. 139 seq.)" (pp. 153–154)

PENTECOST ISLAND (New Hebrides)

(Data identical with those on *Gaua Island.*)

PIMA

AH

"Among the Pima, as with some other tribes, there are remarkably few half-breeds. It is said that this is partly due to the fact that in most cases where a woman becomes pregnant by a white man an abortion is induced. One well-known attempt of this nature occurred very recently. . . . Mr. Alexander, the agent, was told by the Indians of another case where abortion was induced by burying the woman up to her waist in the earth.

"In the eighteenth century Pima confessionary are the following suggestive questions: "Have you drank, from a desire to kill the child within you, *sanari* or anything else?" "Or have you placed (with the same object in view) a very hot stone upon your abdomen?" "Or have you lain for a length of time upon your front?" "Or have you lain a long time in the sun?" "Have you abstained for a long time from eating, wishing that the baby in you dies of hunger?" "Have you aided another woman to kill her unborn infant?" (p. 164)

"Among the Pima, according to Chief Antonio's sister, infanticide is rare. Quite recently one of the educated girls became pregnant by a white man. As the gestation advanced to near the end, she was observed to have a rope hanging from the roof, upon which she pulled herself up and then dropped down. On another occasion she was seen to run wildly against the door and strike it with her abdomen. Finally a live child was born, but it died the same night. The cause of death was not learned." (p. 166)

GROSSMANN, F. E. "The Pima Indians of Arizona," *Smithsonian Institution, Annual Report* 26:407–409, Washington, D. C., 1871.

RUSSELL, FRANK. "The Pima Indians," *Bureau of American Ethnology, Annual Report* 26, Washington, D. C., 1908.

PARSONS, E. C. "Notes on the Pima," *American Anthropologist* n.s. 30:445–64, 1928.

Since at the death of the husband all his property is destroyed, some wives fear that they might be left widows with many children. Hence abortion and infanticide occur frequently. This is not considered a crime and the old women of the tribe procure abortions. (Grossmann, p. 415) The Pima sometimes nurse children until they are six or seven years old. If the woman gets pregnant while lactating, she aborts by pressure on the belly. The unborn is sacrificed to the interests of the previous baby "which the mother loved more because she could see it." Bastards are aborted at three to four months. One was aborted in the seventh month, with the help of a medicine man. Abortion is usually successful and only in a small percentage of cases does it cause death of the woman. (Russell, p. 186) There was infanticide, especially of children with alien fathers. Since the Pima are patrilineal, the bastard, if permitted to live, took the gens of his putative father. Bastards were not respected, though according to tradition a bastard will be a great man or chief. (Parsons, p. 455)

(See also *Southwest U. S. Indians.*)

POLYNESIA (in general)

BROWN, GEORGE. *Melanesians and Polynesians.* London, 1910.

"I was not able to get any trustworthy information as to the extent to which abortion is practiced, beyond the statement that it is frequently done."

[Further discussion by this author points out that in all of the Polynesian and Melanesian islands the natives believe that a certain plant, a long creeper, that grows commonly on beaches there, is the specific for abortion. He says,] "In practice, however, the administration of the 'specific' is generally accompanied by vigorous kneading or shampooing [sic] which probably effects the desired results. . . . The same plant is used for suppressed menstruation." (pp. 33–34)

POMO (Central)

LOEB, E. M. *Pomo Folkways.* University of California Publications in American Archaeology and Ethnology, 19, #2, Berkeley, 1926.

"The majority of informants were somewhat reticent on the subject of abortion and infanticide. Drew (Coast informant) said that children were killed in the olden days if they were not wanted. The mother killed them by strangulation. If an unmarried woman was getting a child she was apt to commit abortion (ku dasamatca, C, baby squeeze). Bastards (ku baba etco, C, baby fatherless), were brought up by the maternal uncle, who treated them in every way as if he were their father. The use of this word was an insult if you said it in a nasty manner. The boy or girl bastard had no difficulty in getting married, but the mother was ashamed to give birth to a bastard." (p. 255)

POMO (Clear Lake and Russian River)

POWERS, STEPHEN. "The Tribes of California," *U.S. Geographical and Geological Survey,* Vol. 3, Washington, D. C., 1877.

(*Kabinapek,* Clear Lake Basin) "But even if they were not originally addicted to infanticide, they were sometimes guilty of foeticide, which was accomplished, not by drugs, but by violent physical means." (p. 207)

PONAPE

CHRISTIAN, F. W. *The Caroline Islands.* London, 1899.

HAHL, DR. "Mittheilungen über Sitten und rechtliche Verhältnisse auf Ponape," *Ethnologisches Notizblatt,* 2:1–13, 1901.

HAMBRUCH, P., AND EILERS, A. "Ponape, Part II," *Ergebnisse der Südsee-Expedition 1908–1910*, G. Thilenius, ed., II, B, vii, XI, 1–386, Hamburg, 1936.

The people of Ponape deny that they have techniques of abortion or that they practice it. They do, however, profess to know a sterilizing drug. (Hambruch-Eilers, p. 83) Abortion by massage is frequent and is allegedly a fairly recent [1901] introduction from the Gilberts. (Hahl, p. 11) Abortion is fairly common in the first year of marriage. They first drink kava to drug themselves and then they massage the uterus. This may explain the rule that kava is not approved for women. However, women do take it secretly. They are not punished for this, although it is deemed improper for them to do so. Abortion is considered very wrong indeed and the lovers usually marry when the girl gets pregnant. (Hambruch-Eilers, p. 83) "*Iol, Yol.* A species of giant convolvulus growing on the hill-slopes: flowers, large, white with sulphur-yellow centre. A decoction of the leaves and seeds possesses properties akin to those of ergot of rye. Much used by the native women for procuring abortion." (Christian, p. 352) [In Ponape the killing of a priest's child is honorable.]

RIESENBERG, S. H. "Magic and Medicine in Ponape," *Southwestern Journal of Anthropology*, 4:406–429, 1948.

"kawɛ · la-lisé · yan ("destroys pregnancy")—an abortifacient (Informant Takio): 1. pwá · kɛ t, six, eight, or ten terminal buds; 2. í · law, a handful of leaves. Pounded together, squeezed with ínɛ pal or cloth. One bottle of liquid is sufficient. Effective up to three months' pregnancy. (p. 421)

"í · law = *Clerodendron inerme* (L.) Gaertn. (p. 427)

"pwá · kɛ t = *Procris pedunculata* (Forst. f.) Wedd." (p. 428)

PONCA

DORSEY, J. O. "Omaha Sociology," *Bureau of American Ethnology, Annual Report*, 3, Washington, D. C., 1884.

(The data are identical with those for the *Omaha*.)

PUEBLO (in general)

NH

"Induced abortion is reported as infrequent." (p. 15, quoting: Aberle, S.B.D., "Frequency of Pregnancies and Birth Interval among Pueblo Indians," *American Journal of Physical Anthropology,* 16:63–80, 1931)

(See also *Southwest U. S. Indians.*)

PUKAPUKA

BEAGLEHOLE, ERNEST AND PEARL. *The Ethnology of Pukapuka.* B. P. Bishop Museum, Bulletin 150, 1938.

"The pregnant woman should be careful not to bring on miscarriage after the fourth month of pregnancy. Though there is no record of deliberate attempts to produce miscarriage by physical means, miscarriage is easily produced by psychological means. When a woman is dissatisfied with her husband, or commits adultery in thought or deed, or does not love her husband as she ought, or does not desire a child by him, or is in general mental distress, a miscarriage is likely to follow. No preventive is known to ward off the possible effects of such a psychological upset, save only the counsel to the married woman to be of good cheer and of easy heart.

"As to the frequency of abortion, it was impossible to gain any information. There is a fairly well established technique for securing abortion, however, and informants could give many cases where it might be desired:

"If the child is the result of incest; if the woman is tired of the man who is the father of her child and wishes to marry another man; if the woman fears that her husband will not wish to be the sociological father of her child or will despise her because she is pregnant by another man; if a married woman becomes pregnant by another man and is afraid that her husband will thereby discover her intrigue; if a woman is pregnant by a man who is ugly or physically deformed, and is afraid her child may be born with the deformities of its father. For all these reasons a woman might decide on an abortion. A well-informed woman informant knew of none of her friends who had had an abortion, but she thought it occurred nowadays among unmarried girls.

"The method of securing abortion is by physical manipulation, called *lomi te wita* (pressure on the fetus) or *lomi yapu* (pressure on the pregnant woman). A medicine man is rarely employed because it is shameful to get an outsider to do this.

The father or mother of the pregnant woman gives her a prolonged and severe *lomilomi* (deep pressure) using the *wakatele* technique, rubbing from the top of the abdomen toward the thighs. 'The blood inside gets all mixed up, it flows outward from the body, and carries the child with it!' is the rationalization given by Pau. He said this *lomilomi* method would be sure to work up to the fourth month of pregnancy. Another informant believed that the efficacy of the *lomilomi* would be improved if the hands were dipped in hot water before being applied to the abdomen. This informant also recommended that the pregnant woman should drink plenty of hot water." (p. 267)

[If lightning strikes or a meteor falls, it is thought that the unborn child was incestuously conceived and it is therefore aborted. (*passim*)]

PURARI

WILLIAMS, F. E. *The Natives of the Purari Delta.* Territory of Papua Anthropology Report, 5, Port Moresby, 1924.

"Women say they are in great fear of the pains of labour, and abortion by self-inflicted violence is certainly practised." (p. 62)

"The latter is usually brought about (I am told) by climbing a tree; the kind called *Pairu,* which is tall and smooth, is most in favour for the purpose. This process will kill the *foetus.* To produce the actual abortion the woman must chew the bark of a tree called *Kunu,* and then, sitting in her canoe, paddle away a good distance. But it was insisted she must go westwards towards the River Baroi. Should she go north or east, the desired effect would not ensue. . . . There are other kinds of abortifacients and prophylactics but, like the above, they seem to be either mechanical or magical, or a curious blend of the two." (p. 235)

QUAPAW

CURRIER, A. F. "A Study Relative to the Functions of the Reproductive Apparatus in American Indian Women," *Transactions of the American Gynecological Society,* 16:264–94, 1891.

"At the Quapaw Agency (Indian Territory) one abortion was reported as resulting from the kick of a horse. Criminal abortions among the full-bloods are rare at this agency, but among the mixed they are about as frequent as among whites." (p. 278)

RHADÉ MOI

JOUIN, B. Y. *La Mort et la Tombe, etc.* Travaux et Mémoires de l'Institut d'Ethnologie, 52, Paris, 1949.

[The French term "avorter" applies both to abortion and miscarriage. Only a reference to the "discrete burial" of fetuses suggests that this passage may also refer to intentional abortion. G. D.] "The aborted foetus is called proh plè. Wrapped in an old blanket, it is buried in the cemetery, or else, if during an attack of malaria the woman miscarries in the fields or near a path, it is buried any place handy. In either case the ground is levelled, to hide the place. If possible, the woman herself does this as rapidly and secretively as feasible. The ghosts of such fetuses are most dangerous, and are addressed in prayer, as follows: 'You, genii of the ghosts of aborted fetuses, you to whom rice has not been offered, to whom water has not been given, for whom the fire has not been stoked, you who were left in the orchid of the brač tree, don't get angry.' These ghosts have access to heaven and to the ear of Aé Dié, master of the Universe, who readily listens to them, so that they can send mankind many misfortunes. They are also under the care of the nourishing goddess H'bia Dung Day, who takes care of their feeding and mothers these children who never lived on earth." (pp. 124–26)

RIFF

COON, C. S. *Tribes of the Riff.* Harvard African Series, Vol. IX. Cambridge, Massachusetts, 1932.

The women's market sells contraceptives and abortifacients, but their sale and possession are kept secret from men, because their use is cause for divorce. A woman who bears no child after a reasonable period is accused of using such substances, simply on general suspicion, and is divorced. (p. 110)

ROTUMA

GARDINER, J. S. "The Natives of Rotuma, Part II," *Journal of the Anthropological Institute,* 27:457–524, 1897.

"Herbs to procure abortion are not unknown, but the more usual method used to be for the woman to go into the water and deliver herself there." (p. 480)

RWALA

MUSIL, ALOIS. *The Manners and Customs of the Rwala Bedouins.* New York, 1928.

"Many a Rwala girl becomes pregnant before the wedding. As soon as this is noticed by her relatives, they try to help her by various means, even if injurious to her health. Should the girl die from an abortion nobody will ever hear of it, as the women keep silent and the men as a rule pay no attention to matters concerning women. If the girl cannot rid herself of the foetus, she presses her lover to marry her at once, but in case he refuses or is absent at the time she often commits suicide. For should her father or brother find that his daughter or sister is with child, he would coax her on some pretext outside of the camp, kill her, cut her body in ten pieces, and then bury them. Nobody will take the girl's part, nobody asks the reason, they simply talk of her as if she had died a natural death. Her kin, *ahl,* would not allow a single girl who had become a mother to stay among them. Her child would not be a member of the kin, and, because it would not be acknowledged by the father on account of its illegitimacy, it would be without a kin and would stand in the clan like a stranger, without protection, without help. But a position of this nature is so contrary to the views and customs of the Bedouins that it is never allowed to arise. A pregnant girl may escape from her tribe and seek refuge in the settled territory or in a large town and try to make a living there. If she disappears without making herself conspicuous, no one will pursue her; she is soon forgotten, yet must never return. Her kinsfolk consider her dead and would kill her should she come back to them. The girls, of course, know the punishment meted out to them, and therefore place a saber between themselves and their lovers at their night meetings, with the warning: 'I am a maiden! Fear Allah . . .' " (p. 240)

"Only when the girl has been raped . . . will her relatives spare her, but in this case they kill both the violator and the child without mercy, and then demand from the murdered man's kin the blood price for the child. This cannot be left alive, as it would have no kin, *ahl,* and compensation for it is asked because it has weakened the girl, a member of their kin." (p. 240)

"A woman who has miscarried, or the fruit of whose womb has perished, is an object of fear." (p. 243)

SAC and FOX

CURRIER, A. F. "A Study Relative to the Functions of the Reproductive Apparatus in American Indian Women," *Transactions of the American Gynecological Society,* 16:264–294, 1891.

"At the Sac and Fox Agency (Indian Territory) my correspondent had never known of abortion, either accidental or induced, among the pure bloods." (p. 278)

SAMOA

TURNER, GEORGE. *Samoa a Hundred Years Ago.* London, 1884.

"*Infanticide,* as it prevailed in Eastern Polynesia and elsewhere, was unknown in Samoa. . . . But the custom of destroying them [infants], *before* that [before birth] prevailed to a melancholy extent. Shame, fear of punishment, lazy unwillingness to nurse, and a dread of soon being old-looking, were the prevailing causes. Pressure was the means employed, and in some cases proved the death of the unnatural parent." (p. 79)

KRÄMER, AUGUSTIN. *Die Samoa-Inseln,* Vol. II. Stuttgart, 1903.

"Turner rightly stresses that infanticide was a rarity in Samoa while abortion by means of massage and kneading is practiced today as it was formerly, as I repeatedly had the occasion to ascertain by an observation of my patients." (p. 53)

PB

"Samoan women abort their children so that their breasts should not become flaccid and wilted." (2:512)

"It is reported of the Samoan Islands that they abort by mechanical means." (2:527)

"In Samoa infanticide is something altogether unheard of. By contrast, abortion by the use of mechanical means is extensively practiced. The motives for abortion are variable: sometimes it happens due to shame, sometimes due to fear of premature aging, and sometimes also because of their unwillingness to undertake the trouble of rearing children." (2:512)

NH

This work contains a statement written by Margaret Mead, according to which Samoans abort by mechanical means. Sometimes this consists in expert manipulations performed by old masseurs, but sometimes the boy simply places his foot against the girl's side, and applies pressure rather roughly. The Samoans also believed that, if chewed in large enough doses, kava could act as an abortifacient. (p. 23 fn.)

SANPOIL and NESPELEM

RAY, V. F. The Sanpoil and Nespelem. *University of Washington Publications in Anthropology*, 5. Seattle, 1932.

Abortifacients and contraceptives are common knowledge. (p. 215) They use the Western Yarrow (Achillea Millefolium L. var. lanulosa Nutt). They also use Piper's upper portions: A strong potion is made by boiling the leaves and stems in water. (A hot decoction of the roots of this plant is used to cure colds.) (p. 218) Abortion, and other crimes, are punished by lashes on the back. The chief holds a hearing and determines the number of lashes to be given, the punishment ranging from a few strokes up to a hundred lashes. Old offenders are treated more severely than young ones. (p. 113)

SEDANG MOI

DEVEREUX, GEORGE. "Sedang Field Notes." MS, 1934–35.

As regards voluntary abortion, the Sedang abort by hitting the abdomen, but, unlike the *Naga*, not with a stone, because it would be fatal to the woman. One informant denied that abortion was practiced, but immediately added that hot water poured on the abdomen would kill both the baby and the mother. Another informant declared in this connection that before a child is born, and even until it is suckled, it is "like a piece of wood." After nursing for the first time it becomes truly human. Infanticide—and probably also abortion—are penalized by the payment of a fine to the village.

"Informants: Mbra:o, the approximately 80-year-old former chief of the village of Tea Ha, and A-Rua, an approximately 50-year-old medicine woman, who played with, and massaged, her naked breasts while telling the story.

"(1) Tcak, of Tea Tlang, had a daughter named A-Tham, with whom he regularly cohabited before she married. Tcak's wife slept in the fields (to protect the crops) while her husband

and daughter cohabited in the house.* The 'next day' (i.e., presumably 'sometime later') the father and his daughter went to sleep in the fields. When other people went after them (i.e., joined them in the fields in the morning) they saw the father step on his daughter and then give her hot water to drink, so that she would not have a (full term) child.† After that he let her go home. When she reached the village, people said: 'Why is your skirt bloody?' A-Tham replied: 'There were many leeches.‡ They bled me at night.' People believed her. The next day she married Tha of Tea Prong—a village which has since then merged with Tȧ Hnj@—who came to live with A-Tham at her village.§ On her wedding-night, milk came from A-Tham's breasts. Her husband asked her: 'Why are you wet?' He thought that A-Tham had cohabited with another man before her marriage, and told her that this was not good. He did not know she had committed incest with her father. The next day Tha said: 'Today I won't go to the fields. I had evil dreams.' All the others went to the fields while he stayed behind, all alone. He then stole—as a "fine"—the following objects belonging to his father-in-law: One (imported) jacket, one Annamese blanket, and two Kaseng râmoa blankets worth a buffalo,|| and went back to his own village. Then Tha's father went to see Tcak, and said to him: 'If you claim you did not cohabit with your daughter, let us have a water-ordeal. If we lose, we will pay you two buffa-

* Surprisingly enough, apparently the village-house, which has no partition between the hearths of the various families, is meant, rather than the field-guardian's hut. Were the latter meant, it would imply that the mother actually slept outdoors, which is inconceivable.

† Hot water is said to be an abortifacient, believed to dissolve the unborn fetus, which is thought to be little more than a bloodclot. Mechanical abortion, by hitting the abdomen with a stone, was denied by some, because "it would kill the woman."

‡ Cf. the *Persian* abortifacient technique of bleeding oneself with leeches. (PB)

§ The Sedang are neither preferentially patrilocal nor matrilocal, the residence of the spouses being that which is most advantageous to them. The matrilocality of this marriage suggests either that Tha was of little account, or that Tcak was a well-to-do man. The former is improbable in view of the aggressively self-confident manner in which Tha behaved subsequently—a thing no poor boy would dream of doing. By contrast, the hypothesis that Tcak was unusually wealthy is probable, since, among the Moi, rich people often exhibit much *hybris* and defy the mores.

|| Only a well-to-do and ostentatious Moi would own so much imported clothing.

loes.' * Then Tcak became angry and said: 'My daughter cohabited with other men! Why do you say she cohabited with me? Let us take spears, and fight!' Then A-Tham spoke up and said: 'My father is doubly guilty. First, because he wants to spear these people,† and second, because he accuses other boys. Therefore I will confess, because I don't want fights. Father always cohabited with me and I had a child.' A-Tham then paid one pig to her husband's village and there was a divorce. When an abortion is performed, the woman's belly is big, and the child is born dead, with all its bones broken. This really did happen.

"After a pause, the informants—and more particularly A-Rua —told the following additional story:

"(2) A-Nde(y), a medicine woman from Tả Kảnong, could hit a woman lightly on the abdomen, so that the child died inside her and the mother aborted it. Later on Ri:ang, a man from Ko Kom, killed this witch, because she always ate the souls of fetuses.‡ The first time she did it, it happened as follows: Mbriang's wife, A-Ngi:u, who was pregnant, went to the forest. A-Nde(y) was hidden in the forest, and touched her lightly. Some time later A-Ngi:u's husband asked her: 'Why don't you give birth?' A-Ngi:u replied: 'I don't know! I did nothing!' That is how A-Nde(y) did it the first time, and she kept on doing the same thing time and again. She also aborted A-V@, wife of Mbrong, A-Vien, wife of Mbay, and A-N@y, wife of He:a (ng). After she touched a pregnant woman's belly, it became as flat as that of a nullipara (*vînjoh*), or of a man. After she did it the third or fourth time, she was unmasked."

SEMANG

SCHEBESTA, PAUL. *Among the Forest Dwarfs of Malaya.* London, 1928.

They know abortifacients but do not use them themselves. The Malays ask the Semang for abortifacients. (p. 102) [They also know contraceptives and aphrodisiacs.] The *Kenta* know and use both abortifacients and aphrodisiacs. (p. 229)

(See also *Negritos of Malaya.*)

* No poor man would dare to speak this way, because the rich man's big soul would cause his small and weak soul to cringe and be ashamed (*ca:u* and *lim*). Also, two buffaloes represent great wealth.

† This suggests that Tha's father had enough influence to muster a following for such an errand.

‡ Witchcraft consists in eating souls and is equated with cannibalism.

SHASTA

PB

"The Shasta Indians of Northern California use, according to Bancroft, large quantities of the root of a parasitical fern which grows on the tip of their fir trees." (2:525, quoting Bancroft, H. H., *Native Races of the Pacific States,* New York, 1874–75)

SHORTLANDS (Solomon Islands)

BROWN, GEORGE. *Melanesians and Polynesians.* Cambridge, 1910.

"In the Shortlands group (Solomon Islands) there are certain old women who are recognized as infallible abortionists. They make the patient swallow certain leaves, one of which is a small leaf with three lobes, which grows on a vine near the seashore. Then a stone is heated and wrapped up in leaves. This is pressed heavily against the navel for some hours if necessary." (pp. 33-34)

SHUSHWAP

TEIT, JAMES. "The Thompson Indians of British Columbia," in *Jesup North Pacific Expedition Publications.* American Museum of Natural History, New York, 1900.

"Abortion was rarely practiced." (II:584)

SIBERIA

HK

PB

They use the root of *Adonis* species as an abortifacient. (HK, 2:542)

"In Siberia girls use the root of *Adonis vernalis* and *Adonis apennina* in order to abort." (PB, 2:525, quoting Frank)

SINAUGOLO

SELIGMAN, C. G. "The Medicine, Surgery, and Midwifery of the Sinaugolo," *Journal of the Anthropological Institute,* 32:297–304, 1902.

"Abortion. Connection often takes place before menstruation is established, and in any case it is customary for a girl to dispose of her favours as she chooses before she is married. Some keep a tally of their intrigues by knots made in a string fringe commonly attached to neck ornaments. Pre-conjugal children are, however, rare, and were stated to depreciate seriously the girl's value; hence abortion is commonly attempted, and if this fails the girl's mother often kills her unwelcome grandchild soon after its birth. To induce abortion violent exercise, especially jumping or applying hot stones to the abdomen or lying prone while another woman stands on the patient's back, are the methods usually adopted. These are stated to be effectual only before the bones are formed, while the child is *rara,* i.e., blood; this period may be assumed to cover the first three or four months of pregnancy. Abortion is practiced more or less secretly, but besides this there is another and far more secret ceremony which a woman who had already had children but wishes to have no more may undertake. The ceremony is known as *ginigabani,* and considerable difficulty was experienced in eliciting details, so much so that I am indebted for the following account to A. C. English, who kindly investigated the matter for me after I had left the district. There is generally a woman in the village or one of the surrounding villages who is supposed to be gifted with a power inherited from her mother of causing women to become *hageabani,* literally incapable of having more children. Suppose a woman considers she has enough children, she will by stealth seize an opportunity of consulting such a woman and will pay her for her services. The woman gifted with the power sits down behind and as close as possible to her patient, over whose abdomen she makes passes while muttering incomprehensible charms. At the same time herbs or roots are burnt, the smoke of which the patient inhales. The latter in paying passes the fee behind her own back to the operator without looking round, and she is told not to mention her name or see her again. The exact ritual observed varies according to the power inherited by the practitioner; often a vegetable infusion is drunk by the patient as part of the charm. The operator at the time of arranging what payment she is to receive should in honour ask if the woman's husband had given his consent, and refuse to operate in the contrary event. A woman gifted with the above powers is generally supposed to be able to cause conception to take place, and would sometimes be called upon for that purpose by wives who were jealous of their husband's infidelities. The operator seated first in front and then behind her patient makes passes over the latter's stomach, muttering charms and expectorating chewed areca nut over her patient's abdomen." (pp. 302–303)

SINKIYONE (South Fork of Eel River)

DRIVER, H. E. *Culture Element Distributions: X, Northwest California.* Anthropological Records, 1, #6, Berkeley, 1939.

"Medicine eaten or drunk." (p. 350)

SINKIYONE (of Upper Mattole River)

DRIVER, H. E. *Culture Element Distributions: X, Northwest California.* Anthropological Records, 1, #6, Berkeley, 1939.

"Blows or pressure on abdomen." (p. 350)

SIOUX (Dakota)

KEATING, WILLIAM H. *Narrative of an Expedition.* London, 1825.

"Women are, in their opinion, bound at all times, whether single or married, to be chaste. If an unmarried female proves otherwise, she usually endeavors to conceal her shame by procuring abortion; this is held to be highly criminal; but it is the cause and not the act of abortion which is censured; for married females frequently obtain miscarriages with the knowledge and consent of their husbands, and to this no objection is made. Widows that prove with child seldom resort to the same means, but they endeavor to conceal the birth of their offspring; and this is considered equally criminal." (p. 411)

SCHOOLCRAFT, H. R. *History, Condition and Prospects of the Indian Tribes.* Philadelphia, 1853.

"They are acquainted with some plants, which, taken by pregnant women, in many cases cause abortion, and sometimes prove fatal to the mother, as well as the child. It is commonly taken by those who have become pregnant without a husband, and not infrequently by those who have husbands but do not wish to be encumbered with another child, mostly because they have already as many as they can carry, unable to follow them in moving." (p. 252)

DENIG, E. T. "Indian Tribes of the Upper Missouri," *Bureau of American Ethnology, Annual Report* 46, Washington, D. C., 1930.

"Cases of infanticide are very common. . . ." (p. 521) [The context shows that abortion is meant.]

(See also *Assiniboine.*)

SISSANU

NEUHAUSS, RICHARD. *Deutsch Neu-Guinea,* Vol. I. Berlin, 1911.

"In Sissanu, women use internal means as well as a massage of the body." (p. 151)

SIWAH

CLINE, WALTER. *Notes on the People of Siwah and El Garah in the Libyan Desert.* General Series in Anthropology, 4, 1936.

Abortion is a common practice. The woman carries heavy burdens, runs fast, drinks gunpowder in water or swallows the foam that gathers at the camel's mouth. (p. 43)

SOCIETY ISLANDS

PB

"Abortion, according to Bemet, replaced the formerly prevalent infanticide." (2:512)

(See also *Tahiti.*)

SOLOMON ISLANDS (in general)

ROMILLY, H. H. *The Western Pacific and New Guinea.* London, 1887.
HOPKINS, A. I. *In the Isles of King Solomon.* London, 1928.

They kill most children, especially in the North, soon after they are born—the author does not quite know why. They buy children from the other tribes, but not children who are too young. Thus, the women are constantly seen suckling puppies and little pigs. They also do this if their child just happens to die—or else they will suckle a four- or five-year-old child. Bastards are killed at birth—and perhaps their mothers as well. They also kill twins, being "ashamed" of them. (Romilly, pp. 68–70) The women abort either by means of a concoction made of plants, or else by external (mechanical) means. Death often results from abortion. In culturally still vigorous Mala abortion is condemned by "public conscience," so that it is an exceptional occurrence. When infanticide is suppressed [by Europeans] vigor declines and the abortion rate increases. (Hopkins, p. 70)

SONGOSOR (Western Caroline Islands)

EILERS, ANNELIESE. "Westkarolinen (Songosor, Pur. Merir)," *Ergebnisse der Südsee-Expedition 1908–1910,* G. Thilenius, ed., II, B, IX, i, 1–405, Hamburg, 1935.

There is no abortion, but after coitus the woman expects the man to remove his semen from her vagina with his finger. If he refuses to do this, she will not cohabit with him again. Bastardy is no shame for the mother. (p. 60)

SOUTH AFRICA (in general)
WGS

"In South Africa abortion is a common custom. Abortion and infanticide are so nearly universal in savage life either as egoistic policy or group policy, that exceptions to the practice of these vices are noteworthy phenomena." (p. 315, quoting Fritsch, G., *Die Eingeborenen Süd-Afrikas*, Breslau 1872, p. 96)

SOUTHWEST U.S. INDIANS (in general)
AH

". . . Artificial abortion, the people believe, is apt to be followed by sterility." (p. 54)

"X. Notes on Social Abnormalities. The foregoing chapter concludes the necessarily deficient physiological observations, and the writer will now approach the pathology of the tribes. In this connection it is necessary to touch on, first of all, the unpleasant subject of social abnormalities, which often have a direct connection with disease, injury, or even death.

"Artificial Abortion. Desire for and love of children are universal among the Indians. Nevertheless artificial abortion is practised among all the tribes visited, and is told of by the older men or women without much hesitation. The causes of the practice are shame or fear in the unmarried, and among married women inability through poverty to provide for the family, or a loss of many previous children, or a desire to be rid of concomitant physical difficulties and necessary subsequent cares. The occurrence is more frequent in the unmarried, notwithstanding the fact that among most of the tribes early illicit sexual intercourse is not very uncommon and the additional fact that the bearing of children by unmarried women brings no particular discredit and is but a slight obstacle to future marriage.

"Nothing definite was learned as to the period of gestation at which abortion is preferably induced; but it seems probable that no efforts are made before the fetus has betrayed viability. The means employed are mainly some form of direct physical violence applied to the abdomen; occasionally one hears of an ingestion of some 'medicine.' In most instances it appears that the prospective mother is aided in the execution of her design by another woman, by a medicine man, or by the husband. There was found nowhere much fear of serious bodily consequences, which suggests that these may be more limited than under similar circumstances among white women." (p. 163)

"Among the Navaho, Hopi, and other tribes manual or bandage (sash) pressure is applied to the woman's abdomen with the object of crushing or expelling the fetus." (p. 164)

SPANISH-AMERICAN COLONIES (in general)

PB

"The excessive amount of work, which the Spaniards imposed upon them, is alleged to have driven the women [to abortion] because they did not wish to let their children fall into a similar misery." (2:516. Cf. Las Casas, Bartolomé de, *Oeuvres* (Llorente, ed.), Paris, 1822, and Petrus Martyr, *De Rebus Oceanicis,* Köln, 1574)

SWAHELI

VELTEN, CARL. *Sitten und Gebräuche der Suaheli.* Göttingen, 1903.

"*Faux pas of a young girl.* If a young girl finds someone outside her home who takes her virginity, the whole town laughs at her. If, on top of that, she gets pregnant, the people say of her: 'She sold her virginity from too great a desire.' Her parents too soon notice the signs of her pregnancy. For example, if she has a craving for this or that, especially for lemons, bananas, sugar cane, sugar, or good fruit, her parents soon realize what it is all about and ask her: 'Why do you have such a special craving for these things?' She gives them no answer. She usually hates some young man or some other young girl living in the house; her breasts increase in size, the color of her forehead becomes lighter, and when, on top of that, the menses no longer appear, the parents inquire into the matter and discover that her navel has begun to protrude somewhat; these are the surest signs that a pregnancy has occurred.

"As soon as this happens, the parents ask her: 'Who did it?' She is no longer able to conceal things and denounces her seducer. If her parents deem the matter worth the trouble they appeal to the parents of the young man. If they are able to reach an agreement, the young man marries the seduced girl, but the child is fundamentally not rated as a *mtoto wa balâli,* a real child. Nonetheless, the Swaheli say: 'I will (retroactively) make the pregnancy into a permissible one.' If the seducer is a slave and they do not wish the shame to become known on the outside, they give the young girl a beverage which destroys the pregnancy. They often make her drink gunpowder mixed with water, or else she gets an herb medicine. After taking these drugs for seven days, her pregnancy is disposed of." (pp. 100-101) "Another reason why we find so few children on the Coast is that the women, when they feel the nefarious signs of pregnancy, destroy it; if they do not wish to give birth, they say: 'If I bear a child I will age too much and no man shall desire me any more; such being the case, it is better if I remain as though I were single.' " (p. 29)

HK

The Swaheli use as abortifacient the following preparation: They dissolve a crystal of copper sulfate the size of a plum kernel in one and a half liters of water and drink the solution morning and evening. (p. 543)

PB

"They deem abortion of the fetus possible between the second and fourth month of pregnancy." (2:516, quoting Kersten [sic! Perhaps Kersting, Herman, "Arzeneien und Zaubermittel des Mganga 'Fuaga,' " in Götzen, G. A. Graf von, *Durch Afrika von Ost Nach West,* 2nd ed., Berlin, 1899, appendix, p. 412, is meant.]

TAHITI

ELLIS, WILLIAM. *Polynesian Researches During a Residence of Nearly Eight Years in the Society and Sandwich Islands,* Vol. I. London, 1853.

"The greatest source of amusement to the people, as a nation, was most probably the existence of a society, peculiar to the Islands of the Pacific, if not to the inhabitants of the southern groups. This was an institution called the *Areoi* society." (p. 229)

"It has been already stated that the brothers, who were made gods and kings of the *Areois* lived in celibacy; consequently they had no descendants. On this account, although they did not enjoin celibacy upon their devotees, they prohibited their having any offspring. Hence, one of the standing regulations of this institution was, the murder of their children. . . . To them, also, the gods whom *Oro* had placed over them delegated authority, to admit to their order all such as were desirous to unite with them, and consented to murder their infants." (pp. 232–33)

"They were a sort of strolling players, and privileged libertines, who spent their days in travelling from island to island, and from one district to another, exhibiting their pantomimes, and spreading a moral contagion throughout society." (p. 234)

'In addition to the seven regular classes of *Areois,* there were a number of individuals, of both sexes, who attached themselves to this dissipated and wandering fraternity, prepared their food and their dresses, performed a variety of servile occupations, and attended them on their journeys, for the purpose of witnessing their dances, or sharing in their banquets. These were called *Fanaunau,* because they did not destroy their offspring, which was indispensable with the regular members." (pp. 238–39)

"Infanticide, the most revolting and unnatural crime that prevails, even amongst the habitations of cruelty which fill the dark places of the earth, was intimately connected with the execrable Areoi institution." (p. 248)

". . . The horrid deed was always perpetrated before the victim had seen the light, or in a hurried manner, and immediately after birth." (p. 254)

[Note: With Ellis, as with most writers on the subject of the *Areoi,* there is good reason to take the information with a grain of salt. Quite a bit has been written on it, but most contemporary Polynesian specialists with whom I am acquainted are inclined to be suspicious of not only the writers but also their informants for fanciful imaginations. There does not seem to be very much factual data on them (the *Areoi*). In this book, Ellis speaks only of infanticide, but it is very probable that abortion was also practised. According to my own field research infanticide is, of course, a thing of the past, but abortion seems quite widely practised. Marianne L. Stoller]

PB

"It is reported of the female inhabitants that they abort the children so that their breasts would not become flaccid and wilted." (2:512)

STOLLER, MARIANNE L. "Unpublished Field Notes on Tahiti." Collected on the Peabody Museum of Salem Expedition to Polynesia, 1952. (Statement specially prepared for this volume, 1954.)

"*Case No. 1:* The woman is a native from one of the outer Islands; the man is a European. The information was furnished by the man, and the incident occurred several years ago. The couple have been living together for some years and have three children; the oldest is sixteen or seventeen, the youngest has been in school only one or two years. At the time, the man was more than sixty years old, and the woman past thirty-five. According to him, the woman informed him that she was two or three months pregnant and he was displeased at the news. He felt another child would mean too much trouble in the household, and he was too old to be further bothered by "wailing babies." He told the woman that she must get rid of the baby—he did not want it. Apparently there was some controversy over his feelings, but the woman yielded to his orders. Her objections were a 'nod' toward her religion, he said, 'but really she didn't want to be bothered with another child either.' He left the means of the abortion to her and she obtained a native prescription and part of the medicine from the local Tahitian doctor. The recipe he related is only partially recorded. It included the juice from green pineapples boiled with the leaves of some herbs which grew in a certain valley. She obtained the remainder of the ingredients herself with considerable trouble, for some of them had to come from specific localities. It is not clear who prepared the concoction, but she drank it and a few hours later became quite ill with abdominal pains, nausea, etc. The abortion occurred shortly afterwards, and she was ill in bed for three or four days. The only other effect was that her menstrual periods for the succeeding few months were irregular and accompanied by much pain.

"*Case No. 2:* Information in this example came directly from the woman herself, a Tahitian about thirty years old. She had been having an affair with a Tahitian man some seven or eight years her junior. The romance went on for the better part of a year; she was 'very much in love with him' and felt that he really loved her. He lived in a different district of the island and would visit her at night. When his visits suddenly stopped she heard that he had been called into the army and was confined to the barracks. Several weeks later he let her know by devious means that he would visit her on a specific evening. By this time she knew she was pregnant, and awaited his visit with happy anticipation for she felt he would share her joy over the news. However, when he came they quarrelled violently, he left in a rage, and she was very upset. After several days of reflection she decided that she did not want the baby, and felt that having an abortion would 'show' him. She decided she could not appeal to her mother for advice because her mother would be angry and would also want her to have the child. Therefore, she went to a friend who is married to a European and 'would know about such matters.' The friend advised her to go to a certain pharmacist in town and tell him what she wanted. This the girl did and the pharmacist gave her a liquid to drink and verbal instructions. By the time she had returned home she had forgotten part of the instructions but took part of the medicine. A few hours later she became extremely ill with severe abdominal cramps, nausea and diarrhea. She went out to the toilet, and fainted there. When she recovered she began to hemorrhage. She remained there for 'three or four hours' and finally felt well enough to leave; she was still hemorrhaging, but not as much. She was too weak to walk, and called her sister-in-law to help her. This occurred in the afternoon, and she slept until about midnight. When she awoke she felt much better, but was seized with fear that she had done herself great damage and had not really produced the abortion. Consequently, she took the remainder of the bottle of medicine and, to assuage her worries, some wine also. About dawn she became ill again—'much worse than the first time.' Again she was very nauseated and went to the toilet; the diarrhea returned, and pains in her abdomen, back and legs became acute. She said she thought she was going to die—she 'never hurt so much before.' After a while she began to hemorrhage again—from her bowels she thought—but several large clots of blood 'came down.' Rather than tell her mother why she was ill, she simply said she had eaten some spoiled fish. Her mother helped her back into bed, gave her some aspirin and put hot towels on her stomach. The illness receded slightly, but she began to have a bad headache. She also continued to hemorrhage a little. Through the day waves of nausea and diarrhea returned, her abdomen was very sore and she had muscular cramps. Finally her mother confronted her with a suspicion of the truth, which she then acknowledged. Her mother was very angry, but said she would go to a native doctor to get some medicine. The medicine (the ingredients of which were unknown to the informant) consisted of a liquid and an ointment. The liquid again made her violently ill and apparently caused a temporary paralysis, for she said she could not walk and the women had to lift her. The ointment was 'spread between my legs and made me itch very much, but it was cold.' By the third day the hemorrhaging had ceased and during the following two or three days the nausea and diarrhea gradually diminished. She remained in bed for about ten days, but even at the end of that time her abdomen was still sore. She menstruated in about two or three weeks and 'it smelled very bad.'

"When the man heard, via the grapevine, that she had had an abortion he was extremely angry. She had not told him she was pregnant. About a month after the abortion he came out to see her, and they had a fight during which she was bruised and received a black eye. This made her so angry that she felt she had been quite justified in producing the abortion, although she said she would never do it again: it made her much too ill, and at the time she was very much afraid that she was going to die.

"In addition to these two specific cases, there were also several pieces of gossip about women who had had abortions. In two examples the women became so ill that they were taken to the hospital and have never had any more children. Two other women obtained medicine from the pharmacists, but the opinion was that native medicine was best, because aftereffects were not as severe and it never failed. One woman went to a Chinese herbalist, but the medicine did not work; this was given as the explanation of why her child had a cleft palate and a malformed head. Twice the story of a woman who had died as a result of an abortion was mentioned. In two of these incidents the reason for wanting to abort was given as revenge on the man in a broken love affair. There were no reasons stated in the other cases. It would seem, from the tenor of the gossip, that the procedure was censored in theory but condoned in practice."

(See also *Society Islands.*)

TAMI (New Guinea)

KEYSSER, CH. "Aus dem Leben der Kaileute," in Neuhauss, Richard, *Deutsch Neu Guinea,* Berlin, Vol. 3, 1911.

" 'In Tami the woman who aborted her child has, for a short while, a mourning net, which corresponds approximately to "court mourning for 24 hours" or "half-mourning." ' " (p. 151)

"Abortion, like all matters pertaining to birth, is the exclusive concern of women about which men have nothing to say. The child in the womb is the property of the woman." (p. 150)

NEUHAUSS, RICHARD. *Deutsch Neu-Guinea,* Vol. III. Berlin, 1911.

"Free development is artificially impeded by abortion and infanticide. Fertility is present. My list of births mentions various women who have 5, 6, 8, and 9 children. However, the two-child system is their ideal: 'A boy to replace the father, a girl to replace the mother.' In the year 1890, the mission found in Tami approximately 180 people, in Wonam a little over 100, and a few more than 70 on Kalal. This number was maintained for approximately fourteen years (until 1904), i.e., until the people accepted Christianity. In the next six years the population increased by 25. One can conclude from this that in a short time a few families can populate a small island." (p. 524)

TANALA

LINTON, RALPH. *The Tanala.* Field Museum of Natural History Anthropological Series, 22, 1933.

"There is little stigma attached to bastardy. They do kill infants born on a bad birth date, or if divination gives bad results. Unmarried girls occasionally procure an abortion, but the Tanala were reticent about this and the method used could not be learned." (p. 282)

LINTON, RALPH. Personal Communication, 1952.

"Abortion was not prevalent. I am under the impression that some kind of herbal remedies were used. Whatever these remedies may have been, they do not seem to have been particularly effective ones."

(Cf. also NH, pp. 7–8.)

TARAHUMARA

BENNETT, W. C., AND ZINGG, R. M. *The Tarahumara.* Chicago, 1935.
LUMHOLTZ, CARL. *Unknown Mexico,* Vol. I. New York, 1902.

Abortion and infanticide are practiced to avoid social disgrace. Abortion is deemed "ugly" and is rarely done. The woman does it herself, through a violent massage of the belly in advanced pregnancy. In other cases she fills a heavy olla with water and places it on her belly. Infanticide is not common, but does occur. (Bennett and Zingg, p. 348) In rare instances, right after birth they sit down on the neonate, to save themselves the trouble of bringing it up. (Lumholtz, p. 243)

(See also *Southwest U. S. Indians.*)

TARASCO

(See also *Southwest U. S. Indians.*)

TASMANIA

BONWICK, JAMES. *Daily Life and Origin of the Tasmanians.* London, 1870.

"Few women, especially in the later times, bore any children until they had been several years married, especially if they had any reputation for beauty. . . . Abortion, too, was frequently practiced; and for the same reason as in Europe and Africa, to preserve elegance of figure, and save the lady the petty annoyances of maternity. The old women, by vigorously thumping the reclined figure of the *enceinte* would produce the required result. The earliest colonists of Australia in 1788, observed the same practice, and found it spoken of at Port Jackson as *meebra.*" (p. 76) [Port Jackson—the early name for Sydney. G. D.]

TATARS

PB

"Tatar women use *menyantes trifoliata* and amber or amber water." (2:531, quoting Demič, V. E., "Uber Volkmedicin in Russland," *Wiener klinische Wochenschrift,* 2:902–908, 1889)

TAULIPANG

KOCH-GRÜNBERG, THEODOR. *Vom Roroima zum Orinoco,* Vol. III. Stuttgart, 1923.

This tribe has six techniques for causing abortion: (1) A large globular gourd, such as women use to fetch water, is put on the fire. If it bursts, the fetus too bursts and comes out. This is a magical analogy. (2) Pregnant women cause the large Toncadira ants to bite their bodies. (3) They take Tocandira ants, pound them, and in the morning drink this paste in cold water, which was out of doors during the night. (4) They drink lemon juice mixed with water. (5) They grind the bark of the līkaua tree and drink it with water. (6) They rub wetezág leaves of a tree, which 'burn like nettles,' over the body. There are allegedly also other abortifacients. They are probably used mostly by girls who can do with their bodies as they please. (pp. 131–32)

THOMPSON INDIANS

TEIT, JAMES. "The Thompson Indians of British Columbia," in *Jesup North Pacific Expedition Publications.* American Museum of Natural History, New York, 1900.

"Abortion was rarely practiced, and was effected by the drinking of medicine. Newly born babies were sometimes, but very rarely summarily disposed of by strangling or drowning, but women who did so were thought very severely of, and publicly reprimanded." (I:305)

THONGA

FRAZER, SIR J. G. "Taboo and the Perils of the Soul," in *The Golden Bough.*

"The Ba-Thonga, a Bantu tribe of South Africa in the valley of the Limpopo River, attribute severe droughts to the concealment of miscarriages by women, and they perform the following rites to remove the pollution and procure rain. A small clearing is made in a thick and thorny wood, and here a pot is buried in the ground so that its mouth is flush with the surface. From the pot four channels run in the form of a cross to the four cardinal points of the horizon. Then a black ox or a black ram, without a speck of white on it, is killed and the pot is stuffed with the half-digested grass found in the animal's stomach. Next, little girls, still in the age of innocence, are sent to draw water, which they pour into the pot until it overflows into the four channels. After that the women assemble, strip off their clothes, and covering their nakedness only with a scanty petticoat of grass they dance, leap and sing, 'Rain, fall!' Then they go and dig up the remains of the prematurely born infants and of twins buried in dry ground on the hill. These they collect in one place.

No one may approach the spot. The women would beat any male who would be so indiscreet as to intrude on their privacy and they would put riddles to him which he would have to answer in the most filthy language borrowed from the circumcision ceremonies; for obscene words, which are usually forbidden, are customary and usual on these occasions. The women pour water on the graves of infants and of the twins in order to 'extinguish' (timula) them as the natives phrase it; which seems to imply that the graves are thought to be the source of the scorching heat which is blasting the country. At the fall of evening they bury all the remains which they have discovered, poking them away in the mud near a stream. In these ceremonies, the pouring of water into channels which run in the direction of the four quarters of heaven is clearly a charm based on the principles of homeopathic magic to procure rain. The supposed influence of twins over the waters of heaven and the use of foul language at rain-making ceremonies have been illustrated in another part of this work. (Cf. 'The Magic Art and the Evolution of Kings,' Vol. I, pp. 262 seq. 278)" (p. 154)

TIKOPIA

FIRTH, RAYMOND. *We the Tikopia.* New York, 1937.

Abortion, while not frequent, does occur. It is practiced by single girls only. Married women do not abort; "they have no need" to do it. (p. 414) Pregnancy not followed by marriage creates the problem of the unwanted child. One solution is to abort the fetus. A certain girl was pregnant, judging by the state of her belly and breasts. She was a promiscuous person and hence the father of her unborn child was unknown. This girl caused her child "to descend" (meaning to abort) by the use of hot stones. After her abortion she remained in her house for a few days. This incident was common talk because the girls in the village are quick to detect such signs of pregnancy. Girls abort especially if several men could be the father of the unborn child. If only one man could possibly have impregnated her, the lovers are usually quick to marry. Married women also abort, if they have many children and the land is scarce. This is an alternative to infanticide. The prospective father may say: "The orchard is small, let the babe therefore be put to death because, if it lives, there will not be enough orchard to support it." Abortion is achieved by manipulation: the fingers and thumbs pressed downward on the belly. In other instances they heat stones and place them on the abdomen and rub downward with them. They also use leaves—concerning which no details were obtained—but it is not clear whether these leaves are effective abortifacient drugs or simply magic. The women of Tikopia abort at all stages of pregnancy. Sometimes they pass only blood, sometimes an incomplete embryo, and sometimes a child near its time. Occasionally the mother dies as a result of an abortion. (pp. 527–528)

TIV

ABRAHAM, R. C. *The Tiv People.* The Government Printer, Lagos, 1933.
DOWNES, R. M. *The Tiv Tribe.* The Government Printer, Kaduna, 1933.
EAST, RUPERT, ed. *Akiga's Story: The Tiv Tribe as seen by One of Its Members.* The International Institute of African Languages and Cultures, London, 1939.

When the imborivungu becomes public property, they kill a human being, and not merely a mouse, as is done when it is private property. Some say they kill a man, while others say they kill a baby or a foetus procured from a woman who has aborted and who is a primipara. In the latter case they proceed as follows: If a young girl is pregnant when they desire to "set right the land" with an imborivungu, the elders confer and plot how to get the child from her womb by stealth. They determine to make her abort. As soon as she feels quickening and complains of sensations in the womb, the old ones are pleased. One of them fetches a medicine for causing abortion, grinds it up and gives it to her, saying that it will cure her. The girl takes the medicine without knowing what it will do to her, and will miscarry. Even if this should happen in daytime, the fetus will not be buried. The boys who should bury the fetus are told by those in the secret to wait, because so-and-so has been sent for and the fetus must not be buried until that person arrives. This is done to keep the fetus unburied until nightfall, when the rite begins. Then they tell the boys to bury it, pretending that they have waited long enough for the person allegedly sent for. When the small children take the fetus, to bury it in back of the village, one of the elders goes there quickly, takes the fetus from them and sends them away, saying: "Go home! It is too late for you children to bury it. I myself will do it properly." The children, who are afraid of darkness, run home. The elder then takes the fetus and hides it. When all are asleep, the elders meet and the keeper of the imborivungu brings it to them. Then they perform the rite with the dead fetus. The elder who had hidden it puts it on the ground, and places beside it the imborivungu and a calabash of water. First he takes the fetus and makes passes with it, and then cuts its throat with a knife. They then take the blood and smear it on the imborivungu, wash their hands in the calabash bowl, and, finally, take the bloody water and pour it into the well and over the farm of the keeper of the imborivungu. Thus good crops are produced and the first woman who, next morning, draws water from the well will conceive at once and bear a son even if up till then she was barren. If a normally born baby is to be killed for this rite, it is killed by blowing a certain powder into its nose. (East, pp. 227–29) In discussing earth-rites, Downes states that the medicine which induces abortion in the primipara is brought from the Uke, which may mean either the Jukun or the Hausa. (Downes, pp. 52–53) Abraham also describes this rite and specifies that it requires not a spontaneous but an induced abortion. One drug used is the powdered bark of a tree: "That which pushes out the fetus." It is given to the pregnant woman without her knowledge, and has very rapid effects. The woman passes blood in her urine and soon thereafter aborts. No woman is aborted more than once and she does not have to be the wife of one of the mba tsav. A woman who has been aborted in this manner is held to be especially favored by A'ondo and will soon be pregnant again and bear a healthy offspring. The foetus' ears, feet, hands, nose and liver are cooked in a pot. Then bits of this cooked flesh are scattered, while they say: "The sun is a boy, the moon is a girl." The initiates present at the rite wash their hands in the pot, and then plunge into it the imborivungu. Then the imborivungu is taken out of the pot and the drops of water dripping from it are shaken over the field, and into the well. The fetus' navel-cord is preserved and is immersed annually into water which is then sprinkled on the farms and wells by means of the wet imborivungu. (Abraham, p. 76)

TOBA

KARSTEN, RAPHAEL. "The Toba Indians of the Bolivian Gran Chaco," *Acta Academiae Aboensis, Humaniora* 4, Åbo, 1923.

Abortion and infanticide are frequent and socially not disapproved. Single girls especially tend to abort and always do it when the baby's father is not known. Married women abort if their husbands abandon them. Abortion is mechanical. The woman herself presses out the fetus with her thumbs, sometimes after killing it first by striking her stomach. Generally she is assisted by an old woman. Usually a girl aborts after four or five months of pregnancy. There is some pain, but no damage to health. No drugs are used. Abortion is not felt to be immoral, since the child is not considered an independent person. Abortion is therefore a private matter, about on a par with the extraction of a tooth. (pp. 23–24)

TOBELORESE

PB

(Same data as for the *Galela.*)

TOLOWA

DRIVER, H. E. *Culture Element Distributions: X, Northwest California.* Anthropological Records, 1, #6, Berkeley, 1939.

"Medicine eaten or drunk. Blows or pressure on abdomen. Hot stones on abdomen. (?) Lifting, hard work. (?)" (p. 350)

TORADJA (Tolage, Topebato, Ampana)

KRUYT, A. C. "Beobachtungen an Leben und Tod, Ehe und Familie in Zentralcelebes," *Zeitschrift für Socialwissenschaft,* 6:707–714, 1903.

"The number of children is decreased not only by the aforementioned mortality of children, but fairly frequent use is also made of abortifacients, especially in the Tolage tribe, and less so among the Topebato. A very widely used abortifacient of the Toradja is the mastication of the stem of the leaf of the *wongoli* or *pu' apa'a* tree (probably Polyscias nodosa Seem, cf. Koorders, *Verslag eener botanische dienstreis door de Minahassa,* p. 491) The motives for this frequency of abortion are the following two: Shame or else dread of the burden of child care.

"In general, among the Toradja it is accounted a shameful

thing for an unwed woman to bear children. The feeling of shame is far less strong among the Topebato than among the Tolage. No one esteems such a girl less than before on this account and an extramarital child is never the reason why a girl does not get a man. But she is ridiculed. These jibes, which everyone feels entitled to make about such a mother, induce her to get rid of the fetus by every possible means. In this area people are very sensitive to ridicule, though their jibes seem very harmless to us. When internal means do not induce an abortion, one lets one's abdomen be compressed and rubbed, nay, one makes someone step on one's belly.*

"The reason why abortion is more common among the Tolage than among the Topebato is to be sought in the fact that the Tolage keep slaves, while the Topebato do not. Since the slaves are more numerous than the freeborn, it happens not seldom that freeborn girls cohabit with slaves, and the girl must often pay with her life for such a pregnancy, since cohabitation between a slave and a freeborn woman is severely prohibited. In addition, through the leisure which the keeping of slaves affords the Tolage, this tribe has acquired an external civilization which sees nothing shameful in free intercourse between young people—only in its consequences. Among the Topebato the situation is entirely different. There they know no fear of miscegenation [between social classes? G. D.] because in that tribe all, save only isolated bought or war-prisoner slaves, are free.

"In addition to the ridicule which such a young girl has to endure, she also greatly dreads the burden of raising such a child, which has no father; because no one will bring firewood for her, no one will share with her the task of keeping an eye on the child, or perform such small jobs for her as her husband would, were she married. This motive is valid for both tribes.

"In addition many married women also get rid of the fruit of their womb, in order to avoid the burden of caring for the little bellower. Regardless of how unnatural this may be, I can name many such cases among Toradja women. One learns such things only by overhearing conversations, because one never speaks of such matters in public. The cause of this unnatural procedure

* Several Toradjas told Mr. Kruyt that when girls of the Ampana tribe become pregnant, they hang themselves if they do not succeed in aborting the fetus. (From a letter to the German translator, H. J. Nieboer.)

is, once more, the slavery system of the Tolage. While among the Topebato married couples desire children, since these will later on be their sole help, the free Tolage woman does not experience this need, since she has her slaves to work for her. In addition, slavery makes the Tolage woman more inclined to take it easy than the Topebato woman, and she is therefore also more inclined to avoid all inconveniences. Among married slave women there is the additional motive for abortion that they have no desire to bear and to raise children for someone else, i.e., for their masters. I know more than one slave woman who aborts every time she gets pregnant, and who flatly declares that she has done so for the abovementioned reason.

"I dare say that if nature were often not stronger than the abortifacients, the families would be even smaller. However, they do not know absolutely effective [abortifacient] devices, and means for the prevention of pregnancy seem totally unknown to the Toradja. Only the Mohammedans believe themselves to possess such contraceptives in their *doa*-s or magic formulas. If the attempt to abort does not succeed, it sometimes happens that the mother kills, or seeks to kill, her child after it is born." [At this point the author gives details about the actual murder of newborn infants, about infanticide by planned neglect and starvation and about the exposing of children.]

"The abovementioned cases show that it is the mother herself who aborts the fetus or kills her newborn child, and that she herself, and only she, is motivated to do such things." [The author adds that infanticide, being a crime within the family, is not punished in a society where murder is dealt with by means of vendettas. Only a slave woman, who kills her child, may experience the wrath of her master, but even he will not kill her.] (pp. 711-13)

TORRES STRAITS (in general)

HA

Girls abort from shame or else to save themselves the trouble of raising a child. Older women also abort, because old parents are ridiculed; hence, after a certain number of births, they destroy their children. It is proper to have the same number of boys and girls, but female children are killed more often than male children, because they need more looking after when they are grown up, since young men come to see them in the gardens. This means that parents do not get enough rest, because they have to be on the alert to keep their daughters from being stolen by the men of their choice. (pp. 67–68, quoting *Cambridge Anthropological Expedition to Torres Straits,* Vol. VI, p. 107, Cambridge, 1908)

The inhabitants practice both abortion and infanticide. However, recently both practices have almost disappeared, because it is now profitable to have children. Indeed, nowadays the sons are able to get jobs, which means luxury for their parents, and the daughters are sold to the highest bidders among the young men. As a result, children are more desired than ever before. (pp. 41–42, quoting *ibid,* Vol. VI, p. 110)

TORRES STRAITS (Eastern Islands)

HADDON, A. C. in *Reports of the Cambridge Anthropological Expedition to Torres Straits,* Vol. VI, Cambridge, 1908.

"Abortion is procured by medicinal and mechanical means. The leaves of the shore convolvulus, *wakor* (Ipomaea pes-caprae), which grows on the beach, are used for this purpose and it is also said to be a preventive. . . .

"Mr. Bruce has given me the following details. If a woman, who finds herself pregnant, wishes to induce abortion, she ties a vine around her body or a rope made of coco-nut fibre; or she climbs a coco-nut palm and bumps her stomach against the trunk in ascending and descending; or when she goes to her gardens she will fill a basket full of yams or sweet potatoes, lie on her back and put the heavy basket on her abdomen. In some cases she presses a bamboo on her abdomen, or strikes it with something heavy and hard. The old women also recommend the simple expedient of carrying heavy loads from the gardens." (p. 107)

TORRES STRAITS (Western Tribes)

HADDON, A. C. "The Ethnography of the Western Tribe of Torres Straits," *Journal of the Anthropological Institute,* 19:297–440, 1890.

"Abortion was very frequently procured; for this they had several methods. There were two or three medicinal plants used for this purpose, or when a woman was big with child, she would lie on her belly and bump it up or down on some stones—or lying on her back she, or her friends, would pound her abdomen with smooth stones. Again the mother might press upon the head of the foetus, through the wall of the abdomen, with a hot stone. (In Daudai compression by means of a cord was used to destroy the foetus.)" (p. 359)

TROBRIAND

MALINOWSKI, BRONISLAW. *The Sexual Life of Savages in North-Western Melanesia,* 3rd ed. London, 1932.

". . . They never practise *coitus interruptus,* and still less have any notion about chemical or mechanical preventives.

"But though I am quite certain on this point, I cannot speak with the same conviction about abortion, though probably it is not practised to any large extent. I may say at once that the natives, when discussing these matters, feel neither fear nor constraint, so there can be no question of any difficulties in finding out the state of affairs because of reticence or concealment. My informants told me that a magic exists to bring about premature birth, but I was not able either to obtain instances in which it was performed, nor to find out the spells or rites made use of. Some of the herbs employed in this magic were mentioned to me, but I am certain that none of them possess any physiological properties. Abortion by mechanical means seems, in fine, the only effective method practised to check the increase of population, and there is no doubt that even this is not used on a large scale.

". . . It is amusing to find that the average white resident or visitor to the Trobriands is deeply interested in this subject, and in this subject only, of all the ethnological problems opened to him for consideration. There is a belief prevalent among the white citizens of eastern New Guinea that the Trobrianders are in possession of some mysterious and powerful means of prevention or abortion." (pp. 168–69)

TRUK

GLADWIN, THOMAS. "Truk Field Notes." MS, Yale University Human Relations Area Files.

In the olden days, girls were sometimes aborted by their mothers to keep them from getting old too fast. This was accomplished by downward massage. They rub the abdomen vigorously downward. This may be done by the husband himself. They sometimes also jump vigorously up and down on the belly. If this does not work, nothing else is possible. This is no longer done, because nowadays [1947] the women of Romonum desire children. Women did abort in olden days so that they could continue to engage in sexual relations. Women pound and massage the abdomen, being perhaps assisted therein by their husbands "if they want to." They also jump up and down. If this fails, nothing else can be done. Abortion is no longer practiced—the informant did not know why. Bollig does mention abortifacient herbs but the informant denied this. Women used to abort because they desired to continue cohabiting and also from laziness. They also jumped off high places in order to abort. Public opinion disapproved of abortion and the woman's relatives, if they knew that she had aborted, were angry with her.

GLADWIN, THOMAS, AND SARASON, S. B. *Truk: Man in Paradise.* Viking Fund Publications in Anthropology, 20, New York, 1953.

". . . The techniques of abortion are widely known and consist in violent jumping or massage of the abdomen. However, while this used to occur in the past it is said not to be practiced any more. This statement must be considered suspect: not only do the doctors in the administration hospital report cases of women with entirely normal pregnancies who suddenly lose their babies, but it is also hard to understand how the women so anonymously [sic] reported not to want children can realize this wish and still maintain a high level of sexual activity, for contraceptives are—or were at the time of this study—unknown.

"*Miscarriage.* After the first three months of pregnancy less concern need be felt over the possibility of spontaneous abortion. The foetus has now taken definite form and is therefore better implanted in the uterus. If a miscarriage takes place it is usually the work of a ghost. Ghosts may plant in the woman's abdomen a black trepang (also known as bêche de mer or sea cucumber, a fat worm-like organism a few inches to a foot long found on the sea bottom) which eventually aborts; its presence can sometimes be diagnosed and it is then deliberately aborted. Sometimes the foetus itself turns out to be a ghost; these usually are born shortly before the full nine-month term and are identified by their distorted features, short arms, and other characteristics. In other words, the Trukese have observed the characteristics of the developing foetus when it appears at varying stages of prematurity, but have accounted for its appearance variously as being just blood, a trepang, or a small ghost. Babies born at full term but in some respect abnormal are also considered to be ghosts and are disposed of in the same fashion as a premature "ghost" or "trepang." Most commonly this is stated to be by throwing them in the sea, sometimes in a weighted box; burning is also mentioned. Culturally this is not defined as infanticide and the suggestion of infanticide horrified the Trukese; a ghost is not a person and cannot actually be killed in any case. However, Andy was born with his cranium almost entirely unossified; the midwife pronounced him a ghost and his mother agreed. When they were preparing the box in which he would be thrown into the sea, a "father" of hers looked at Andy, denied he was a ghost, and refused to permit his disposal. Her "father" brought some medicine and Andy developed normally. In this situation his mother reported she was frightened at having given birth to a ghost, but at the same time felt he was her baby and was very reluctant to have him thrown away.

"Because such abnormalities are predetermined by the work of a ghost rather than being a result of faulty development, no treatment is available which will assure the birth of a healthy and normal child except for early diagnosis and abortion of the ghost's work." (p. 133)

TRUMAI

HDBK

"Sexual intercourse is forbidden among the Trumai during the last months of pregnancy and until the child can walk. (Quain MS.) Abortion is often practiced, either by manipulating the abdomen or by drinking magic medicines." (3:337)

TSIMSHIAN

(Data identical with those on the *Nesqually*.)

TUBATULABAL

VOEGELIN, E. W. *Tubatulabal Ethnography*. Anthropological Records, 2, #1, Berkeley, 1938.

This tribe practices contraception, abortion, and infanticide. When the woman first knows that she is pregnant, she aborts by boiling the leaves of a tree and drinking this decoction. (p. 45) Abortion is procured by means of herbal decoctions. (p. 60)

TUCUNA

HDBK

"Abortion and infanticide are practiced, especially when the father is a Neo-Brazilian, as the child would be disqualified for sib and moiety membership. Otherwise, it is believed that infanticide is a sin and that Taé punishes the soul of the perpetrator after death." (3:717)

"TULAPI" *

STONE, ERIC. *Medicine among the American Indians.* New York, 1932.

The Tulapi used a decoction of cedar sprouts, hops, and bearberry. (p. 77)

TUMLEO

ERDWEG, P. M. J. "Die Bewohner der Insel Tumleo, Berlinhafen, Deutsch-Neu-Guinea," *Mitteilungen der Anthropologischen Gesellschraft in Wien,* 32:274–310, 317–99, 1902.

"The last of this type of plants [which produce sterility] is the worst; it is called lapalet. The root of this plant is peeled, cut into small slices and then eaten in alternation with the kernels of coconuts. No one dares to chew this substance, because it has too bitter a taste; they have to swallow it whole. The poison which is in this plant is so harmful that it not only causes sterility, but is capable of killing even a three or four months old fetus. We still do not know why people desire to cause sterility or even abortions. Even the males don't quite know what to say about this. They are ignorant both of the secret devices of the females, and of the means which makes this sterility possible. They only know that the women know such things, and also that they ingest poisons derived from plants in order to achieve their ends. The married women are the only ones who know these secrets, but are completely silent about the more personal details thereof." (p. 383)

* The identity of the "Tulapi" (perhaps pronounced Tulapai—cf. Walapi for Walapai in the same book) could not be determined.

TUPINAMBA

THEVET, ANDRÉ. *Les Singularitéz de la France Antarctique, Autrement Nommée Amérique: et Isles Découvertes de Notre Temps,* Paris, 1878.

CARDIM, FERNÃO. *A Treatise of Brasil and Articles Touching the Dutie of the Kings Majestie our Lord, and to the Common Good of all the Estate of Brasill, Hakluytus Posthumus or Purchas His Pilgrimes,* Vol. XXVI. Glasgow, 1906.

MAGALHÃES DE GANDAVO, PEDRO DE. *History of the Province of Santa Cruz, Documents and Narratives Concerning the Discovery and Conquest of Latin America: The Histories of Brazil,* Vol. II. New York, 1922.

If a husband makes his pregnant wife angry, she will take "instead of this fruit" a certain herb which causes abortion. (Thevet, p. 173) The caraguata, a kind of thistle, bears a fruit as long as the finger and yellow in color. Raw, it blisters the lips, but is all right if roasted or boiled, though if a pregnant woman eats it she aborts as a rule. (Other caraguata leaves which are like very long flags, two or three fathoms in length, bear an "artichoke" [Hartichocke] like the Nana, but do not taste good. These leaves "laid in steepe" (i.e., steeped) yield a fine flax. (Cardim, pp. 480–481) A local girl is sometimes given to a prisoner of war, so that he will make her pregnant. The parents of the girl then eat this baby, as an act of vengeance against the enemy prisoner. But since the girl knows what end is in store for her baby, she will often abort it, so it cannot be cannibalized. (Magalhães de Gandavo, pp. 107–108)

UGANDA

GPM

"Amongst royalty, however, totems descend in the female line; a prince takes the totems of his mother and is considered a member of her clan. Kings, consequently, may and do belong to different clans. The members of certain clans, however, are ineligible to the throne; if one of their women is taken to wife by the king, all her sons are killed at birth." (p. 523)

"No princess, however, may marry or have children on penalty of death. This fact, coupled with their prestige and their complete liberty of movement, results in a degree of sexual license which amounts practically to promiscuity. If a princess has an illegitimate child, it is secretly put to death. 'There can be no doubt that the object of this stringent law was to end the old and regular law of succession through the female line, when the sister's son inherited the throne.' " (p. 530)

[The index lists these items as referring also to *abortion*. G. D.]

UGI (Solomon Islands)

ELTON, F. "Notes on the Natives of the Solomon Islands," *Journal of the Anthropological Institute,* 17:90–99, 1888.

"On the island of Ugi the women often procure abortion. I have known several cases of three to seven months' pregnancy, where abortion was procured, but could never find out exactly what they used to procure the same. I am aware that there is a certain shrub growing in the islands, the leaves whereof they use for this purpose, by making a drink of them; likewise they wear tight bandages around their waist. There are only a few women who understand this, and they make rather a profitable trade by it." (p. 93) In Ugi and on the beach of San Cristoval they also commit infanticide, because it is too much trouble to raise children. It is better to buy a grown child from the bush people, who keep their children with the sole object of selling them to the beach people. In the other Solomon Islands there is no infanticide, except the killing of bastards. (p. 93)

ULIASE

PB

"Abortifacients are extensively used." (2:513)

ULITAO (Marianas)

PB

"Abortion seems to have been practiced, though precise details about it are not available." (2:513)

U.S. INDIANS (in general)

PB

Engelmann, speaking of the Indians of the United States, says: "Abortion is often found among the Indians and especially among those who, as a result of the contact with civilization, have laxer morals. Some tribes are well justified in doing this, in view of the fact that the birth of a half-breed child endangers the mother, since it is usually so large that it is usually impossible for such a baby to pass through the pelvis of an Indian mother." (2:520, quoting, apparently, Engelmann, G. J. *Labor Among Primitive Peoples,* St. Louis, 1882)

UTE

STEWART, O. C. *Culture Element Distributions, XVIII, Ute-Southern Paiute.* Anthropological Record, 6, #4, Berkeley, 1942.

Moanunt band: "Unmarried mothers and married women with young children abort by means of pressure, lying on a rock or stick. As regards drinking hot water, the informant either denied knowledge of it or refused to discuss it. A hot concoction was drunk as an abortifacient." (p. 303) "It was made of clover seed (sawarĭnt)." (p. 346)

Tömpanöwöts band: "Unmarried mothers and married women with young children abort by means of pressure, lying on a rock or stick. They drank hot water or a hot concoction as an abortifacient." (p. 303)

Taviwatsiu band: "Unmarried mothers and married women with young children abort by means of pressure, lying on a rock or stick. They drank hot water as an abortifacient." (p. 303)

Möwataviwatsiu band: "Unmarried mothers abort by means of pressure, lying on a rock or stick." (p. 303)

Möwatci band: "One informant stated that unmarried mothers and married women with young children abort by means of pressure, lying on a rock or stick. Another informant denied that married women with young children aborted, and added the drinking of hot concoctions to the first informant's list of abortion producing techniques." (p. 303)

Wimönuntci band: "Unmarried mothers aborted by means of pressure, lying on a rock or stick." (p. 303)

VENDA

STAYT, H. A. *The Bavenda.* London, 1931.

The fear of abortion is so deeply rooted in this tribe that a man believes that if he cohabits with a woman who has aborted, he will die of consumption. After aborting, women must not go near cattle, lest their contact make the cattle sterile. After the woman aborts, no further cohabitation takes place until the husband takes his wife to the medicine man for purification. He makes a small incision on the neck or wrist of each spouse, rubbing the drops of blood into the other spouse's wound, thus signifying that they are of one blood. Then they are placed on opposite sides of a tree, back to back, and are tied together with bark string, with the tree between them. Next, both urinate into the same vessel and the powdered root of the mukhundandou tree—which is so strong that even the elephant can't break it—is added to the urine. Each spouse is then given some of this to drink, the remainder being rubbed on their legs. The string is then cut, to signify the cutting away of disease. Abortion is usually practiced by female adulterers. (p. 90)

WALAPAI

KROEBER, A. L., ed. *Walapai Ethnography.* American Anthropological Association, Memoir 42, Menasha, 1935.

"(L) Formerly there was no deliberate abortion. Natural abortion sometimes came from lifting heavy things; just too hard work.

"(J) There was no abortion in former times because the husband and the old women in a family watched the girls so closely that they always knew when they were pregnant. I know of one case, four or five years ago, where the girl was unmarried. She waited until the baby was born, then just let it lie and die. Then she took it and buried it.

"(P) I know nothing about infanticide in the old times or nowadays.

"There are no plants which will cause abortion. Sometimes a woman works too hard and lifts heavy things on purpose. Sometimes a man treads on his wife's belly and kills the child. This is still done." (p. 136)

WANKONDE

JOHNSTON, SIR H. H. *British Central Africa.* London, 1897.

"The children of an adulterous intercourse are killed in the Wankonde tribe. The people also practise the adoption of children extensively, especially where couples are childless.

"Children that are born deformed or defective are almost invariably killed. Respect for the life of very young children is not great though of course the mother from natural instincts is loath to lose her child. It was related to me once of the head wife of some man that, being extremely angry with one of the junior wives, and seemingly for good reason, she punished her by taking her young baby and throwing it in the fire where it burned to death. This fact was told to me to indicate that the woman in question was a person of determined character but it did not seem to strike my native informant that it was a particularly wicked or cruel thing to do. Yet children on the whole are kindly treated if they are reared at all. They grow up much like children do in all uncivilised countries—treated somewhat heedlessly but seldom harshly. The mother will place a charm round her baby's neck, and in some cases ornaments. As a rule the child that can walk is allowed to run about naked and dirty so that it may not be bewitched; but babies in arms are scrupulously washed and kept clean.

"In spite of their desire to honour their husbands with offspring it is not at all a rare thing for women to bring about abortion between the third and fifth month, either to spite their husbands with whom they may have quarrelled, or who have given them cause for jealousy, or because the child is the result of illicit intercourse. Abortion is procured by drinking a decoction of the bark of certain trees, or else by the insertion of a sharply pointed piece of bamboo." (p. 417)

WAPPO

DRIVER, H. E. *Wappo Ethnography*. University of California Publications in American Archaeology and Ethnology, Berkeley, 36, #3, 1936.

"Woman 'rolled around on her belly' or drank concoctions from certain plants to induce menstruation." (p. 199)

WAREGA

DELHAISE. "Les Warega," in van Overbergh, Cyril, *Collection de Monographies Ethnographiques*. Bruxelles, 1909.

"The pregnant woman who accords her favors to a man other than her husband must die unless she causes her child to disappear.

"Cases of abortion are frequent even without motive, by a simple *caprice* of the woman." (p. 147)

WATUBELA ISLAND

PB

"Abortifacients are extensively used. . . . The women thus create a two-child system." (2:513)

WITOTO

WHIFFEN, THOMAS. *The North-West Amazons.* London, 1915.
TESSMANN, GÜNTER. *Die Indianer Nordost-Perus.* Hamburg, 1930.

"Foeticide is not practiced and abortion is probably unknown except to medicine men, who would only procure it for their own purposes or protection." (Whiffen, pp. 149–50) Abortion is practiced by a few women who do not want children. (Tessman, p. 326)

WIYOT

DRIVER, H. E. *Culture Element Distributions, X, Northwest California.* Anthropological Record, 1 #6, Berkeley, 1939.

Abortion denied, but the author deems the information not wholly reliable. (p. 350)

WOGEO

HOGBIN, H. I. "Puberty to Marriage: A Study of the Sexual Life of the Natives of Wogeo, New Guinea," *Oceania,* 16:185–209, 1946.

A pregnant girl is condemned. Thus, Sanamuk's sisters, though nowise personally harmed by her pregnancy, beat her when her attempted abortion failed. Her third sister, Yam, did come to her rescue, but even she scolded her, and ridiculed her for being unable to make her lover marry her and for being "only good to lie with." Sanamuk's parents observed an icy silence, and insisted that the child be given out for adoption. As to brothers, some beat their erring sisters, while others are sympathetic. Gwaramun even expressed his pleasure over his sister Sanamuk's delivery, saying that, since no one would marry her now for a long time, she could remain by his side. The villagers were at first skeptical about whether he really meant this, but later on agreed that he was very fond of his sister and therefore maybe spoke the truth. Since Sanamuk's child resembled several men, the brother did not make himself ridiculous by asking all these men to help support it. Since in Wogeo illegitimate children are always believed to result from intercourse with several men, when a girl gets pregnant her lover usually refuses to marry her, because he feels that the child can only be partly his. Even if the girl swears that she was faithful to him, he does not believe her. Nonetheless, if a girl is pregnant, she first tries to persuade her lover to marry her. If he refuses, she eats a special kind of bark, chosen as an abortifacient because of its oily and slippery surface. The ingestion of this bark is followed by illness and by a general poisoning of the organism, which causes abortion. (pp. 207–209)

WOLOFF

PB

"Abortion is frequent." (2:516, quoting Rochebrune, A. T. de, "La Race Onolove," *Revue d'Anthropologie*, 4:283, 1881.)

"Among the Woloff there are certain fetish men, and especially those from the region of Cayor, who enjoy a special reputation for their ability to abort children." (2:531, quoting Rochebrune, *ibid.*)

XOSA

PB

"Four to five heads of cattle must be paid for the intentional abortion of a married woman, regardless of whether this has been done with or without the consent of the husband. The person who prepares or gives the drug used for this purpose is also punishable. The fine goes to the chief, because, by this act, he lost one human life. The wife's fine may be demanded from her husband, if he knew about it, or from her parents or else from the man whose child it was, if it was not that of the husband." (2:537, quoting Kropf, Albert, *Das Volk der Xosa Kaffern*, Berlin, 1889)

YAHGAN

COOPER, J. M. *Analytical and Critical Bibliography of the Tribes of Tierra del Fuego*. Bureau of American Ethnology, Bulletin 63, Washington, 1917.

HDBK

"Deliberate abortion is common (Hahn, a 805; Martial, 198; Th. Bridges, cited by Hyadès, p. 376) and infanticide not rare. . . ." (Cooper, p. 171)

"In some cases abortion—by mechanical, not medicinal, means —was resorted to by unmarried mothers." (HDBK 1:97)

YAKUT

PRIKLONSKII, V. L. "Three Years in the Yakut Territory," *Behavior Science Translations* [32:14, 1953].

PB

"Demič mentions as an abortifacient of the Yakut a tea made of *ledum palustre*." (PB, 2:525, quoting Demič, V. E., "Über Volkmedicin in Russland," *Wiener klinische Wochenschrift,* 2:902–908, 1889)

[Priklonskii (32:14) denies the occurrence of abortion among the Yakut.]

YANA

GIFFORD, E. W., AND KLIMEK, STANISLAW. *Culture Element Distributions, II, Yana.* University of California Publications in American Archaelogy and Ethnology, 37, #2, 1936.

"The Northern Yana practice abortion. The Central Yana do not. (p. 83)

"Northern Yana do it 'with thumb—or fingernails.' " (p. 92)

YAP (Caroline Islands)

SALESIUS, PATER. *Die Karolinen-Insel Yap.* [1907].

SENFFT, A. "Die Rechtssitten der Jap-Eingeborenen," *Globus,* 91:139–143, 149–153, 171–175, 1907.

MÜLLER, W. "Yap," *Ergebnisse der Südsee-Expedition 1908–1910,* G. Thilenius, ed., II, B, II, 1–811 (1–380). Hamburg, 1918, 2 vols.

GERMANY: Reichstag. Denkschrift über die Entwickelung der deutschen Schutzgebiete in Afrika und in der Südsee, 1901/1902. *Stenographische Berichte über die Verhandlungen des Reichstages.* x. Legislaturperiode, 2. Session, 1900/03. VIII. Anlageband, No. 814, pp. 5301–5311. Appendix F II; Missionsberichte, pp. 5482–84; H: Medizinalberichte VII: West-Karolinen (Dr. Born), pp. 5519–34. Berlin, 1903.

HRAF

Illegitimacy is bad luck but not a disgrace. (Müller, p. 232) Though the women are fond of children, they have no great desire to give birth to them. As a result, they practice abortion very generally. The massage of the belly is quickly successful. No other details have been learned. (Germany: Reichstag, p. 5524) They have drugs to make them fertile but quite frequently sterility is desired and is artificially induced through abortifacient media, the recipe of which the author was unable to learn. (Müller, p. 224) The girls in the "bäwai" are careful not to get pregnant because, in that case, they must leave the house and must marry. Consequently, such girls practice abortion most intensively. (Germany: Reichstag). Abortion and contraception are widely practiced by young women lest they should lose their beauty. "As a means of procuring an abortion, or menstruation immediately after it has failed to occur, boiled sea water is drunk. Abortion is looked on as shameful and is a reason for divorce but is not a legally punishable action." (Senfft, p. 153) Infanticide does not exist but women, in the first years of marriage, are known to abort, "their aim being to preserve themselves." (Salesius, p. 69) The people of Yap are frantically trying to have children because they are in the process of becoming extinct. Where missionaries impose sexual morals and increase the population, the Yap people say: "Those are people of inferior clay, i.e., former tribute payers. There is no need to tend the vulgar coconut—one should check it rather. It is the noble papaya that does need tending." That is morality for you! They view Christian morality as an attempt to cause their extinction. (HRAF)

YORUBA

WARD, EDWARD. *Marriage among the Yoruba.* Catholic University of America, Anthropological Series, 4, Washington, D. C., 1937.

"Very often a man finds after he has completed the 'bride price,' and has remained with his wife for some time, that she cannot conceive. This is sometimes due or thought to be due, to the fact that she has brought on this state of barrenness by hindering the course of nature before marriage (native doctors are adepts at compounding medicines to cause abortion)." (p. 30)

YUMA

(See *Southwest U. S. Indians.*)

YUMU

(Data identical with *Ngali.*)

YURACARE

HDBK

"Abortion and infanticide were very common among ancient Yuracare, who killed illegitimate and crippled children. The Yuracare are said to have practiced a kind of birth control, each family limiting the number of its children." (3:498)

YUROK

KROEBER, A. L. *Handbook of the Indians of California.* Bureau of American Ethnology, Bulletin 78, Washington, 1925.

"As a girl's property value was greatly impaired if she bore a child before marriage, and she was subject to abuse from her family and disgrace before the community, abortion was frequently attempted. Hot stones were put on the abdomen, and the foetus thrown into the river. There is little doubt that parents guarded their girls carefully, but the latter give the impression of having been more inclined to prudence than to virtue for its own sake. Probably habits differed largely according to the rank of the family. Poor girls had much less to lose by an indiscretion." (pp. 44)

YUROK (vicinity of Martin's Ferry)

DRIVER, H. E. *Culture Element Distributions, X, Northwest California.* Anthropological Record, 1, #6, Berkeley, 1939.

"Lifting, hard work." (p. 350)

ZAMBESI

MAUGHAM, R. C. F. *Portuguese East Africa: The History, Scenery and Great Game of Manica and Sofala.* London, 1906.

"Although the people of this territory are exceedingly productive, I am told that childbirth is often deliberately frustrated by the women between the third and fifth month of pregnancy, either where their condition may have been the result of infidelity to the husband, or where the latter may have given real or fancied cause for jealousy. This is brought about by drinking the juice of the Pawpaw (Carica papaya) or some other astringent liquid, or else by violent means, the woman experiencing scarcely any ill effects." (p. 271)

ZAPAROAN TRIBES of Peruvian and Ecuadorian Montana (Maina, Zaparo, Zapa, Gae and Semigáe, Andoa, Coronado, Oa, Roamaina, Awishira, Iquito, Pinche, Canelo, Alabano, Neva, Asaruntoa, Aunale, Curizeta, Coronado of the Aguarico River, Inemo-dikama)

HDBK

"Abortion is evidently common." (3:645)

ZUNI

STEVENSON, M. C. "The Zuni Indians," *Bureau of American Ethnology, Annual Report,* 23, Washington, D. C., 1901.

"A young pregnant woman, becoming alarmed, called in the theurgist. He examined the abdomen, and declared that she was carrying three children and that should they reach full development she would surely die. He produced premature birth; and it was claimed by the doctor that the first two born breathed a few times and that the third was stillborn. Abortion is rarely practiced on married women; but it is not uncommon among the fallen women, who are always pointed at with the finger of scorn, except when they are on a bed of illness; they then receive the same consideration as others. Their infants are not discriminated against in any way." (p. 296)

STEVENSON, M. C. "Ethnobotany of the Zuni." *Bureau of American Ethnology, Annual Report,* 30, Washington, D. C., 1915.

"Gaertneria acanthicarpa (Hook). Britton. Ragweed. Ambrosiaceae. Ragweed family. . . . The entire plant is made into tea, which is drunk warm for obstructed menstruation. The tea is also rubbed over the abdomen while it is massaged. The Zuni claim that the tea taken sufficiently strong will produce abortion. While this vice exists in Zuni, cases are very rare." (pp. 51–52)

AH

Artificial abortion, the people believe, is apt to be followed by sterility. (p. 54)

". . . The Zuni woman drinks some decoctions, but if these fail, has recourse to pressure." *

* "A restraining influence in this tribe is the belief that the woman who induces abortion is likely to lose the capacity of having more children. According to information given to the writer by Dr. E. J. Davis, the agency physician, so great is this fear that as soon as a mother becomes aware that her daughter is pregnant

BENEDICT, RUTH. *Zuni Mythology,* Vol. I. New York, 1935.

Bastards were ridiculed but not killed. They therefore sometimes abandon bastards at birth, and, in order to be able to do so, they seek to conceal their illegitimate pregnancies. There are legends about the exposure of infants. (pp. xvi–xvii)

(See also *Southwest U. S. Indians.*)

APPENDIX I. SOUND NEGATIVE EVIDENCE

ISNEG

VANOVERBERGH, MORICE. *The Isneg Life Cycle. I. Birth, Education, and Daily Routine.* Catholic Anthropological Conference, Publications, 3, #2, Washington, D. C., 1936.

"Voluntary abortion seems to be neither known nor practised. Here of course one is treading upon dangerous ground when inquiring into the matter, but nevertheless it was told me very emphatically by persons whose entire confidence I possessed that such practices were never resorted to. Do not some Isneg at least know about it, and does it not happen occasionally in some spot or another of the extensive Apayaw district? I do not know. It should be taken into consideration though that to the Isneg all

---

with an illegitimate child she at once assures her that all will be well and that she must not interfere with it. When the old women learn of a recent case of abortion on the part of a young woman, they place her at once in warm sand for ten days to prevent her 'drying up.'

"A method favored in this tribe [Zuni] is for the woman to grasp her gravid uterus through the abdominal wall and twist and squeeze it until she succeeds in detaching the fetal connections." (p. 164)

children are welcome, and even in the case of a child that would be born out of wedlock, its premature death would not save the girl from the anger of her parents, nor the boy from his duty to marry the girl or to suffer some terrible punishment, so that as far as I understand the Isneg mind, a living child will result more to the satisfaction of everybody concerned than a dead one." (pp. 100–101) *

* [This item, which contains only negative evidence, is reproduced *in extenso*, because it is the only such item which seems convincing to the present writer. G. D.]

PART FOUR

TABULATION OF TRAITS

1. KEY TO TABULATION

Due to the spottiness of data, it seemed undesirable and unfeasible to attempt a mapping of various traits or to undertake a statistical study of correlations between various traits listed in the following tabulation and various aspects of social structure. Instead, it was attempted to tabulate some 50-odd traits for the tribes on whom data are included in the sourcebook. These traits have been divided into seven groups. The occurrence of a given trait is represented by the appearance of a symbol in the column to which that given trait belongs. In some instances a symbol has been placed between parentheses to indicate that we are dealing here with matters of interpretation, with uncertainty, or with ambiguous wording. Otherwise it is felt that the tabulation is self-explanatory.

SYMBOLS

I. *Motive*

- A adultery
- B beauty, husband's love is to be preserved
- C coitus taboo during pregnancy and/or lactation
- D dreams and omens
- E economic system of the group
- F fear of penalties, including shame if specified
- G government (native); politics, dynastic matters, class, slavery, wife of prisoner of war
- H health, strength, prophylaxis, fear of pain, eugenics
- I illegitimacy or posthumous child

J joy, desire for amusement
M missions, whites, conquest, acculturation, halfbreeds, slavery to whites
P poverty
Pc cannibalism due to poverty
Q quarrels, anger, spite, desertion usually involving husband or lover
R religion and magic
S social factors, war, etc.
T trouble of raising children, "laziness," rejection of parental role
W wealth quest

II. *Involuntary or Forced*

A assault
C coitus
G government or legal process
H husband
I informal family and public pressures
J jealousy of other women and co-wives
L lover
M magic or religious purposes
P penalty, automatic
S supernaturals, devils, ghosts, not motivated by human agent
W witchcraft

III. *Techniques*

A anal, clyster
B belt, constricting
C coitus
D drugs
E effort
H heat, external
I instruments
J jolts
L leaps, jump up and down
M mechanical
O organism weakened by bleeding or starvation
P pessaries, packs

Ψ psychogenic
R religious and magical
S skin irritants and baths
T topical, local medication
V vaginal manipulations

IV. *Attitudes*

\+ approved
— disapproved
C conditional approval
O neutral, tolerant

V. *Penalties and Consequences*

C criminal or civil legal procedures including divorce
N natural consequences involving health
P private or informal social procedures
S supernatural penalties including expiatory rites
o involving others than the aborting woman
w involving the woman who aborts

VI. *Penalty for Not Aborting*

VII. *Abortion as Penalty*

TRAIT LIST

TRIBES	I	II	III	IV	V	VI	VII
Ababua			D	–	Co, Cw		
Abipones	BC		(M)	(–)			
Abyssinia			D				
Achewa	ACR	M	D				
Achomawi			M				
Admiralty Islands	IF		L				
Africa (west?)	(A)F(I)		D			*	
Agaria			(D)(R)				
Ainu	IJM(S)		BDLMR		(C) Nw		
Akamba	IJ		D		Nw		
Alaska Indians			M				
Aleut			(R)				
Alorese	QT		EJLM	–			
Amazon River Indians	(C)(I)(T)			(C)			
Ambon			(D)				
Angami Naga	(I)	(I)	M	(–)			
Ao Naga	I		M	(+)			
Apache, Jicarilla	I		D(M)				
Mescalero			DIM				
San Carlos			DM	(–)			
White Mountain			M				
Apinayé	HQ		D				
Aranda	MPT		B (R)S				
Arapaho				–	(Sw)		
Araucanians	(I)(Q)		D	(–)			
Arawaks (Antilles) in general	M		D	(+)			
Aru	(G)(M)						
Ashanti	A(H)	GW	D				*
Assiniboine	QT	H	IM	O	(Nw)(Pw)		
Atjeh	(S)	(H)	D	(+)			
Australia in general	(P)						
New South Wales	M						
Portland Bay, Victoria	P(T)						
Queensland, North West Central			BM				
Sydney area	BT		M				
Victoria	Q		M				
West Arnheim Land	AI						

	I	II	III	IV	V	VI	VII
ans	ACHIM	GM	D	C			
‹orth Borneo				(–)			
east Borneo	R		D				
casteaux in general	(T)		DM	(O)			
	CI(T)		DLM	(–)	Pw		
Bay	I(T)		DM				
	DQ		DM(S)				
tone Island	I		BHMRST				
Island			D	(–)			
	(C)T		DM				
	DH		ADP		(Nw)		
ino	IJT						
mo, Baffin Land, Hudson Bay					So		
opper		A	(M)				
Iudson Bay	P(T)	H					
Koyukuk	I		(I)(M)		Nw		
Polar	P		M				
Smith Sound Inuit			IM				
spiritu Santo	IHM	(H)	DEM		Pw		
iji	CEFGHIM PQST	HIJ	DIM Ψ SV	C	CwNoNw		
lathead	FI			–			
Formosa, aborigines	FR		M	+		*	
Futuna	GQ	HI	M			*	
Galela (Gilolo)			D				
Gaua			DMR				
Gilbert Islands	I(P)(T)		BM				
Gilyak	(M)						
Guaycuru, general	C						
Pampas, Brazil	BE(H)(I)				Nw		
Paraguay	I			O			
Guianas in general			DM				
Gunantuna	FI	GI	BDLMR			*	
Haida							
Haiti, Arawak of	M		D	(+)			
Hawaii	BGR	GI	DIM(R)(S)	C			
Hehe	C						
Herero	Q(T)		BDM				
Hopi	FI		BDM(R)Ψ	–	Sw		
Hottentot (South West Africa)	(T)		BDM				
Nama	(I)		BD	–	CoCw		
Huichol	(FHIPT)		(DM)				
Ila	(T)	C	D	–	CoCw		*
Inca			(M)				
India, Aboriginal Tribes in general	R						
Iroquois of Canada	T	H	D				
Jakun	IT			–	Pw		

TRIBES	I	II	III	IV	V	VI	VII
Aymara	I		BI				
Azande	A	H	D				
Azimba			D				
Aztec, ancient	GH(S)		D				
modern	I		DR				
Babar	C		DM				
Bafiote	H		DM				
Baholoholo	(G)(H)		(D)				
Bahuana	C		D				
Bakairi			(D)				
Bakongo	AF(I)Q		D(R)				
Bali	GI		D(R)	–			
Bangala	AF						
Barotse				(–)			
Baru	(T)						
Batak			I				
Bergdama	(T)		BDM				
Bontoc Igorot	IT		HMS	(O)			
Borneo, North	(G)	J					
Brazilian Amazonas	BT		D(M)(O)				
Brunei	(B)GI						
Buin	BIT		DHM		Nw		
Buka	AF		DMS				
Bukaua	HT		DMO	O			
Buna	I		D				
Buru			D	O			
Bushmen, S. W. Africa	(T)		BDM				
Caduveo	T						
Cahita			DM				
Canary Islands			D(M)				
Caraya		H	M		Nw		
Catawba	I						
Celebes, Central (Toradja?)	H			(–)			
Chaco Tribes	CHIPQ		(D)M	(+)			
Chagga	ACDF(R)	HI	DIM		So		
Cherokee				–			
Cheyenne	C(I)T			–	Cw		
Chichicastenango			(D)	(–)			
Chimariko					Pw		
Chinook	I		DM				
Chippewa	IQT		DELM	–	Nw		
Chontal	M						
Choroti	I		M	C			
Chukchee	?	?	?	?	?	?	?
Comanche	I						
Congo in general			DM				
Cootch	(I)						
Cora	(FHIPT)		(DM)				
Creek			(D)	–			
Crow	Q	H	IM		NwPw		
Cuna	IM	G		C			

TRIBES
Dahome
Dayak,
South
d'Entre
Djuka
Dob'u
Doreh
Dusu
Eddy
Eeta
Efat
Efik
Eng
Esk

TRIBES	I	II	III	IV	V	VI	VII
Dahomeians	ACHIM	GM	D	C			
Dayak, North Borneo				(–)			
Southeast Borneo	R		D				
d'Entrecasteaux in general	(T)		DM	(O)			
Djuka							
Dobu	CI(T)		DLM	(–)	Pw		
Doreh Bay	I(T)		DM				
Dusun	DQ		DM(S)				
Eddystone Island	I		BHMRST				
Eetar Island			D	(–)			
Efate	(C)T		DM				
Efik	DH		ADP		(Nw)		
Engano	IJT						
Eskimo, Baffin Land, Hudson Bay					So		
Copper		A	(M)				
Hudson Bay	P(T)	H					
Koyukuk	I		(I)(M)		Nw		
Polar	P		M				
Smith Sound Inuit			IM				
Espiritu Santo	IHM	(H)	DEM		Pw		
Fiji	CEFGHIM PQST	HIJ	DIM Ψ SV	C	CwNoNw		
Flathead	FI			–			
Formosa, aborigines	FR		M	+		*	
Futuna	GQ	HI	M			*	
Galela (Gilolo)			D				
Gaua			DMR				
Gilbert Islands	I(P)(T)		BM				
Gilyak	(M)						
Guaycuru, general	C						
Pampas, Brazil	BE(H)(I)				Nw		
Paraguay	I			O			
Guianas in general			DM				
Gunantuna	FI	GI	BDLMR			*	
Haida							
Haiti, Arawak of	M		D	(+)			
Hawaii	BGR	GI	DIM(R)(S)	C			
Hehe	C						
Herero	Q(T)		BDM				
Hopi	FI		BDM(R)Ψ	–	Sw		
Hottentot (South West Africa)	(T)		BDM				
Nama	(I)		BD	–	CoCw		
Huichol	(FHIPT)		(DM)				
Ila	(T)	C	D	–	CoCw		*
Inca			(M)				
India, Aboriginal Tribes in general	R						
Iroquois of Canada	T	H	D				
Jakun	IT			–	Pw		

TRIBES	I	II	III	IV	V	VI	VII
Aymara	I		BM	–			
Azande	A	H	D	C	CoCwPw		(*)
Azimba			D		(Nw)		
Aztec, ancient	GH(S)		D	–	Cw		
modern	I		DR	–	Co		
Babar	C		DM				
Bafiote	H		DM				
Baholoholo	(G)(H)		(D)				
Bahuana	C		D				
Bakairi			(D)				
Bakongo	AF(I)Q		D(R)				
Bali	GI		D(R)	–			
Bangala	AF						
Barotse				(–)	(Cw)(So)(Sw)		
Baru	(T)						
Batak			I				
Bergdama	(T)		BDM				
Bontoc Igorot	IT		HMS	(O)			
Borneo, North	(G)	J					
Brazilian Amazonas	BT		D(M)(O)				
Brunei	(B)GI						
Buin	BIT		DHM		Nw		
Buka	AF		DMS				
Bukaua	HT		DMO	O			
Buna	I		D				
Buru			D	O			
Bushmen, S. W. Africa	(T)		BDM				
Caduveo	T						
Cahita			DM				
Canary Islands			D(M)				
Caraya		H	M		Nw		
Catawba	I						
Celebes, Central (Toradja?)	H			(–)			
Chaco Tribes	CHIPQ		(D)M	(+)			
Chagga	ACDF(R)	HI	DIM		So		
Cherokee				–			
Cheyenne	C(I)T			–	Cw		
Chichicastenango			(D)	(–)			
Chimariko					Pw		
Chinook	I		DM				
Chippewa	IQT		DELM	–	Nw		
Chontal	M						
Choroti	I		M	C			
Chukchee	?	?	?	?	?	?	?
Comanche	I						
Congo in general			DM				
Cootch	(I)						
Cora	(FHIPT)		(DM)				
Creek			(D)	–			
Crow	Q	H	IM		NwPw		
Cuna	IM	G		C			

TRIBES	I	II	III	IV	V	VI	VII
Java			DM				
Jivaro	AIR	H	DMR	C			
Jukun		P					(*)
Kabyle				(–)	Pw		
Kaffir				–	CoCw		
Kagoro			D				
Kai	H		DMR	O			
Kaingang							
Kalmuck	(I)		HMS				
Kamchadal	T		D(J)M				
Kasai	(I)M	(I)	D	(C)			
Kato			DM				
Kazak	I						
Keisar	(T)		D	–			
Kgatla	AI	L	D	–	CoCwNwSo		
Kiowa Apache	C						
Kiwai			BH(M)		Nw		
Klikita			D				
Kling			D				
Knisteneaux	QT		D				
Koita				O			
Kroë			DHM				
Kuanyama Ambo	I		DT				
Kusaie	I		M				
Kwakiutl	HIT		DEM	–	(Cw)		
Lamba	(D)						
Lampong	(I)		DMRS				
Lengua	(C)(T)						
Lepcha		S			So		
Lesu			D				
Lkungen (Songish)			D				
Loango							
Loyalty Islands			D				
Machiguenga	M						
Macusi	BT		DR				
Mafulu	IPRT		BM				
Mailu	(I)						
Mairapa	M	M(S)		(+)			
Malagasy	IT						
Malay				(–)			
Malekula	CMW		DEL				
Mam							
Mambowe				(–)	(CwSoSw)		
Mangareva							
Mangbetu		(H)	I				
Manja			DH(R)				
Mano and Mandingo		J	D				
Manus			B		Nw		
Maori	(B)(H)	S	BDIMR				*
Marianas	IMT		D	(+)			
Maricopa	(M)		BD				

TRIBES	I	II	III	IV	V	VI	VII
Maronites	P		E				
Marquesas	S	JW	DI				
Marshall Islands	IS		MS	O			
Masai	FHI	CH	DI	C	PoPw		*
Massawa	FI		D				
Massim (Southern)							
Mataco	IQ		DM	C			
Mattole			D				
Mbaya	BT		M		Nw		
Mbundu	FI		D				
Melanesia in general	ADQT		DM(S)	O			
Menomini			D(R)				
Merir, Pulo Ana, Sonsol			D				
Mexican Indians of N. W. Mexico			D(M)				
Micronesia in general			MS				
Miriam	FI		BDELM		Nw		
Mohave	IM(Q)	(G)(I)W	M(R)V	–			
Mojo and Baure				–	Cw		
Mongol (Yuan Dynasty)				–	C		
Mongol-Oirat (Kalmuck)				–	Co		
Montana and Bolivian East Andes	M						
Monumbo			BDEJ				
Moriori	I			O	Nw		
Mount Hagen	CT		M				
Munda-Kolh	P			–	Pw		
Mu'ò'ng			M	(–)			
Muria	I	I	DR	C	Nw	(*)	
Murngin	T		M	–			
Mythuggadi	(I)		M				
Nahua	I		DR	–	Co		
Navaho,	AHIP(R)T	I	BE(L)M	–	NwPw		
Northwestern			(D)				
Negritos of Malaya			D				
Nesqually	IT						
New Britain, Duke of York Island	(C)T		DIM				
Gazelle Peninsula	I						
Western tribes							
New Caledonia	BFIT		D	(–)			
New Guinea, territory of, in general	BHT						
New Hebrides, in general	(M)		DM				
New Ireland	T		BDLM		(Nw)		
Ngali	Pc						
Nias		S					
Nigeria, in general	I	W	D				
Southern			D				
Niue	IFS		DM	–	Cw		
Nongatl			E				

TRIBES	I	II	III	IV	V	VI	VII
Nootka	T			–	Pw		
North American Indians, in general	(M)(T)		(I?)				
Nufor			BDM				
Nukuoro	GP		M				
Omaha	(H)I(T)	H	D				
Ona	Q						
Opata	IP		DJM				
Orinoco tribes	B						
Otomi	(FHIPT)		(DM)				
Ottawa			D				
Owambo	IR	I	DM		Nw		(*)
Pacific Islands, in general							
Paiute, Harney Valley	Q		M	–			
Northern	IM		M				
Surprise Valley			M				
Palau	BI		D				
Palaung			D	–			
Papago	(FHIPT)		(DM)				
Papuans, Geelvink Bay	T						
New Guinea, territory of	T		LM				
Payagua	T		M				
Pedi					(Cw)So		
Pentecost Island			DMR				
Pima	CIM		DEHLMO	O			
Polynesia in general			DMS				
Pomo, Central	I			–			
Clear Lake and Russian River			M				
Ponape	IRT		DM	–			
Ponca	(H)I(T)	H	D				
Pueblo in general	(FHIPT)		(DM)				
Pukapuka	ADFHI(Q)	?	DM Ψ				(*)
Purari	H		DEMR				
Quapaw	M						
Rhadé Moi				(–)	(S)		
Riff			D	–	Cw		
Rotuma			D(S)				
Rwala	FI	I		–	NwPwSo		
Sac and Fox	M						
Samoa	BFT		DM		Nw		
Sanpoil and Nespelem			D	–	Cw		
Sedang Moi	I	W	HM	–	CoCw		
Semang			(D)	–			
Shasta			D				
Shortlands (Solomon Islands)			DHM				
Shushwap							
Siberia	(I)		D				
Sinaugolo	I(T)		DEHLM	(–)			
Sinkiyone, South Fork and Eel River			D				
Upper Mattole River			M				

TRIBES	I	II	III	IV	V	VI	VII
Sioux	(C)IT	(H)	D	(–)			
Sissanu			DM				
Siwah			DE				
Society Islands in general	M						
Solomon Islands in general	M		DM	(–)	Nw		
Songosor	(I)		(V)				
South Africa in general	(G)(T)						
Southwest U.S. Indians	FHIPT		(B)D(M)		Nw		
Spanish American Colonies in general	M						
Swaheli	BG		D				
Tahiti	BGMQ(R)T	H(L)(M)	D	(–)	NoNwPw		
Tami	(T)			O			
Tanala	(D)I						
Tarahumara	FI(T)		M	–			
Tarasco	(FHIPT)		(DM)				
Tasmania	BT		M				
Tatars			D				
Taulipang	I		DRS	O			
Thompson Indians			D	–	Pw		
Thonga				–	So		
Tikopia	IPT	H	DHM(R)		Nw		
Tiv		M(W)	DR	(C)			
Toba Indians	I		M	O			
Tobelorese			D				
Tolowa			(D)(E)(H)(M)				
Toradja	FGIST		DM				
Torres Straits in general	FIT	I					
Eastern Islands			BDEJM				
Western tribe			BDM				
Trobriand Island			(DMR)	(O)			
Truk	BC(H)T	MS	DLM	–	Pw		
Trumai	(C)		DMR				
Tsimshian	IT						
Tubatulabal			D				
Tucuna	I			C			
"Tulapi" (unidentified)			D				
Tumleo			D	(O)			
Tupinamba	GQ		D				
Uganda	G					(*)	
Ugi	T		D				
Uliase			D				
Ulitao							
U.S. Indians in general	IHM						
Ute, Moanunt	(C)I(T)		DM				
Tömpanöwöts	(C)I(T)		DM				
Taviwatsiu	(C)I(T)		DM				
Möwataviwatsiu	I		M				
Möwatci	(C)I(T)		DM				
Wimönuntci	I		M				

TRIBES	I	II	III	IV	V	VI	VII
Venda	A			–	NoSoSw		
Walapai	IM		EM	–			
Wankonde	AQ		DI				
Wappo			DM				
Warega	AF(T)						
Watubela	(T)		D				
Witoto	T	(W)					
Wiyot							
Wogeo		I	D			*	
Woloff			(R)				
Xosa	A		D		CoCw		
Yahgan	I		M				
Yakut			D				
Yana			M				
Yap	BI		DM	–	Cw		
Yoruba	I		D		Nw		
Yuma	(FHIPT)		(DM)				
Yumu	Pc						
Yuracare	I(T)						
Yurok	GI		H(M)	–			
vicinity of Martin's Ferry			E				
Zambesi	AQ		DM				
Zaparoans of Peruvian and Ecuadorian Montana							
Zuni	HI		DMS		Nw		
ADDENDA							
Australia (Melville Island)					N		
Kpelle			D	–	CoCw		

Note: The tabulation of data regarding the *Hottentot* (*Nama*) also includes material published by Schapera, which was located too late to be incorporated into the Sourcebook.

BIBLIOGRAPHY

BIBLIOGRAPHY

1. Ackerknecht, E. H. "Primitive Autopsies and the History of Anatomy," *Bulletin of the History of Medicine,* 13:334–39, 1943.
2. Bastian, Adolf. *Der Völkergedanke im Aufbau einer Wissenschaft vom Menschen und Seine Begründung auf ethnologische Sammlungen.* Berlin, 1881.
3. Bettelheim, Bruno. *Symbolic Wounds.* Glencoe, Illinois, 1954.
4. Brock, J. F., and Autret, M. *Kwashiorkor in Africa.* World Health Organization Monograph, Series 8, Geneva, 1952.
5. Cornford, F. M. *The Origin of Attic Comedy.* Cambridge, 1934.
6. Deutsch, Helene. *The Psychology of Women.* New York, 1944–45.
7. Devereux, George. "A Sociological Theory of Schizophrenia," *Psychoanalytic Review,* 26:315–42, 1939.
8. ——— "Mohave Beliefs Concerning Twins," *American Anthropologist,* n. s., 43:573–92, 1941.
9. ——— "Social Structure and the Economy of Affective Bonds," *Psychoanalytic Review,* 1942.
10. ——— "The Mental Hygiene of the American Indian," *Mental Hygiene,* 26:71–84, 29:303–14, 1942.
11. ——— and Loeb, E. M. "Antagonistic Acculturation," *American Sociological Review,* 7:133–47, 1943.
12. ——— "Mohave Orality: An Analysis of Nursing and Weaning Customs," *Psychoanalytic Quarterly,* 16:519–46, 1947.
13. ——— "Mohave Pregnancy," *Acta Americana,* 6:89–116, 1948.
14. ——— "Mohave Coyote Tales," *Journal of American Folklore,* 61:233–55, 1948.
15. ——— "The Function of Alcohol in Mohave Society," *Quarterly Journal of Studies on Alcohol,* 9:207–251, 1948.
16. ——— "Mohave Paternity," *Samiksa, Journal of the Indian Psycho-Analytical Society,* 3:162–94, 1949.
17. ——— "Post-Partum Parental Observances of the Mohave Indians," *Transactions of the Kansas Academy of Science,* 52:458–65, 1949.

18. ——— "Heterosexual Behavior of the Mohave Indians," in Róheim, Géza, ed., *Psychoanalysis and the Social Sciences,* V. 2, New York, 1950.
19. ——— "Catastrophic Reactions in Normals," *American Imago,* 7:343–49, 1950.
20. ——— "The Psychology of Feminine Genital Bleeding: An Analysis of Mohave Indian Puberty and Menstrual Rites," *International Journal of Psycho-Analysis,* 31:237–57, 1950.
21. ——— "Education and Discipline in Mohave Society," *Primitive Man,* 23:85–102, 1950.
22. ——— *Reality and Dream: The Psychotherapy of a Plains Indian,* New York, 1951.
23. ——— "Why Oedipus Killed Laius: A Note on the Complementary Oedipus Complex," *International Journal of Psycho-Analysis,* 34:132–41, 1953.
24. ——— "Cultural Factors in Psychoanalytic Therapy," *Journal of the American Psychoanalytic Association,* 1:629–55, 1953.
25. ——— *Primitive Genital Mutilations in a Neurotic's Dream, Journal of the American Psychoanalytic Association,* 2:484–493, 1954.
26. ——— *Culture and Mental Disorder.* (in press).
27. Durkheim, Emile, and Mauss, Marcel. "De Quelques Formes Primitives De Classification," *Annèe Sociologique,* 6:1–72, 1901–02.
28. Elwin, Verrier. *The Baiga.* London, 1939.
29. Feldman, S. S. Notes on the "Primal Horde," in Róheim, Géza, ed., *Psychoanalysis and the Social Sciences,* I, New York, 1947.
30. Festetich de Tolna, Rodolphe de. *Chez les Cannibales.* Paris, 1903.
31. François, H. K. B. von. *Napoleon I.* Berlin, 1929.
32. Freud, Sigmund. *The Taboo of Virginity.* Collected Papers, IV. London, 1952.
33. ——— *Leonardo da Vinci.* New York, 1932.
34. ——— *Totem and Taboo.* New York, 1938.
35. Fürer-Haimendorf, Christoph von. *The Naked Nagas.* Calcutta, 1946.
36. Goldenweiser, Alexander. "The Principle of Limited Possibilities in the Development of Culture," *Journal of American Folklore,* 26:261–90, 1913.
37. Hallowell, A. I. "Ojibwa Personality and Acculturation," *Proceedings and Papers of the Twenty-ninth International Congress of Americanists,* 2:105–112, 1949.
38. Holmberg, A. R. *Nomads of the Long Bow.* Smithsonian Institution, Institute of Social Anthropology Publication, 10, Washington, 1950.
39. Horton, Donald. "The Functions of Alcohol in Primitive Societies," *Quarterly Journal of Studies on Alcohol,* 4:199–320, 1943.
40. Jones, Ernest. *Papers on Psychoanalysis,* 3rd. ed. New York, 1923.

41. Jordan, Pascual. *Verdrängung und Komplementarität.* Hamburg, 1947.
42. ——— "Reflections on Parapsychology, Psychoanalysis and Atomic Physics," *Journal of Parapsychology,* 15:278–81, 1951.
43. Kluckhohn, Clyde, and Leighton, Dorothea. *The Navaho.* Cambridge, Massachusetts, 1946.
44. Kobler, Fritz. "Description of an Acute Castration Fear based on Superstition," *Psychoanalytic Review,* 35:285–89, 1948.
45. Kroeber, A. L. "Olive Oatman's Return." *Kroeber Anthropological Society Papers,* 4:1–18, 1951.
46. LaBarre, Weston. "Social Cynosure and Social Structure," *Journal of Personality,* 14:169–83, 1946.
47. Leighton, Dorothea, and Kluckhohn, Clyde. *Children of the People,* Cambridge, Massachusetts, 1947.
48. Lévi-Strauss, Claude. *Les Structures Elémentaires De La Parenté.* Paris, 1949.
49. Linton, Ralph. *The Sacrifice to the Morning Star by the Skidi Pawnee.* Chicago, 1922.
50. ——— "The Comanche." in Kardiner, Abram, *The Psychological Frontiers of Society.* New York, 1945.
51. Lowie, R. H. *Are We Civilized?* New York, 1929.
52. ——— *The Crow Indians.* New York, 1935.
53. ——— *The History of Ethnological Theory.* New York, 1937.
54. Mead, Margaret. *Coming of Age in Samoa.* New York, 1928.
55. Merton, R. K. "The Self-Fulfilling Prophecy." in *Social Theory and Social Structure.* Glencoe, Illinois, 1949.
56. Montagu, M. F. A. *Adolescent Sterility.* Springfield, Illinois, 1946.
57. Reuss, H. "Ein Fall von anatomischen Narzismus (Autocohabitatio in urethram)," *Deutsche Zeitschrift für die gesamte gerichtliche Medizin,* 28:340–46, 1937.
58. Róheim, Géza. "The Nescience of the Aranda," *British Journal of Medical Psychology,* 17:343–63, 1938.
59. Seligman, C. G., and B. Z. *Pagan Tribes of the Nilotic Sudan.* London, 1932.
60. Strehlow, C. *Die Aranda und Loritjastämme.* Frankfurt-am-Main, 1907–08.
61. Temesváry, Rezsö. *Volksbräuche und Aberglauben in der Geburtshilfe und der Pflege des Neugebornen in Ungarn.* Leipzig, 1900.
62. Thomas, W. I., and Znaniecki, Florian. *The Polish Peasant in Europe and America,* Vol. III, Boston, 1919.
63. Vanoverbergh, Morice. *The Isneg Life Cycle. I: Birth, Education and Daily Routine.* Catholic Anthropological Conference Publications, 3:81–186, 1936.

64. Whiting, J. W. M., and Child, I. L. *Child Training and Personality.* New Haven, 1953.
65. Whorf, B. L. "The Relation of Habitual Thought and Behavior to Language." in Spier, Leslie, ed., *Language, Culture and Personality.* Menasha, Wisconsin, 1941.
66. Wulfften-Palthe, P. M. van. "Koro. Eine merkwürdige Angsthysterie," *Internationale Zeitschrift für Psychoanalyse,* 21:249–57, 1935.
67. Yates, S. L. "An Investigation of the Psychological Factors in Virginity and Ritual Defloration," *International Journal of Psychoanalysis,* 11:167–84, 1930.

SUBJECT INDEX

SUBJECT INDEX

NOTE: The subject index only covers Parts One and Two, since the tabulation of traits constitutes a systematic index of the Sourcebook (Part Three).

AUTHOR INDEX

AUTHOR INDEX

NOTE: This index does *not* pertain to the Sourcebook. In addition, it does not list authors in the following connections:

1 Data also found in the Sourcebook section.
2 Additional data on tribes cited in the Sourcebook.

Thus, *Ralph Linton* is listed in connection with certain *theoretical* statements, and in connection with statements about the *Skidi Pawnee,* but *not* in connection either with data on *Tanala* abortion or on *Tanala* homosexuality, though the latter data are not in the Sourcebook, because they can be found in the work cited in the Sourcebook.

INDEX OF ETHNIC GROUPS AND LOCALITIES

INDEX OF ETHNIC GROUPS AND LOCALITIES

NOTE: The present index lists only those ethnic groups which do not appear in the Sourcebook, since the latter is, in a sense, an index in itself.